W9-BNT-253

Alastair
Sawday's

Special Places
to Stay

Spain

"This book will become
your best friend."
Spanish Magazine

Edited by Keidie Burton

Alastair
Sawday's

Special Places
to Stay

French
Bed & Breakfast

"Long the definitive voice
on French B&Bs."
The Daily Mail

Edited by Emma Carey & Florence Oldfield

Alastair
Sawday's

Special Places
to Stay

Green Europe

"Attractive, easy to use and
unashamedly eco-centric."
Daily Telegraph

Edited by Kate Shepherd

Alastair
Sawday's

Special Places
to Stay

French Châteaux
& Hotels

"Sawday unearths the
most beguiling châteaux,
auberges and hotels."
The Daily Telegraph

ipa
Publisher
of the Year

Alastair
Sawday's

Special Places to Stay

Sixth edition
Copyright © 2010 Alastair Sawday
Publishing Co. Ltd
Published in 2010
ISBN-13: 978-1-906136-33-8

Alastair Sawday Publishing Co. Ltd,
The Old Farmyard, Yanley Lane,
Long Ashton, Bristol BS41 9LR, UK
Tel: +44 (0)1275 395430
Email: info@sawdays.co.uk
Web: www.sawdays.co.uk

The Globe Pequot Press,
P. O. Box 480, Guilford,
Connecticut 06437, USA
Tel: +1 203 458 4500
Email: info@globepequot.com
Web: www.globepequot.com

All rights reserved. No part of this
publication may be used other than for the
purpose for which it is intended nor may
any part be reproduced, or transmitted, in
any form or by any means, electronically or
mechanically, including photocopying,
recording or any information storage or
retrieval system, without prior written
permission from the publisher. Requests
for permission should be addressed to:
Alastair Sawday Publishing in the UK; or
The Globe Pequot Press in North America.
A catalogue record for this book is
available from the British Library. This
publication is not included under licences
issued by the Copyright Agency. No part of
this publication may be used in any form of
advertising, sales promotion or publicity.

*We have made every effort to ensure the accuracy
of the information in this book at the time of
going to press. However, we cannot accept any
responsibility for any loss, injury or
inconvenience resulting from the use of
information contained therein.*

Series Editor Alastair Sawday
Editor Florence Oldfield
Assistant Editor Cristina Sánchez González
Editorial Director Annie Shillito
Writing Alex Baker, Viv Cripps,
Jo Boissevain, Monica Guy, Abigail Hole
Florence Oldfield, Jennifer Telfeyan
Inspections Richard & Linda Armspach
Abbi Greetham, Jill Greetham,
Abigail Hole, Florence Oldfield,
Cristina Sánchez González,
Jennifer Telfeyan
*Thanks to those people who did a few inspections
or had a go at a write-up*
Accounts Bridget Bishop,
Shona Adcock, Rebecca Bebbington,
Christine Buxton, Amy Lancastle,
Sally Ranahan
Editorial Sue Bourner,
Angharad Barnes, Jo Boissevain,
Roxy Dumble
Production Jules Richardson,
Rachel Coe, Tom Germain,
Anny Mortada
Sales & Marketing & PR Rob Richardson,
Sarah Bolton, Bethan Riach, Lisa Walklin
Web & IT Dominic Oakley
Chris Banks, Phil Clarke,
Mike Peake, Russell Wilkinson,

Alastair Sawday has asserted his right to
be identified as the author of this work

Maps: Maidenhead Cartographic Services
Printing: Butler, Tanner & Dennis, Frome
UK distribution: Penguin UK, London

Alastair Sawday's

Special Places to Stay

Italy

4 Contents

The buildings

Beautiful as they were, our old offices leaked heat, used electricity to heat water and rooms, flooded spaces with light to illuminate one person, and were not ours to alter.

So in 2005 we created our own eco-offices by converting some old barns to create a low-emissions building. We made the building energy-efficient through a variety of innovative and energy-saving building techniques, described below.

Insulation We went to great lengths to ensure that very little heat can escape, by laying thick insulating board under the roof and floor and adding further insulation underneath the roof and between the rafters. We then lined the whole of the inside of the building with plastic sheeting to ensure air-tightness.

Heating We installed a wood-pellet boiler from Austria, in order to be largely fossil-fuel free. The pellets are made from compressed sawdust, a waste product from timber mills that work only with sustainably managed forests. The heat is conveyed by water, throughout the building, via an under-floor system.

Water We installed a 6000-litre tank to collect rainwater from the roofs. This is pumped back, via an ultra-violet filter, to the lavatories, showers and basins. There are two solar thermal panels on the roof providing heat to the one (massively insulated) hot-water cylinder.

Photo: Tom Germain

Lighting We have a carefully planned mix of low-energy lighting: task lighting and up-lighting. We also installed sun-pipes to reflect the outside light into the building.

Electricity All our electricity has long come from the Good Energy company and is 100% renewable.

Materials Virtually all materials are non-toxic or natural. Our carpets are made from (80%) Herdwick sheep-wool from National Trust farms in the Lake District.

Doors and windows Outside doors and new windows are wooden, double-glazed and beautifully constructed in Norway. Old windows have been double-glazed.

We have a building we are proud of, and architects and designers are fascinated by. But best of all, we are now in a better position to encourage our owners and readers to take sustainability more seriously.

What we do

Besides having moved the business to a low-carbon building, the company works in a number of ways to reduce its overall environmental footprint.

Our footprint We measure our footprint annually and use it to find ways of reducing our environmental impact. To help address unavoidable carbon emissions we try to put something back: since 2006 we have supported SCAD, an organisation that works with villagers in India to create sustainable development.

Travel Staff are encouraged to car-share or cycle to work and we provide showers (rainwater-fed) and bike sheds. Our company cars run on LPG (liquid petroleum gas) or recycled cooking oil. We avoid flying and take the train for business trips wherever possible. All office travel is logged as part of our footprint and we count our freelance editors' and inspectors' miles too.

Our office Nearly all of our office waste is recycled; kitchen waste is composted and used in the office vegetable garden. Organic and fairtrade basic provisions are used in the staff kitchen and at in-house events, and green cleaning products are used throughout the office.

Working with owners We are proud that many of our Special Places help support their local economy and, through our Ethical Collection, we recognise owners who go the extra mile to serve locally sourced and organic food or those who have a positive impact on their environment or community.

Engaging readers We hope to raise awareness of the need for individuals to play their part; our Go Slow series places an emphasis on ethical travel and the Fragile Earth imprint consists of hard-hitting environmental titles. Our Ethical Collection informs readers about owners' ethical endeavours.

Ethical printing We print our books locally to support the British printing industry and to reduce our carbon footprint. We print our books on either FSC-certified or recycled paper, using vegetable or soy-based inks.

Our supply chain Our electricity is 100% renewable (supplied by Good Energy), and we put our savings with Triodos, a bank whose motives we trust. Most supplies are bought in bulk from a local ethical-trading co-operative.

For many years Alastair Sawday Publishing has been 'greening' the business in different ways. Our aim is to reduce our environmental footprint as far as possible, and almost every decision we make takes into account the environmental implications. In recognition of our efforts we won a Business Commitment to the Environment Award in 2005, and in 2006 a Queen's Award for Enterprise in the Sustainable Development category. In that year Alastair was voted ITN's 'Eco Hero'. In 2009 we were given the South West C+ Carbon Positive Consumer Choices Award for our Ethical Collection.

In 2008 and again in 2009 we won the Independent Publishers Guild Environmental Award. In 2009 we were also the IPG overall Independent Publisher and Trade Publisher of the Year. The judging panel were effusive in their praise, stating: "With green issues currently at the forefront of publishers' minds, Alastair Sawday Publishing was singled out in this category as a model for all independents to follow. Its efforts to reduce waste in its office and supply chain have reduced the company's environmental impact, and it works closely with staff to identify more areas of improvement. Here is a publisher who lives and breathes green. Alastair Sawday has all the right principles and is clearly committed to improving its practice further."

Becoming 'green' is a journey and, although we began long before most companies, we still have a long way to go. We don't plan to pursue growth for growth's sake. The Sawday's name – and thus our future – depends on maintaining our integrity. We promote special places – those that add beauty, authenticity and a touch of humanity to our lives. This is a niche, albeit a growing one, so we will spend time pursuing truly special places rather than chasing the mass market.

That said, we do plan to produce more titles as well as to diversify. We are expanding our Go Slow series to other European countries, and have launched *Green Europe*, both bold new publishing projects designed to raise the profile of low-impact tourism. Our Fragile Earth series is a growing collection of campaigning books about the environment: highlighting the perilous state of the world yet offering imaginative and radical solutions and some intriguing facts, these books will keep you up to date and well-armed for the battle with apathy.

Photos: Tom Germain

I spent two weeks in Italy recently and was reminded what a grand role this book can play. We began in a B&B near Genoa, and we were immediately made to feel special. This was the work of the blessed Rosanna and Domenico in their oasis, La Traversina. Then we headed to the Cinque Terre, those celebrated 'five towns' of Liguria, outrageously picturesque on their rocky headlands but overloaded with travellers. So we gave up exploring, settled into our Special Place – the Villanova and made friends with the owners. Then rain drove us north to the shores of Lake Maggiore, where we stayed in the exquisite Polidora, its 18 acres of garden on the shores of a lake whose shimmering loveliness has seduced travellers for centuries. Across the water are the foothills of the Alps, snow whitening the peaks beyond the unfolding layers of green. Around the lake are villages and towns where strolling is a joy and eating a delight. There are islands rich in history, and pottering by boat from one to the other is one of the sweet pleasures of Maggiore.

So I am a big fan of this book. But planning an Italian holiday with it in your hand can be an exercise in frustration. Which special place to choose, of so many? To make things harder, we have many places in the cities, too: Venice, Florence, Rome, Naples, Turin, each awash with magnificent museums, beautiful streets and squares and delectable food.

Poor old Italy has taken a bashing recently and is feeling the crisis: fewer English tourists are travelling because of the weak pound. The trick is, of course, to eat out less frequently, move around a little less, cut down on the espressos and gelatos. Then there was the earthquake in Abruzzo in 2009, and many of our owners' businesses suffered as a result. But Italy is as much fun as ever, and the landscape and architecture have not changed.

These pages are packed with resourceful owners offering more than just a bed for the night. There are courses galore: we have three new B&Bs in Puglia alone offering art and pottery workshops, while wine and cookery courses, photography courses and guided tours abound. There's truffle and mushroom hunting, too.

Our Ethical Collection is new to this edition and there are lots of awards for food. I would love, one day, to have awards for sheer colourfulness, too. Italians would win them in droves. This is a country with that rare knack still, to make the visitor feel valued and alive.

Alastair Sawday

Until really quite recently, the thought of holidaying in Italy conjured up images of 'la bella Toscana' and the fashionable north. Think of cypress-lined avenues; David's perfectly carved torso; the treasures of Florence and Venice; vineyards stretching from Piedmont to Lazio... Beyond the glitzy Amalfi coast and Pompeii's fallen columns, Italy's rougher but beautiful southern half barely got a look in. These days, however, tourism in Italy is breaking through the north-south divide, infiltrating even the deepest, most remote corners of the south. More people than ever are heading southwards to the foot of Italy's slender boot – and the triangular-shaped 'ball' of Sicily, pitched into the Mediterranean.

With each new edition comes a stronger presence 'down south', and, in this sixth

edition, we have more special places than ever before. Those pages that cover flat, blue-skied Puglia, the heel of Italy's boot, are stuffed with the iconic cone-shaped 'trulli' houses and 'masserie' (fortified farmhouses). The fertile lands of Campania are peppered with agriturismi, a B&B concept that marries the twin industries of the south – agriculture and tourism. And, in wild, intriguing Sicily, is an exciting selection of small B&Bs, swanky hotels and quirky self-catering places to suit every pocket.

But this book is not just about landscape and bricks and mortar but also our owners. It is, of course, their hard work and spirit that make a self-catering house feel like home, a grand hotel welcoming, and a stay on a no-frills farm memorable. The southerners' focus on agriculture and their reliance on the land goes some way towards explaining their down-to-earth attitude: life is to be lived simply, to be relished, and the pace is slow. Thankfully, they are showing no signs of changing; spend a week here and you'll see what I mean. Whilst swathes of the country are being swept along in a 'slow' revolution, southern Italy doesn't appear to have even thought about the pursuit of a faster life.

While on the subject of Slow, you might consider taking the train when planning your trip. Don't assume it is compulsory to jump in a plane. If you catch the Eurostar from London in the afternoon you will be pulling into Rome the

Photo left: Agriturismo Alla Madonna del Piatto, entry 224
Photo right: Castello di Ripa d'Orcia, entry 169

following morning. Savour the journey, not just the arrival. Travelling through Italy by train is a rewarding, inspiring and, above all, exciting way to explore the country – and it beats hopping from one airport lounge to another.

Of course, it goes without saying that the Giotto-beautiful regions of northern Italy and the Renaissance cities of Florence, Venice and Rome are as popular as ever; and we have unearthed more gorgeous places for this edition. All our owners, from north to south, are characterised by the warmth of their welcome, the love of what they do and the way in which they do it. Still, if you haven't yet sampled a Neapolitan pizza in Naples, wandered Sicily's ancient ruins, basked on Puglia's sun-baked beaches or encountered the slowest of 'slow' Italy without fear of being dragged into the fast lane, follow your nose south and give it a go. You'll never look back.

Florence Oldfield

Photo: Bosco della Spina, entry 173

It's simple. There are no rules, no boxes to tick. We choose places that we like and are fiercely subjective in our choices. We also recognise that one person's idea of special is not necessarily someone else's so there is a huge variety of places, and prices, in the book. Those who are familiar with our Special Places series know that we look for comfort, originality, authenticity, and reject the insincere, the anonymous and the banal. The way guests are treated comes as high on our list as the setting, the architecture, the atmosphere and the food.

We have selected the widest range of places, and prices, for you to choose from – castles, villas, city apartments, farmhouses, country inns, even a monastery or two. It might be breakfast under the frescoed ceiling of a Renaissance villa that is special, or a large and boisterous dinner in a farmhouse kitchen, or a life-enhancing view. We have not necessarily chosen the most opulent places to stay, but the most interesting and satisfying. But because Italy has, to quote Lord Byron, "the fatal gift of beauty" it is easy to forget that it hasn't all been built with aesthetics in mind. Don't be put off when you discover that there are swathes of industrial plant (yes, even in Tuscany). These things can't be airbrushed out, but acknowledge that they exist and they won't spoil your fun.

Inspections

We visit every place in the guide to get a feel for how both house and owner tick.

We don't take a clipboard and we don't have a list of what is acceptable and what is not. Instead, we chat for an hour or so with the owner or manager and look round. It's all very informal, but it gives us an excellent idea of who would enjoy staying there. If the visit happens to be the last of the day, we sometimes stay the night. Once in the book, properties are re-inspected every few years, so that we can keep things fresh and accurate.

Feedback

In between inspections we rely on feedback from our army of readers, as well as from staff members who are encouraged to visit properties across the series. This feedback is invaluable to us and we always follow up on comments.

So do tell us whether your stay has been a joy or not, if the atmosphere was great or stuffy, the owners and staff cheery or bored. The accuracy of the book depends on what you, and our inspectors, tell us.

Photo: Casa Rosa, entry 225

A lot of the new entries in each edition are recommended by our readers, so keep telling us about new places you've discovered too. Please use the forms on our website at www.sawdays.co.uk, or later in this book (page 406).

However, please do not tell us if your starter was cold, or the bedside light broken. Tell the owner, immediately, and get them to do something about it. Most owners, or staff, are more than happy to correct problems and will bend over backwards to help. Far better than bottling it up and then writing to us a week later!

Subscriptions

Owners pay to appear in this guide. Their fee goes towards the high costs of inspecting, of producing an all-colour book and of maintaining our website. We only include places that we find special for one reason or another, so it is not possible for anyone to buy their way onto these pages. Nor is it possible for the owner to write their own description. We will say if the bedrooms are small, or if a main road is near. We do our best to avoid misleading people.

Disclaimer

We make no claims to pure objectivity in choosing these places. They are here simply because we like them. Our opinions and tastes are ours alone and this book is a statement of them; we hope you will share them. We have done our utmost to get our facts right but apologise unreservedly for any mistakes that may have crept in. The latest information we have about each place can be found on our website, www.sawdays.co.uk.

You should know that we don't check such things as fire alarms, swimming pool security or any other regulation with which owners of properties receiving paying guests should comply. This is the responsibility of the owners.

Finding the right place for you

All these places are special in one way or another. All have been visited and then written about honestly so that you can take what you want and leave the rest. Those of you who swear by Sawday's books trust our write-ups precisely because we don't have a blanket standard; we include places simply because we like them. But we all have different priorities, so do read the descriptions carefully and pick out the places where you will be comfortable. If something is particularly important to you then check when you book: a simple question or two can avoid misunderstandings.

Maps

Each property is flagged with its entry number on the maps at the front. These maps are a great starting point for planning your trip, but please don't use them as anything other than a general guide – use a decent road map for real navigation. Most places will send you detailed instructions once you have booked your stay. Self-catering places are marked in blue on the maps; others are marked in red.

Ethical Collection

We're always keen to draw attention to owners who are striving to have a positive impact on the world, so you'll notice that some entries are flagged as being part of our 'Ethical Collection'. These places are working hard to reduce their environmental footprint, making significant contributions to their local community, or are passionate about serving local or organic food. Owners have had to fill in a very detailed questionnaire before becoming part of this Collection – read more on page 400. This doesn't mean that other places in the guide are not taking similar initiatives – many are – but we may not yet know about them.

Symbols

Below each entry you will see some symbols, which are explained at the very back of the book. They are based on the information given to us by the owners. However, things do change: bikes may be under repair or a new pool may have been put in. Please use the symbols as a guide rather than an absolute statement of fact and double-check anything that is important to you – owners occasionally bend their own rules, so it's worth asking if you may take your child or dog even if they don't have the symbol.

Wheelchair access – The ♿ symbol shows those places that are keen to accept wheelchair users and have made provision for them. However, this does not mean that wheelchair users will always be met with a perfect landscape. You may encounter ramps, a shallow step, gravelled paths, alternative routes into some rooms, a bathroom, perhaps even a lift. In short, there may be the odd hindrance and we urge you to call and make sure you will get what you need.

Photo: Green Manors, entry 317

Limited mobility – The limited mobility symbol 𝄅 shows those places where at least one bedroom and bathroom is accessible without using stairs. The symbol is designed to satisfy those who walk slowly, with difficulty, or with the aid of a stick. A wheelchair may be able to navigate some areas, but these places are not fully wheelchair friendly. If you use a chair for longer distances, but are not too bad over shorter distances, you'll probably be OK; again, please ring and ask. There may be a step or two, a bath or a shower with a tray in a cubicle, a good distance between the car park and your room, slippery flagstones or a tight turn.

Children – The 𝄉 symbol shows places which are happy to accept children of all ages. This does not mean that they will necessarily have cots, high chairs, etc. If an owner welcomes children but only those above a certain age, we have put these details at the end of their write-up.

These houses do not have the child symbol, but even these folk may accept your younger child at quiet times. If you want to get out and about in the evenings, check when you book whether there are any babysitting services. Even very small places can sometimes organise this for you.

Pets – Our 🠾 symbol shows places which are happy to accept pets. It means they can sleep in the bedroom with you, but not on the bed. It's really important to get this one right before you arrive, as many places make you keep dogs in the car. Check carefully: Spot's emotional wellbeing may depend on it.

Owners' pets – The 🐕 symbol is given when the owners have their own pet on the premises. It may not be a cat! But it is there to warn you that you may be greeted by a dog, serenaded by a parrot, or indeed sat upon by a cat.

Photo: Locanda Casanuova, entry 161

Types of places

Each entry is simply labelled (B&B, hotel, self-catering) to guide you, but the write-ups reveal several descriptive terms. This list serves as a rough guide to what you might expect to find.

Agriturismo: farm or estate with B&B rooms or apartments; Albergo: Italian word for an inn, more personal than a hotel; Azienda agrituristica: literally, 'agricultural business'; Casa (Cà in Venetian dialect): house; Cascina: farmhouse; Castello: castle; Corte: courtyard; Country house: a new concept in Italian hospitality, usually family-run and akin to a villa; Dimora: dwelling; Fattoria: farm; Locanda: means 'inn', but sometimes used to describe a restaurant only; Podere: farm or smallholding; Palazzo: literally a 'palace' but more usually a mansion; Relais: an imported French term meaning 'inn'; Residenza: an apartment or house with rooms for guests; Tenuta: farm holding, or 'tenancy'; Villa: country residence.

Rooms

Bedrooms — We tell you about the range of accommodation in singles, doubles, twins, family rooms and suites, as well as apartments and whole houses. A 'family' room is a loose term because, in Italy, triples and quadruples often sleep more than the heading suggests; extra beds can often be added for children, usually with a charge, so check when booking.

Where an entry reads '4 + 2' this means 4 B&B rooms plus 2 self-catering apartments/villas/cottages.

Bathrooms — Assume that bathrooms are en suite unless we say otherwise. Italian bathrooms often have a shower only.

Meals

Eating in Italy is one of life's great pleasures. There is plenty of variety, and each region has its own speciality and its surprises. Many owners use organic, home-grown or locally grown ingredients, and more often than not will have produced some part of your meal themselves.

Vegetarians — Although fresh, seasonal vegetables are readily available in Italy,

Photo: Fattoria di Pietrabuona, entry 109

most Italian dishes contain meat and some Italians still find the concept of vegetarianism quite bizarre. All of our owners who offer a good range of vegetarian options have a special symbol – but don't be surprised if those without it struggle to understand a meal without meat.

Breakfast – What constitutes breakfast varies hugely from place to place. Many hotels don't offer it at all, especially in towns, where it is normal to walk to the nearest bar for your first espresso. (Prices double or triple as soon as you sit down, so if you want to save money, join the locals at the bar.) If you are

confronted with a vacuum-packed breakfast it's because B&Bs are only allowed to serve fresh ingredients if they meet certain strict regulations. On farms, however, you should find homemade jams and cakes as well as home-produced cheeses and fruit.

Dinner – Hotels and other places with restaurants usually offer the widest à la carte choice. Smaller places may offer a set dinner (at a set time) and you will need to book in advance. Many of our owners are excellent cooks so, if you fancy an evening sitting two steps from your bedroom on your host's terrace overlooking Tuscan hills or Umbrian

Photo: Su Dandaru, entry 344

valleys, be sure to ask your hosts — on booking or on arrival — if they are able to share their culinary skills and serve up a sumptuous dinner on site. Sometimes you will eat with the family; sometimes you will be eating in a separate dining room, served by a member of the family. Small farms and inns often offer dinners which are excellent value and delicious, so keep an open mind. But be aware that laws in some regions of Italy do not allow B&Bs to serve dinner to their guests.

Prices

The prices we quote are the prices per night per room unless otherwise stated, breakfast included. For self-catering, we specify if the price is per week. For half-board, it may be per person (p.p.). Meal prices are always given per person; we try to give you an approximate price and say if wine is included. Prices quoted are those given to us for 2010-11 but they may change before the next edition is published in 2012. Treat them as a guideline rather than as infallible. We try to list any extra hidden costs — eg linen, towels, heating — but always check on booking.

Booking and cancellation

Hotels will usually ask you for a credit card number at the time of booking, for confirmation. Remember to let smaller places know if you are likely to be arriving late, and if you want dinner. Some of the major cities get very full (and often double in price) around the time of trade fairs (e.g. fashion fairs in

Milan, the Biennale in Venice). And book well ahead if you plan to visit Italy during school holidays.

Some cancellation policies are more stringent than others. It is also worth noting that some owners will take the money directly from your credit/debit card without contacting you to discuss it. So ask them to explain their cancellation policy clearly before booking so you understand exactly where you stand; it may well avoid a nasty surprise. And consider taking out travel insurance (with a cancellation clause) if you're concerned.

Payment

The most commonly accepted credit cards are Visa, Eurocard, MasterCard and Amex. Many places in this book don't take plastic because of high bank charges. Check the symbols at the bottom of each entry before you arrive, in case you are a long way from a cash dispenser!

Tipping

In bars you are given your change on a small saucer, and it is usual to leave a couple of small coins there. A cover charge on restaurant meals is standard. A small tip ('mancia') in family-run establishments is also welcome, so leave one if you wish. But do.

Closed

When given in months this means for the whole of the month stated. So, 'Closed: November–March' means closed from 1 November to 31 March.

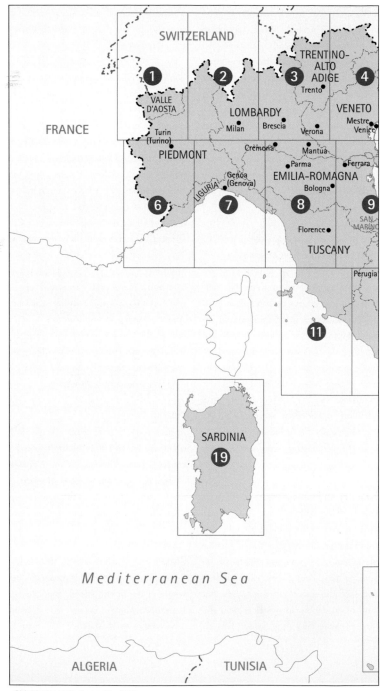

©Maidenhead Cartographic, 2010

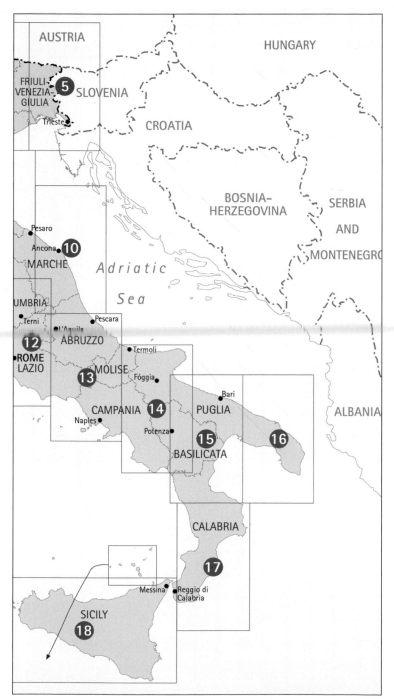

©Maidenhead Cartographic, 2010

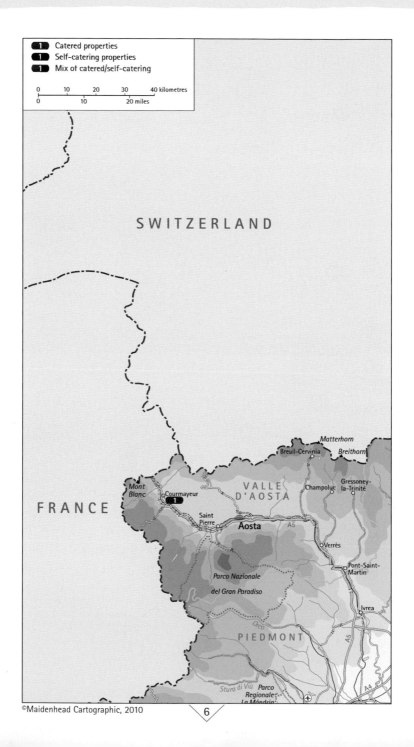

©Maidenhead Cartographic, 2010

Map 2   23

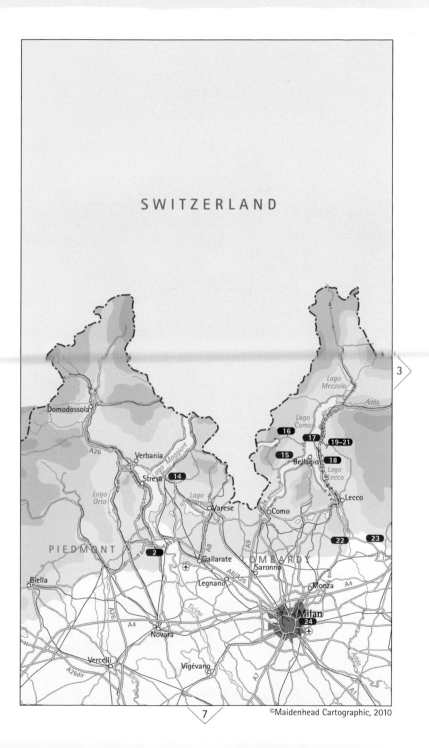

SWITZERLAND

Lago
Mezzola

Adda

Domodossola

Lago
Comos

16

17

19-21

A26

Verbania

Lago Maggiore

15

Bellagio

18

Lago
Lecco

Stresa

14

Lago
Orta

Lago
Varese

Lecco

Varese

Como

PIEDMONT

2

A8

A9

Gallarate

LOMBARDY

22

23

Biella

A8/A26

Saronno

Legnano

Monza

A4

A26

Ticino

A4

Milan

24

Novara

Vercelli

A26dir

Vigévano

A7

Adda

A1

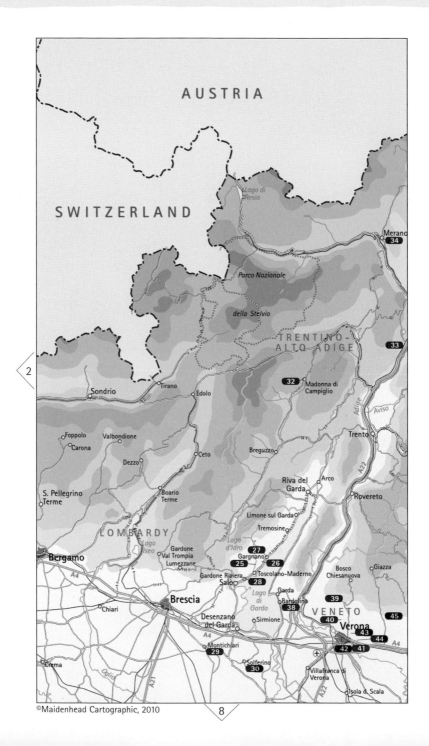

Map 4   25

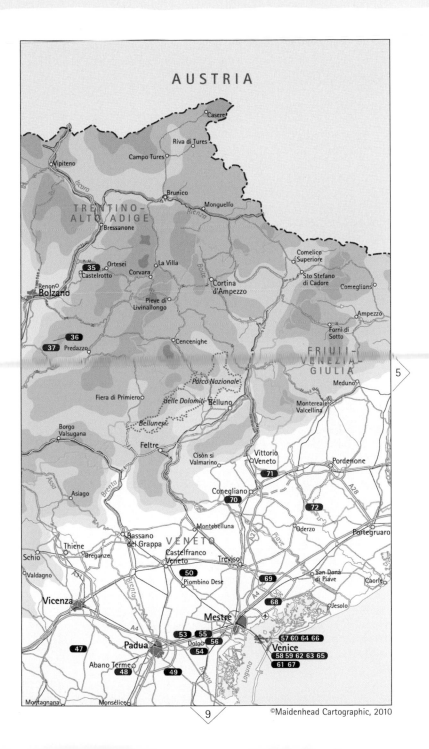

©Maidenhead Cartographic, 2010

AUSTRIA

Tarvisio

A23

Tolmezzo

Gemona di Friuli

FRIULI-
VENEZIA-
GIULIA

Faedis

75

Povoletto

74

Udine

Codroipo

A23

Palmanova

Gorizia

A4

A4

Monfalcone

SLOVENIA

73

Lignano
Sabbiadoro

Grado

Lignano Riviera

Bibione

Trieste

CROATIA

4

©Maidenhead Cartographic, 2010

When asked by Sawday's to swap my mode of travel from plane to train, I thought about what I would be giving up — stagnant fluorescent airports, humourless staff and cramped seating. These are things that my Italian experience could do without.

This guide is concerned with finding special places. We don't usually mention the journey because, let's face it, budget flying is not exactly a special experience — rather something we have to endure before delving into the wonders awaiting us at the other end. Perhaps the journey by train would be different, a journey we could actually call 'special'.

Throughout our books we celebrate owners who are making an effort to be green and encourage readers to consider their carbon footprint. So we're very aware that it is important we keep our 'compilation carbon' to a minimum, too. When I considered the train journey I felt excited. Not only would I be avoiding those tedious queues and robotic frowns, I would be saving carbon emissions and going a little way to lessen the global contribution to climate change.

My fourteen-hour overnight journey from London to Rome was, as I had imagined it to be, special indeed. After a pan-European dinner in the restaurant car with its crisp white tablecloths, I returned to my shared cabin where water was offered at no extra charge; blankets were duly delivered.

I imagined the countryside outside my window: the French and Swiss towns we would pass (why, I asked myself, had I not chosen the cheaper option and travelled by day?). I fell into a deep sleep with the train droning peacefully beneath me and awoke just in time for breakfast. Twenty minutes later I was rested, relaxed and pulling in to the station in Rome. My Italian experience had been extended by fourteen enjoyable hours and, as the back of my train ticket told me, I had saved a mass of carbon.

A special experience that helps the environment deserves a page in this book and I urge you to try the experience for yourself — you'll be surprised to find the difference it can make.

Kate Shepherd

• www.seat61.com offers fantastic advice on fares and bookings for all European sea and land travel, and has a special section on Italy.

• www.ferroviedellostato.it is the Italian rail website for train timetables and fares. Remember to type in Italian names for places (eg Firenze not Florence).

• www.raileurope.co.uk is the place to book tickets. If you prefer to speak to a human being, call +44 (0)870 5848 848 and book over the phone.

• www.tgv-europe.com

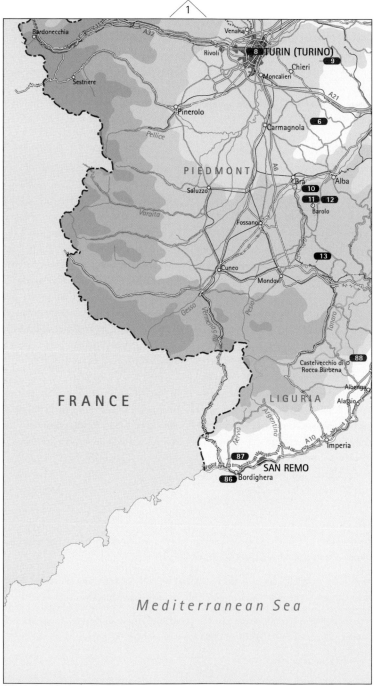

©Maidenhead Cartographic, 2010

Map 7   29

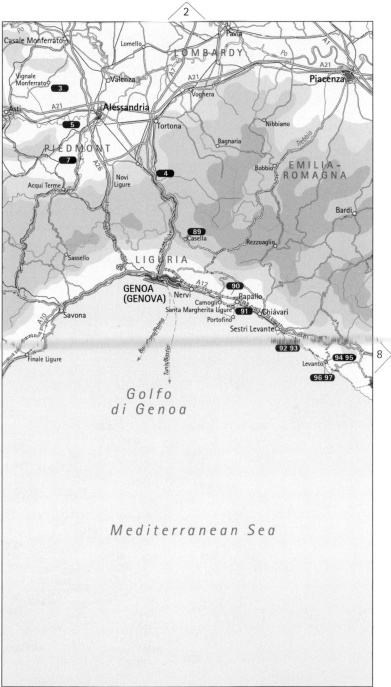

©Maidenhead Cartographic, 2010

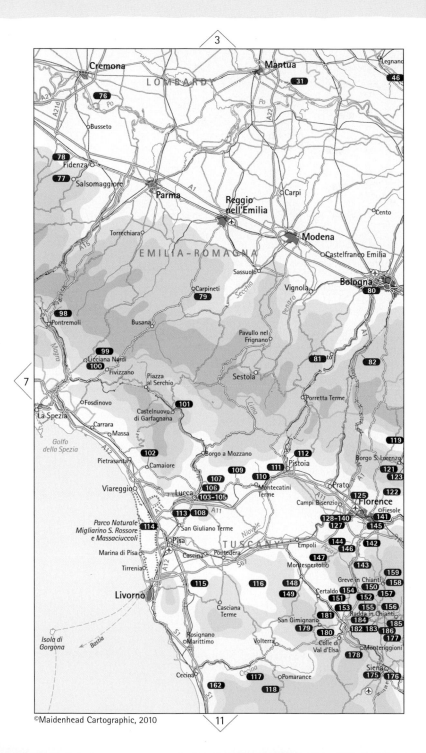

3

Cremona
Mantua
Legnano
LOMBARDY
46
31
76
Po
A21d
A22
Po
A22
oBusseto
78
Fidenza o
77
Salsomaggiore
A1
Carpi
Parma
Reggio
nell'Emilia
oCento
Torrechiara o
EMILIA-ROMAGNA
Modena
A15
Castelfranco Emilia
Sassuolo o
Bologna
Carpineti
Secchia
Vignola o
80
79
A1
98
o Pontremoli
Busana
Pavullo nel
Frignano o
Magra
99
Licciana Nardi
100
o Fivizzano
81
82
7
Piazza
al Serchio
Sestola
Panaro
o Fosdinovo
101
Porretta Terme
La Spezia
Castelnuovo
di Garfagnana
Lima
119
Carrara
o Massa
Golfo
della Spezia
A12
102
o Borgo a Mozzano
112
Borgo S. Lorenzo
Pietrasanta
o Camaiore
109
111
Pistoia
121
123
Viareggio o
107
110
Prato
122
106
Montecatini
Terme
A11
125
Florence
Lucca
103-105
Campi Bisenzio
o Fiesole
113
108
A11
128-140
141
Parco Naturale
Migliarino S. Rossore
e Massaciuccoli
114
o San Giuliano Terme
127
145
o Pisa
144
142
Marina di Pisa o
Cascina
Pontedera
TUSCANY
Empoli
146
147
143
Tirrenia o
A12
S67
Montespertoli
159
158
115
116
148
Greve in Chianti
150
149
Certaldo o
154
157
152
Isola di
Gorgona
Bastia
Casciana
Terme
153
155
156
San Gimignano
181
Radda in Chianti
184
185
o Rosignano
Marittimo
179
180
182 183
186
177
Volterra o
Colle di
Val d'Elsa
178
Monteriggioni
Cecina
Cecina
Siena
162
117
o Pomarance
175
176
118

©Maidenhead Cartographic, 2010

11

Map 9

31

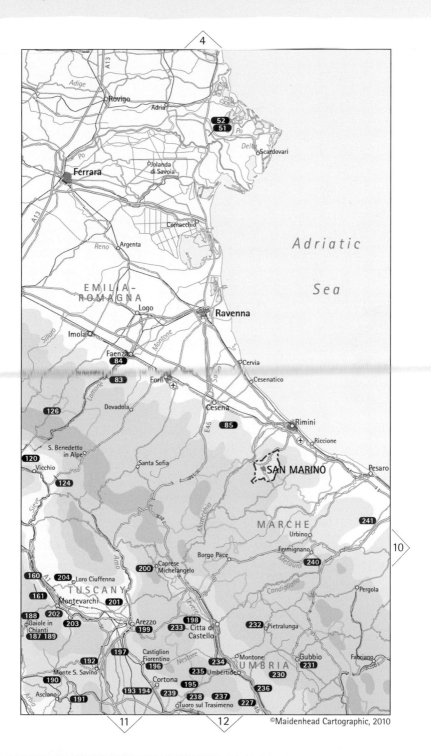

©Maidenhead Cartographic, 2010

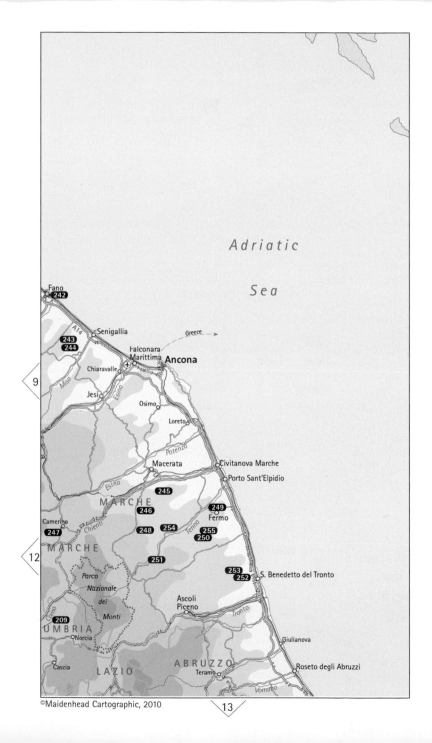

©Maidenhead Cartographic, 2010

Getting around Italy 33

Public transport is excellent in Italy. Many of our special places lie within ten miles of a bus or train station, and if owners are willing to arrange collection you may not need to hire a car.

A train journey in Italy can be as slow (and cheap) or as fast (and more expensive) as you want it to be, but one thing is sure: city-to-city travel is faster, easier and cheaper by train than by car. The state-run network *Ferrovie dello Stato* (FS) operates many different types of train: *Inter Regionale* (slow but cheap), *Intercity* (excellent) and the fast but relatively costly *Eurostar* (not to be confused with the London–Paris Eurostar). You pay per mile.

Seat reservations, compulsory on *Eurostar*, are strongly recommended on all routes at peak hours and in high season. Automatic ticket machines are plentiful in most major stations, but you must validate your ticket by stamping it (*convalida biglietto*), either here or in the

machines provided on platforms. If you don't, you could get a fine (*multa*) – also highly likely if you buy your ticket on board rather than beforehand.

A few mainline and most regional trains in Italy now take bikes, and you need to purchase a ticket for the bike as well as yourself. The bike ticket will be valid for 24 hours and can be used anywhere, so buy a few if you plan to travel with a cycle for several days. Usually there's a bike symbol on the bike carriage and, if you're lucky, a bike rack too.

Travel by train is not always the best choice though, particularly in the south where west–east networks are slow or non-existent, and you must always check times. You might be better off booking a seat on a coach; *agenzia viaggi* (travel agents) are found in nearly all towns across the country and will book coaches and trains for you.

Urban buses, metros, trains and trams are also reliable and cheap. Buy a day ticket in advance, at a ticket machine or a local news kiosk (*tabacchi*).

Driving in Italy is challenging for the British driver – Italian drivers are skilled but scary and like nothing better than to sit on your tail. Mountain roads can be steep and narrow with precarious drops and hair-pin bends; although we try to mention in our write-ups when roads are particularly difficult, please keep this in mind when choosing your hire car.

Photo: istock.com

©Maidenhead Cartographic, 2010

Map 12

35

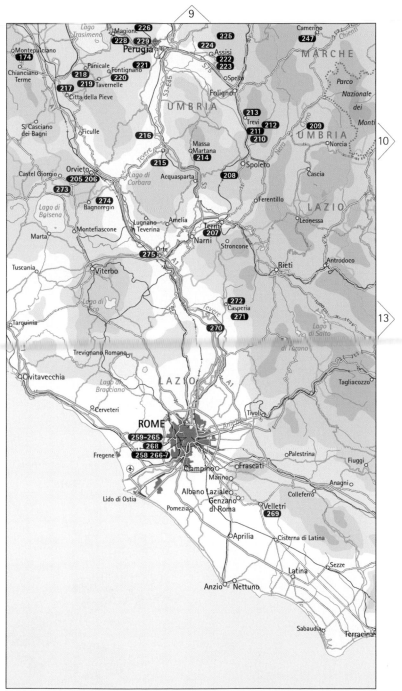

©Maidenhead Cartographic, 2010

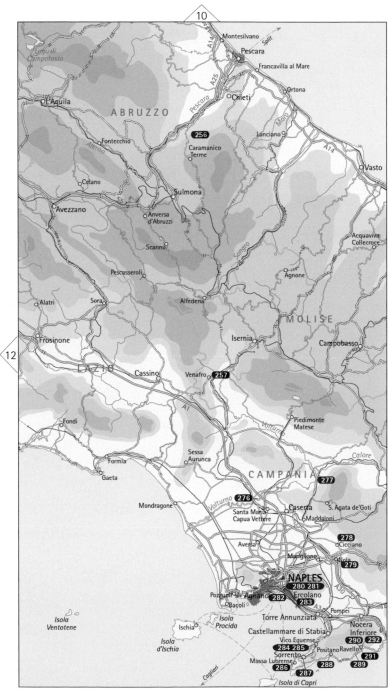

©Maidenhead Cartographic, 2010

Map 14   37

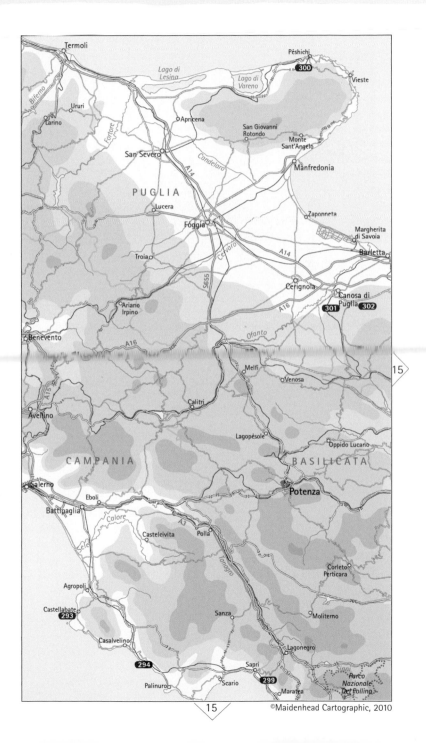

©Maidenhead Cartographic, 2010

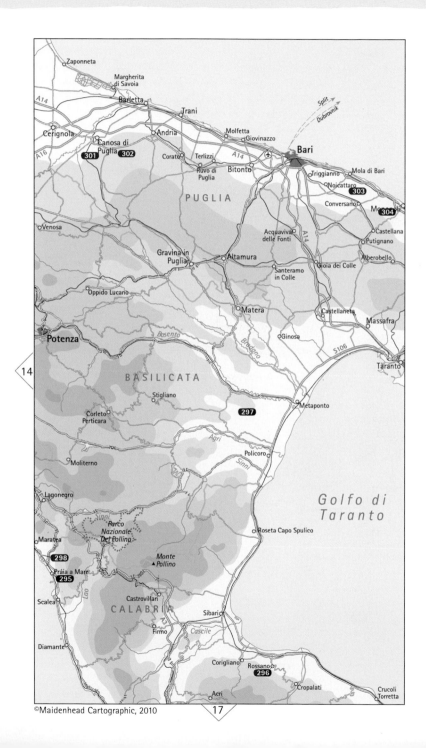

Map 16

39

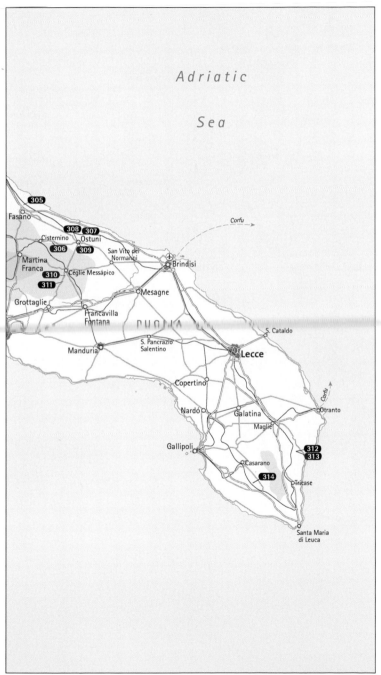

Adriatic

Sea

Corfu

305

Fasano

308 307

Cisternino Ostuni

306 309 San Vito dei Normanni

Martina Franca

310 Ceglie Messápico Brindisi

311

Mesagne

Grottaglie

Francavilla Fontana PUGLIA

S. Cataldo

Manduria S. Pancrazio Salentino

Lecce

Copertino

Corfu

Nardó Galatina Otranto

Maglie

Gallipoli 312

Casarano 313

314 Tricase

Santa Maria di Leuca

©Maidenhead Cartographic, 2010

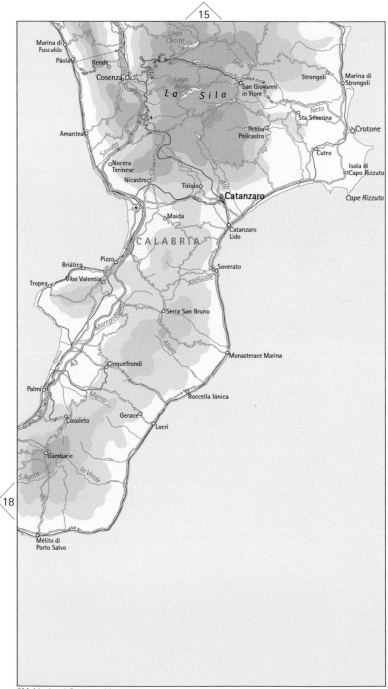

©Maidenhead Cartographic, 2010

Map 18

41

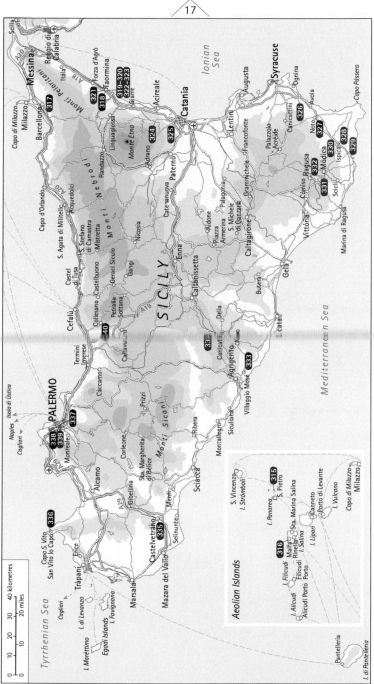

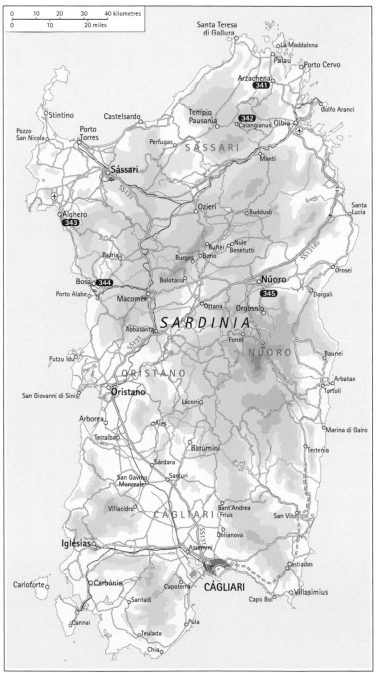

| 0 | 10 | 20 | 30 | 40 kilometres |
| 0 | | 10 | | 20 miles |

Santa Teresa
di Gallura

La Maddalena

Palau

Porto Cervo

Arzachena
341

Golfo Aranci

Stintino

Castelsardo

Tempio
Pausania

342
Calangianus   Olbia

Pozzo
San Nicola

Porto
Torres

Perfugas

SASSARI

Monti

Sássari

SS131

Ozierí

Buddusò

Santa
Lucia

Alghero

343

Bultei   Nule
Benetutti

SS131dir

Padria

Burgos   Bono

Orosei

Bosa   **344**

Bolotaria

Núoro

Porto Alabe

Macomér

345

Dorgali

Ottana   Orgòsolo

SARDINIA

Abbasanta

Fonni

Putzu Idu

NUORO

Baunei

ORISTANO

Arbatax
Tortoli

San Giovanni di Sinis

Oristano

Láconi

Arborea

Ales

Marina di Gairo

Terralba

Barúmini

Tertenia

Sárdara

San Gavino
Monreale

Sanluri

Villacidro

CAGLIARI

Sant'Andrea
Frius

San Vito

SS131

Dolianova

Iglésias

Assemini

Castiadas

Carloforte

Carbónia

Capoterra

CÁGLIARI

Villasimius

Santadi

Capo Boi

Cannai

Púla

Teulada

Chia

©Maidenhead Cartographic, 2010

Valle d'Aosta · Piedmont

Photo: istock.com

Auberge de la Maison

What a setting! You're in the old part of the village of Val Fenet, three kilometres from Courmayeur, in sight of Mont Blanc, surrounded by gentle terraces, gardens, meadows and majestic views. The Auberge has a quietly elegant and exclusive feel yet is not in the least intimidating, thanks to the cheerful (and efficient) staff. Bedrooms are uncluttered, stylish and comfortable with mellow colours. Many have a third bed disguised as a sofa; nearly all have balconies and views ranging from good to superb. A Tuscan influence is detectable in the décor; the owner is from Florence. His impressive collection of images of the Valle d'Aosta, from old promotional posters to oil paintings, makes a fascinating display, while a reassembled wooden mountain house is a most unusual feature of the reception and sitting area. There's a fitness centre, too, with a sauna and hydromassage. Come in any season: to fish for trout or play a round of golf, or to ski (right to the ski lift) or don crampons for a winter ascent.

Price	€140–€310. Half-board €195–€340.
Rooms	33: 14 doubles, 3 suites, 3 family rooms, 13 triples.
Meals	Dinner €38. Wine €12.
Closed	15 days in March & 15 days in November.
Directions	From south, direction Entreves; signed. From France, signed after Mont-Blanc tunnel.

Alessandra Garin
Fraz. Entrèves, 11013 Courmayeur

Tel	+39 0165 869811
Email	info@aubergemaison.it
Web	www.aubergemaison.it

Cascina Motto

Flowers everywhere: spilling from the balcony, filling the patio, clasping the walls of the cottage... wisteria, vines, azaleas, roses. It's an immaculate garden, with lawns, spreading trees, boules court and a discreet summer pool. Roberta's lovely, too, so warm and friendly; you are made at once to feel part of the family. They came here years ago – she and David, their daughters, Roberta's parents Sergio and Lilla, four dogs. They clearly love the house, which they've restored and filled with paintings and beautiful things. In a quiet street, in a quiet village, this is a happy and restful place to stay. The twin room, named after Roberta's grandmother, has windows facing two ways – over the garden and towards Monte Rosa – plus whitewashed walls, blue cotton rugs, blue-painted iron beds, books, a comfy sofa, a big bathroom. The cottage, its bedroom in the hayloft, is bright, airy, charming, with country furniture, a well-equipped kitchenette, a balcony; it's completely independent of the main house. Breakfast is a feast, and the lakes of Orta and Maggiore are a 20-minute drive. *Minimum stay two nights.*

Price	€75. Cottage €85–€150.
Rooms	1 + 1: 1 twin. 1 cottage for 2-4.
Meals	Restaurants 1km.
Closed	December–February.
Directions	From Milano A4 (Laghi); after Gallarate, A26 for Alessandria exit Castelletto Ticino. Signs for Novara SS32, 3rd exit for Divignano (via Boschi di Sopra). At Divignano, 2nd left for Via Marzabotto.

	Roberta Plevani
	Via Marzabotto 7, 28010 Divignano
Tel	+39 0321 995350
Email	cascinamotto@interfree.it
Web	www.cascinamotto.com

Ethical Collection: Food.
See page 400 for details

Cascina Alberta Agriturismo

This attractive hilltop farmhouse in this famous wine-producing area. Marked by two stately cypress trees, the house is two kilometres from the town centre and has 360° views of the surrounding vineyards and hills – sensational. The business is run on agriturismo lines by smiling, capable Raffaella, who lives just across the courtyard with her town-planner husband and their 16 year-old son. Tiled guest bedrooms are extremely pretty: an old marble-topped table here, a country wardrobe there, beds painted duck-egg blue, walls in soft pastel and many pieces beautifully painted by Raffaella. Both the bedrooms and the frescoed dining room lie across the farmyard from your hosts; if you choose to eat in, you dine at your own table on local dishes at reasonable prices, with wines from the estate — some of them have been aged in wooden barrels and are hard to find outside the area. Raffaella speaks excellent English and is happy to help guests get the most out of this enchanting area. Just an hour's drive from the coast.

Price	€64-€75. Triple €80-€90.
Rooms	5: 4 twins/doubles, 1 triple.
Meals	Dinner with wine, €16-€22.
Closed	20 December-February; August.
Directions	From Vignale, follow signs to Camagna. After 2km left at roadside shrine. Cascina Alberta is 400m on right.

Raffaella de Cristofaro
Loc. Ca' Prano 14,
15049 Vignale Monferrato
Tel   +39 0142 933313
Email   cascinalberta@netcomp.it
Web   www.cascinalberta.it

Entry 3   Map 7

La Traversina Agriturismo

Come for the roses, the irises, the hostas! You'll find over 230 different varieties of plant here – they are Rosanna's passion. With drowsy shutters, buzzing bees and walls festooned in roses, the house and outbuildings appear to be in a permanent state of siesta. As do the seven cats, basking on warm window sills and shady terraces. There's a touch of *The Secret Garden* about the half-hidden doors, enticing steps and riotous plants, and the air is fragrant with lavender, oregano and roses, many from France. The house and farm, on a wooded hillside, have been in Rosanna's family for nearly 300 years; she gave up a career as an architect to create this paradise 40 minutes from Genoa. Homely, imaginatively decorated, bedrooms have handsome furniture, books, pictures; bathrooms come with baskets of goodies. Everyone eats together at a long table in the conservatory or outside, where lights glow in the trees at night. Rosanna, Domenico and young Vijaya are the most delightful hosts and the home-grown food is a revelation: agriturismo at its best. *Children over 12 welcome. Courses on roses February-May.*

Price	€90–€110. Half-board €70–€80 p.p. Apartments €115–€135. All prices per night.
Rooms	2 + 3: 1 double, 1 family room. 3 apartments for 2.
Meals	Dinner €25–€35, by arrangement. Wine €8. Restaurant 7km.
Closed	Rarely.
Directions	A7 Milan-Genova exit Vignole Borbera for Stazzano; 4km; signed.

Ethical Collection: Food.
See page 400 for details

Rosanna & Domenico Varese Puppo
Cascina La Traversina 109,
15060 Stazzano

Tel	+39 0143 61377
Email	latraversina@latraversina.com
Web	www.latraversina.com

Casa Isabella

What a renovation! Computer programmer and whizz-at-cocktails Alessandro, and architect/designer Monica, alive with happiness and creativity, gave up lives in Turin for this dream: to renovate a village farmhouse in lovely Piedmont with glorious vineyard views. Casa Isabella is heaven. Doors and tiles have been reclaimed and walls painted in classic hues (ochre, slate blue, a dash of claret); elegant 1920s furnishings mix with unusual paintings and contemporary quirkery; lights have been inserted into stone stairs, bathrooms have exquisite hand-made mirrors, and coloured candles illuminate grandmother's cutlery. Bedrooms are huge and two have balconies. Monica's food is delicious, the breads and pastas homemade, the menus regional, the wines local; a sample of salami or a snack of crudités from the kitchen garden are yours whenever you like. Heavenly breakfasts are served, when you want them, in the dining room or in the shade of a tree; in winter, logs smoulder. Books by the score, boules in the garden, a charmingly natural pool for swimmers, and a bustling market town 15 minutes down the road.

Price	€120.
Rooms	4: 2 doubles, 2 twins.
Meals	Dinner €30. Wine €9-€38.
Closed	Rarely.
Directions	A26 Alessandria-Genova; exit Alessandria Sud. Follow signs for Nizza Monferrato; signs to Vaglio Serra on SP40. After 4km in Vaglio Serra, signs for Casa Isabella.

Monica Molari & Alessandro Barattieri
Via La Pietra 5, 14049 Vaglio Serra
Tel   +39 0141 732201
Email info@casa-isabella.com
Web   www.casa-isabella.com

Cascina Papa Mora Agriturismo

Authentic agriturismo in northern Italy. Adriana and Maria Teresa run grandmother's old house, speak fluent English and make you truly welcome. The farm produces wine, vegetables and fruit; the pantry overflows with oil, wine, chutney and jam. (This is one of the main regions for Barbera, Dolcetto, Bracchetto, Spumante.) We can't say that the farmhouse has been lovingly restored – more razed to the ground and rebuilt, then bedecked with simple stencils of flowers. Bedrooms, some hiding in the roof area, have no-nonsense 1930s furniture and light floral spreads. There's a little sitting room for guests with a wood-burning stove and, outside, a garden with roses, lavender and herbs sloping down to the pool and stables. The sisters also run a restaurant here and are passionate about their organic credentials. Dinner is a feast of gnocchi and tagliatelle, pepperoni cream puffs, anchovies in almond sauce, all delicious, and fun. Don't leave without sampling some homemade organic ice cream. Breakfast on the veranda where the blossom is pretty, the hills surround you, the bread comes fresh from the wood oven.

Price	€70. Singles €40. Triple €85. Quadruples €95. Half-board €60 p.p.
Rooms	7: 4 twins/doubles, 1 triple, 2 quadruples.
Meals	Lunch/dinner with wine, €25-€30.
Closed	December-February.
Directions	A21 exit Villanova d'Asti & for Cellarengo. On outskirts of village left into Via Ferrere, past small chapel to farm.

Adriana & Maria Teresa Bucco
Via Ferrere 16, 14010 Cellarengo

Tel	+39 0141 935126
Email	papamora@tin.it
Web	www.cascinapapamora.it

La Granica

When Karen, with Mark, went in search of her Italian roots, their adventure ended in an 18th-century grain barn in a secluded dell surrounded by rolling vineyards. Enter the beautifully renovated *granica* through a foyer of limestone floors, a wet bar and exposed brick walls: to the left is the library with deep leather sofas and chocolate and lime colours; to the right is the dining room, sleekly minimalist with polished marble floors and Lithuanian oak chairs. Here, fresh buffet-breakfasts and seasonal four-course dinners are served. Beneath a high cathedral ceiling, the four bedrooms are luxuriously furnished with lashings of silk, velvet chenille armchairs (or chaise-longue), splashes of raspberry tones, Egyptian cotton sheets. In the more traditional rooms are mahogany sleigh beds and resplendent bohemian chandeliers. The self-catering terrace house holds a diminutive sitting room, a fully equipped kitchen and double and twin bedrooms in house style – the former with a 'Jacobean' four-poster. Trees and lawns neatly frame the discreet swimming pool. *Minimum stay two nights in cottage.*

Price	€110–€165. Cottage €150–€200 (€635–€1,150 per week).
Rooms	4 + 1: 4 doubles. Cottage for 2-4.
Meals	Breakfast €10 for self-caterers. Dinner with wine, €30–€35. Buffet supper €10. Snacks €5–€8. Restaurant 3km.
Closed	Rarely.
Directions	From A26 exit Alessandria Sud for Nizza Monferrato; signs for Fontanile.

Ethical Collection: Environment.
See page 400 for details

Karen Langley
Cascina Mulino Vecchio 5,
Regione Mulino Vecchio, 14044 Fontanile
Tel   +39 0141 739105
Email   info@lagranicahotel.com
Web   www.lagranica.com

Alla Buona Stella

Turin: grandiose home to baroque architecture and art, irresistible cafés, divine chocolatiers, prestigious opera house… and capital of the aperitivo. Here, in a respectable residential street in the heart of the old town, is Roberta's B&B. Up the lift of this very elegant building to a wide landing on the fourth floor and there is Roberta to greet you, with her lovely big smile and infectious laugh. There's an elegant oval dining table for breakfast, a cluster of shiny blue matching sofa and chairs, a little computer corner and a comforting, comfortable décor. Then there are the guest quarters on the floor above, high under the eaves, reached by a wooden open-tread stair. Expect three big, friendly, generous, traditional rooms, all polished antiques, gleaming floors, patterned rugs and easy chairs. The suite has its own little terrace, looking right down to the courtyard below, and the bathrooms are excellent, with showers and baths, bottles of shampoo, coloured towels. Roberta is super-organised, loves the city, loves her B&B, knows all there is to know. You could not be in better hands.

Price	€100–€110.
Rooms	3: 1 twin/double, 1 suite for 2-3, 1 triple.
Meals	Restaurants nearby.
Closed	Rarely.
Directions	10-minute walk from centre of Turin. Train station Porta Susa (1km) and Porta Nuova (5km). Airport A. Pertini of Torino Caselle (35km).

Roberta Simonetti
Via del Carmine 10, 10122 Turin

Tel	+39 0111 9710823
Email	info@allabuonastella.it
Web	www.allabuonastella.it

Entry 8   Map 6

Viavai

Alberto and Francesca inherited a big country house in hilltop Casalborgone, exploited the family's talent, taste and respect for Viavai's origins, renovated and then moved in. Now three generations live here, cheerfully spread across the big first floor. The second and third floors, reached via a small lift and a beautiful stone stair, are devoted to six uncluttered guest rooms, four with lush valley views. At ground level is a huge courtyard with a pool to one side and a courtyard garden dotted with wicker chairs. The stylishness spreads into the bedrooms, all harmonious colours, perfect wooden floors and striking textiles — linen, silk, organza, hessian. Bathrooms have plaster and brick walls, eco soaps and fluffy colour-matched towels. On this level you'll also find the dining room for (delicious) breakfasts. And then there's Francesca, full of life and ideas, keen to introduce you to the highlights (cultural, oenological, gastronomic) of this undiscovered region. There are eco walks from the village, personal shoppers (just ask!) and special prices at the little restaurant down the hill. A treat for all seasons.

Price	€70–€95.
Rooms	6: 3 doubles, 2 suites, 1 family room for 4.
Meals	Restaurant 5-minute walk.
Closed	Rarely.
Directions	From Chivasso, SS590 to San Sebastiano da Po; right onto SS458. At Casalborgone, right onto Corso Vittorio Emanuele II; signs to "centro storico".

Francesca Guerra Vai
Via Valfrè 7, 10020 Casalborgone

Tel	+39 0119 174406
Email	info@viavai.to.it
Web	www.viavai.to.it

Agriturismo Erbaluna

On a hot summer's day the old cellars have a musty but blissful perfume, redolent of decades of good red wine. This working vineyard is run by the Oberto family and guests are capably and sensitively looked after by two husband and wife teams: Severino and Carla, and Andrea and Monica. Mamma Letizia makes sure everything is as it should be. The house is a typical late 1800s cascina, a long, two-storeyed white building fronted by a paved and gated courtyard, across from which are the cellars; all state-of-the-art and, work permitting, open for guided viewing. Begin the day with a homemade breakfast in country surrounds, retreating later, once the sun has softened, to the shared roof terrace for an aperitif over the balustrade, Immaculately clean bedrooms hold a collection of rustic and antique walnut furniture, faux-brocade bedspreads and old family photographs. The two-storey apartments have tiled and beamed living areas with extra sofabeds, well-equipped kitchens and dining tables that seat up to eight. In every room, wine, bottle-opener and glasses come as standard – naturally.

Price	€70–€85 (€450 per week). Apartments €550 per week.
Rooms	5 + 2: 5 doubles. 2 apartments for 2-4.
Meals	Restaurant 1km.
Closed	Rarely.
Directions	A21 Torino-Piacenza exit Asti east. M'way for Alba, dir. Barolo. 2nd sign for La Morra, Fraz. Annunziata.

	Severino Oberto
	Fraz. Annunziata 43, 12064 La Morra
Tel	+39 0173 50800
Email	agriturismo@erbaluna.it
Web	www.erbaluna.it

Il Gioco dell'Oca Agriturismo

People love Raffaella: her home is full of tokens of appreciation sent by guests. She spent much of her childhood here – the farm was her grandparents'. She is happy to be back, looks after her guests beautifully, feeds them well, and has tampered with the pretty, 18th-century farmhouse as little as possible. The well-worn, welcoming kitchen, much as it must have been 50 years ago, is for you to use as and when you like – the warm hub of a sociable house. Next door is a breakfast room set with little tables, but if it's fine you'll prefer to breakfast under the portico in the garden, which is big enough for everyone to find their own secluded corner. The bedrooms are simple and cosy, with family furniture and wooden beds, one with a hob, sink and fridge – a bonus if you have little ones. Bathrooms are bright and new. The farm, up in the hills near Barolo – a wonderful area for cheeses and wines – produces wine, fruit and hazelnuts. A pity the road is so close but you'll forgive that for the pleasure of staying at such a relaxed, welcoming and thoroughly Italian agriturismo.

Price	€65-€75. Triple €75-€85.
Rooms	7: 6 twins/doubles, 1 triple.
Meals	Restaurant 500m.
Closed	January.
Directions	From Asti (east) exit autostrada TO-PC. Follow sign for Alba & Barolo. Left 2km before village, 50m on right sign for house.

Raffaella Pittatore
Via Alba 83, 12060 Barolo
Tel   +39 0173 56206
Email   info@gioco-delloca.it
Web   www.gioco-delloca.it

Hotel Castello di Sinio

Sitting atop the tiny village of Sinio surrounded by rolling hillsides, hazelnut plantations and a multitude of vineyards, this 12th-century castello belonged to the noble Carretto family for some 600 years. On the village side, the stone façade appears impregnable, but move to the courtyard and a different mood prevails: lush green lawn, colourful flower beds, cascades of geraniums falling from windows boxes…a delicious little swimming pool has been tucked to one side of the castle. Americans Denise and Jay (Giacomo to the locals) have done a tremendous job of restoration, at the same time becoming ardent Piemontesi exponents of the region's wines, gastronomic delights and traditions. Denise is the chef, personally creating the memorable meals, while Jay holds court in the dining room. Good-sized bedrooms have terracotta floors, many with exposed stonework, beams and individual examples of beautiful vaulted stonework and fine Barocco furniture. Bathrooms are equipped with shower cabins and handy magnifying mirrors. Stunning. *Minimum stay two nights at weekends in October.*

Price	€150–€325.
Rooms	18 doubles.
Meals	Dinner, 4 courses, €45; by arrangement. Wine from €15.
Closed	8 January–February; 2 weeks mid-August.
Directions	From Alba dir. Cuneo, Barolo & Gallo. At Gallo, dir. Grinzane Cavour; immed. left for Sinio, 7km. Signed.

	Denise Pardini
	Vicolo del Castello 1, 12050 Sinio
Tel	+39 0173 263889
Email	reservations@hotelcastellodisinio.com
Web	www.hotelcastellodisinio.com

Cascina Adami - Il Nido

A short drive down a country lane, the 17th-century farmhouse is set into its hill with superb views over gentle hills patchworked with wheat fields and vineyards – leading the eye to snowy peaks beyond. This is the best wine-producing area of Italy, and opposite the lane is a dairy where you can stock up on the sheep's cheese – soft, mild, delicious – Murazzano. Discreetly distant from the main house, down a steep unpaved track – watch your wheels! – is a four-square, two-storey stone structure, once a goats' shed. Il Nido (the nest) is a delicious bolthole for two. Owner Paolo is a master at putting salvaged finds to unusual use so expect pale new stone floors and chunky old rafters, a delicate wooden fretwork door, a stylish steel table and chairs, a charming kitchen tucked under a chunky white stone stair, a bedroom with a big cream bed and small blue shutters, driftwood and pebbles prettifying quiet corners. Outside is smart wooden furniture from which to gaze on the views and a huge linen parasol. Contemporary rusticity, ancient peace. *Minimum stay two nights.*

Price	€680 per week (€350 for weekend). Heating extra.
Rooms	House for 2.
Meals	Restaurants in Murazzano, 1.5km.
Closed	October–March.
Directions	A6 from Turin exit Carrù dir. Clavesana, Murazzano.

Paolo & Flavia Adami
Fraz. Mellea 53, 12060 Murazzano

Tel	+39 0118 178135
Email	flavia.adami@yahoo.it
Web	www.cascinaadami.it

Lombardy • Trentino–Alto Adige

Photo: istock.com

Polidora

From the botanical garden on the shores of Lake Maggiore, where islands hover on the glistening water and the Alps stand protectively in the distance, you will feel at total peace with the world. The changing light mischievously catches rare species of plant, flower and tree in moods you would not think possible, in supernatural shades. What luck that GianLuca decided to convert the stables in the grounds of his elegant 1900s villa into a spacious and stylish B&B. Now the WWF-protected acres are yours to explore: with lonely benches, pebble beaches and shady patches inviting you to unwind, we defy you to read a book without being distracted by the beauty – or to not swim in the cool waters of the lake the moment you see their enticing ripples. While GianLuca is away, Barbara and Alan are on hand for breakfasts and conversation; following careers in gardening for the National Trust and running a heritage house, the care of Polidora and guests was too good an opportunity to miss. Lunch in the nearby village of Cerro or picnic in the grounds; the great thing is, you can stay here all day.

Price	€140–€280.
	Whole house €3,000 per week.
Rooms	3: 2 doubles, 1 suite for 5.
Meals	Restaurants 1-3km.
Closed	Rarely.
Directions	From Milan, A8 exit Sesto Calende; follow shores of Lake Maggiore, through Angera. Entrance before Cerro di Laveno Mombello.

GianLuca Sarto
Via Pirinoli 4,
21014 Cerro di Laveno Mombello

Tel	+39 0332 629239
Email	info@polidora.com
Web	www.polidora.com

Alberghetto La Marianna

On the banks of Lake Como, this family-run hotel is housed in a villa simply modernised and redecorated with a relaxing feel. Bedrooms are strictly functional, with cheery tiled shower rooms; most have lakeside views. Some have balconies, one has its own little terrace (but no lake view). A road runs between you and the busy lake, so if you're a light sleeper, it might be worth giving up those beautiful watery views for a room at the back, at least in summer. Paola is a delight and, in her own words, treats guests as friends. Breakfasts include homemade bread, cakes and jams; she's also a good cook and a "mistress of desserts" – try them out in the restaurant for dinner, run by husband Ty. You can eat inside and admire the ever-changing local art work lining the walls or outside where you can embrace the lake views on the terrace that juts onto the shimmering water. You won't be short of advice here on things to do: visits to gardens and villas, boat tours to Isola Comacina, day trips to St Moritz and the Engadine.

Price	€85–€95. Single €60–€65.
Rooms	8: 7 doubles, 1 single.
Meals	Dinner with wine, €30.
Closed	Mid-November to mid-March (open 26 December–6 January).
Directions	From Como direction Menaggio on west lakeside road to Cadenabbia 30km; 300m after ferry port to Bellagio.

	Paola Cioccarelli
	Via Regina 57,
	22011 Cadenabbia di Griante
Tel	+39 0344 43095
Email	inn@la-marianna.com
Web	www.la-marianna.com

Entry 15   Map 2

Villetta Il Ghiro & Villetta La Vigna

Wisteria was growing through the old convent when Ann and her husband fell in love with it. The roof had fallen in too but, undeterred, they went ahead and turned it into the lovely place it is today. They thoroughly enjoy welcoming guests to these two apartments, traditional, comfortable, homely and quiet, with their big airy rooms, well-equipped kitchens and independent outside stairs. Il Ghiro is on the first floor of a former hay barn; La Vigna is above the garages, its second bedroom opening off the first, and its little balcony catching the afternoon sun. Best of all is the garden with its big lawns and fenced pool and tennis court discreetly tucked away; it's a treat to stroll amongst the shrubs and the trees, lie back on a lounger with a view to the river, take tea on the terrace. Birdsong and water are the only sounds and yet you are no distance at all from the excitements of Menaggio and Como. The position is wonderful, on the isthmus between two grand lakes, on the edge of a cobbled village, surrounded by mountains, meadows and winding country lanes. *Flexible rental periods.*

Price	€450–€900 for 2-3; €900–€1,800 for 4-6. €200-300 for extra double room. Prices per week.
Rooms	2 apartments: 1 for 2-3, 1 for 4-6.
Meals	Restaurants 5-minute walk.
Closed	October–April.
Directions	From Menaggio N340 for Porlezza to Grandola, towards Porlezza & Lugano. Right at bakery; immediately right for Cardano. Right into Via al Forno.

Ann Dexter
Via al Forno 5, Cardano,
22010 Grandola ed Uniti

Tel	+39 0344 32740
Email	ann.dexter@libero.it

Albergo Olivedo

An easy walk from the centre of Varenna, Laura's quayside hotel, soft orange-hued with balconies and Art Nouveau lamps, has a jaunty air. There are polished parquet floors, grandmother's furniture, starched cotton on firm beds and, from many rooms, wonderful views over the lake; the little reception with burr maple counter and speckled floor could grace a French pensione. Just a few steps away is the family's more recent acquisition, a classic, 19th-century villa, the Toretta, with large lovely bedrooms and more superb views of the harbour. Frescoes, decorative iron staircase and lofty ceilings have been carefully restored, while traditional tiles, handsome beds and fine old furniture give the rooms a distinguished air. It stands in its own pretty garden, so relax in the shade of the trees or bask on the terrace – before wandering over to the Olivedo for a tasty and traditional meal (Laura's brother is chef); inside or out you have a view of the harbour and the charming Como ferry. The hotel has been in Laura's family for 60 years and the staff are warm and friendly.

Price	€110-€155. Half-board €150-€190 for 2.
Rooms	19: 14 doubles. Villa Torretta: 5 doubles.
Meals	Dinner €25. Wine from €7.
Closed	2 November-20 December.
Directions	From north, SP72 from Colico to Varenna.

	Laura Colombo
	Piazza Martiri 4, 23829 Varenna
Tel	+39 0341 830115
Email	info@olivedo.it
Web	www.olivedo.it

Albergo Milano

Colourwashed houses cluster round the church on a little, rocky promontory. The lake laps gently on three sides; on the fourth, mountain slopes rear steeply upwards. Wander along a cobbled street, catching glimpses of the lake down every side alley, and you come to Albergo Milano, smack on the waterfront. It's pretty, traditional, disarmingly small, and Bettina and Egidio are engaging people, thrilled to be running their own little hotel. Everywhere is freshly and stylishly furnished, with dashes of colour to add warmth and some lovely country furniture, and each bedroom with a balcony or terrace and a lake view. The dining room's big new windows open onto a wonderful wide terrace where you eat out on fine days, the lake stirring beside you. The food is divine gourmet-Italian, the wine list heavenly. A step away, in the old part of town, is a charming room with great views, and the apartments with kitchenette and living room. Bettina is a mine of information about this area and there's a regular train service into Bergamo and Milan. A little gem. *Book garage parking in advance.*

Price	€130-€185. Apartments €120-€260.
Rooms	11 + 2: 10 doubles, 1 triple. 2 apartments for 2-5.
Meals	Dinner €29. Wine from €18.
Closed	December-February.
Directions	From Lecco SS36 to Sondrio; 1st exit for Abbadia Lariana. After 15km, before tunnel, left for Varenna. Park in Piazza San Giorgio. 150m to hotel (map in piazza).

Bettina & Egidio Mallone
Via XX Settembre 35, 23829 Varenna

Tel +39 0341 830298
Email hotelmilano@varenna.net
Web www.varenna.net

Agriturismo Castello di Vezio - Casa Pupa

The *castello* of Vezio, a must-see for visitors to the area and with 360° panorama of the lake, belongs to the Greppi family; everyone staying here has free and private access. So here you have it all: activities for the family, well-kept gardens and a pool with views over what is debatably Italy's most beautiful lake; and a slice of history to boot. The castle goes back to the Middle Ages and stands high above the shore, with a sheer drop down to lovely Varenna. Admire the owls and hawks who reside in the battlements; imagine barbaric invaders approaching from Como, or aggressors advancing from Lecco. When you've had your fill of history, return to Casa Pupa to rest and unwind. The Greppi family themselves lived in the house in the 1970s and photos of their sailing days line walls. There's a light-hearted boating theme throughout, even a rope to help you up the spiral stair. At the top: light-filled, slightly faded bedrooms. A great place to stay for a large party; the two simple *mansarde* (loft-apartments) have their own kitchens. *Minimum stay three nights.*

Price	€1,900–€5,100 per week.
Rooms	House for 7–15 (min. 8 people in high season).
Meals	Breakfast €15, by arrangement. Restaurant 100m.
Closed	Never.
Directions	Directions on booking.

Maria Manuela Greppi
Via del Castellano 16, 23828 Varenna

Tel	+39 0258 190940
Email	vezio@robilant.it
Web	www.agriturismocastellodivezio.it

Entry 19 Map 2

Agriturismo Castello di Vezio - Casa Milena & Casa Giovanni

Spectacularly secluded from the other houses inside the entrance gates of Castello di Vezio (and 700 metres down a steep path) the two-up, two-down Casa Milena, crouches in a cliff yards from the craggy edge and then… there's the lake, inviting deep breaths and wide eyes every time you open the front door. The cottage is one of the most romantic places to stay in this guide and it would be impossible not to feel inspired here: your gaze falls on that dazzling lake from wherever you are: bed or kitchen sink. One of the bedrooms has a terrace for those who wish to share the experience – but you'll feel alone with those views. Back up the path and you can play a spot of tennis with the other guests staying in the castle grounds. There are also secret spots for those who like their privacy. Casa Giovanni (photo above) is set in its own orchard below the castle; it, too, feels private and is suitable for a family of four. The grey granite of both these new buildings is softened inside by floral bed spreads and friendly, modern kitchens. The setting is a dream. *Minimum stay one week Oct-May. Children over 8 welcome at Casa Milena.*

Price	€1,000-€1,400 per week.
Rooms	2 houses for 4.
Meals	Breakfast €15, by arrangement. Restaurant 100m.
Closed	Rarely.
Directions	Directions on booking.

Maria Manuela Greppi
Via del Castellano 16, 23828 Varenna

Tel	+39 0258 190940
Email	vezio@robilant.it
Web	www.agriturismocastellodivezio.it

Agriturismo Castello di Vezio - Casa Cima & Casa Selva

With views stretching over Lake Como from your dining room, a balcony hugging the outside of the house and sun-trapped terraces at every turn, Casa Cima is a delightful family getaway high up in the historic hamlet of Vezio. Behind the entrance gates, the lake far below, is a small, friendly holiday village. Shared by just five places to stay are a tennis court and a huge games room with table football. And space! The children may play football or rounders on the lawn while you doze in the shade of one of numerous trees, or sunbathe in peace beside your very own pool (Casa Cima); you also have access to the 12th-century castle. If the party is a large one, you can rent its ground-floor companion, Casa Selva, too. Both apartments have 18th-century floral designs in pretty bedrooms and simple but functional bathrooms. There are eating areas inside and out, and heaps of storage. Shop in the delicatessens of Perledo, dine in the neighbouring restaurant, or motor down to beautiful Varenna below. A superb place for families. *Minimum stay three nights.*

Price	Cima €2,000-€2,800. Selva €800-€1,200. €2,800-€4,000 for both rented together. Prices per week.
Rooms	2 houses: 1 for 4, 1 for 8. Can be rented together (sleeps 12).
Meals	Breakfast €15, by arrangement. Restaurant 100m.
Closed	Never.
Directions	Directions on booking.

Maria Manuela Greppi
Via del Castellano 41, 23828 Varenna
Tel   +39 0258 190940
Email   vezio@robilant.it
Web   www.agriturismocastellodivezio.it

Il Torchio

Marcella's happy personality fills the house with good cheer. She and Franco are artists – she an animator, he a painter; if you like the bohemian life you will like it here. Franco also has an antiquarian bookshop in Milan, which explains all the shelves in the sitting room. Their home began life in 1600 as the stables of the noble Calchi family; you enter through a fine stone archway into a courtyard. Franco's bold paintings adorn the walls and every corner is crammed with curios that Marcella has picked up on her flea market forays. Bedrooms are endearingly old-fashioned – no frills but good, comfortable beds. The big, private suite, entered via French windows, has green views down to Calco, a great big bed, family photos on the walls, and a cabinet filled with children's old toys. The bathrooms are basic but have lovely hand-painted tiles. The whole family is a delight – including the cats – and Marcella's cooking is superb. Active types can canoe in summer and ski in winter (just a one-hour drive); or visit Verona, Lake Como, and the stunning shops of Milan. *Ask about massage.*

Price	€50.
Rooms	3: 1 suite; 2 doubles sharing bath.
Meals	Dinner €15, by arrangement.
Closed	Rarely.
Directions	From Milan to Calco; right at r'bout, over 2 speed bumps, right onto Via Ghislanzoni; follow signs for Vescogna; at top of hill.

Ethical Collection: Food.
See page 400 for details

Marcella Pisacane
Via Ghislanzoni, Loc. Vescogna,
23885 Calco
Tel +39 0399 274294
Email il_torchio@hotmail.com
Web iltorchio.wordpress.com

Agriturismo Casa Clelia

The hotel has been sculpted out of the 11th-century convent, using the principles of eco-bio architecture. Cows peer from sheds as you arrive, chickens, geese and sheep bustle – this is a working farm. The main house stands proud against wooded hills and beyond are convent, outhouses, orchards and barns. Rosanna is a dear and looks after you as well as she looks after her large family. She is a talented cook and has taught a fantastic team of local cooks everything she knows; one of her treats is her taster menu, your chance to sample – guilt-free   several delicacies all at once. The bedrooms, a good size, are stunning and warmly original, all wood, stone and bold colours; bathrooms are modern, lighting subtle. Heat comes from a wood-burner integrated with solar panels; cork and coconut ensure the sound-proofing of walls. Children will be welcome, free to run wild in the gardens, orchards and eight hectares of woods. Hard to imagine a more wonderful place for families… or for a get-away-from-it-all weekend. There's horse riding nearby, too, and Bergamo, mid-way between Lake Como and Lake Iseo, is a cultural treat.

Price	€95-€125.
Rooms	10: 6 doubles, 2 doubles/quadruples, 2 triples.
Meals	Lunch/dinner with wine, €20-€35. Closed Mondays.
Closed	Never.
Directions	From A4 exit Capriate; signed.

Ferruccio Masseretti
Via Corna 1/3,
24039 Sotto il Monte Giovanni XXIII
Tel   +39 0357 99133
Email   info@casaclelia.com
Web   www.casaclelia.com

Antica Locanda dei Mercanti

Entering the gloomy, cavernous courtyard, you wouldn't imagine the lightness and charm of this small, discreet boutique hotel on the second floor of an 18th-century building in the heart of Milan. Heavy glass doors slide open to a simple reception where chic Italians and visitors mingle; young staff whisk you off to rooms whose individuality and style promise country-house comfort rather than the spartan modernity associated with this energetic city. This is an enterprise run by real people with passion. From the smallest room with its elegant Milanese fabrics and wicker chair with cherry striped and piped cushions to the largest, airy room with its muslin-hung four-poster, terrace, olive tree and scented climbers, each space surprises. Fine linen, deep mattresses, dramatic murals, fresh posies, stacks of magazines, small, gleaming shower rooms – and, soon, ceiling fans giving way to air conditioning: each room bears the distinctive hallmark of Paola, the engaging and energetic owner. No communal space, so breakfast is delivered to your room. Chic simplicity, and La Scala a heart beat away.

Price	From €205; from €375 with terrace.
Rooms	14 doubles (4 with terrace).
Meals	Breakfast €10 (€15 in bedroom). Light lunch & dinner in room on request. Restaurants nearby.
Closed	Rarely.
Directions	Via S. Tomaso is a small street off Via Dante, halfway between the Duomo and Piazza Castello. No sign, just a brass plate.

Bruce Scott
Via San Tomaso 6, 20121 Milan
Tel   +39 0280 54080
Email   locanda@locanda.it
Web   www.locanda.it

Agriturismo Cervano B&B

Surrounded by wild orchids and violets at the highest point of the garden, the sun splashing colour across the sky as it sets over majestic Lake Garda, you could be fooled into believing you were a 19th-century wine merchant returning from Milan for the harvest of your country estate. What a pleasant surprise you would have on entering your house if that were true. Anna and her husband Gino have mastered the restoration of Gino's once-crumbling family home, a fine example of Lombard 'fort' design, and the interior is stylish and contemporary: bathrooms are slick Italian, new beds are dressed in handmade linen, there's a marble breakfast bar in the luminous kitchen and a huge American-style fridge packed with breakfast goodies. Despite the modernity, Anna and Gino have constantly kept the 1800s in mind: exposed beams have been perfectly restored, floors imitate the original style and the marble is Verona's most rare: speckled pink and red. Wine is still produced on site but now it's organic, and solar panels heat water. A superb restoration in a beautiful and peaceful setting.

Price	€100–€150. Whole house €500–€900. Apt for 4 €110–€130 (€15 per extra person). Apt for 10 €150–€300 p.p. Prices per night.
Rooms	3 + 2: 2 doubles (1 with sofabed), 1 triple. 2 apartments: 1 for 4, 1 for 10.
Meals	Restaurant 1km.
Closed	Never.
Directions	From Gargnano, right towards golf club; signed. If you're following GPS, look for Via Golf in Toscolano Maderno, then Via Sassello 30 (car entrance).

Gino & Anna Massarani
Via Cervano 14, 25088
Toscolano Maderno

Tel	+39 0400 548398
Email	info@cervano.com
Web	www.cervano.com

Ethical Collection: Environment; Food.
See page 400 for details

Entry 25   Map 3

Hotel du Lac

The hotel oozes old-fashioned charm. A 1900s townhouse, it shares the same street as the villa from which D H Lawrence eulogised about the "milky lake" of Garda. The ox-blood façade, with white relief and green shutters, is as striking as the view from the patio that overhangs the water; you can swim from here. Valerio's grandparents owned a piano shop in Milan and lived in the house until 1959; much of their furniture remains. The family could not be more helpful. Roomy bedrooms are wonderfully old-fashioned with big beds and wardrobes, Thirties' lights and polished terrazzo floors; beds are deeply comfortable and dressed in crisp cotton. Six rooms look onto the lake and have small balconies or terraces. The dining room, around a central courtyard with a palm that disappears into the clouds, looks directly onto the water. You can also dine upstairs on the open terrace, where metal tables and chairs are shaded by an arbour of kiwi – a magical spot at night, the water lapping below, the lights twinkling in the distance. There's even a small music room with a piano to play – guests sometimes do.

Price	€96–€140.
Rooms	12 doubles.
Meals	Menu à la carte, from €30. Wine from €13.
Closed	1st week of November; week before Easter. Out of season call +39 0365 71269.
Directions	From Brescia-Salò dir. Riva del Garda. After Bogliaco, 400m slip road on right to Via Colletta. Parking at hotel.

Valerio Arosio
Via Colletta 21, 25084 Villa di Gargnano

Tel	+39 0365 71107
Email	info@hotel-dulac.it
Web	www.hotel-dulac.it

Hotel Gardenia al Lago

Jasmine-scented gardens and green lawns reach to Lake Garda's edge; an immaculate terrace makes the most of the views. The hotel stands, a feast of colour and design, against the steep, wooded foothills of Mount Baldo. It was bought by the Arosio family as a summer home in 1925. They were piano-makers from Lodi – note the original piano in the music room – and in the 1950s turned the house into a guesthouse. Today it is a small, restful, civilised hotel. The bedrooms have been renovated – some frescoes being uncovered in the process – and are beautiful, with distinctive Empire antiques, exquisite floor tiles and muslin billowing at French windows. Many have balconies or terraces; bathrooms are Edwardian-style and superior. The dining room has a more Sixties flavour and in summer you eat under the trees, by candlelight. The entire family – parents and sons – are delightful, and many guests return. Lemon and olive trees surround you – they produce wonderful olive oil – and a grassed garden hugs the lakeside. Take a dip off the small beach further along: the water is said to be the purest in Italy.

Price	€78–€214. Singles €54–€149.
Rooms	25 doubles.
Meals	Menu à la carte, from €30. Wine from €12.50.
Closed	1st week of November; week before Easter. Out of season call +39 0365 71269
Directions	From Brescia-Salò dir. Riva del Garda. After Bogliaco, 400m slip road on right to Via Colletta. Parking at hotel.

Giorgio & Andrea Arosio
Via Colletta 53, 25084 Villa di Gargnano
Tel +39 0365 71195
Email info@hotel-gardenia.it
Web www.hotel-gardenia.it

Dimora Bolsone

Film-like, the lake glitters between the cypress trees — an expanse of blue far below. Gaze in wonder as gentle, cultured, charming Raffaele — and spaniels Rocky and Glenda — settle you on the terrace with a jug of freshly squeezed orange juice. Economist, lecturer, sailor, antique collector, big game hunter and green aficionado, Raffaele is the lifeblood of this property, meets and greets you and gives you free run of these 46 acres, a glorious mix of of protected parkland and terraced gardens. The 15th-century house reposes gracefully among jasmine-strewn loggias and lemon trees; step in to a cool, ordered calm. Big, dark, immaculate bedrooms have light polished floors, soft washed walls, family portraits, delicious linen. All are different — gilt cornices and flirty rococo in one, sober masculinity and a 15th-century bed in another. Start the day feasting on almond cookies, local cheeses, cold meats, fresh fruits; tour Verona, or the lake; return to a salon/library with green leather armchairs and huge stone fireplace. An essay in perfection, a feast for the senses. *Children over 12 welcome. Min. stay two nights.*

Price	€200. Singles €170.
Rooms	5 doubles.
Meals	Restaurants 1km.
Closed	30 November-28 February.
Directions	A4 exit Desenzano del Garda or Brescia Est, then 45 Bis for Gardone Riviera. Left at Il Vittoriale, signed San Michaele; 2km, on left.

Raffaele Bonaspetti
Via Panoramica 23, 25083 Gardone Riviera
Tel   +39 0365 21022
Email info@dimorabolsone.it
Web   www.dimorabolsone.it

Villa San Pietro Bed & Breakfast

A splendid 17th-century home. Annamaria, warm, vivacious, multi-lingual, is married to Jacques, French and charming; they have a young son, and Anna's mother lives in self-contained splendour at the far end. It's a rather grand name for a house that is one of a terrace, but once inside you realise why we have included it here. This is an immaculate home and no expense has been spared. There are oak beams, ancient brick floors, fine family antiques, floral fabrics, not a speck of dust. Guests have their own sitting room with a frescoed ceiling, the bedrooms are delightful and, to the excitement of Annamaria and Jacques, frescoes were discovered in the newly restored *sala di pranzo*. Another exceptional thing about the house is the large garden and terrace. There is also a pretty ground-floor loggia for memorable meals – Annamaria's dinners are sophisticated regional affairs, we are told. You are close to the town centre yet in a quiet road, and Montichiari is perfectly sited for forays into Garda, Brescia, Verona and Venice.

Price	€90–€110.
Rooms	5 doubles.
Meals	Dinner with wine, 4 courses, €30. Restaurants 200m.
Closed	Rarely.
Directions	From Milan motorway A4 exit Brescia east towards Montichiari, city centre & Duomo. Via S. Pietro leads off corner of central piazza.

Jacques & Annamaria Ducroz
Via San Pietro 25, 25018 Montichiari
Tel   +39 0309 61232
Email villasanpietro@hotmail.com
Web   www.abedandbreakfastinitaly.com

Tenuta Le Sorgive - Le Volpi Agriturismo

One cannot deny the beauty of Lake Garda, but it's a relief to escape to the unpopulated land of Lombardy. This 19th-century *cascina* has been in the Serenelli family for two generations. The exterior, crowned with pierced dovecote and flanked by a carriage house and stables, remains impressive, even if some character has been lost during restoration. Vittorio is justly proud of his 28-hectare farm: everything is organic, solar panels provide electricity, wood-chip burner the heating. Big guest rooms, with wooden rafters, are a mix of old and new. Some have attractive, metalwork beds, some a balcony, two have a mezzanine with beds for the children, all are crisp and clean. This is a great place for families to visit as there's so much to do: horse riding and mountain biking from the farm, go-karting and archery nearby, watersports, including scuba diving courses, at Garda. There are also a large gym and a well-maintained pool. Vittorio's sister, Anna, runs Le Volpi, the *cascina* only a stroll away where you can sample gnocchi, Mantovan sausages and mouthwatering fruit tarts. *Min. stay three nights in high season; one week in apt.*

Ethical Collection: Environment.
See page 400 for details

Price	€85-€105.
	Apartments €550-€900 per week.
Rooms	8 + 2: 8 twins/doubles.
	2 apartments for 4.
Meals	Breakfast €5 for self-caterers.
	Dinner with wine, €15-€28.
	Closed January & Mon/Tues evening.
Closed	Never.
Directions	Exit A4 Milano-Venezia at Desenzano
	for Castiglione delle Stiviere; left at
	lights; left after 20m to Solferino.
	At x-roads, left. Signed.

Vittorio Serenelli
Via Piridello 6, 46040 Solferino
Tel   +39 0376 854252
Email   info@lesorgive.it
Web   www.lesorgive.it

B&B Antica Locanda Matilda

Home of the Gonzaga family, patrons of art and architecture during the Renaissance, Mantua is one of Italy's finest cities: surrounded on three sides by lakes, brimming with palazzi that sing with intricate frescoes. The Locanda, situated in an uninspiring industrial area on the outskirts of the city (the centre a ten-minute drive on the ringroad; light sleepers beware) catches the distant skyline view – wonderfully dramatic at night. Inside is stylish, cool and delightful, and lovely Cristina, the perfect hostess, has thought of everything, from a mini fridge in the corridor to free bikes to borrow to a shuttle bus to and from the station. Each of the bedrooms is spacious, clean, comfortable and air conditioned, with white walls and a big chunky-raftered ceiling; one room is ensuite. Not everyone loves dogs but the family's quartet of Shar Peis adds to the homely atmosphere. The pretty breakfast sun room overlooks the garden's infinity pool – lovely to get home to in summer. The local gastronomy is quite something and you are a ten-minute walk from an excellent restaurant.

Price	€80-€90.
Rooms	3: 1 double; 2 doubles sharing bath.
Meals	Restaurant 700m.
Closed	Never.
Directions	Modena-Brennero exit Mantova Nord; over r'bout thro' industrial area; after 500m (immed. after underpass), right; on to Ostiglia. At r'bout, straight on, over flyover; signed Castelletto Borgo, keep left; on left after 200m.

Cristina Parma
Via F. Rismondo 2, 46100 Mantua

Mobile   +39 335 6390624
Email   info@locandamatilda.it
Web   www.locandamatilda.it

Bio-hotel Hermitage

It's not often that a bio-hotel comes with such a splash of luxury. Built a century ago, the old Hermitage has been entirely refashioned – with a modern 'eco' eye and a flourish of decorative turret. A wooden floor spans the reception area; behind is a vast and comfortable living room. A Tyrolean-tiled wood-burner dominates the centre; windows open onto a balcony with the best views in the Alps. You eat at red-clothed tables on Trentino dishes and homemade pasta in the *stübe*, with its lovely panelled ceiling of old, recycled wood. The main restaurant is larger but as beautiful. Bedrooms are serene, some are under the eaves, most have a balcony and the suites are huge. Wooden floors are softened by Persian rugs or pale carpets from Argentina, curtains and bedspreads are prettily checked. There's a superb wellness centre and an indoor pool with a ceiling that sparkles. Bars and chic boutiques are a ten-minute walk, and the hotel has its own bus that shuttles you to the slopes. Santa tips up at Christmas distributing presents for the children from a little cabin at the end of the garden.

Price	Half-board €140-€340 p.p.
Rooms	25: 18 twins/doubles, 7 suites for 3-4.
Meals	Half-board only. Wine from €15.
Closed	April-June.
Directions	Exit A22 St Mich & Mezz for Madonna di Campiglio for 75km; at Madonna di Campiglio, bypass through mountain; next exit. Signed on left.

Barbara Maffei
Via Castelletto Inferiore 63,
38084 Madonna di Campiglio
Tel   +39 0465 441558
Email   info@biohotelhermitage.it
Web   www.biohotelhermitage.it

Schwarz Adler Turm Hotel

All around are the soaring, craggy Dolomites – nothing like them to give a sobering perspective on man's place in nature's scheme. If you do feel overawed, you'll be soothed on arrival – Manfred, Sonja and their staff are so delighted to see you, so eager to do all they can to please. Though the hotel is young, it is a faithful reproduction of a 16th-century manor house and blends in well with the village. The roomy, light bedrooms are carpeted and hotel-comfortable, with glorious alpine views; each has a loggia, a balcony or direct access to the garden. The pretty village of Cortaccia (known as 'Kurtasch' by the locals) stands at 300 metres and looks down over a wide valley floor studded with orchards. This was Austria (the area turned Italian in 1919) and the hotel's cuisine, served in the beautifully restored family restaurant opposite, reflects this – a tour de force of Italian and South Tyrolean dishes. A fascinating example of German Renaissance architecture, the restaurant has a well-stocked bar: the perfect place to gather after a day of walking and a visit to the hotel's sauna and steam room.

Price	€140–€190. Half-board €78–€105 p.p.
Rooms	24 doubles.
Meals	Dinner, 3 courses, €25–€40. Wine from €15. Restaurant 20m.
Closed	2 weeks in February; 22-27 December.
Directions	From A22 exit Egna/Ora. On for 8km dir. Termeno; left for Cortaccia; immed. after church on left.

Famiglia Pomella
Kirchgasse 2,
39040 Kurtatsch/Cortaccia

Tel	+39 0471 880600
Email	info@turmhotel.it
Web	www.turmhotel.it

Relais & Châteaux Hotel Castel Fragsburg

Stay in May and you'll see and smell the glory of the wisteria that drapes itself the length of the loggia where meals are served. The Fragsburg, built as a shooting lodge for the local gentry, perches on the side of a wooded hill with a crystal-clear view across the valley – mountains and valley unfurl. Perhaps the most magnificent spot from which to enjoy the view is the pool. Sun yourself on the screened deck on a hot day, then wander the grounds, beautiful with sub-tropical trees, surrounded by vineyards. Big bedrooms and huge suites have been redecorated and the combination of rugs, wood and some antique painted headboards softens any newness. Beds are deeply inviting with piles of pillows; white bathrooms are stunning. And then there's the wellness centre, studded with treatments, purifying products, aromatic smells and white robes. The whole feel of the place is Tyrolean, from the staff costumes to the delicious teatime strüdel. The fairytale castles and scenery of this northern region are not to be missed, and the Ortner family ensure you get the most out of your stay. Truly delightful.

Price	€250-€400.
	Half-board €140-€350 p.p.
Rooms	20: 6 doubles, 14 suites.
Meals	Dinner à la carte, €40-€120.
	Restaurant 5km.
Closed	15 November-25 March.
Directions	Exit A22 Bolzano Sud; Merano Sud. Right to Merano; 1.5km; right at Shell petrol station to Scenna. On for 2.5km, bridge on right, signed Labers; over and on for 5km.

	Alexander Ortner
	Via Fragsburger Strasse 3, 39012 Merano
Tel	+39 0473 244071
Email	info@fragsburg.com
Web	www.fragsburg.com

Hotel Cavallino d'Oro

The village is postcard Tyrolean, and Cavallino d'Oro (Little Gold Horse) has been welcoming travellers for 680 years. The market still runs every Friday in summer: farmers set up their stalls at the foot of the 18th-century bell tower (that still chimes through the night!). This was Austria not so very long ago: the local customs are still alive, and regular concerts take place at the inn over dinner. Bedrooms are mostly delightful, though a few have roof lights only. Others look onto the medieval square, the best have balconies with incredible views. There's a fascinating mix of antique country beds – some hand-decorated, some four-poster, some both. Many of the doors are painted, as are the beams in the green and peach sitting room; room 9 has the original ceiling. Dine in the sparkling dining room, breakfast in the rustic stübe, a wood-panelled room with geraniums at the window and checked tablecloths. Susanna and Stefan are as friendly as they are efficient. Go swimming, walking and biking in summer, sleigh riding and skiing in winter, and you can take the free shuttle to the new cable car and Alpe di Siusi.

Price	€80–€100. Singles €50. Half-board €58–€78 p.p.
Rooms	18: 5 doubles, 2 twins, 4 singles, 3 suites, 4 triples.
Meals	Lunch €12. Dinner €23. Wine from €14.
Closed	November.
Directions	A22 motorway, exit Bolzano Nord. Castelrotto signed at exit. Hotel in market square in town centre.

Susanna & Stefan Urthaler
Piazza Kraus 1, 39040 Castelrotto
Tel   +39 0471 706337
Email   cavallino@cavallino.it
Web   www.cavallino.it

Entry 35   Map 4

Hotel Zirmerhof

The Sound of Music in the peaks of South Tyrol. Alto Adige is a stunning area, and still more Germanic than Italian. The Perwanger family were here when it was still part of Austria and survived all the changes. Sepp, fourth generation – the hotel started in 1890 – runs a calm and happy ship. Much of the furniture is original to the house including 101 hand-carved dining chairs... Discover nooks and crannies, creaky floors and hand-painted doors, each with a chalked blessing by the priest. A fire crackles in the little library's grate, the snug panelled stübe is warmed by a tiled stove and the walls are sprinkled with family portraits – all is as *gemütlich* as can be. Bedrooms, including those in the annexe, have a wholesome country feel, some with balconies, many with panoramas; all are warm, friendly and snug. The food is south Tyrolean and delicious, much of the produce from their own happy cows, and is accompanied by their gewürztraminer wines – what a treat after a day in the mountains. Heaven for hikers and sybarites alike: delicious massages in the spa and a decked 12m pool.

Price	€142-€232. Half-board €89-€159 p.p.
Rooms	35 + 3: 24 twins/doubles, 6 singles. 5 suites. 3 log cabins for 3-5.
Meals	Breakfast €16. Dinner €40. Wine à la carte. Restaurant 300m.
Closed	7 January-10 May; 5 November-26 December.
Directions	A22 Modena-Brennero exit Neumarkt; SS48 dir. Cavalese. On for 10km, left to Radein. In Radein dir. "centro"; signed.

Josef Perwanger
South Tyrol, 39040 Radein

Tel	+39 0471 887215
Email	info@zirmerhof.com
Web	www.zirmerhof.com

14 Suiten Hotel Berghofer

At the end of the meandering track: birdsong and fir trees, cowbells and meadows, the scent of larch and pine. The tranquillity continues: there are shelves of books and magazines beside the fire, light modern furniture, an abundance of flowers, a cuckoo clock to tick away the hours. Bedrooms, named after the peaks you can see from large windows, have glazed doors leading to private balconies, and breathtaking Dolomites views. Rugs are scattered, pale pine floors and light walls are offset with painted wardrobes and stencilled borders. Some rooms have an extra store room, a few can be linked – ideal for a family; all have a separate seating area and a large bathroom. Dine in the charming 1450 *stübe*, purchased from a local farmer and painstakingly moved, timber by timber, up the hill. The restaurant displays a wonderful 18th-century stove; the food is regional and stylish. Ski in winter, hike among the alpine flowers in summer, return to a massage or hay-sauna, catch the sunset over the mountain.

Price	Half-board €222–€312 for 2.
Rooms	14: 13 suites for 2, 1 chalet for 4.
Meals	Half-board only. Wine from €20. Restaurant 1km.
Closed	Certain weeks in February & November.
Directions	A22 exit Neumarkt/Auer; SS48 to Kaltenbrunn; 200m after garage, left for Radein; on to Oberradein; signed.

Ethical Collection: Food.
See page 400 for details

Renate Ortner-Huber
Oberradein 54, South Tyrol,
39040 Radein

Tel	+39 0471 887150
Email	info@berghofer.it
Web	www.berghofer.it

Veneto • Friuli–Venezia Giulia

Photo: istock.com

B&B

Veneto

All'Eremo Relais Agriturismo

Far from the madding crowds, you are ensconced in a solid 1970s farmhouse overlooking Lake Garda – what a setting! Adorable Elena, ex-lawyer from Verona, loves her guests, loves the country life and bakes a different cake for breakfast each day. The open-plan downstairs is the heart of the house, all chunky beams, wall paintings and agrarian artefacts on white walls, while outside is a small summer kitchen in the garden with a barbecue – a great extra addition for guests. Now that Elena's parents have moved to Verona you have three bedrooms to choose from, two with magnificent views, all with very comfortable beds and charmingly decorated in palest pinks and creams by Elena. Terraces have been furnished with loungers on every level: settle back and absorb the tranquillity and the views with a glass of Bardolino rosé. Elena is full of recommendations of where to go and what to do, and which restaurants to try – slip off to the lake, dine on fabulous fish, sample the opera in Verona, come and go as you please. Brilliant value – you'll love this place.

Price	€80–€110.
Rooms	3: 2 doubles, 1 family room for 2-4.
Meals	Guest kitchen & barbecue. Restaurants 1km.
Closed	Never.
Directions	A22 exit Affi; to Garda for 3.5km. In Albare, left at lights towards Bardolino; after 3km, 'Corteline'; 500m on right, take minor road Sem e Pigno until end; follow dirt track on left to house. Unsigned.

Elena Corsini Piffer
Strada delle Rocca 2, Loc. Casetta Rossa,
37011 Bardolino

Tel	+39 0457 211391
Email	info@eremorelais.com
Web	www.eremorelais.com

Relais Ca' delle Giare

Enrico and Giuditta are a cultured and elegant couple who have made their B&B rooms, in the rose-clad coaching house and converted barn, as homely as their own. They welcome you with an old-fashioned, easy charm and their friendly pets like to pad around and say hello too. An old stone archway leads to the guest quarters. All have chunky ceiling beams, antique Sicilian furniture, shiny tiled floors and colourful rugs. The two upstairs rooms look over rolling wine groves; the garden room, with its own entrance and kitchenette, has French windows leading to a courtyard, and a sofa to snuggle on in front of an open fire. Bathrooms are luxurious: bright spotlighting, showers over baths, sumptuous thick towels. Enormous Sicilian urns ('giare') dot the pretty, sloping garden bordered by woods and hydrangeas. Tuck into breakfast on the well-kept lawn, then find a peaceful spot on a sunlounger with a view of Verona. Veronese Giuditta is a font of knowledge on concerts and exhibitions, and if you fancy a Valpolicella wine tour, you're in the right place: Enrico will happily take you.

Price	€120-€130.
Rooms	3: 2 doubles, 1 suite (with kichenette).
Meals	Restaurants 3km.
Closed	Rarely.
Directions	A4/A22 exit Verona Nord; signs to Tangenziali. At end, left dir. Borgo Trento. At lights left dir. Quinzano; over r'bout, thro' Quinzano, up hill & hairpin bends. At top after 5km sign for Negrar, left; house immed. right.

Enrico & Giuditta Corpaci
Via Campi di Sopra 1,
37024 Negrar - Verona
Tel +39 0456 015059
Email info@cadellegiare.it
Web www.cadellegiare.it

Ca' del Rocolo

Such an undemanding, delightful place to be and such a warm, enthusiastic young family to be with. Maurizio ran a restaurant in Verona, Ilaria was a journalist and has three cookbooks to her name; they gave it all up for a country life for their children. Their 1800s farmhouse is on the side of a hill overlooking forested hills and the vast Lessinia National Park. Over a decade has passed since their move; Maurizio did much of the renovation himself and the result is authentic and attractive. Simple cotton rugs cover stripped bedroom floors, rough plaster walls are whitewashed, rooms are big and airy, with solid country furniture and excellent beds and bathrooms. There's also a shared kitchen. Breakfast is at the long farmhouse table or out on the terrace, making the most of the views: delicious food, seasonal cakes, home-grown fruits, happy conversation. Dinner, mostly vegetarian, is an occasional affair. This is a seven-hectare, all-organic farm, with olives and fruit trees, hens, horses and beehives; there are nature trails galore, a saltwater pool in the offing, and always something going on.

Price	€63–€75 (€410–€450 per week).
Rooms	3: 2 doubles, 1 family room.
Meals	Light meals €15. Wine €6–€8.
	Shared guest kitchen. Restaurant 4km.
Closed	Rarely.
Directions	Directions on booking.

Ilaria & Maurizio Corazza
Via Gaspari 3, Loc. Quinto,
37142 Verona

Tel	+39 0458 700879
Email	info@cadelrocolo.com
Web	www.cadelrocolo.com

Ethical Collection: Environment; Food.
See page 400 for details

B&B Domus Nova

Stroll down the Via Mazzini, lined with Gucci and Bulgari. People-watch on the Piazza delle Erbe, where the crowds throng until 2am. Soak up grand opera beneath a starry summer sky at the Roman amphitheatre. And return to the warmth and classicism of the Domus Nova, in the car-free heart of Verona; it is wonderfully quiet. This is a grand family house that has been restored to its former splendour. Giovanni grew up here, three relatives are architects and his wife's sister is an interior designer – no wonder it's perfect. The look is luxy hotel, the feel is B&B and the views are fabulous: onto the large and lovely Piazza dei Signori and its historic tower. Bedrooms, on the third and top floors, are spacious yet cosy, immaculate yet friendly... natural pigments on walls, rich fabrics, painted beams, fine antiques, and one with a balcony so you can be Juliet for a day. The salon is equally inviting, with its comfortable leather armchairs and elegant breakfast tables, classical music and antique books. You'll imagine yourself in another century staying here! *Minimum stay two nights. Parking available.*

Price	€230-€260. Suite €280-€310. Extra bed €60.
Rooms	4: 1 double, 2 twins/doubles, 1 suite (with kitchenette).
Meals	Restaurants nearby.
Closed	Epiphany-February.
Directions	In "centro storico", next to Piazza delle Erbe.

Anna & Giovanni Roberti
Piazza dei Signori 18,
37121 Verona

Mobile	+39 380 707 1931
Email	info@domusnovaverona.it
Web	www.domusnovaverona.it

Antica Verona

Stay for a few days and enjoy a slice of Veronese life. Opening off the street, this tall, 16th-century, grey-shuttered palazzo stands in the old quarter, midway between the Piazza delle Erbe and the Duomo. It is owned and lived in by Signor Aletti and his lovely wife, who have created a guest apartment on the second floor. This is reached by a small lift and is serene, delightful and simply furnished, with gentle colours and family antiques. Sig. Aletti, quiet and softly spoken, with a huge smile, painted the murals himself. The beamed, white-walled double bedroom is cool and attractive, the little sitting/dining room has a sofa that unfolds to make two single beds (fine for children) and the old-fashioned bathroom is immaculate. There are some great food shops and restaurants in the area but if you're inspired to eat in, the little kitchen has all the mod cons. And you needn't fear the cold in winter: there's central heating too. Never mind the lack of an outside space – that hardly matters when the delights of Verona lie outside your door, and there are bikes to rent a few streets away. *Minimum stay six nights.*

Price	€50–€90.
Rooms	1 apartment for 2-4.
Meals	Restaurants within walking distance.
Closed	Never.
Directions	Train station 2km from apartment: Piazza Bra; Via Oberdan; Corso P. Borsari; Via Fama; Via S. S. Vecchio.

Carlo Alberto Aletti Alemagna
Via San Salvatore Vecchio 6a,
37121 Verona

Tel	+39 0458 065076
Email	caaletti@gmail.com
Web	www.anticaverona.altervista.org

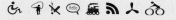

Agriturismo Musella Relais & Winery

There's a canoe at your disposal, to ply the small river that runs through – and bikes for the roads, towels for the plunge pool and different pastries for breakfast each day. Such is the generosity of the Pasqua di Bisceglie family, two of whom live within the walls of Musella; the rest live on the estate. Sweep through the electric gates, park under the pergola and there's Paulo to greet you, with impeccable English and an irresistible smile. This 16th-century estate, built around a vast courtyard of grass, has become a modern winery and superb B&B; there are also four apartments should you wish to do your own thing. Expect chunky rafters and country antiques, wrought-iron beds and crisp cotton sheets, harmonious colours and art on the walls. Some rooms are on the upper floors, others have their own outdoor space, yet others have open fires. Bathrooms are fabulous, and spacious. You may replenish your fridges from the small shop a walk away, make friends in the guest sitting room (books, open fire), savour the olive oils and the valpolicella, fish on the river (bring your rod). *Minimum stay two nights. Wine-tasting.*

Price	€135–€155. Single €90. Triple €165. Apts €210–€280.
Rooms	11 + 4: 9 doubles, 1 single, 1 triple. 4 apts for 2-4.
Meals	Breakfast for self-caterers included.
Closed	15 December–15 February.
Directions	A4 exit Verona Est dir. Valpent; exit Via Mattarana (Borgo Venezia, white sign). Left at exit, straight on for 2km; in Ferrazze right at end; Musella courtyard on left after 250m.

Famiglia Pasqua di Bisceglie
Via Ferrazzette 2,
San Martino Buon Albergo,
37036 Verona

Mobile	+39 335 7294627
Email	paulo@musella.it
Web	www.musella.it

La Rosa e Il Leone

Everything about La Rosa e Il Leone – from the ancient Roman columns in the flower-filled garden to the Juliet-style balcony of the marbled-floor master bedroom – breathes sentiment and romance. Named after Valeria's Veronese father and Milanese mother – the Rose of Lombardy, the Lion of the Veneto – the villa is an ode to their love both for each other and for the arts. The walls sing with framed musical scores and programmes from nights at La Scala, Milan and L'Arena, Verona, while adjoining first-floor sitting rooms celebrate the juxtaposition of the masculine (hard lines, dark colours, stacks of leather-bound books) and the feminine (curves, pastel colours, a passion for music and dance). The soft hand-woven sheets on antique framed beds were part of Valeria's mother's dowry, the furniture part of her parent's lifetime collection. Stroll under leafy pergolas; listen to the history humming in the leaves of ancient cypresses; breakfast al fresco admiring an extraordinary replica of the Louvre's winged Victory of Samothrace. Like her house, Valeria is a gold-mine of high culture. A must for anyone visiting Verona.

Price	€135. Whole house €1,890 per week.
Rooms	3: 1 double; 2 doubles sharing bath.
Meals	Restaurants 1-4km.
Closed	Mid-October to mid-March.
Directions	From Verona dir. Vicenza to Caldiero; left for Illasi. Right after 2km, then right again, then left at end.

Valeria Poli
Via Trieste 56,
37030 Colognola ai Colli
Tel   +39 0457 650123
Email   vvpoli@libero.it

Massimago

You get the best of both worlds here: the independence of a private apartment and the personality of a B&B. Lovely young agronomist Camilla and her mother Lorenza have opened up the doors of the family farm to guests and go out of their way to make your holiday a dream. An evening at the opera in Verona? They'll sort out tickets and transport, by Vespa or vintage car. Olive/wine/cherry harvesting on the farm, followed by a feast? Book in. This beautifully restored country retreat, with unspoilt valley views, has been in the family since 1883. Next door is a long cream house divided into three elegant apartments for guests, furnished with a charming mix of family heirlooms and modern treats, lovely old fireplaces, delicious trompe l'oeils and plenty of books. Buy their wines and oil, help yourselves to their vegetables and fruits. Breakfasts are on the house, romantic poolside dinners are on request, and the pool, unfenced, floodlit at night, is bliss. Note that L'Olivo and Il Ciliego have hobs not ovens, and little ones must watch La Vite's bannister-free stair. Exceptional place, exceptional people.

Price	€120–€210.
Rooms	4 apartments: 3 for 2, 1 for 2-3.
Meals	Breakfast included. Restaurant within walking distance.
Closed	Rarely.
Directions	A4 Milan-Venice exit Verona Est; follow dir. Vicenza, then Vago. Thro' San Pietro di Lavagno, Mezzano di Sotto. Signed.

Camilla Rossi Chaovenet
Via Giare 21, 37030 Mezzane

Mobile	+39 349 7899985
Email	info@massimago.com
Web	www.massimago.com

Agriturismo Tenuta La Pila

Raimonda and Alberto will soon have you chatting over a welcome drink; he speaks a clutch of languages, she's bubbly, both are committed to the green way of life. Each B&B room is named after a fruit and smartly decorated: cream walls, exposed brick, crisp linen, fluffy towels, and antique furniture to add a homely touch. Two of the apartments are in a separate building once used for drying tobacco; they have immensely high beams and are decorated in a similar style. You get a table, chairs and sofabed in the large central living area, and a neat corner kitchen; cheerful bedrooms have flower prints and checked bedspreads; two further apartments have oak floors and country antiques. Breakfast is a spread of home produce: kiwi jam, eggs, fruit, bread, yogurt. The farm is surrounded by fertile fields, trees and kiwi vines meandering across the plains, with the beautiful towns of Rovigo and Chioggia close by. Return to a peaceful patio-garden, a dip in the pool, and skittles and boules beside the huge magnolia. A happy place. *Minimum stay two nights.*

Price	€65–€80. Singles €45–€55. Apts €658–€898 per week.
Rooms	5 + 4: 2 twins/doubles, 3 triples. 4 apts: 2 for 2-4, 2 for 4-5.
Meals	Breakfast €5 for self-caterers. Dinner €20. Wine €5-€10. Restaurants 2km.
Closed	Rarely.
Directions	From SS 434 Verona-Rovigo exit Carpi. Left at stop; after 500m left onto Strada dell'Argine Vecchio della Valle & onto Via Gorgo da Bagno. After 1km along asphalt road, left into farm.

Raimonda & Alberto Sartori
Via Pila 42, Loc. Spinimbecco, 37049
Villa Bartolomea

Tel	+39 0442 659289
Email	post@tenutalapila.it
Web	www.tenutalapila.it

Il Castello

A narrow, winding road leads up to the *castello* at the foot of the Berici hills. Also known as the Villa Godi-Marinoni, the castle was built by Count Godi in the 15th century, on the ruins of an old feudal castle. Massive hewn walls enclose the compound of terraced vines, orchard, Italian garden and panoramic views stretching to Padua; you enter via an arched entrance, ancient cobbles beneath your feet. The villa itself is still lived in by the family: Signora Marinoni and her son, courteous and attentive, run this vast estate together. Guest apartments (one with its kitchen on the far side of the courtyard) are in an outbuilding with curious gothic details in the plastered façade; furnishings are a mix of dark antique and contemporary. Hidden below the castle walls is the garden with fish pond; in spring, hundreds of lemon trees are wheeled out to stand grandly on pedestals. The climate is mild and the hillside a mass of olive groves. Olive oil is produced on the ten-hectare estate – there's a wine cellar in the bowels of the castle, and a *cantina* where you can buy. *Minimum stay three nights.*

Price	€58.
Rooms	4 apartments for 2-4.
Meals	Restaurant 500m.
Closed	Never.
Directions	A4 exit Vicenza Est; at r'bout follow signs to Riviera Berica for 15km. In Ponte di Barbarano, at lights right towards Barbarano. In main square, left to Villaga; villa 500m on left.

Elda Marinoni
Via Castello 6,
36021 Barbarano Vicentino

Tel	+39 0444 886055
Email	info@castellomarinoni.com
Web	www.castellomarinoni.com

B&B Casa Ciriani

Set back from the road, the gated villa looks cool and inviting: shaded by trees, shuttered against the sun. Signora Ciriani and her husband built it 30 years ago; now she and her daughter run their charming B&B. Nothing is too much trouble. The entrance hall of this peaceful family home has a traditional mosaic floor that sweeps into the drawing room – designed (and partly laid!) by Mariantonietta. Upstairs is a family room with some country antiques and paintings by nieces and nephews. In one room, a beautiful old yellow chest catches the eye, and a private terrace. Brush up your Italian with Silvana (though she also speaks excellent English) at breakfast on the portico in summer, delightful with wrought-iron furniture and earthenware jars. The owners are passionate gardeners and are happy for you to gather a picnic and bring it back here; they'll provide the rest! Enjoy wine tours in the lush Euganean hills, hop on a bus for Venice, take a stroll round Padua. Mariantonietta has also arranged special prices for guests at the exquisite thermal spa nearby. Wonderful. *Minimum stay two nights.*

Price	€65–€80. Singles €40–€50.
Rooms	3: 2 doubles, 1 family room.
Meals	Restaurants 2km.
Closed	Christmas & New Year.
Directions	Firenze-Venezia, exit Padova Sud after toll for Padova; 1st lights, main road left for Rovigo; 3km; 2nd lights, right for Abano; 1km; 3rd lights, right Via S. Maria d'Abano; 700m, left into Via Guazzi; 200m.

Silvana & Mariantonietta Ciriani
Via Guazzi 1,
35031 Abano Terme

Tel +39 0497 15272
Email bb.casaciriani@gmail.com
Web www.casaciriani.com

Villa Mandriola

A charming surprise when, after the modern village of Albignasego, the unassuming gates swing open to Via San Caboto, a leafy statue-lined avenue, a peaceful pocket of 18th-century Italy. Villa Mandriola is the country home of one of the oldest families in Italy: the San Bonifacios, Earls of Padova. Thick ancient walls surround the charming park garden preserving the remarkable calmness that the San Bonifacio family would have enjoyed in the 1700s. From the vaulted vestibule of the approach to the chapel and frescoed ballroom, the landing and halls patrolled by family portraits, the panelled bedrooms with their faded bathrooms, the villa is steeped in history yet still provides comfort and relaxation. Feast on the half-board option and be treated as nobility would, retreating from town for respite. A large group may take on the whole house, a smaller group may choose between the two-floored apartment at the villa gates or the beautiful cottage overlooking the swan-sprinkled lake. Padua is the shortest of drives. *Minimum stay three nights.*

Price	€2,300–€4,000 per week. Half-board €35 extra p.p.
Rooms	Villa for 12 (2 doubles, 3 twins, 2 singles).
Meals	Breakfast from €15. Dinner €30–€40. Wine from €8.
Closed	Never.
Directions	Directions on booking.

Ethical Collection: Food.
See page 400 for details

Nicolò San Bonifacio
Via S. Caboto 10,
35020 Albignasego
Tel   +39 0496 81246
Email   info@villamandriola.com
Web   www.villamandriola.com

Ca' Marcello

Venice owes her history of great Renaissance naval battles partly to the long line of military captains in the Marcello family: many lead the fleet to victory, thus securing Venice her wealth and beauty. Ca'Marcello, a magnificent Palladian-style villa set in a perfectly manicured and historic garden, represents the Marcello legacy. Stroll around the peaceful, statue-lined park; take a private tour of the main house and its fresco-filled ballroom; peer in awe at the ancestral portraits of the Marcellos. Despite its history and significance Ca'Marcello is still the family home – and behind the formal façade the atmosphere is wonderfully relaxed. Kind, softly spoken Jacopo grew up here and will ensure a luxurious stay: you have the whole west wing at your disposal. Expect beeswax, polished wooden stairs and floors; rooms over two floors, virtually untouched since the 18th-century yet in perfect condition; a well-equipped kitchen (but do ask if you'd prefer meals cooked for you); a sitting room; and an exquisite pool in a private garden. Unique.

Minimum stay one week in high season.

Price	€2,250–€3,500 per week.
Rooms	Apartment for 8.
Meals	Breakfast €10. Dinner €30–€40.
	Wine from €10. Children's menu €15.
Closed	Never.
Directions	From Venice-Treviso airport, left until Quinto; right & follow signs to Badoere. Signed from Badoere.

Jacopo Marcello
Via del Marcello 13,
35017 Levada di Piombino Dese

Tel	+39 0499 350340
Email	info@camarcello.it
Web	www.camarcello.it

Agriturismo La Presa

The agriturismo is Lucia's baby – she looks after both farm and guests wonderfully. So bowl along the flatlands of the Po delta, pass the chicken factory by, approach the silver poplar lined drive – Lucia has planted hundreds – and sweep through open gates to a peaceful farmstead scented with jasmine. These 400 acres of maize, soya, wheat and cattle have been in the family for 30 years; Lucia has received guests for three. Brick pathways link the main house (two bedrooms) to the rest which lie in a converted farm building. Inside, all feels clean, simple, spacious and cool. Shower rooms are new, floors are wooden or tiled and softened by rugs, walls are light green, and the 'single' beds in the annexe – two beds up, two down – are more like small doubles. The beamed dining room, where meat roasts on the fire before supper, is most inviting. Breakfasts promise homemade tarts and the chestnut table seats 16. Friend Alberto's knowledge of the delta is superb – let him take you up the river and catch oysters. Or borrow the bikes: this flat reclaimed countryside is brilliant for cycling. *Minimum stay two nights.*

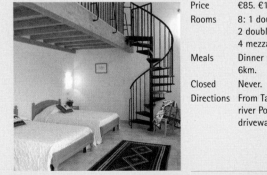

Price	€85. €140 for 4.
Rooms	8: 1 double, 1 suite for 2 + cot; 2 doubles sharing bath. Annexe: 4 mezzanine suites for 4-6.
Meals	Dinner with wine, €30. Restaurant 6km.
Closed	Never.
Directions	From Taglio di Po follow right bank of river Po for 5km until poplar lined driveway.

Lucia La Presa
Via Cornera 13,
Taglio di Po, 45019 Rovigo
Tel   +39 0426 661594
Email   info@lapresa.it
Web   www.lapresa.it

Entry 51   Map 9

Tenuta Ca' Zen

Lord Byron's passionate affair with an earlier owner's wife inspired many lines. It's all terribly romantic and Elaine's delight in her remarkable home shines through; her Irish eyes twinkle as she regales you with tales of almost-as-illustrious guests. Chapel, stable and cottages are typical of Venetian agricultural architecture; the villa itself is sombre and impressive. Family antiques, stunning terrazzo floors, old wooden doors and chandeliers fill this spacious house and imbue the air with romance and history. Elegant bedrooms are enormous and keep their wonderful 'lived in' feel. The bathrooms, newly restored, are large and inviting. Meals are served in the majestic dining rooms where, in *Fawlty Towers* style, Sergio swaps his gardening clothes for a waiter's jacket and serves delicious local dishes cooked by his wife. Remote rivers, wetlands and sand dunes create an ideal spot for nature lovers seeking a holiday away from the crowds. It's also excellent country for horse riding, a sport Elaine and her daughter offer here. An alluring fusion of Italian creativity and Irish charisma.

Price	€90-€125.
Rooms	5: 3 twins/doubles, 1 suite for 4, 1 family room for 4.
Meals	Light supper €25. Dinner, 3 courses, €45; by arrangement. Wine €7-€30. Restaurants 2km.
Closed	Mid-November to mid-February.
Directions	SS Romea exit Taglio di Po; right at 1st lights, straight on until river bank; left with river on right, on for 3km to house.

Ethical Collection: Community.
See page 400 for details

	Elaine & Maria Adelaide Avanzo Taglio di Po, 45019 Rovigo
Tel	+39 0426 346469
Email	info@tenutacazen.it
Web	www.tenutacazen.it

Villa Rizzi Albarea

Hidden behind the house is the loveliest wild garden, where exciting pathways thread their way past statues and trees, and bridges span a romantic lake with an island and swans. To the front is a lawn next to an art-filled chapel, with roses in the cloisters, pines, palms, peonies and ancient magnolias. The house is intriguing, too: the oldest Palladian villa between Venice and Padua. Once a convent for the Giudecca nuns, it looks back ten centuries. Though wars and fire have meant much restoration, it's still a beautiful place. Bedrooms are a fresh mix of traditional and flounced, with delectable antiques and comfortable beds, some with old frescoes, others with stunning rafters. Shower rooms sparkle, Persian rugs glow on stone or wooden floors, and there's a fire for winter. This is deep in the country but not isolated, barely touched by the nearby motorway; all birdsong and roses in summer. In spite of breakfasts served by uniformed maids – and sauna, gym, pool and lake – the atmosphere is personal, thanks to these generous hosts. *Minimum stay two nights.*

Price	€180-€280. Apartment €200-€280.
Rooms	7 + 1: 7 suites. Apartment for 2-4.
Meals	Restaurants nearby.
Closed	Rarely.
Directions	From autostrada A4 Milano-Venezia, exit Dolo, over lights, 1.5km. Right at Albarea sign, 1km; signed.

Aida & Pierluigi Rizzi
Via Albarea 53,
30030 Pianiga di Venezia

Tel	+39 0415 100933
Email	info@villa-albarea.com
Web	www.villa-albarea.com

Villa Colloredo

Handsomely ranged around a courtyard, these 18th-century Venetian buildings – all peachy stone and olive shutters – hold a cool surprise. Bold paintings, modern sculptures and colourful collages dot their interiors – part of the private collection of the Meneghelli family. Architecturally, these former stables and grain stores, next to the family villa, fuse modern styling with original features. Beamed ceilings and wooden or tiled floors contrast with streamlined kitchens, simple rustic furniture and artwork on white walls. Spaces have been imaginatively used – a shower, perhaps, in a glass-topped cube – to maximise the open, airy feel. Upper floors have lovely low windows, with views to fields, orchards or courtyard. Two of the larger apartments can be joined together – great for families. The outdoor cloisters are a tranquil place to sit and read, or set out lunch; behind the villa are wonderful natural gardens to explore. Drop in on Padua – or drive to Fusina and catch the water bus to Venice! Family-run with a homely and welcoming feel. *Minimum stay two nights.*

Price	€60–€80. Apartments €80–€110.
Rooms	1 + 4: 1 double. 4 apartments for 4.
Meals	Restaurant 200m.
Closed	7 January–4 February; 17 February–26 March; 3 November–20 December.
Directions	From A4, exit Dolo dir. Sambruson; right opp. church.

Andrea Meneghelli
Brusaura 24,
30030 Sambruson di Dolo

Tel	+39 0414 11755
Email	info@villacolloredo.com
Web	www.villacolloredo.com

Villa Tron Carrara Mioni

You're in a wonderfully central spot – perfect for exploring the delightful towns of the Veneto. Gabriella and Sandro are a considerate, charming couple who love to share their home with guests. Standing on the site of a palace destroyed by Napoleonic troops, it's typical of the grand villas built by Venetian patrician families in the early 19th century. They travelled by water; now a busy road sweeps between the house and the river. But the house is set well back and is surrounded by five hectares of elegant gardens and woodland, including an ice house and a lake. Inside, the rooms are big and beautifully proportioned, filled with fresh flowers, antiques and gracious sofas. Old family photos record generations of the Carrara and Mioni families (ask for the full story!). The super airy double room on the first floor has its own small terrace and two views onto the garden; there's a faint hum of traffic but nothing serious. On the second floor is the family suite. Gabriella serves you a lovely breakfast of homemade cakes, jams and fruit, out under the trees in summer, elegantly presented. *Minimum stay two nights.*

Price	€120–€170.
Rooms	2: 1 double, 1 suite for 3 (1 twin, 1 single).
Meals	Dinner €32–€38, on request. Restaurants 200m.
Closed	Rarely.
Directions	A4 exit Mirano-Dolo. At r'bout dir. Dolo; after 8km left at x-roads in front of church dir. Venice; on for 1km, house on left, 4th gate.

Alessandro & Gabriella Mioni
Via Ca' Tron 23,
Dolo - Riviera del Brenta

Tel	+39 0414 10177
Email	villatron@libero.it
Web	www.villatron.it

Hotel Villa Alberti

Pluck fruit from the orchard, wash it in the fountain, pick a quiet spot in the walled garden. This 17th-century villa, once the summer residence of Venetian nobility, has been restored by the delightful Malerbas to combine grand features with a warm and unstuffy mood. Beautiful shutters and floors, Murano lights and chandeliers, decorative ironwork lamps and balconies... all has been reclaimed and revived. And it is no wonder Gianni is proud of his garden, its box-lined paths, statues and century-old trees, its exceptional roses, its carpets of wild flowers; it develops as it matures. The reception hall – a sweep of dark polished wood, rich rugs and deep sofas – leads to three floors of bedrooms furnished in a simple but refined style: wooden or stone floors, silky bedspreads, a few antiques; ask for one overlooking the garden rather than the road. The rooms in the *barchessa* are more rustic and somewhat blander. Feast on delicious risottos on the terrace in the summer; you could get used to the aristocratic life! A direct bus runs to Venice from Dolo; here you are peacefully out of town.

Price	€90–€130.
Rooms	20 doubles.
Meals	Dinner €25. Wine €12. Restaurant 300m.
Closed	Rarely.
Directions	A4 exit Dolo-Mirano. At lights in Dolo, left, direction Venice. 2km along river, over bridge & cont. in same direction along opp. bank for 1.5km. Hotel on right.

	Famiglia Malerba
	Via E. Tito 90, 30031 Dolo
Tel	+39 0414 266512
Email	info@villalberti.it
Web	www.villalberti.it

Dune Agriturismo Relais

Why stay in Venice, when half an hour away, by boat or train, lies this peaceful estate, deeply rural and a sandal-clad stroll from a private beach space at Eraclea Mare? The family farm (mostly beef) is going strong but it's daughter Francesca who runs the show. And what a splendid show it is: an airy reception bright with art by cousin Lorenzo; a huge garden with barbecue and big swimming pool; an inexpensive restaurant whose young chef cooks with passion (absolutely worth the half-board option); and a little shop selling home-grown produce you can cook yourself. The apartments are fabulously well-equipped: simple stylish bedrooms dressed in earthy tones, luxurious bathrooms, dreamy kitchens. You can tell the family care about the environment and love seasonal, organically grown food – some of the produce comes from the fields outside. Local staff give a slick performance, smile spontaneously and do their utmost to make you feel part of the family, even when they're packed out in summer. A poster in reception sums it all up: "Good company, good wine, good welcome: good people." *Minimum stay three nights in apts. Flexible out of season booking.*

Price	€90–€190. Apts €70–€160 for 2; €100–€200 for 4.
Rooms	15 + 11: 5 doubles, 2 singles, 2 suites, 2 family rooms for 4, 4 triples. 11 apts: 3 for 2, 4 for 4, 4 for 4-6.
Meals	Breakfast €7 for self-caterers. Dinner €20–€30. Restaurant 100m.
Closed	Rarely.
Directions	A4 Trieste-Venezia exit San Donà di Piave/Noventa. Follow directions for Eraclea Mare, then Dune Verde, until Via dei Fiori.

	Francesca Pasti Via S. Croce 6, Eraclea Mare, 30020 Venice
Tel	+39 0421 66171
Email	info@adriabella.com

B&B Corte 1321

Down a narrow alleyway, through a large and lovely courtyard, tall walls towering above, and enter a 15th-century palazzo. The apartment is on the ground floor, the B&B on the first. Catch your breath inside, at this calm, eclectic décor of Persian rugs, silk curtains, fresh flowers and influences from Bali and Morocco. Amelia is a Californian artist and her paintings hang on every wall. She and her mother Deborah live nearby, so there's no need to tiptoe around your hosts. Most guests are English speaking and bedrooms have been designed to meet American expectations: the best linen, mattresses and showers; hand-crafted beds; the internet. One room looks onto the canal, the other two onto the courtyard. In the apartment downstairs the style is uncluttered, the whitewashed walls making the most of the light. Breakfast is a pretty basket of brioche and bread in the courtyard. The little vaporetto is five minutes away – no bridges! – the local shop is across the square and the Rialto, markets and Accademia are nearby. *Minimum stay two nights.*

Price	€125–€175 for 2; €150–€190 for 3; €175–€220 for 4. Apt €125–€220.
Rooms	3 + 1: 3 family rooms: 2 for 2-3, 1 for 2-4. Apartment for 4.
Meals	Restaurants nearby.
Closed	Rarely.
Directions	From Piazzale Roma, water bus towards Lido; exit San Silvestro; walk towards Campo San' Aponal; 3rd left; 3rd right.

Amelia Bonvini
San Polo 1321, 30125 Venice
Tel +39 0415 224923
Email info@corte1321.com
Web www.corte1321.com

Oltre Il Giardino

A corner of paradise in off-beat San Polo – take a water taxi to the door! What a joy to find, behind the iron gates, a dreamy courtyard garden scented with jasmine and lavender; to breakfast under the pergola – April to October – is quite a treat. This enchanting cream stone villa once belonged to Alma Mahler, the composer's widow; now it is the home of Signora Muner and her son Lorenzo, and is run by the sweetest staff. Gaze from your bedroom window onto a magnolia, an olive and a pomegranate tree – wonderfully restorative after a day discovering Venice. Each room is elegant, spacious and filled with light, each has its own charm; three have sitting rooms and the ground-floor suite its own lovely piece of garden terrace. Colours range from vibrant turquoise to dark chocolate to pale ivory, there are family antiques and art on the walls and lovely mosaic'd bathrooms with Bulgari products. Deep green sofas in the lounge, the international papers on the table: all feels calm, inviting, intimate. The Rialto is a 15-minute walk; artisan shops and eateries wait outside the door.

Price	€150-€250. Suites €200-€500.
Rooms	6: 2 doubles, 4 suites.
Meals	Restaurant 200m.
Closed	Never.
Directions	Vaporetto to San Tomà; cross Campo San Tomà. Exit left into Calle del Mandoler; right, then left to end. Right into Campo dei Frari; over bridge, left. Over 2nd bridge, right; hotel at end.

Lorenzo Muner
San Polo 2542,
30125 Venice

Tel	+39 0412 750015
Email	info@oltreilgiardino-venezia.com
Web	www.oltreilgiardino-venezia.com

Palazzo Tiepolo

Old-fashioned grandeur at its best, but the approach down a narrow alley gives nothing away. This 16th-century beauty has been in the Tiepolo family forever and friendly Lelia oversees the ongoing restoration. Tiepolo, the ground-floor studio, has been cleverly thought out. A beautifully equipped and stocked kitchen tucks behind cupboard doors, the shower room is in a corner and the gem of a dining area overlooks the life and bustle of the Grand Canal. Valier, an apartment in a separate building, is perfect peace; enjoy a glass of wine and music from the CD collection in its courtyard garden. Cream and pale terracotta walls bedecked with prints and gilt mirrors set off rich rugs and Venetian furniture in the living room, the walk-in shower and kitchen are in opposite corners and wide wooden stairs lead to the mezzanine's bed, encased in embroidered linen. For grand old style, go B&B and take the antique-filled suite in the house. Breakfast is formally served on bone china and the history of the Tiepolos surrounds you. *Minimum stay three nights in apts.*

Price	Suite €1400–€1750. Apartments €700–€800. Prices per week.
Rooms	1 + 2: 1 suite. 2 apartments for 2.
Meals	Restaurants nearby
Closed	Never.
Directions	Vaporetto 1 to San Tomà; straight on, right at end. Cross Campo San Tomà, right into Campiello San Tomà. Over canal into Calle dei Nombolithen, right Calle Centani; house at end on left. Bell marked M. Passi.

Lelia Passi
Calle Centani, San Polo 2774,
30125 Venice

Tel	+39 0415 227989
Email	leliapassi@gmail.com
Web	www.cortetiepolo.com

Casa San Boldo - Grimani, Loredan & Manin

Your own tennis court – in Venice! Borrow a racket, or watch others from the jasmine-covered bandstand in the garden. Francesca's parents live on the ground floor and share both court and garden. These well-restored apartments are elegant yet cosy, with family antiques, fresh flowers, smart sofas and Persian rugs on parquet floors. There are intriguing quirks too: an original window and its glass preserved as a piece of art, a 1756 dowry chest from Alto Adige. And you're never far from a window with bustling canal views. The smaller apartment on the first floor has a sweet twin/double tucked away beneath the rafters, and a larger double room downstairs with modern paintings by a local artist. The little kitchen is beautifully equipped, the dining room has high ceilings and a Venetian marble floor. Grimani has a bedroom on the ground floor with garden views and another up; the super new Manin is also on the ground floor. Multi-lingual Francesca who lives nearby is kind, friendly and runs cookery courses that include buying the produce from the Rialto market, just around the corner. *Minimum stay three nights.*

Price	Grimani €1,550-€1,950. Loredan €1,150-€1,550. Manin €900-€1,200. Prices per week.
Rooms	3 apartments: 1 for 4, 2 for 4-6.
Meals	Restaurants 200m.
Closed	Never.
Directions	Park at Piazzale Roma nearby. Details on booking.

Francesca Pasti
San Polo 2281,
30125 Venice
Tel   +39 0421 66171
Email   info@adriabella.com
Web   www.adriabella.com

Pensione La Calcina

Catch the sea breezes of early evening from the terrace butting out over the water as you watch the beautiful people stroll the Zattere. Or gaze across the lagoon to the Rendentore. Ruskin stayed here in 1876, and for many people this corner of town, facing the Giudecca and with old Venice just behind you, is the best. The hotel has been discretely modernised by its charming owners; comfortable bedrooms have air con, antiques and parquet floors. Those at the front, with views, are dearer; the best are the corner rooms, with windows on two sides. A small top terrace can be booked for romantic evenings and you can breakfast, lunch or dinner at the delightful floating restaurant, open to all – delicious dishes are available all day and the fruit juices and milkshakes are scrummy. Pause for a moment and remember Ruskin's words on the city he loved: "a ghost upon the sands of the sea, so weak, so quiet, so bereft of all but her loveliness, that we might well doubt, as we watched her faint reflection on the mirage of the lagoon, which was the City and which the shadow." The vaporetto is a step away.

Price	€110–€310. Singles €90–€150.
Rooms	27: 20 doubles, 7 singles.
Meals	Lunch/dinner, with glass of wine, €26–€35. Restaurant closed Mondays.
Closed	Never.
Directions	Water bus line 51 or 61 from Piazzale Roma or train station; line 2 from Tronchetto.

Alessandro Szemere
Fondamenta Zattere ai Gesuati,
Dorsoduro 780, 30123 Venice

Tel	+39 0415 206466
Email	info@lacalcina.com
Web	www.lacalcina.com

Fujiyama Bed & Breakfast

Jasmine, wisteria, shady trees – hard to believe this pool of tranquillity is minutes from the hurly-burly of Venice's streets and the grandeur of the Rialto and St Mark's Square. Even more unusual – for this city – is to step through an oriental tearoom to reach your bedroom. The four bedrooms are on the upper two floors of this tall, narrow 18th-century townhouse and continue the gentle Japanese theme. Carlo worked in Japan for eight years – also Algeria, Egypt, Holland – and his love of the Far East is evident throughout. With views over the garden or the lovely Venetian rooftops, the rooms exude a light, airy and ordered calm with their polished dark wood floors, white walls, Japanese prints and simple oriental furnishings. Shower rooms are small but neat and spotless. Breakfast on the terrace in summer or in the tea room in winter. A charming and warm host, full of stories and happy to chat, Carlo will recommend good local restaurants – especially those specialising in fish. Retreat here after a busy day exploring this magical city and sip a cup of jasmine tea on the shady terrace.

Price	€70–€150.
Rooms	4 doubles.
Meals	Restaurants next door.
Closed	Never.
Directions	From station, water bus line 1. Get off at stop Cà Rezzonico & walk to end of Calle Lunga San Barnaba.

Carlo Errani
Calle Lunga San Barnaba 2727A,
Dorsoduro, 30123 Venice
Tel   +39 0417 241042
Email   info@bedandbreakfast-fujiyama.it
Web   www.bedandbreakfast-fujiyama.it

Terrazza Veronese

You're in a creative corner of 'La Serenissima' — the City otherwise known as Venice. In fact, you would be forgiven for missing the little red door altogether, hemmed in as it is between one art gallery (parading a mouthwatering collection of Venetian treasures) and another. Inside, at the top of the staircase, awaits a delightful top-floor flat. In the little red sitting room are glistening crystal chandeliers, their reflections bouncing off pretty mirrors; in the bedroom, ornate French armoires and matching side tables; in the bathroom, pretty blue and white tiling from top to toe. Striking orange walls express the colours of the Mediterranean in the kitchen, and then it's out onto a narrow terrace where window boxes perch on sills, spilling red geraniums in summer — a sunny spot for a morning coffee. It's very central here, yet quiet; the street leads to a vaporetto stop so there's no through traffic, and the Rialto is five minutes away. Sara has compiled a bumper pack of information: essential reading for the first time visitor and Venice buff alike. *Minimum stay three nights. Cot available.*

Price	€150.
Rooms	1 apartment for 2-4.
Meals	Restaurants nearby.
Closed	Never.
Directions	Vaporetto 82 to S. Samuele; up Calle delle Carozze (Palazzo Grassi on left) into Salizzada San Samuele; house between Profumo Santa Maria Novella & Venice Design Art Gallery, on right.

Sara Tidy
3147 Salizzada San Samuele,
San Marco, 30124 Venice

Tel   +44 (0)1484 435974
Email   sara.tidy@btinternet.com
Web   www.terrazzaveronese.com

Bloom & Settimo Cielo Guest House

In the heart of Venice, yet not overwhelmed by tourists, is a perfectly restored house and boutique hotel. You check in round the corner, then delightful reception escorts you to your room. No lift, so be prepared to carry bags to the second (Settimo Cielo) and third (Bloom) floors; on the fourth is the sitting room – books, guide books, your own prosecco in the fridge. From here, step out onto the roof top terrace, a privileged spot with panoramic views, magically lit at night. Back down to the six bedrooms – what fun the owners had in their creation! Spacious and filled with light, named after colours not numbers, they are a beguiling mix of funky and grand. Bows in navy, lilac, cerise attach themselves to doors behind which a heady mix of Venetian baroque and modern minimalism lies; romantic too, though Cream takes the biscuit. Expect raw silk and floating organza, button-back leather and pale painted beams, gilt mirrors and glass-fronted fridges, fine antiques and bathrooms small but exquisite. Buffet breakfasts are elegant and the Chiesa San Vidal is three minutes away – a peerless setting for Vivaldi.

Price	€90–€220.
Rooms	6: 4 doubles, 2 triples.
Meals	Restaurants nearby.
Closed	Never.
Directions	Vaporetto 1 to Sant'Angelo. Walk until tall redbrick building, then 1st turning on left of building (Ramo Narisi); on until small bridge then left. Along Calle del Pestrin until courtyard on right (Campiello Nuovo); hotel just in front.

Alessandra Vazzoler & Paolo Battistetti
Campiello Santo Stefano,
San Marco 3470, 30124 Venice
Mobile   +39 340 1498872
Email   info@bloom-venice.com

Locanda al Leon

Such friendly people and such a perfect spot: three minutes walk from everything that matters (like the Basilica end of St Mark's Square, the airport bus and the vaporetto stops). This small, unpretentious, family-run hotel, its characterful old entrance down a tiny alley, is an excellent choice if you're visiting Venice on a tightish budget but want to be at the centre of it all. It's been modestly modernised. Clean, carpeted bedrooms (the biggest on the corner of the building, looking onto the Campo San Filippo e Giacomo and the Calle degli Albanesi) have Venetian-style bedheads with scrolled edges and floral motifs; there are matching striped counterpanes and curtains, modern Murano chandeliers and neat shower rooms. The new flat, a five minute walk from the hotel, is ideal for families. Breakfast is taken at a handful of tables on the big, first-floor landing (no lift) buffet-style: breads and croissants, yogurts and fruit juice – what you'd expect for the price. And there's no shortage of advice – one or two members of the delightful dall'Agnola family are always around. *Minimum stay two nights at weekends.*

Price	€80–€210. Singles €60–€130. Triple €100–€250. Apt €100–€300. All prices per night.
Rooms	11 + 1: 8 doubles, 2 singles, 1 triple. Apartment for 4.
Meals	Restaurants nearby.
Closed	Rarely.
Directions	Water bus line 1 or 82 to San Zaccaria. Follow Calle degli Albanesi until last door on left; signed.

	Marcella & Giuliano dall'Agnola Campo Santi Filippo e Giacomo 4270, Castello, 30122 Venice
Tel	+39 0412 770393
Email	leon@hotelalleon.com
Web	www.hotelalleon.com

Giudecca Mare Riva

On the site of an old gondola boathouse, on the southern side of the island of Giudecca, is a luxurious new waterfront development with spectacular views. Life's quieter this side of the lagoon, but there are still plenty of trattorias, shops and bars, the vista of islands is a dream and in eight minutes you can be stepping out of the vaporetto and onto the square of San Marco. If you have your own boat, you'll be glad of the private jetty. Inside: huge sheets of glass pulling in water and sky, polished marble sweeping from living room-kitchen to bathroom, Italian furniture, clean lines, white walls and pictures in gold frames. White and duck-egg blue is the kitchen, contemporary and cool. In the bedroom, the floor is of pale ash, the wardrobe of fitted glass and the bed is vast. Almost every modern luxury you can think of is here: air conditioning, underfloor heating, American style fridge freezer, DVD and CD players, flat-screen TV. Outside, a courtyard from which a metal stair spirals its way up to a roof terrace tangled in jasmine with two perfect loungers… the sunsets are fabulous. *Minimum stay three nights. Two vaporetto stops from Piazza San Marco.*

Price	£1,330 per week.
Rooms	Apartment for 2-3.
Meals	Restaurants within walking distance.
Closed	Never.
Directions	Private water taxi from Marco Polo airport or vaporetto from Piazzale Roma to Zitelle; walk length of Calle Michelangelo to lagoon end.

Nick & Wendy Parker
D3 Giudecca Mare Riva,
Calle Michelangelo, 30133 Venice

Tel	+44 (0)2380 456710
Email	info@venicefortwo.com
Web	www.venicefortwo.com

Relais Ca' Maffio

The delightful young Levi Morenos welcome you to their huge villa in the Sile nature reserve; they live at one end, their parents at the other and the guests in between. They're a family with a history: in 1939 they bought Jesurum, legendary producers of Venetian lace; some historic examples are on display here. The guest bedrooms are on the first floor, classically elegant, harmoniously colour-themed, immaculately furnished. Imagine the best of new (gleaming wooden floors, luxurious fabrics) and a touch of the old (an antique bibelot, a gilt-framed botanical print) and bathrooms that are top of the range. The villa's round-arched façade is striking, its vast open 'veranda' furnished with sofas, tables and an open stone fireplace; breakfast out here in summer and let Nicolò help you plan your day. The house is perfectly placed for birdwatching rambles and bike rides along the river Sile, as well as for cultural forays into Treviso and Venice (drive to Quarto d'Altino, then take the train). Or ask Nicolò to ferry you on his little boat down the river – it flows by at the end of the garden.

Price	€135–€165. Suite €190–€230.
Rooms	4: 3 doubles, 1 suite for 2-4.
Meals	Restaurant 2km; choice 8km.
Closed	Occasionally.
Directions	A4 Milano-Trieste, exit Quarto d'Altino. Follow signs for centre, left at r'bout for Roncade, right after bridge onto Via Principe; after 2km, right.

Nicolò Levi Morenos
Via Principe 70,
31056 Roncade
Tel   +39 0422 780774
Email   info@camaffio.com
Web   www.camaffio.com

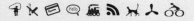

Castello di Roncade Agriturismo

An imposing entrance, a garden full of statues and roses and a 16th-century villa do not mean impossible prices. A stately double room furnished with antiques is available in the house itself and there are five simply furnished apartments in the corner towers, some ideal for families. All have big wardrobes and dark wooden floors, heating for winter, air con for summer, and thick walls to keep you cool. The newly refurbished garden apartment is bright and airy, a perfect little place for two with its own terrace. Surrounding the castle and village are the estate vineyards which produce some excellent wines; try the Villa Giustinian Rosso della Casa or the Pinot Grigio and you'll be tempted to take a case home; at the very least make sure you join a tasting session. The owners and their son Claudio are helpful hosts and proud of their wines. No dinner but you're welcome to throw a rug on the lawn for a picnic for an evening meal. Don't take the car to Venice but catch instead the bus to Treviso – an ancient place of cloisters and canals, frescoes and churches – then the train.

Price	€85–€110. Apartments €70–€100.
Rooms	1 + 5: 1 double. 5 apts: 2 for 2, 3 for 4.
Meals	Occasional dinner, €50. Restaurants 500m.
Closed	Rarely.
Directions	Exit A27 Venice-Belluno at Treviso sud, follow Roncade. You can't miss the castle's imposing entrance and magnificent gardens.

Vincenzo Ciani Bassetti
Via Roma 141,
30156 Roncade

Tel	+39 0422 708736
Email	vcianib@tin.it
Web	www.castellodironcade.com

Maso di Villa Relais di Campagna

Under an hour from Venice, high on a hill, Maso di Villa is a stylish step up from the usual agriturismo set-up. Chiara Lucchetta, the owner, has renovated this glorious old farmhouse with breathtaking attention to detail. Everything, from the beautifully restored Veneto furniture and the stripped wooden beams to the light switches salvaged from antique shops in the original style has been put in place to produce a quiet symphony of rural Italy. Huge and sprawling on the outside, the house couldn't be cosier or more inviting within. The bedrooms are comfortable and painted in warm colours, some with stunning ornate headboards designed by Chiara's father, and carved locally. Knotted old wooden pillars shore up the ceiling in the sitting room, which is scattered with armchairs and bathed in sunlight. And, from every window, astonishing views: on one side, the Dolomites, on the other, the unbroken expanse of vineyards and woodland that is the Prosecco wine region. Enjoy abundant breakfast on the terrace, wander in the gardens: unwind in this magical place.

Price	€130-€165. Singles €110.
Rooms	6: 5 doubles, 1 twin.
Meals	Trattoria 300m (closed Mondays & Tuesdays).
Closed	Rarely.
Directions	A4 Venice-Trieste; dual c'way 10km; A27 for Belluno; past Treviso Sud; exit Treviso Nord; right for Treviso Conegliano, SS13 Pontebbana; 18km; in Susegana left at lights for Collalto, 5km; on left, entrance in Via Morgante II, green gate.

Chiara Lucchetta
Via Col di Guarda 15, Loc. Collalto,
31058 Susegana
Tel +39 0438 841414
Email info@masodivilla.it
Web www.masodivilla.it

Giardino di Mezzavilla

In a town with a history – it was the site of the Italian victory over the Austro-Hungarian forces: the end of the First World War – is a house of bohemian beauty owned by the nicest people. The pretty 17th-century courtyard is still intact, as are the haylofts, the wine cellar and the greenhouse, all enveloped by acres of garden, theirs and their neighbours'. And a big old tree that fell in last year's storm has been kept, roots and all. The character continues inside, up to two big guest rooms with sober planked floors, colourwashed walls, old-fashioned radiators and the odd antique; no safes or gadgets, just good books, natural soaps, extremely comfortable beds. Janine (who speaks five languages) will lend you maps for free council bicycles – yes, really; her breakfasts, organic feasts of homemade everything, set you up beautifully. Or you could jump in the car and visit the Dolomites or the sea. Return to Aga-cooked dinners that are pure pleasure – fruit and veg from the garden, local meats, Angelo's well-chosen wines. All this and fresh mountain air at night… you'll sleep like a baby.

Price	€70–€110.
Rooms	3: 1 single, 1 family room for 2, 1 family suite for 4.
Meals	Dinner with wine, €20. Restaurant 300m.
Closed	Never.
Directions	S. Giacomo di Veglia by church after Albergo da Carlo, 1st left at bread shop onto Via Mezzavilla; on right.

Janine Raedts & Angelo Vettorello
Via Mezzavilla 26,
31029 Vittorio Veneto

Tel	+39 0438 912585
Email	info@giardinomezzavilla.com
Web	www.giardinomezzavilla.com

Hotel Villa Luppis

Still the grand country mansion it became in the early 1800s, when Napoleon secularised the monastery that had been here for centuries; the present owner's ancestors later made it a base for diplomatic activities. Geographically, it feels in limbo, too – on the border between Veneto and Friuli and surrounded by acres of flat farmland. The hotel, all creamy peeling stucco and terracotta roof tiles, is reached via an imposing gateway. Twelve acres of grounds include lawns and venerable trees, gravel paths and a fountain. Inside, the various formal reception and dining areas are graced with antiques and presided over by dignified staff. Bedrooms are elegantly old-fashioned, with comfortable beds and excellent bathrooms. You can go for walks along the river bank but really this place works best as a centre for day excursions. There's a daily shuttle into Venice and the staff will organise trips to other towns and cities, as well as to the Venetian and Palladian villas along the river Brenta. Cookery courses are on offer – and wine tastings in what was once the monks' ice-cellar.

Price	€220–€265. Singles €115–€125. Suites €280–€320.
Rooms	39: 27 doubles, 2 singles, 10 suites.
Meals	Dinner from €55. Wine from €15.
Closed	Never.
Directions	From Oderzo towards Pordenone. Right at Mansue, signed. From A4, exit Cessalto (12km) for Motta di Livenza & Meduna di Livenza. Hotel before village of Rivarotta.

Giorgio Ricci Luppis
Via San Martino 34,
33080 Pasiano di Pordenone

Tel	+39 0434 626969
Email	hotel@villaluppis.it
Web	www.villaluppis.it

Tenuta Regina Agriturismo

Views stretch to Croatia on a clear day. Great for a sociable family holiday: an hour to Treviso, Trieste (beloved of James Joyce) and Udine, a 12m x 6m pool with snazzy loungers and a big garden with volleyball. Table tennis, bikes and a children's playground too; the owners, who have children themselves, are proud of their restoration. Now grandfather's farmhouse and grain store are manicured outside and in, and there's a distinct small-resort feel, but the lovely old ceiling rafters remain. The most homely apartment is the largest, on the western end of the farmhouse: two storeys of wooden floors and gleaming doors, pristine white kitchen, four immaculately dressed beds, a sprinkling of family pieces. Perhaps even a bunch of fresh roses – Giorgio's passion. The other apartments, some in front of the pool, some just over the road, feel more functional. Comfortable and open-plan, two on the ground floor, they come with spotless showers, dishwashers and safes, and top-quality linen. A relaxed and untouristy spot for families who love to make new friends. *Flexible rental periods.*

Price	€80-€120. Apts €400-€1,360 per week.
Rooms	3 + 4: 3 suites.
	4 apts: 3 for 2-4, 1 for 4-5.
Meals	Breakfast €7 for self-caterers.
	Restaurants 1.5km.
Closed	Rarely.
Directions	A4 Venezia-Trieste, exit Latisana; signs for Trieste. At Palazzolo, right at 1st lights for Piancada; continue for 7km.

Alessandra Pasti
Casali Tenuta Regina 8,
33056 Palazzolo dello Stella

Tel   +39 0431 587971
Email   tenutaregina@adriabella.com
Web   www.adriabella.com

Agriturismo La Faula

An exuberant miscellany of dogs, donkeys and peacocks on a modern, working farm where rural laissez-faire and modern commerce happily mingle. La Faula has been in Luca's family for years; he and Paul, young and dynamic, abandoned the city to find themselves working harder than ever. Yet they put as much thought and energy into their guests as into the wine business and farm. The house stands in gentle countryside at the base of the Julian Alps – a big, comfortable home, and each bedroom delightful. Furniture is old, bathrooms new. There is a bistro-style restaurant where wonderful home-reared produce is served (free-range veal, beef, chicken, lamb, just-picked vegetables and fruits); on summer nights there may be a barbecue. An enormous old pergola provides dappled shade during the day; sit and dream awhile with a glass of estate wine or acquavita. Or wander round the vineyard and *cantina*, watch the wine-making in progress, practice your skills with a golf club on the residents' driving range, cool off in the river, visit the beaches of the Adriatic. Perfect for families. *Minimum stay two nights.*

Price	€80. Apartments €455 per week.
Rooms	9 + 4: 9 twins/doubles.
	4 studio apartments for 2-4.
Meals	Lunch/dinner €18. Wine €10.
	Restaurant 500m.
Closed	16 September-14 March.
Directions	A23 exit Udine Nord dir. Tarvisio &
	Tricesimo. From SS13 Pontebbana dir.
	Povoletto-Cividale. At r'bout, right dir.
	Povoletto. At Ravosa, pass Trattoria Al
	Sole on left; right after 20m. Signed.

Paul Mackay & Luca Colautti
Via Faula 5, Ravosa di Povoletto,
33040 Udine

Mobile   +39 334 3996734
Web   www.faula.com

Ethical Collection: Environment;
Community; Food. See page 400 for details

Casa del Grivò Agriturismo

This is the house that Toni built – or, rather, lovingly revived from ruin. The smallholding sits in a hamlet on the edge of a plain; behind, wonderful, high-wooded hills extend to the Slovenian border, sometimes crossed to gather wild berries. Your lovely hosts have three young children. Simplicity, rusticity and a 'green' approach are the keynotes here; so you'll sample traditional wool-and-vegetable-fibre-filled mattresses. Beds are comfy and blanketed, some with wonderful quilts. Your children will adore all the open spaces, the animals and the little pool that's been created by diverting a stream. Adults can relax with a book on a bedroom balcony, or in a distant corner of the garden. Maps are laid out at breakfast, and there are heaps of books on the region; the walking is wonderful, there's a castle to visit and a river to picnic by. Paola cooks fine dinners using old recipes and their own organic produce. There's a lovely open fire for cooking, and you dine by candlelight, sometimes to the gentle accompaniment of country songs: Paola was once a singer. *Minimum stay two nights; five in high season.*

Price	€60. Half-board €50 p.p.
Rooms	4: 1 double, 2 family rooms sharing 2 bathrooms; 1 family room with separate bathroom.
Meals	Lunch in summer only. Picnic by arrangement. Dinner with wine, from €25.
Closed	Mid-December to April.
Directions	From Faédis, Via dei Castelli for Canébola. After 1.5km right, over bridge; 2nd house on left.

Toni & Paola Costalunga
Borgo Canal del Ferro 19,
33040 Faédis

Tel	+39 0432 728638
Email	casadelgrivo@libero.it
Web	www.grivo.has.it

Emilia-Romagna

Photo: istock.com

Antica Corte Pallavicina Relais

As you turn down the estate's driveway, ancient breeds of cattle and horse pause their grazing, and geese and hens shuffle out of your way. You have arrived at the home of one of Italy's most cherished salami producers, the Spigarolis, who opened their relais with the intention of winning tourists over to the gastronomy of the region. Elegant guest rooms nod to the past in their traditional guise, but have an exquisitely modern edge thanks to their round zinc basins, medusa-like lamps whose bulbs cascade to the floor, and delicious poplar-wood decked showers. Days can be spent in the kitchen with inspiring Massimo learning how to chop and stir, or out exploring the area on one of the estate's bikes. But you cannot leave without visiting the castle's famed cellars, where thousands of culatelli di Zibello and Parmigiano Reggiano cheeses are left to age. Savour both delights at either of the family's two restaurants here. Then finish your day with an aromatic bath in your suite's tub, right next to the glowing fire. Look forward to fresh brioches at breakfast beneath frescoed ceilings.

Price	€140–€250.
Rooms	6: 4 doubles, 2 suites.
Meals	Dinner €50–€75.
Closed	Rarely.
Directions	From A1, exit Fidenza. Follow signs to Busseta, then Polesine Parmense.

Massimo Spigaroli
Strada del Palazzo Due Torri 3,
43010 Polesine Parmense
Tel   +39 0524 936539
Email relais@acpallavicina.com
Web   www.acpallavicina.com/relais

Antica Torre Agriturismo

Two golden labradors ambling across the pristine gravel paths in the lee of the 14th-century tower and enormous colonnaded barn, covered in vines, exude a peaceful contentment – which belies the energy that the family pour into this enterprise. From sweeping flagstones at dawn to the final flourish of a delicious bottle at dinner, this family is devoted to agriturismo. Don't expect to stumble across farm machinery or be set upon by winsome lambs: Antica Torre, with its many buildings, has the air of a model farm. The big rooms in the *casa rustica*, with their ancient polished brick and tile floors, have strange and wondrous rustic furniture, and curly metal bedheads inject a light-hearted air. Otherwise, expect simple bathrooms, immaculate housekeeping and an honest rurality. With its huge fireplace and long tables covered in red gingham, the barn, where generous breakfasts are served, has a distinctly alpine air. In the evening, deep in the ancient Cistercian cellar, to the strains of plain chant and Puccini, feast with locals and guests on Vanda's astonishingly good cooking. *Wine-tasting.*

Price	€110. Half-board €75 p.p.
Rooms	8 twins/doubles.
Meals	Dinner €20. Wine €5–€12.
Closed	December–February.
Directions	From Salsomaggiore centre, SP27 for Cangelasio & Piacenza. Fork left (signed Cangelasio); 1.5km; left for Antica Torre. Driveway left after 1.5km.

	Francesco Pavesi
	Case Bussandri 197, Loc. Cangelasio,
	43039 Salsomaggiore Terme
Tel	+39 0524 575425
Email	info@anticatorre.it
Web	www.anticatorre.it

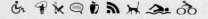

Villa Bellaria

Off the track, but not isolated, tucked under a softly green hillside, this cream-painted *casa di collina*, with its wide hammock'd veranda and well-established garden, has been a retreat from summer heat since 1900. Having moved here 15 years ago, Marina, warm and kind, herself a keen traveller, decided to throw open its doors and share her enthusiasm for this lovely, little-known area with its medieval villages, castles and thermal cures. On the stairs, etchings of The East India Company recall the Raj. A much-loved, ornately carved mirror, made by her cabinet maker father at his renowned atelier in Milan, graces a wall. Immaculate bedrooms are a happy mix of wrought-iron bedsteads, delicately embroidered blinds, tile floors and contemporary art. After breakfast alfresco – and delectable homemade tart – head off through leafy lanes to the walled hill town Castel Arquato, or Piacenza and Parma. After a hard day exploring or being sporty, contemplate the area's gastronomic delights: nothing sums up Emilia-Romagna so well as its food. This is a comfortable, civilised bolthole – and great value.

Price	€60-€70. Singles €40-€50.
Rooms	4 doubles.
Meals	Restaurant 300m.
Closed	Rarely.
Directions	At lights after Alseno on to Vernasca. On for 5km, right into small street for Cortina; house 2km with green gate on left.

	Marina Cazzaniga Calderoni
	Via dei Gasperini,
	29010 Cortina di Alseno
Tel	+39 0523 947537
Email	info@villabellariabb.it
Web	www.villabellariabb.it

B&B Valferrara

On an ancient road between Canossa and Carpineti, this 17th-century travellers' lodge sits in the silent hamlet of Valferrara. Weary merchants would rest their heads in peace – and absorb the calm and protection of the surrounding forested hills and distant castle of Carpineti. Ruined when Giuliano and Cosetta discovered it in 1994, the *casa di scale* ('tiered house'), complete with flat-roofed Emilian tower – where a clutch of apartments are almost ready – has been completely and masterfully restored with local materials, and parquet flooring fashioned from recycled beams of oak. Cosetta restores local antique furniture and the house is full of it; crisp cotton envelops large, beautifully framed beds and an eye-catching walnut writing desk stands elegantly near one of her several finely polished wardrobes. Expect a warm welcome and a delicious breakfast – under the cool portico, in the walled garden or in the dining room: a fabulous conversion of the old stables. Fresh parmesan can be sampled locally and smiling Cosetta, also a great cook, provides dinner on request.

Price	€76–€90.
Rooms	3: 1 double; 2 doubles sharing bath.
Meals	Restaurants 1-4km.
Closed	Rarely.
Directions	A1 Bologna-Milano exit Modena Nord. SS via Emilia to Reggio Emilia, exit Scandiano to Viano; to Carpineti, dir. Casina, thro' Cigarello. After 1.5km, right at small Valferrara sign; 100m on left.

Cosetta Mordacci & Giuliano Beghi
Via Valferrara 13, Pantano,
42033 Carpineti

Mobile	+39 340 1561417
Email	info@bb-valferrara.it
Web	www.bb-valferrara.it

B&B a Bologna

Before it became a B&B, nuns lived here – but don't expect cloisters. This is a modern Italian no-frills apartment block with a central lift and a winding stair. The position, not the street, is the thing. What you have here is a simple four-bedroom B&B, its bedrooms off a narrow, white-painted corridor enlivened with the occasional picture. Furniture is plain, beds are floral and there's lots of space. Two rooms share a big bathroom down the hall, with a washing machine – ideal for a family. The feeling is cosy, homely, unfake, unforced; there are books and Slow Food magazines for guests' taking. Your hosts, gregarious, generous Signora de Lucca and her husband – who also have an agriturismo outside town – set up a buffet breakfast the night before so guests can help themselves as early or late as they like in the morning. It's all very flexible, you have your own keys so you may come and go as you please. The Piazza Maggiore is a ten-minute walk and a bi-weekly market is a short stroll. A very decent budget-friendly base for those undeterred by old-school décor and silk flowers!

Price	€65–€110. Triple €95–€120.
Rooms	4: 1 double, 1 triple; 2 doubles sharing bath.
Meals	Restaurants nearby.
Closed	Never.
Directions	Right out of train station; 1st left onto Via Amendola; 2nd right onto Via Milazzo; 100m, left onto Via Cairoli. 2nd floor; ring bell.

Signora de Lucca
Via Cairoli 3, 40121 Bologna

Tel	+39 0514 210897
Email	takakina@hotmail.com
Web	www.traveleurope.it/bolognabb

La Piana dei Castagni Agriturismo

Write, paint, read or potter: here, deep in the woods, there's nothing to distract you. This is a secret little Hansel and Gretel house with a vegetable patch, demure shutters and lace-trimmed curtains. It stands isolated among chestnut and cherry trees, reached via a long, wriggling track; below are bucolic meadows, falling to a farm or two, and a further distant descent along the yawning valley. An old stone farmhouse converted and adapted for B&B, La Piana is a modest place to stay. The bedrooms, named after local berries, are a good size and painted in clear pastel colours; tiny pictures hang above beds and little windows set in thick walls look out over the glorious valley. The shower rooms – one of them a restyled chicken shed! – are simply tiled. Valeria lives ten minutes away at La Civetta. She is gentle, kind, spoiling; even the breakfast *torte di noci* are homemade. She will also help organise everything, from trekking to truffle hunting. An ideal spot for those who love the simple pleasures of life: good walks by day, good food by night. *Minimum stay two nights.*

Price	€70-€95. Singles €40. Triples €80-€100.
Rooms	5: 2 doubles, 1 single, 2 triples.
Meals	Dinner €19-€21. Wine €8-€20. Restaurant 3km.
Closed	November-March.
Directions	From Tolè, follow signs for S. Lucia & Castel d'Aiano; signed.

Valeria Vitali
Via Lusignano 11,
40040 Rocca di Roffeno
Tel   +39 0519 12985
Email   info@pianadeicastagni.it
Web   www.pianadeicastagni.it

Ethical Collection: Food.
See page 400 for details

Lodole Country House

Here is an exceedingly well-renovated 17th-century stone cottage with views over breathtaking Apennine countryside; it's a treat to arrive. Flowers brighten window boxes, wooden shutters are hung and varnished just so, terracotta planters march up to the front door, and a paved path curves up to a swimming pool from which you can gasp in wonder at the view. Bedrooms – Sun, Sky, Stars – reflect their names, and are wonderfully romantic; Moon has semicircular end tables and in its bathroom a skylight; Dawn, pale pink, faces east; Sunset, pale orange, faces west. All have low lighting, wooden boards, exposed beams, soothing hues. Well-chosen pieces add interest: polished armoires, antique vanities, free-standing antique washbasins and fine wrought-iron beds, some canopied in soft cotton. The living room has a fireplace, big white sofas, a window to the hills, and a raised area beyond for delicious, lovingly sourced breakfasts served at separate tables by Alice. Numerous local trattoria provide discounted meals to guests and the Molino del Pero golf course lies handily next door.

Price	€90.
Rooms	6: 5 doubles, 1 triple.
Meals	Restaurants nearby.
Closed	Rarely.
Directions	A1 exit Rioveggio; left dir. Monzuno/Loiano. To Monzuno; continue to Loiano. After 2km, Borgo Lodole on left. Left; on for 100m to 'Lodole B&B.'

Alice Frontini
Loc. Lodole 325, 40036 Monzuno

Tel	+39 0516 771189
Email	a.zucchi@admcom.net
Web	www.lodole.com

Relais Varnello

Just above the pretty town of Brisighella, but you'll need the car — it's quite a hike! In young gardens, the brick buildings stand sparklingly clean and tickety-boo. Nicely-furnished rooms have views across the valley or garden; the suites are in a separate building, with a sauna. The farm produces Sangiovese DOC wine and olive oil, which you can buy along with Faenza pottery showing the family crest. Giovanni has been producing oil and wine all his life and you won't leave here without a bottle or two — it's delicious. If you speak a little Italian, pick his brains, he has a vast knowledge of Italian grapes (over 1,000 varieties) and will happily tell you about some of the best wines available. Spend your days lounging by the pool: there are wide views over the Padana and to the Adriatic, and there's a private wild park — Giovanni's pride and joy — just a stroll away: a lovely place for a picnic and a book. Higher up the hill is the Parco Carné, with Club Alpino Italiano (CAI) walking trails. *Minimum stay two nights.*

Price	€130. Suites €180.
Rooms	6: 4 twins/doubles, 2 suites.
Meals	Dinner from €20. Restaurant 300m.
Closed	January-15 March.
Directions	From Brisighella on SP23 Montecino & Limisano road, signed to Riolo Terme. After 3km, left after Ristorante Manicômi, signed to Rontana. 1st building on left.

	Giovanni Liverzani
	Via Rontana 34, 48013 Brisighella
Tel	+39 0546 85493
Email	info@varnello.it
Web	www.varnello.it

Azienda Vitivinicola e Agrituristica Trerè

Braided vines stretch as far as the eye can see... in the middle of this flat green patchwork is a compact grouping of rosy buildings and a clump of tall trees to one side. The entertainingly angular farmhouse is surrounded by barns and stables – now modern apartments and a conference room. This is very much a wine-producing estate – around the house are certificates and awards, a shop and a little rose-and-gold wine museum – but in spite of all this, there's a family feel; toys are scattered around and the atmosphere is easy. The bedrooms in the house have a light and pretty elegance, all beamed ceilings, pastel walls, lovely old family furniture and memorable touches – the deep lace trim of a white sheet folded over a jade bedcover, a wall full of books. The apartments are attractive but more functional in feel. Each has French windows opening onto a private patio and a mezzanine with an extra bed tucked under a skylight – fun for kids. The restaurant is open on weekend evenings, and there are other places to eat nearby.

Price	€68-€78. Singles €52. Suite €135-€150. Apts €80-€92 for 2; €108-€190 for 4-6.
Rooms	7 + 4: 4 doubles, 1 twin, 1 suite for 4-6, 1 triple. 4 apts for 2-6 (with kitchenette).
Meals	Breakfast €6.50. Dinner €23 (except Jan/Feb & Mon-Thurs). Wine €7-€22. Restaurants 2km.
Closed	Rarely.
Directions	From Faenza via Emilia SS9 for Imola/Bologna; 3km left after Subaru garage on Via Casale; signed.

Morena Trerè & Massimiliano Fabbri
Via Casale 19, 48018 Faenza

Tel	+39 0546 47034
Email	trere@trere.com
Web	www.trere.com

Quattro Passeri

If the mammoth suit of armour that greets guests at the entrance were the lord of the house, then Stefano would be his loyal squire: he keeps it in tip-top shape. Stone archways, leaded windows, a coat of arms over the fireplace continue the neo-medieval theme, but it's the details you'll appreciate: sweetly painted flowers on porcelain handles, embroidered pillows on quilted beds. Birdsong is everywhere and the rooms are named Skylark, Dove, Swallow; the self-catering apartments have a similarly pretty décor and basic kitchenettes. Buffet breakfast is taken at round café tables in the charming stone-walled kitchen. In cooler months, get cosy by the antique Austrian oven; when the season's right, dive into a bowl of gorgeous cherries (Stefano will have plucked them that morning). You are perched high in the undulating countryside, yet the coast is a quick drive down the hill, and if that seems just too far away, there are a beautifully maintained pool and sauna here. Sporty and ambitious spirits can go biking and trekking; Ravenna is around the corner. *Min. stay six nights first two weeks in August.*

Price	€110-€150. Suite €150-€200. Triple €130-€160. Apartments €160-€200.
Rooms	5 + 3: 3 twins/doubles, 1 suite for 2-4, 1 triple. 3 apts for 2-4.
Meals	Restaurant 1.6km.
Closed	December-February.
Directions	From Milan/Bologna A14 exit Cesena Nord; E45 dir. Rome for 3.5km dir. Cesena centre. Thro' town centre to main road 9 Emilia. Fork right for Longiano and Roncofreddo. Signs for Roncofreddo/Santa Paola.

Stefano & Sandra Samoré
Santa Paola di Roncofreddo,
47020 Forli-Cesena

Tel	+39 0541 949522
Email	info@4passeri.com
Web	4passeri.com

Liguria

Photo: istock.com

Villa Elisa

The climate is kind: visit at any time of the year. The hotel was created in the 20s when Bordighera, a pretty town with sloping tree-lined roads and pastel houses, became a winter retreat. Rita's father-in-law, who ran it for years, was a painter and had artists to stay – bedroom walls are still hung with the works they left him. Some still come, following in the steps of Monet. Your hosts are the nicest you could wish to meet. Rita and husband Maurizio take groups off into the Maritime Alps in their minibus and guide them back on three-hour walks, Rita likes to spoil – she has even provided a playroom for children, and special activities for summer. Bedrooms have parquet floors and are dressed in blue; bathrooms are white-tiled with floral friezes and heated towel rails; larger rooms have terraces with views to the hills. There's a courtyard garden scented with bougainvillea, oranges and lemons, and a wonderful pool area with plenty of quiet corners. The pebbled beach is a ten-minute dash down the hill and the restaurant is charming; fresh fish is on the menu and the wine list is long.

Price	€120-€180. Singles €80-€110. Suite €200-€250. Apt €220-€300.
Rooms	34 + 1: 30 doubles, 3 singles, 1 suite. Apartment for 4.
Meals	Lunch/dinner from €40. Wine €16-€50. Half or full-board option for week-long stays.
Closed	5 November-22 December.
Directions	Via Romana parallel to main road through town (Via Aurelia), reachable by any x-road that links the two. Villa at western end of Via Romana.

Rita Oggero
Via Romana 70, 18012 Bordighera
Tel   +39 0184 261313
Email info@villaelisa.com
Web   www.villaelisa.com

B&B

Casa Villatalla Guest House

Revel in the peace — and the views: they sweep across the wooded valley to the blue-grey mountains beyond. Roger (British) and Marina (Italian-Swiss) moved not long ago to Liguria and had the delightful Casa Villatalla built in traditional style, ochre-stuccoed and green-shuttered. They are wonderfully welcoming hosts — and the cheerful, eclectic décor of the house reflects their warm personalities and love of travel. Through the brick archway, a Swiss armoire presides over a dining room furnished with rustic wooden tables on which seasonal breakfasts and dinners (do book) are served. Upstairs, charming modern bedrooms, some lead to balconies and those views. All are different — in Quercia, a bedstead woven from banana tree fronds, in Corbezzolo, rose tones and a flowery patchwork quilt. Marina, a keen horticulturist, nurtures her garden full of roses, and there's a swimming pool terrace which is crowned by a fine oak tree, beautifully illuminated at night. Together they organise occasional painting and yoga courses: another reason to stay. *Min. stay two nights July & August.*

Price	€80-€90.
Rooms	5: 1 double, 4 twins/doubles.
Meals	Dinner with wine, from €25.
Closed	Never.
Directions	Follow Val Nervia road from coast. 1km after Dolceacqua, left to Rocchetta Nervina. After 3km, left to La Colla. Villatalla on right, after 2km.

Roger & Marina Hollinshead
Loc. Villatalla,
18035 Dolceacqua

Tel   +39 0184 206379
Email   info@villatalla.com
Web   www.villatalla.com

Casa Cambi

You can hardly believe that such a village has survived unspoilt into the 21st century. It's a fairytale tangle of winding cobbled streets and medieval stone houses on a green and rocky hilltop. All around are dramatic mountains and stupendous views. A square, uncompromising castle dominates the hill; right below is Anna's entrancing house. A tiny front door (the house is 700 years old, after all) takes you straight into a delightful, vaulted room – a soothing mix of creams and whites, ochres and umbers. Pale walls contrast with a gleaming wooden floor and old polished furniture, its subtle, restrained country charm sets the tone for the rest. All the rooms are a delight, all full of unexpected touches – jugs of fresh wild flowers, hessian curtains on wrought-iron poles, a rack of old kitchen implements stark against a white wall... vivacious Anna adores her house and has lavished huge care on it. She's bubbly and friendly and loves cooking; her kitchen is a delight. Breakfast out in the pretty terraced garden among olive and fig trees, revel in those mountain views.

Price	€90–€110.
Rooms	4: 2 doubles, 1 twin, 1 family room.
Meals	Dinner with wine, €25–€30.
Closed	5 October–15 May.
	Out of season fax +39 010 812613.
Directions	A10 exit Albenga. S582 Garessio for Castelvecchio di Rocca Barbena, 12km. Free car park outside pedestrianised Borgo, 5-minute walk.

Anna Bozano
Via Roma 42,
17034 Castelvecchio di Rocca Barbena

Tel	+39 0182 78009
Email	casacambi@casacambi.it
Web	www.casacambi.it

Palazzo Fieschi

The name of this elegant townhouse near Genoa commemorates former owners, the distinguished Fieschi family, once a power in the land. Now it belongs to Simonetta and Aldo Caprile, who left the world of commerce for a life of hotel-keeping. They have carefully renovated the old palazzo, adding modern comforts to its *cinquecento* grandeur. The oldest working hotel in Liguria, it overlooks a square and is a short walk to the centre; there's also a shuttle service for guests. The surrounding countryside is steep and wooded, away from the autostradas and with walking nearby. Bedrooms are white-walled and spotless, many with lovely antiques and fabulous carved or painted bedheads. Rooms vary but those on the mezzanine floor in the oldest section of the house have the most character: beautiful tiles, grand doorways, low ceilings. One has access to the tower from where you can peep out over the square. The dining room, with its chandeliers and sweeping red drapes, is popular for weddings. The Capriles are courteous hosts, and you may encounter the odd musical evening in winter.

Price	€90–€220. Singles €70–€110. Family room €140–€280. Triples €120–€250.
Rooms	24: 3 doubles, 10 twins/doubles, 8 singles. 1 family room, 2 triples.
Meals	Dinner €26–€50. Wine list from €10.
Closed	20 December–March.
Directions	From A7 exit to Busalla. In Busalla for Casella; 3.5km, left for Savignone. Hotel in village centre.

Ethical Collection: Food.
See page 400 for details

Aldo, Simonetta & Sara Caprile
Piazza della Chiesa 14,
16010 Savignone
Tel   +39 0109 360063
Email   info@palazzofieschi.com
Web   www.palazzofieschi.com

Sognando Villa Edera

At the top of the winding road from Rapallo is a family agriturismo noted for its spectacular views: they swoop from your deckchair down to the coast. These 1.5 hectares of olive groves and orchards were planted by Sara's grandfather and you can enjoy the fruits at breakfast, along with the most delectable tarts and jams. Rosanna works her magic in the kitchen, daughter Sara makes superb cappuccino, there are well-behaved dogs, cats, a donkey and a pony, and Rosanna's tiered gardens are delightful. Below the gardens, five simple, sunny and spotless guest rooms have been created from the farmworkers' houses, each with its own piece of garden or terrace. You may choose to set off for the day – for the beaches of Portofino, or the peaceful palmed promenade, two harbours and little castle of Rapallo – but you can happily spend all day here too, high up among the birdsong and the roses, the deckchairs and the terraces, the pool and the heavenly views. The beach is three kilometres away, the restaurants are down the hill, the Cinque Terre is 40 minutes by car and the buses run three times a day. *Minimum stay three nights.*

Price	€90-€150. Family room €120-€200.
Rooms	5: 4 twins/doubles, 1 family room for 3-4.
Meals	Restaurants 10-minute walk.
Closed	Rarely.
Directions	A12 Genova-Livorno exit Rapallo. Round central reservation, right onto Via Savagna for 1.5km; into Via Sotto la Croce. Right into Salita S. Giovanni, gate on left.

Sara Piaggio
Salita San Giovanni 3,
16035 Rapallo

Tel +39 0185 260686
Email info@sognandovillaedera.com
Web www.sognandovillaedera.com

Villa Gnocchi Agriturismo

Once you've negotiated the steep, windy and poorly maintained access drive, you are rewarded with fantastic views over Santa Margherita. Roberto, a farmer, trained at Pisa University and inherited the house from his grandfather in a dilapidated state; he's made a few changes! He loves it here, deep in the country but within sight of the sea... so sip a glass of wine from the terrace and gaze down the coast. The views are stunning. Each bedroom is different: white, ochre or saffron; all are simply furnished and decorated with dried flowers. Bright bedcovers dress grandfather's beds, muslin curtains flutter at windows, old framed prints hang on the walls and many shower rooms are tiny. Apart from the hoot of the train and the faint hum of the traffic below, the only sound to break the peace is birdsong. Santa Margherita – a 15-minute walk downhill, a bumpy bus or taxi up – is a charming little town, with beach, fishing boats, shops, bars and restaurants. Paths lead to most of the villages and buses from the gate. *Strict check-in/out times (before 13.00 or between 16.30-19.45).*

Price	€105.
Rooms	9: 5 doubles, 2 twins, 2 family rooms.
Meals	Restaurant 500m.
Closed	Mid-October to Easter.
Directions	From Santa Margherita for S. Lorenzo, 4km. Past big sign 'Genova & S. Lorenzo' on left, Rapallo & A12 on right, 50m ahead, left down narrow road. At red & white barrier ring bell.

Roberto Gnocchi
Via Romana 53,
San Lorenzo della Costa,
16038 Santa Margherita Ligure

Tel	+39 0185 283431
Email	roberto.gnocchi@tin.it
Web	www.villagnocchi.it

Hotel Villa Edera

The villa is perched above the beautiful town of Moneglia and is a quintessential, beautifully run, family owned hotel. Orietta, the elder daughter, is manageress – businesslike yet approachable. She is a mine of information about Ligurian art and history, sings in the local choir and loves meeting people who share her interest in music. Her husband and her sister's husband are waiters; mother Ida is a brilliant cook, preparing Ligurian dishes, some vegetarian, with the freshest organic produce, and fabulous breakfasts; sister Edy is a cake-making genius; and father Lino ensures that it all runs like clockwork. Orietta is a keen walker who may take guests out for real hikes – though you can always catch a boat to Portofino and explore the Cinque Terre by sea. You are fairly close to the railway here (a significant part of the landscape, threading the Cinque Terre villages together) but you'd never know. Lots of treats to come back to: a fitness room, sauna, spa, lovely pool, and the beach a ten-minute walk. *Minimum stay three nights. Gluten-free meals available.*

Price	€130–€280. Singles €85–€135. Half-board €75–€125 p.p.
Rooms	27: 21 doubles, 2 singles, 2 suites, 2 family rooms.
Meals	Lunch/dinner €28–€35. Wine €10.
Closed	10 November–15 March.
Directions	Exit A12 at Sestri Levante; signs for Moneglia tunnel. Immed. after 5th tunnel right (at sports field); signed. Free parking.

Orietta Schiaffino
Via Venino 12,
16030 Moneglia

Tel	+39 0185 49291
Email	info@villaedera.com
Web	www.villaedera.com

Abbadia San Giorgio

Sublimely romantic and peaceful, this 15th-century monastery recalls the life of St Francis in frescoes and sculptures overhung by vaulted ceilings. You can almost hear the sandaled Franciscans padding around the cloistered garden. Dipping into a delicious spread for breakfast — served in the refrectory by candlelight — evokes a further monastic air. As for the bedrooms, Orietta and Francesca, a mother and daughter team, have searched Italy for antique furniture and sensual fabrics to make them both sumptuous and individual. Many of the beds are wrought-iron; one's a four-poster. Floors are of original octagonal terracotta or terrazzo tiles. Benefica Mulier is the large and ethereal honeymoon suite, swathed and festooned with gauze and ivory soft furnishings. Elsewhere, tones range from lavish-red to green, apricot and gold, all opulently matched. Neat marble bathrooms sport spa shower cabins with pretty olive oil-based toiletries. An amorous evening might begin with wine tasting in the cellar, then stepping out for dinner. A haven of peace in the centre of beautiful Moneglia. *Minimum stay three nights.*

Price	€190-€250. Suites €210-€310.
Rooms	6: 3 doubles, 1 twin/double, 2 suites for 4.
Meals	Restaurants 100m.
Closed	November.
Directions	A12 exit Sestri Levante dir. Moneglia; under bridge towards town centre, immed. left down palm tree-lined street, right at end after pharmacy; entrance to Abbadia next to church. Or 5-minute walk from station.

Orietta Schiaffino
Piazzale San Giorgio, 16030 Moneglia

Tel	+39 0185 49291
Email	info@abbadiasangiorgio.com
Web	www.abbadiasangiorgio.com

Villa Margherita by the Sea B&B

Federico is the understated owner of this family hotel, and his bubbly sister Paola. A five-minute walk above Levanto – count the steps! – is the Villa Margherita, built in 1906. It once mingled with the smart set and played its part in the summer seasons between the wars, when Levanto was seriously fashionable. The town is still full of character, still worth exploring; fishermen fish, children build sandcastles, but the glitterati have moved on. Sensitively renovated in classic Liguria ochre and decorative fresco, the house sits in leafy, terraced gardens sprinkled with pots of flowers, tables, loungers and tall palms; lap up the lushness over an aperitivo. White walls, muslin-clad windows and deep armchairs welcome you and charm abounds, in each marble stair, graceful iron bannister and decorative floor tiles. Simply furnished flowery bedrooms, family bathrooms and unfussy style imbue the house with the spirit of a well-loved, long-established *pensione*, and the updated garden rooms, one reached through the (breakfast-noisy kitchen), are delightful, each with its own little terrace.

Price	€85–€160.
Rooms	11: 9 doubles, 2 triples.
Meals	Restaurants 5-minute walk.
Closed	Never.
Directions	From A12 exit Carrodano & Levanto; right after station; left onto main street; right onto Corso Italia up hill; hotel on left; parking, signed.

Federico Campodonico
Via Trento e Trieste 31, 19015 Levanto

Tel	+39 0187 807212
Email	info@villamargherita.net
Web	www.villamargherita.net

Agriturismo Villanova

Villanova is where Barone Giancarlo Massola's ancestors spent their summers in the 18th century; it has barely changed. The villa is a mile from Levanto yet modern life feels far behind as you wind your way up the hills through olive groves. The red and cream villa with its own chapel stands in a small, sunny clearing. Giancarlo, quiet, charming, much-travelled, loves meeting new folk; his cat and golden retriever will welcome you too. Guest bedrooms are in the main house and in a small stone farmhouse behind; all have an elegant, country-house feel and rooms are large, airy, terracotta tiled. Furniture is of wood and wrought iron, beautiful fabrics are yellow and blue. All have private entrances and terraces with pretty views. Two of the apartments are separate, a third is in the farmhouse. Giancarlo grows organic apricots, figs and vegetables and makes his own wine and olive oil; breakfasts are delicious. This is a great place to bring children: swings and table tennis in the garden, space to run around in, the coast nearby.

Price	€95–€140. Suites €125–€170. Triples €135–€160. Apartments €500–€1,080 per week.
Rooms	9 + 4: 4 doubles, 2 suites for 3, 3 triples. 4 apartments for 2-6.
Meals	Breakfast €10 for self-caterers. Restaurants 1.5km.
Closed	Never.
Directions	Exit A12 at Carrodano Levanto dir. Levanto. Signs from junction before town (direction Monterosso & Cinque Terre).

Giancarlo Massola
Loc. Villanova,
19015 Levanto

Tel   +39 0187 802517
Email   info@agriturismovillanova.it
Web   www.agriturismovillanova.it

La Sosta di Ottone III

Legend has it that Otto III stayed here on his way to his coronation in Rome in 996, creating La Sosta, a 'stopover' of some magnificence. Now a listed building, the house's unadorned stone façade stands proudly over the hamlet of Chiesanuova, scanning a vista from all rooms of olive groves, village and vineyard-clad hills, before dropping down to Levanto and the sea. The terrace is a superb breakfast and dinner setting, perfect too at sunset with a glass of chilled vermentino. At night, the glow from a host of illuminated bell towers is enchanting. Angela has taken great care to gather the best local slate, marble and wood in the renovation of dining and sitting rooms. Bedrooms, named after Otto and his family members, come in an elegant range of neutrals and corals. There are parquet floors, antique pieces, indoor shutters and iron beds graced by fine bedspreads… take time to pamper yourself in stylish marble and slate bathrooms. Aficionados of all things Ligurian, Angela and Fabio can be depended on for local information, the freshest ingredients and one of the best wine cellars around. Superb. *Minimum stay two nights.*

Price	€180.
Rooms	4: 1 double, 1 suite for 4, 2 family rooms for 2-4.
Meals	Breakfast €10; €5 for children under 12. Dinner €35. Restaurant 5km.
Closed	November-February.
Directions	From Levanto dir. Cinque Terre. Ignore signs on right for Chiesanuova. After 400m park on left near cement watertank. Follow path for 150m.

Angela Fenwick
Loc. Chiesanuova 39,
19015 Levanto
Tel   +39 0187 814502
Email   lasosta@lasosta.com
Web   www.lasosta.com

L'Antico Borgo

High in green hills and along a winding road is the tiny hamlet of Dosso. Leave the car in the little car park and make the short but intrepid journey by foot down to the B&B. Surrounded by olive groves and pocket vineyards, it's hard to believe you are only four kilometres from Levanto. A pretty pebble-paved square and a stone archway form the entrance to the building, a 1700s *casa padronale* fully restored with a soft-ochre façade and dark green shutters so typical of Liguria. A panoramic terracotta-tiled terrace is a fine place to take breakfast or an aperitif and Cecilia is happy for guests to eat their own food here. Relax in the sitting room with a book from the small library, or breakfast at round tables in the rustic taverna. Bright and generous bedrooms are framed by wooden beamed ceilings, two with sea views; all are comfortably furnished with wrought-iron beds warmed by shades of gentle yellow. Modern bathrooms employ solar-heated water. Siblings Cecilia and Carlo are natural hoteliers, he a local surfing hero, both supporters of the Slow Food movement...they know the best places for dinner.

Price	€80–€105. Family rooms €130–€160. Triples €110–€135.
Rooms	7: 1 double, 1 twin/double, 2 family rooms for 4, 3 triples.
Meals	Restaurant 15-minute walk.
Closed	Rarely.
Directions	A12 Genova-Livorno exit Carrodano-Levanto; on for Levanto. Left after gallery, signs for Dosso; free parking at entrance.

Cecilia Pilotti
Loc. Dosso, 19015 Levanto

Tel	+39 0187 802681
Email	antico_borgo@hotmail.com
Web	www.anticoborgo.net

Tuscany

Photo: istock.com

Podere Conti

Set in an organically certified, 200-acre olive estate beneath the magnificent Appennini mountains, this 17th-century hamlet, procured by Corrado and English Cornelia, recently renovated whilst raising a family, is agriturismo perfection. Follow a winding five-kilometre drive through chestnut, hazelnut and oak forest (ensuring utter seclusion), be greeted by charming Cornelia, decant into rooms beautifully designed with Arabian (not Tuscan) flair; both spent time in Abu Dhabi. Find exquisite rugs on cotto floors, raw beams, antique screen bedheads, richly textured cushions, delicious cotton bedding, little chandeliers, creaky trunks, glass bedside lights, and breezy bathrooms with free-standing tubs and monogrammed towels... all feels uncluttered and balanced. La Tavolata, their restaurant, serves delicious estate-produced meals (game in season) against sensational valley sunsets. There's loads to do both on the estate and off – this is heaven for free-range kids. And, with secluded nooks, poolside daybeds and hammocks in secluded crannies, it's pretty nice for adults too. Oh, and a haunted ruin!

Ethical Collection: Environment.
See page 400 for details

Price	€90–€155. Apartments €150–€260.
Rooms	9 + 3: 6 doubles, 3 suites for 4. 3 apartments: 2 for 4, 1 for 5.
Meals	Lunch/dinner €25.
Closed	Mid-January to March.
Directions	From A15/E31 Parma/La Spezia m'way, exit Pontremoli. Right onto SP31, 1st right Via di Caritá e Lautro; T-junc. left SS62, 1st right Via Dobbiana. Follow signs to Podere Conti (approx. 6km).

Cornelia Conti
Via Dobbina Macerie 3,
51023 Filattiera
Tel   +39 0187 855052
Email   info@podereconti.com
Web   www.podereconti.com

Casa Gisella

In the chestnut-mantled Lunigiana mountains, Bastia village is quaint, cobbled, labyrinth'd with lanes and dominated by an ancient, surely unassailable fort. Sitting on the breakfast terrace at Casa Gisella, distracted by gaspworthy views, you feel on top of the world. In the dream holiday home of Irish owners Ronnie and Alison the bedrooms are cosy, comfortable and classy all at the same time and show exceptional attention to detail; nothing too flash, just carefully considered and harmonious: a clean use of space and the odd contemporary painting; big wrought-iron beds covered with beautiful cream fabrics, textured throws and lots of cushions; power showers, snazzy lighting and WiFi. Thick, exposed medieval walls and beams make rooms snug and the big sitting room has a fire for winter. The very modern kitchen is charming and there are guest discounts to be had at local restaurants. The place is a walkers' paradise — you could veer off in any direction for hours — and, being close to both sea and snow, is family-fabulous all year round. *Minimum stay three nights. Flexible rental periods.*

Price	£550-£890 per week.
Rooms	House for 6.
Meals	Welcome pack. Dinner with wine, €32, by arrangement. Restaurants 3km.
Closed	Never.
Directions	A1 to A15, exit A15 Aulla. Follow signs for Licciana Nardi on SS665. From Licciana, signs for Bastia.

Ronnie & Alison Johnston
Via Bastia 20, Bastia,
54016 Licciana Nardi

Tel	+44 (0)7967 188017
Email	info@casagisella.com
Web	www.casagisella.com

Dimora Olimpia

When they came here it was a ruin; eight years on, Olimpia and Gaetano's 16th-century farmhouse is an exquisitely restored home. For the full force of its charm, approach via the cobbled back street where chickens potter and an archway leads to a neighbouring farmer's house. This is a verdant, very unspoilt part of Tuscany – country roads, tiny villages, good walks, fine wines. Passionate lovers of old things, your hosts are also fluent guides to the region; there are uninterrupted views of fields, woods and rumpled hills from elegant terrace and pool. Gorgeousness abounds: bare beams and exposed brickwork have been lovingly preserved, there are old wall hangings, very fine, early country furniture and, in the snug bedrooms, original shutters at tiny windows. The apartment is small, simple and charming, peaceful and cool, their beds aligned with the Earth's magnetic field to ensure perfect sleep. The shower room is first-class, the kitchen tiny, the pillow cases are lined with lace. You will dine well in nearby restaurants and are most welcome to join B&B guests round the antique Indian table. Special. *Minimum stay two nights.*

Price	€70-€75. Apt €350-€450 per week.
Rooms	2 + 1: 1 double, 1 suite. 1 apt for 4.
Meals	Breakfast €5 for self-caterers. Restaurants 4km.
Closed	Never.
Directions	From Aulla SS62 to SS665, then Monti & Amola. Right for Dimora Olimpia in middle of village; on right.

Olimpia De Caro & Gaetano Azzolina
Via Molesana, 54017 Licciana Nardi

Tel   +39 0187 471580
Email info@dimoraolimpia.it
Web   www.dimoraolimpia.it

La Cerreta

Be different and head for the hills. The chestnut-covered slopes of the Garfagnana region are less well-known, more remote and somewhat wilder than the southern Tuscany everyone knows and loves, but no less captivating. Wind up through the Serchio Valley from Lucca, up and up, until you reach this secluded hideaway with views of the breathtaking variety. Inside it's typical rustic simplicity with beams, open fireplace in the kitchen and a traditional stove in the sitting-room. Sybarites might want to bag the cool (in both senses) third bedroom which has its own entrance and shower room and one of those vast beds that you just have to dive on. There's a pretty terrace at the front for breakfast, but you'll more than likely fancy the shady deck round the back for lunch and supper – you'll feel as if you're dining in the tree tops. If all gets too relaxing, you can always pop down the road to the six-hole golf course with its dinky clubhouse, or pack a picnic and stride off in any direction. Jazz and opera fans can head for arty Barga – an irresistible medieval hilltop town where there's always a festival in the offing.

Price	€500–€1,400 per week.
Rooms	House for 6-8.
Meals	Restaurants 2-3km.
Closed	Winter.
Directions	Directions on booking.

	Sarah Bolton
	Castelnuovo di Garfagnana
Email	info@lacerreta.co.uk
Web	www.lacerreta.co.uk

Peralta

It is an adventure to get here (the steepest ravines, the narrowest bends) and an adventure to stay: Peralta is precariously perched on the foothills of Mount Prana. The sculptress Fiore de Henriquez took it on 40 years ago, a labyrinth of ancient dwellings connected by steep steps and sun-dappled terraces; now it is overseen by British Dinah and a team of international helpers, who draw you all together into one big family. Lemon trees, jasmine and bougainvillea romp on every corner, sculptures peep from crannies, and the chestnut-dense valley swoops to the sea. Rooms are properly rustic, not luxurious but charming, some light, some dim; all have vibrant walls, breathtaking views, perhaps an old red sofa, a simple bed covered in a striped cover, a rag rug on a terracotta floor. Pots and pans are mix and match; four of the apartments have dishwashers. There's a panoramic terrace where guests gather to swap stories, a light-filled studio for art and writing courses, a log-warmed sitting room, a small pool. The whole place hums with creativity. *Minimum stay two nights. Children over 10 welcome.*

Price	€350–€2,125 per week.
Rooms	3 apts for 2, 2 apts for 3, 1 house for 4–5, 1 house for 7–8.
Meals	Restaurants 2km.
Closed	Never.
Directions	From A12 Livorno/Genoa, exit Camaiore. Left after Camaiore for Pieve, uphill, signs for Peralta. Left at fork for Peralta, pass blue sign & onto Agliano. Unsigned. Parking 200m, then climb.

Kate Viti & Dinah Voisin
Pieve di Camaiore, Via Pieve 321,
55041 Camaiore

Tel	+39 0584 951230
Email	peraltusc@tiscali.it
Web	www.peraltatuscany.com

Albergo Villa Marta

The travel book-strewn table in reception, crafted from an Indonesian bed, sets the mood: very elegant, not stuffy. The villa-hotel is the creation of the young Martinellis who personally welcome you and attend to your every whim... a Tuscan Christmas? A wine and chocolate tour? All can be arranged. With two flights of steps leading to an entrance on either side, the elegant, loftily positioned 19th-century villa stands in sweeping lawns enfolded by the Monti Pisani, from whose verdant hills you can spot Pisa's leaning tower. The whole feel is intimate yet there's masses of space, and a terrace for spring and summer wafted by magnolias, jasmine and pines. Bedrooms ooze subtlety and comfort: fabrics with flowers and stripes, peach and grey walls, modern art. Bed linen is delicious, walk in showers luxurious, views bucolic. Return after a day in Lucca (catch the bus) to cocktails in the garden and a dip in the pool. The chef gives an international twist to her delicious Tuscan dishes, and in winter you breakfast by an open fire, on breads and brioche straight from the oven. Gorgeous.

Price	€89–€235. Singles €75–€235.
Rooms	15: 8 twins/doubles. Annexe: 7 twins/doubles.
Meals	Menu à la carte, €28–€40. Wine €20–€80. Restaurants 7-minute walk.
Closed	January.
Directions	A11 Firenze-Mare exit Lucca Est; signs for Pisa onto SS12; signs to Albergo Villa Marta; after 250m, left into Via del Ponte Guasperini; entrance 500m on left. Can be tricky; ask for detailed directions on booking.

	Andrea Martinelli
	Via del Ponte Guasperini 873,
	San Lorenzo a Vaccoli, 55100 Lucca
Tel	+39 0583 370101
Email	info@albergovillamarta.it
Web	www.albergovillamarta.it

Albergo San Martino

What a position: in a secluded corner of Lucca, a minute from bars, restaurants and ramparts. There's a fresh-faced enthusiasm about the little San Martino now that the young Morottis have taken over; smiling faces behind reception and breakfasts that shine. Expect cheese and salami platters, baskets of different breads, homemade cakes, yogurts and fresh fruits every day – enjoyed in the courtyard in summer. No architectural flourishes, no rushes to the head – just a simple, comfortable, family-run hotel in one of Italy's loveliest towns. Gone are the fitted carpets, new are the wooden floors. The traditionally furnished, uncluttered bedrooms have creamy silk-like curtains and soft coloured walls, cute shuttered windows and interesting paintings, refurbished bathrooms, the odd fresco. Two new suites in the adjoining building have hydromassage baths and showers and Room 108 gets its own terrace, but all of them will please you. The Duomo is a stroll, there's a concert in San Giovanni every night, and bike rental – for Lucca's cycle-friendly walls – is nearby. *Min. stay two nights high season. Private car park.*

Price	€80–€110. Suites €120–€160.
Rooms	11: 9 doubles, 2 suites.
	Some rooms interconnect.
Meals	Breakfast €10.
	Special price for guests at osteria, 100m.
Closed	Rarely.
Directions	In the Old Town next to cathedral.
	Ask for directions. Parking 400m;
	€10 per day.

Andrea Morotti
Via della Dogana 9, 55100 Lucca

Tel	+39 0583 469181
Email	info@albergosanmartino.it
Web	www.albergosanmartino.it

Alla Corte degli Angeli

Off the main drag of tourists and shoppers, down a side street named after angels, is a refreshing, very special find. This small, intimate, romantic 'maison de charme' seduces you from the moment you step in. Owner Pietro, born and bred within the city walls, is charming and keen to please. Enter the sitting room/reception and let the lift (rare in such places) deliver you to bedrooms upstairs. Each is named after a favourite flower, with an enchanting trompe l'oeil to match; each is furnished in soft Tuscan colours. Some have delicious silk curtains, others bright bedcovers; some have beams, others tall ceilings; all are elegant and calming, with Orchidea and Ortensia our favourites. Bathroom are state of the art: hydromassage baths from which you can watch telly – or listen to music – as you soak. And throughout, the poetic presence of local artist Possenti; even the 'do not disturb' cards bear his designs. The treats continue at table where, in a beautiful frescoed room, bountiful breakfasts are served. Wonderful restaurants lie outside the door – including their own, two minutes away.

Price	€119–€180.
Rooms	10 doubles.
Meals	Breakfast €10. Restaurants 100m.
Closed	Never.
Directions	In centre of Lucca. Ask about parking.

Pietro Bonino
Via degli Angeli 23, 55100 Lucca
Tel   +39 0583 469204
Email   info@allacortedegliangeli.com
Web   www.allacortedegliangeli.com

Da Elisa alle Sette Arti

Some cities are to be escaped – for cooler breezes, respite from the crowds. Lucca isn't like that. More serene than its Tuscan cousins, it is one of the most beguiling medieval cities in Europe, and it is the locals, not the tourists, who set the pace. The elegant shop fronts – dark wood, gold lettering, sparkling glass – are piled high with cheeses, bread, wines; and the entire city is encircled by a wide city wall along which you may cycle or walk! Da Elisa sits within the embrace of the walls, like a little youth hostel for grown ups (good beds, some flourishes in the décor); a rare place. The big wooden door off the street opens to an unprepossessing staircase; then through a little hall are six rooms and a shared kitchen – a blessing for those on a budget. A note says 'help yourself to supplies and leave something for others, too'. Breakfast is DIY: nip up to the bakery while the coffee brews. It's frill-free, functional and could do with a spruce-up, but good prices and delightful staff make up for these shortcomings. Note their second building is a 600m walk from reception; you may need a cab.

Price	€45–€70.
Rooms	10: 4 doubles; 6 doubles sharing bath.
Meals	Breakfast €7. Restaurants within walking distance.
Closed	Never.
Directions	Follow signs to train station, around walls; after 1st bend, through Porta Elisa gate; on for 50m.

Andrea Mencaroni
Via Elisa 25, 55100 Lucca

Tel   +39 0583 494539
Email   info@daelisa.com
Web   www.daelisa.com

Fattoria Mansi Bernardini

Extra virgin olive oil is pressed from the groves that clothe this ancient estate in rural Lucca, and a cluster of vines produce DOC wine. It doesn't get much more Mediterranean than this: a hamlet of farmhouses immersed in gardens, all stone walls and steps, climbing vines and nodding roses. It's a bucolic scene that could come straight from an easel – indeed, you may meet an artist or two, sketching in the shade of the big magnolia, finding inspiration in the hills around. Generations of the Bernardini family have lived and loved this place; we were equally enamoured. Each of the four villas has a history (one the old farm manager's house, another the old hayloft), all are huge and have been wonderfully renovated, in a palette of Tuscan colours. Original stonework, cotto floors and beams are softly illuminated, kitchens are fitted, each house has its pool and garden and there's maid service most days. Il Borghetto has five smaller cottages, so skip across to the greenhouse for breakfast. The owner lives in the main villa. A taste of Italy you thought no longer existed: elegance, comfort and peace.

Price	€110-€150.
Rooms	15: 8 doubles, 3 twins, 4 suites.
Meals	Dinner €30, on request. Wine €6-€10.
Closed	Never.
Directions	A11 exit Capannori dir. Capannori/Porcari, then Porcari/Bagni di Lucca. After 500m with Esselunga on right, r'bout dir. Pescia/Bagni di Lucca; 2.4km signed Lunata; 200m, Via Pesciatina. Right for Pescia; 600m to lights; yellow sign for Villa Mansi.

Marcello Salom
55018 Lucca
Tel   +39 0583 921721
Email   info@fattoriamansibernardini.it
Web   www.fattoriamansibernardini.com

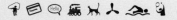

Villa Michaela

A lifetime's treat. Writers, celebrities and a First Lady have all stayed here, in the opulent Tuscan villa with its *House & Garden* interiors. You can even make it your own: indulge family and friends and get married in its chapel. You may have the best luck booking out of season. Come for a few days, join a Slow Food house party, sample local wines, listen to opera. An interior designer has worked his magic on every room, mingling fine English furniture with classic Italian style, while Puccini, Verdi and Dante lend their names to the grander bedrooms, awash with frescoed ceilings, lavish fabrics, king-size beds and double sinks. Also: a family kitchen, a formal dining room, a library and a room for TV, tennis and an outdoor pool. Dine al fresco, on culinary artist Luca's divine concoctions, and let your gaze drift over the floodlit gardens, heady with gardenias, to the 50 acres of pine forests and olive groves beyond. You are bathed in tranquillity yet it's a five-minute walk to the delightful village of Vorno, and unspoilt Lucca is a ten-minute drive. *Coach house for six occasionally available. Minimum stay two nights.*

Price	€150–€310. Whole villa on request.
Rooms	12: 10 doubles; 2 doubles sharing bathroom.
Meals	Dinner with wine, €50. Restaurant nearby.
Closed	Never.
Directions	SS12 from Lucca to Guamo. Follow signs for Vorno; villa behind church.

Vanessa Swarbreck
Via di Valle 8,
55060 Vorno
Tel   +44 (0)7768 645500
Email   vanessaswarbreck@yahoo.co.uk
Web   www.villamichaela.com

Fattoria di Pietrabuona

Hide yourself away in the foothills of the Svizzera Pesciatina – Tuscany's 'Little Switzerland'. Home to a beguiling brood of ancient breed Cinta Senese pigs, this huge estate immersed in greenery is presided over by the elegant Signora – an unlikely pig farmer. The farm buildings have been cleverly divided into apartments that fit together like a puzzle; we liked the three oldest best, near the main villa and each very private. The rest – and the communal pool – are quite a drive up winding hills and some of the roads, though well maintained, are precipitous in parts. not for the faint-hearted nor those worried about heavily-laden hire cars. All have gardens and outside seating. The exteriors are full of character, the interiors are simple and some of the newer apartments have steep stairs. Bring a Tuscan cookbook: the kitchens, some with old sinks but with new everything else, ask to be used, and there's a small shop next to the office selling estate produce. The views are amazing, particularly from the pool, and the villages are worth a good wander. *Minimum stay two nights.*

Price	€450–€1,300 per week.
Rooms	14 apartments: 5 for 2, 5 for 4, 3 for 6, 1 for 8.
Meals	Restaurants nearby.
Closed	Never.
Directions	Exit A11 at Chiesina Uzzanese towards Pescia, then Abetone & Pietrabuona. After P. left for Medicina; left again. After 500m road becomes an avenue of cypresses. Villa & Fattoria at end.

Maristella Galeotti Flori
Via per Medicina 2, Pietrabuona,
51017 Péscia
Tel   +39 0572 408115
Email   info@pietrabuona.com
Web   www.pietrabuona.com

Antica Casa "Le Rondini"

Imagine a room above an archway in an ancient hilltop village, within ancient castle walls. You lean from the window and watch the swallows dart to and fro; there are *rondini* inside too, captured in a 200-year-old fresco. The way through the arch – the via del Vento ('where the wind blows') – and the front door to this captivating house await just the other side. Step into a lovely room, a study in white – fresh lilies and snowy walls and sofas – dotted with family antiques and paintings. Fulvia and Carlo are warm, interesting hosts who have lovingly restored the house to its original splendour. The delightfully different bedrooms have wrought-iron bedheads, big mirrors and some original stencilling. Several, like the Swallow Room, have pale frescoes. All have good views. The little apartment, too, is simple, charming, peaceful. Just across the cobbled street is a walled garden with lemon trees – an idyllic place for breakfast on sunny mornings. A short walk brings you to the square where village ladies sit playing cards, children scamper and the church bell rings every hour, on the hour.

Price	€75–€125. Apartment €65 for 2.
Rooms	5 + 1: 5 doubles. Apartment for 2-4.
Meals	Restaurant 200m.
Closed	December-January.
Directions	A11 Firenze-Pisa Nord. Exit Montecatini Terme. Follow signs to Pescia. Left after 2nd lights, right after petrol station. Follow sign "Colle-Buggiano". Up hill to parking area.

Fulvia Musso
Via M. Pierucci 21,
51011 Colle di Buggiano

Tel	+39 0572 33313
Email	info@anticacasa.it
Web	www.anticacasa.it

Tenuta di Pieve a Celle

Fiorenza welcomes you with coffee and homemade cake, Julie – the retriever – escorts you round the garden, and there are freshly-laid eggs for breakfast. This is pure, genuine hospitality. Off a country road and down a cypress-lined drive, the shuttered, ochre-coloured *colonica* sits amid the family farm's olive groves and vineyards. The Saccentis (three generations) live next door but this house feels very much like home. Bedrooms (one downstairs) are furnished with well-loved antiques, rugs on tiled floors and handsome wrought-iron or upholstered beds. Cesare, Fiorenza's husband, designed the fabrics – pretty country motifs – and his collection of African art is dotted around the rooms. Books, flowers, soft lighting give a warm and restful feel. There's an elegant but easy sitting room, with fireplace, where you eat breakfast if it's too chilly on the patio, and dinner is by request. Sometimes the Saccentis join you: a real family affair. Laze by the pool with views to distant hills, walk in the woods, borrow bikes or visit nearby Lucca.

Price	€130–€160.
Rooms	5 twins/doubles.
Meals	Dinner €30, by arrangement. Wine €10–€25. Restaurant 200m.
Closed	Rarely.
Directions	A11 for Pisa Nord. Exit Pistoia; signs for Pistoia Ovest to Montagnana; 2km, Tenuta on right. Ring bell at gates.

Cesare & Fiorenza Saccenti
Via di Pieve a Celle 158,
51030 Pistoia

Tel	+39 0573 913087
Email	info@tenutadipieveacelle.it
Web	www.tenutadipieveacelle.it

Ethical Collection: Food.
See page 400 for details

Villa de' Fiori

With its formal rose gardens, immaculate lawns and neat box-hedged gravel paths, Villa de' Fiori lives up to its name. Pass through impressive gates and follow the cypress-lined drive to the main house, a renovated, 17th-century confection of peach and white with smart green shutters, a loggia for candlelit dining with live music in the evenings, terraces and, hidden beyond a high hedge, a pool with sophisticated white sun umbrellas, fringed with orange trees. Modernistic awnings provide cover for al fresco dining on the lawns. Inside, simple, uncluttered décor justifies the agriturismo status: vaulted sitting rooms, a music room, original geometric tiles, paintings, good solid furniture, high windows and massive fireplaces. There are six bedrooms in the main house, two of which are large, child-proof family suites. The excellent restaurant is host to a dining club; yoga, ayurvedic treatments and Polynesian massage complete your relaxation; and the olive groves, woodland and vineyards are perfect for exploring – for child and adult alike. Gabriele merrily oversees this lovely, lively place.

Price	€51–€96.
Rooms	6 + 2: 4 doubles, 2 family rooms. 2 apts: 1 for 3-5, 1 for 6-8.
Meals	Half-board option available. Wine €12–€150. Restaurant open to public.
Closed	November–March.
Directions	A11 exit Pistoia, 2nd exit at r'bout; through two sets of lights. 2nd exit at next r'bout; past industrial estate. Right at end of road; signed.

Gabriele Prosperi
Via Bigiano e Castel Bovani 39,
51100 Pistoia

Tel	+39 0573 450351
Email	info@villadefiori.it
Web	www.villadefiori.it

Villa Anna Maria

The wrought-iron gates swing open to reveal a strange and atmospheric haven. You feel protected here from the outside world, miles from the heat and bustle of Pisa. It is an intriguing place. Secret rooms lurk behind locked doors; some bedrooms seem untouched since the 17th century. They are all different, themed and with high ceilings, the most curious being the Persian and the Egyptian. The entrance hall is decked in marble, graced with columns and chandeliers; the library – a touch over the top for some – is nevertheless in tune with the rest, and in tune, it must be said, with its eccentric owner. Claudio and his wife collect anything and everything and rooms are crammed with curios and collectibles. Yes, it's shambolic – but your host cares more about people than about money and there are no rules, so treat it as your home. There's a game room with billiards and videos (3,000 of them), table tennis, a garden with tall palms and woodland paths, a pool with piped music issuing from clumps of bamboo, a barbecue area for those who choose to self-cater, and a romping dog. *Minimum stay two nights.*

Price	€120–€150. Singles €90. Apartments €800–€2,000 per week. Cottage €1,000 per week.	
Rooms	6 + 1: 6 doubles/triples (or 2 apartments for 2-8). Cottage for 2-3.	
Meals	Dinner with wine, €40.	
Closed	Rarely.	
Directions	From Pisa SS12 for Lucca. At S. Giuliano Terme, SS12 left down hill; after Rigoli to M. di Quosa. On right opp. pharmacy.	

	Claudio Zeppi SS dell'Abetone 146, 56010 Molina di Quosa
Tel	+39 0508 50139
Email	zeppi@villaannamaria.com
Web	www.villaannamaria.com

Agriturismo Fattoria di Migliarino

On 3,000 farmed hectares between the Alps and the sea is a gated agriturismo run on well-oiled wheels. This is due to the indefatigable energy of Martino and Giovanna, a young couple with four children who understand the needs of families. The B&B rooms are in the main house: Tuscan beds, soft wall lights and prints, mosquito-proofed windows, big arched sitting areas and a raftered dining room with two sociable tables. In the buildings beyond are 13 two-storey apartments of every shape and size. All have terraces divided by hedges of jasmine, so you may be as private or as gregarious as you like. There's no reception room and breakfasts are basic but those communal rooms are pleasant and the two pools, open from June to September, lie alongside neatly gravelled pathways and lawned spaces with loungers. The well-being centre brims with treatments, the gleaming farm shop specialises in turkey, game, wine and olive oil. Football, tennis and ping-pong are on tap, riding and sailing can be arranged and the sandy beaches are a bike ride away. *Call ahead for access code to entrance gates.*

Price	€100–€130. Apartments €350–€1,500 per week.
Rooms	10 + 13: 10 doubles. 13 apartments for 2-10.
Meals	Breakfast €5 for self-caterers. Agriturismo's taverna 200m. Dinner (min. 15 people) on request.
Closed	Never.
Directions	Exit A11-A12 Pisa Nord, left for Pisa; 1st lights right under r'way bridge to Viale dei Pini. Left after 800m; in Via del Mare.

Martino & Giovanna Salviati
Viale del Mare 1, 56010 Migliarino

Tel	+39 3356 608411
Email	info@fattoriadimigliarino.it
Web	www.fattoriadimigliarino.it

Tenuta Poggio al Casone

You won't forget your first sight of this Tuscan villa, standing alone on top of the world. Alone but for the vast vineyards it oversees; this is wine country and the Castellani family have been in the business since Dante's time. The current generation cultivate organic Chianti and now they've transformed the villa and two cottages into supremely elegant apartments. These would not look out of place in an Italian design show, so sophisticated is their décor, so generous their space. Some apartments have mezzanine levels, others attics or terraces; yet others have jacuzzis and four-posters. The rooms are dressed in gorgeous fabrics and shades of soft ivory and latte, enlivened by splashes of aqua and Tuscan red. If the interiors are finely tuned, the views are utterly untouched. From organising wine tours and tastings to lake fishing and mountain biking, Michela and her team take care of you with consummate professionalism. Swim in the pool, fire up the barbecue, visit Pisa and the Etruscan coast. Fresh, stylish, memorable – a huge treat. *Minimum stay seven nights mid/high season.*

Price	€900–€2,900 per week.
Rooms	9 apartments: 3 for 2, 2 for 3, 2 for 4, 1 for 5, 1 for 6–8.
Meals	Breakfast €12. Restaurant 400m.
Closed	Rarely.
Directions	A1 exit Scandicci then m'way FI-PI-LI dir. Livorno exit Lavoria. Follows signs for Cenaia centre; thro' village for 2km until Quattro Strade, right at lights dir. Crespina. House after 500m on left, big gates.

	Famiglia Castellani
	Via Volpaia 16, 56042 Crespina
Tel	+39 0506 42259
Email	resort@poggioalcasone.com
Web	www.poggioalcasone.com

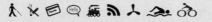

Antica Dimora Leones

A labyrinth of vaulted ceilings, stone fireplaces and original frescoes in the heart of the medieval *borgo* of Palaia. The palazzo was restored in the 1800s but goes way back to AD1000, when it formed part of the castle. Now it is an antique collector's paradise – which is no surprise: the owner's grandparents were antique dealers. It almost feels as though they are still here, wandering the historic corridors and rooms. Specialness is everywhere, from the high frescoed ceilings of the 'noble floor' to the bare beams and rooftop views of the characterful servants' quarters. Every floor has a wonderful sitting room or library, with books, comfy chairs and something precious in each corner. A tray of drinks awaits your arrival; the buffet breakfast (salami, cheeses, homemade cakes) is served in the beamed dining room or under wisteria in the pretty garden. So much history, yet there are some winning modern touches – notably the seven-person hydropool. Restorative, soothing, special – and don't miss the lovely Etruscan town of Volterra.

Price	€95–€120.
Rooms	10: 9 doubles, 1 single.
Meals	Lunch or dinner with wine, €35, on request (small groups only). Restaurants 100m.
Closed	Rarely.
Directions	Superstrada Firenze–Pisa–Livorno, exit Pontedera, follow signs for Palaia centre. Just beyond clock tower on the corner.

Andrea Soldani
Via della Rocca 2,
56036 Palaia

Tel	+39 0587 622024
Email	info@leones-palaia.it
Web	www.leones-palaia.it

Castello Ginori di Querceto

Here's something for families who want the Tuscan sun but don't want to spend the earth. Querceto is a hamlet, a rambling medieval *borgo* on many levels, whose nucleus is a castle around which workers' cottages have evolved (and in the family since 1543!). Leave the car outside the walls and enter a timewarp; the Liscis may own 700 hectares of vineyards and produce a number of important red wines but no-one is in a hurry here. The apartments too will charm you: a clean plain décor in a rustic style, comfort without the frills. There are bright tartan cotton bedspreads, dark shutters to keep out the light, resuscitated floor tiles and nice old doors, simple kitchens with copper pans; the farmhouse sleeping eight (set apart with a small private pool) is brilliant value. The shops are at Ponteginori (4km) but the bread van calls three times a week and the wine is on the spot. The grounds (not the gardens) are yours to roam, the picnic spots are across the way and the big swimming pool is down the steep track, surrounded by olive trees. Friendly Simona, who works here in the summer months, will reveal it all. *Minimum two nights; seven in high season.*

Price	Apartments €450–€750. House €850–1,200. Farmhouse €1,250–€1,950. Prices per week.
Rooms	5 apartments for 2–4. House for 6. Farmhouse for 8.
Meals	Restaurants within walking distance.
Closed	January–February.
Directions	Exit A12 Rosignano; SS1 (via Aurelia) exit Cecina. Follow signs for Volterra & Ponteginori. In Ponteginori, right, cross railway tracks & bridge over river Cecina. At end of road, signed.

	Cristina Sannazzaro Loc. Querceto, 56040 Montecatini Val di Cecina
Tel	+39 0588 37472
Email	info@castelloginoridiquerceto.it
Web	www.castelloginoridiquerceto.it

Relais Guado al Sole Agriturismo

Bump down a lazy track to electric gates and this huge estate of forest and groves, once the hunting lodge of nobility. This is a quiet part of Tuscany, with fewer crowds, where peace reigns in rolling hills and renovated stone buildings, and the views exude serenity. For those seeking solitude it is bliss. Terraces and gardens for strolling give way to tough, hilly walking country: ideal for ramblers and birdwatchers. The apartments here are spacious, spotless and traditional in décor with wooden furniture and neutral washes on walls, well-tiled bathrooms and bedrooms in golds, browns and beiges. Most have open fires in their sitting rooms and almost all the bedrooms have those glorious views. Kitchens are bursting with equipment but if you can't be bothered to use it, wander up to the brick-arched dining room of the big house for local food and wine (served in summer on the terrace). Heaven to laze away a hot afternoon by the infinity pool; there's enough space to feel private, and masses of lush greenery. Laziness may get the better of you: take plenty of novels. *Minimum stay two nights.*

Price	€80-€100. Apartments €110-€190. Cleaning extra.
Rooms	5 + 6: 3 doubles, 2 triples. 6 apts: 3 for 2-4, 2 for 3-5, 1 for 4-6.
Meals	Breakfast €8 for self-caterers. Dinner, 4 courses, €25; by arrangement. Wine €6.
Closed	November-March.
Directions	From SS68 direction Volterra exit Casole D'Elsa-San Dalmazio. At x-roads left dir. Montecerboli; signed.

Annalisa Buzzichelli
Loc. S. Ippolito, 56045 Pomarance
Tel   +39 0588 67854
Email info@relaisguadoalsole.com
Web   www.relaisguadoalsole.com

Il Belvedere

This solid, wysteria-smothered farmhouse set in a ten-acre estate of woods and vineyards houses one big party – and a cosy foursome in the cottage next door. Windows have fantastic views out over the Mugello valley and the small towns of Scarperia and Luco, and of little Grezzano, to which you can walk or cycle through the woods for a morning cappuccino. There's a delicious pool (and decadent hot tub) below, fringed with geraniums and crazily paved flagstones, and, through French windows, a terrace with a huge dining table; imagine yourselves in a Ragu commercial at mealtimes! Indoors, more rustic perfection. Exposed beams, cotto floors, full wine racks, an inglenook fireplace, brass and heavy antiques... and a big functional kitchen and dining room, the friendly heart of this house. A further sitting room on the first floor has panoramic views, an open fire, TV. Bedrooms are cool, shuttered and spacious, some with four-posters swathed in cotton, six heavenly bathrooms, antiques, verandas, natural colours. That cosy outbuilding across the courtyard is self-contained: perfect for teens. A Tuscan treat.

Price	€3,500–€4,900 per week.
Rooms	House for 14.
	Cottage for 4 (let to same party only).
Meals	Restaurants 1km.
Closed	Rarely.
Directions	Exit A1 Barberino di Mugello dir. Borgo San Lorenzo, then Luco and Grezzano. In Grezzano before small bridge, left at church. Up past church until 'Il Belvedere' sign on tree. Left into woods & follow sign until big gates.

Roberto & Flora Lagomarsino
Via di Marzano 117, 50032 Grezzano

Tel	+39 0558 401065
Email	info@ilbelvedere-mugello.com
Web	www.ilbelvedere-mugello.com

Il Poggio alle Ville

Beautiful vistas of sunflowers unfold, until a small hamlet comes into view: welcome to the agriturismo Il Poggio alle Ville. The moment you arrive you know you've chosen well. There's an old cart full of bright geraniums under the trees, roses clambering stone walls and a central green on which guests relax in sun or shade. It is an excellent and thoughtful restoration: the reception in the haybarn, the laundry in the shed, the apartments in the outbuildings, and the consecrated chapel. Step in to find venerable old beams and terracotta floors, white arches and narrow steps, floral bedcovers and snowy towels, perhaps an iron bedstead, a Tuscan fireplace or a picture of the Madonna on the wall. The friendly owners live nearby so there's always someone to look after you (and bottle the tomatoes and make the jams, all for sale along with the olive oil). There's space to roam and it's great for sociable families, with football field, ping-pong and big pool. A short drive up the hill is a huge old stone villa for 16, blessed with views and an elegant pool. Heaps of comfort and charm. *Ask about cookery classes.*

Price	€370–€3,500 per week.
Rooms	8: 7 apartments for 2–6. Villa for 16.
Meals	Dinner with wine, €28, on request. Children (5+) €18.
Closed	Rarely.
Directions	From Borgo San Lorenzo dir. Faenza. After 3km right at the sign for Corniolo/Mucciano; signed, 2km.

Raffaele & Ioana Edlmann
Loc. Le Ville - Mucciano,
50032 Borgo San Lorenzo
Tel   +39 0558 408752
Email info@poggioalleville.it
Web   www.poggioalleville.it

Monsignor della Casa Country Resort

It could be a Giotto landscape: the view of Monte Senario has not changed for 500 years. But the old buildings in the hamlet where estate workers once lived have become an upmarket resort, wonderful for all ages. Run by the charming Marzi family, the complex has a warm, inviting feel. Bay hedges and big terracotta pots of herbs scent the courtyards, there are cherry and olive trees everywhere, established gardens, a playground and two safely fenced pools. The apartments, mostly on two floors, are stylish and uncluttered, with fireplaces, stonework, beams; all have little gardens; the villas have private pools; one is in the old tower with views over the landscape. Airy bedrooms are painted in soft colours; some have four-posters with fine linen drapes, others wrought-iron beds. You can eat in the restaurant bar where hams hang from the beams – the menu is Tuscan, the wine list long. Then burn off the calories in the Wellness Centre, splendid with sauna, jacuzzi and gym. Close by is the Renaissance villa where Monsignor Giovanni Della Casa, a descendant of the Medici, was born in 1503. *Spa.*

Price	€160–€480 (€700–€2,500 per week). Villas €2,000–€6,000 per week.
Rooms	26 + 2: 26 apartments for 2, 4, 6 or 8. 2 villas: 1 for 8–12, 1 for 12–16.
Meals	Dinner €35–€50. Restaurants 3km.
Closed	9 January–5 March.
Directions	From m'way exit A1 Barberino di Mugello; signs to Borgo S. Lorenzo; signs to Faenza; right after 2.7km, signs to Mucciano and Corniolo. After 1km left to villa.

Alessio Marzi
Via di Mucciano 16,
50032 Borgo San Lorenzo

Tel	+39 0558 40821
Email	booking@monsignore.com
Web	www.monsignore.com

Ethical Collection: Food.
See page 400 for details

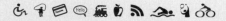

Casa Palmira

A medieval farm expertly restored by charming Assunta and Stefano who, being Italian, have a flair for this sort of thing. You are immersed in greenery yet half an hour from Florentine bustle. The views on the road to Fiesole are stunning; Stefano will ferry you around neighbouring villages in his mini-van, or you could hire mountain bikes and take one of Assunta's wonderful picnic baskets with you. The log-fired sitting room sets the tone: the *casa* has a warm, Tuscan feel, and bedrooms open off a landing with a brick-walled 'garden' in the centre – all Stefano's work. Two have four-poster beds dressed in Florentine fabric, all have polished wooden floors and pretty views, either onto the gardens where Assunta grows her herbs and vegetables or onto vines and olive trees. You are 500 metres above sea level so… no need for air conditioning, no mosquitoes! Breakfast on apricots and home-produced yogurt; dine on Tuscan food. There is also an excellent restaurant up the road. *Minimum stay two nights. Ask about cookery classes.*

Price	€85–€110. Single €65–€75. Triple €110–€130. Apt €135–€145 (€750–€950 per week).
Rooms	7 + 1: 4 twins/doubles, 1 twin, 1 single, 1 triple. Apt for 3-4.
Meals	Breakfast €10 for self-caterers. Dinner with wine, €30. Restaurant 700m.
Closed	10 January–10 March.
Directions	Directions on booking.

Assunta & Stefano Fiorini–Mattioli
Via Faentina 4/1, Loc. Feriolo,
Polcanto, 50030 Borgo San Lorenzo

Tel	+39 0558 409749
Email	info@casapalmira.it
Web	www.casapalmira.it

La Campanella

The green gates are a welcoming sight after the steep crawl up the unmade road, and the views across the valley and the breezes are a joy. The delightful Jill will soon have you seated in her farmhouse kitchen (or under the parasol on the patio): a glass of homemade lemonade, a slice of something sweet; you can't help but feel there's nowhere else you'd rather be. The airy sitting room has high ceiling arches interrupted by the odd beam, and deep sills; white walls are busy with paintings, puffed-up white sofas sit under mounds of cushions, fresh flowers rest on polished tables; there's more than just a touch of Englishness about the place. Pretty bedrooms have terracotta floor tiles, patchwork quilts and more views. Children will entertain themselves for hours in the charming garden, on the swing under the mulberry tree or in the pool. Adults may flop into the hammock with a chilled glass of the neighbour's organic wine; the peace is broken only by the faint shuffles of next door's hens. Walk straight into the woods carpeted in spring with orchids, or pop into Borgo, an eight-minute drive.

Price	€75-€95.
Rooms	2: 1 twin/double, 1 family suite for 2-4. Cot available.
Meals	Lunch €12. Dinner with wine, €30. Restaurant nearby.
Closed	Rarely.
Directions	A1 exit Barberino di Mugello; signs for Borgo San Lorenzo; SP41 to Sagginale; 1st right into Via di Zeti. Follow track up & fork right; 1st yellow house on right at top.

Ethical Collection: Food. See page 400 for details

Jill Greetham
Via Romignano 9, Loc. San Cresci,
50032 Borgo San Lorenzo

Tel	+39 0558 490373
Email	info@atuscanplace.com
Web	www.atuscanplace.com

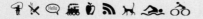

Le Due Volpi

Twenty miles from Florence, yet utterly unspoilt: the gentle hills of the Mugello valley have escaped development and the drive from Borgo is truly lovely. At the end of a long white track is a big house strewn with ivy; outside two snazzy little foxes – 'le due volpi', – splash water into a trough. Step into spaciousness and light and a charming Tuscan interior. Heidi is Italian, well-travelled and speaks perfect English; Lorenzo has a passion for old radios and antiques. They are naturals at looking after guests, love cooking on their Aga, dispatch meals to the loggia in summer and are embarking on a greener lifestyle, introducing solar panels and wood-fired central heating. The bedrooms, with their wooden floors and chunky rafters, couldn't be nicer. Beds are large and lighting soft, wood-burners keep you cosy in winter, Chini-tiled shower rooms have a stylish rusticity. Note that the two top-floor rooms are reached via several stairs. Vicchio, full of history, is a ten-minute drive and there's a riding stables down the road. Bliss. *Minimum stay two nights.*

Price	€80-€95. Extra bed €20-€30.
Rooms	3 doubles (one with kitchenette).
Meals	Picnic with wine, €15.
	Dinner, from €25. Restaurant 3km.
Closed	Rarely.
Directions	A1 exit Barberino; SS551 to Vicchio. From town square, Molezzano/Caselle road. 2km after Caselle, over bridge; at x-roads, right up track signed Villa Poggio Bartoli for 900m; cypress trees on right.

Heidi Flores & Lorenzo Balloni
Via di Molezzano 88,
50039 Vicchio del Mugello

Tel	+39 0558 407874
Email	info@leduevolpi.it
Web	www.leduevolpi.it

Casa Valiversi

The old pharmaceuticals laboratory, perched on a hill, painted in pretty pink, has become a distinctive, distinguished B&B. Just four rooms – one with a balcony, one with an open fire – and Mirella, warm, friendly and living next door. Tired of commuting to Florence every day she has opened her Casa to guests, popping in to serve generous breakfasts. Inside are 20th-century antiques from her years of dealing, sprinkled over three floors with originality and taste. Armchairs range from cream Thirties' Art Deco to Sixties' bubblegum pink, bold art beautifies pale walls, a white Fifties' lamp dominates a glass dining table, six dining chairs are immaculately upholstered. Bedrooms are serene spaces that ooze comfort and class and monogrammed linen, big arched windows overlook groves of olives. For self-caterers, the kitchen is fitted in contemporary style (plus one perfect antique cupboard from France), opening to garden, pergola and large terrace. Here in the hillsides of Sesto Fiorentino, five miles from Florence's centre, a relaxing, refreshing and peaceful place to stay. *Airport 3km.*

Price	€100–€120.
	Whole house €3,000–€5,000 per week.
Rooms	4 twins/doubles.
Meals	Use of kitchen €10.
	Restaurants nearby.
Closed	Never.
Directions	A1 exit Sesto Fiorentino dir. Centro & Colonnata; signed. Ring for further directions.

Mirella Mazzierli
Via Valiversi 61,
50019 Sesto Fiorentino

Tel	+39 0553 850285
Email	mirella@casavaliversi.it
Web	www.casavaliversi.it

Locanda Senio

Food is king here: genuine home cooking from Roberta, and, in the restaurant, much gastronomic enthusiasm from Ercole. Echoing a growing movement to bring lost medieval traditions back to life, they are passionate about wild herbs and 'forgotten' fruits. Enrol on one of their cookery courses (stay three nights and join one at no extra cost). The prosciutto from rare-breed *maiale medievale* is delicious; breakfast is a feast of homemade breads, cakes, fruits and jams; dinner a leisurely treat served in the restaurant with nine tables and cosy log fire. The little inn occupies a stunning spot in a quiet town in the Mugello valley, surrounded by rolling hills… there are guided walks through the woods, gastronomic meanders through the valley. Bedrooms are comfortable and cosy and it is worth paying extra for the suites if you can; they're in the 17th-century building with original fireplaces. There's a relaxation centre of which Roberta and Ercole are very proud – the jacuzzi, sauna and Turkish bath have a delicious aroma. Steps lead up to a pool with blue loungers; body and soul will be nurtured.

Price	€115-€200. Suites €190-€230. Half-board €100-€145 p.p.
Rooms	8: 6 twins/doubles, 2 suites for 2-3.
Meals	Dinner from €45. Wine from €10.
Closed	6 January-13 February.
Directions	From Bologna A14, exit Imola for Rimini; 50m; for Palazzuolo (40 mins). House in village, right of fountain & Oratorio dei Santi Carlo e Antonio.

Ercole & Roberta Lega
Via Borgo dell'Ore 1,
50035 Palazzuolo sul Senio

Tel	+39 0558 046019
Email	info@locandasenio.com
Web	www.locandasenio.com

Casa Howard Guest Houses - Florence

A five-minute walk from the bus and train station is this handsome palazzo, the talk of the town. No reception staff, no communal space, just a big fur throw on a welcoming divan and smiling housekeepers who serve breakfast in your room. On each floor, too, an honesty fridge stocked with soft drinks, wine and champagne. But best of all are the bedrooms, designed with style, originality and humour. If you can splash out on a larger, more lavish room, do, though all are delightful. One, with a sunken bath and Japanese prints on the walls, is a deep sensual red; another is 18th-century elegant, with a black velvet sofa and gold taffeta curtains. The apartment, its queen-size bed residing at the top of a spiral stair, is ultra-modern. There's a room specially for those who arrive with their pooches (dogs' beds, baskets, large terrace), and another, the Play Room, for families (Disney videos, a climbing wall!). Bathrooms are memorable; nights are air-conditioned and peaceful, providing you keep windows shut. A breath of fresh air, and decent value for the heart of old Florence. *Minimum stay two nights at weekends.*

Price	€120-€250. Apartment €1,500-€2,200 per week.
Rooms	12 + 1: 10 doubles, 2 suites. Apartment for 2-3.
Meals	Breakfast €12. Restaurants nearby.
Closed	Never.
Directions	50m from Santa Maria Novella train station.

	Via della Scala 18, 50123 Florence
Mobile	+39 335 266017
Email	info@casahoward.it
Web	www.casahoward.com

Palazzo Niccolini al Duomo

One minute you're battling with tourists in the Piazza del Duomo, the next you're standing inside this extraordinarily lovely palazzo. The *residenza* is on the second floor (with lift); two small trees, a brace of antique chairs and a brass plaque announce that you've arrived at the friendly reception. Ever since it was first built by the Naldini family in the 16th century, on the site of the sculptor Donatello's workshop, the building's grandeur has been steadily added to. And the recent restoration hasn't detracted from its beauty, merely added some superb facilities. It's all you hope staying in such a place will be – fabulously elegant and luxurious, with 18th-century frescoes, trompe l'oeil effects, fine antiques and magnificent beds... but in no way awesome, thanks to many personal touches. Relax in the lovely drawing room and look at family portraits, books and photos. Two signed photos are from the King of Italy, sent in 1895 to Contessa Cristina Niccolini, the last of the Naldini. She married into the current owner's family, bringing the palazzo as part of her dowry. A gem. *Parking available.*

Price	€180-€380. Singles €150-€220. Suites €300-€500.
Rooms	10: 5 doubles, 5 suites.
Meals	Dinner, by arrangement. Restaurants nearby.
Closed	Never.
Directions	In Florence "centro storico". A1 exit Firenze south; head for town centre & Duomo; Via dei Servi off Piazza del Duomo. Park, unload & car will be taken to garage: €25-€30.

Filippo Niccolini
Via dei Servi 2, 50122 Florence

Tel	+39 0552 82412
Email	info@niccolinidomepalace.com
Web	www.niccolinidomepalace.com

Residenza d'Epoca - Palazzo Galletti B&B

At the reception desk, a 17th-century altar. In the entrance hall, a Samurai robe. Up the marble stairs (two storeys), oriental carvings of dragons and proud warriors. The owners' passion for travel brings a sparkle to their eyes. Palazzo Galletti will beguile you: filled with secrets, it's history begins in the 12th century. Walls display frescoes restored to their former glory, along with exciting oriental touches. Bathrooms, encased in marble, fabulously lit, are heaped with towels. Bedrooms are divine, named after the planets, terracotta tiled, topped with rugs, their walls crisply colourwashed or ragged; each opens to a narrow balcony overlooking the inner courtyard. The lofty suites are full of antiques; Cerere is surely the noblest room in this book – 40 sq. metres of frescoed gorgeousness (mythical battle scenes, Roman deities) in creams, yellows and golds. The breakfast room with low vaulted ceilings dates from 1550. Bio energetic aromas waft through the windows from the spa downstairs. An amazing surprise in an unsurprising back street in Florence, a short trot from the Duomo. *Combined stays at Fattoria Bacio in Chianti possible.*

Price	€95–€160. Suites €175–€230.
Rooms	11: 7 doubles, 4 suites.
Meals	Restaurants 100m.
Closed	Never.
Directions	From SMN train station, bus No. 17, 11, 10 or 6. Get off at Via Martelli, right onto Via di Pucci; straight on until Via S. Egidio.

Samuele Minucci & Francesca Cascino
Via San Egidio, 50122 Florence
Tel +39 0553 905750
Email info@palazzogalletti.it
Web www.palazzogalletti.it

Mr My Resort

Here's something different: a small B&B with a luxurious décor and a theatrical flourish. One room is called Actor, another Diva, all exude glitter and glam. Step off the street into a wonderful courtyard – a sun-dappled surprise with seats, plants, flowers and objets – off which the swish bedrooms lie. There are antique majolicas and evocative lighting, mirrors in abundance, velvet and stucco, big beds and sumptuous cushions, and black lava stone in shower rooms to create a fantastic effect. And history to match – lunatics were once housed in the medieval cloisters below. (Anything less like an asylum is hard to imagine today…). Instead: a fresh, cool and charming little spa with jacuzzi, sauna and hammam. Friendly, cosmopolitan owners Cristina and Giuseppe have thought of everything: a sitting area with guidebooks, teas, coffees, WiFi and a fridge at your disposal; breakfast coupons to a stylish café nearby. Outside are fascinating streets to wander while the famous sites are a ten-minute stroll. A refreshing escape from the enticements of Florence. *Minimum stay two nights.*

Price	€95–€170.
Rooms	5: 4 doubles, 1 single.
Meals	Breakfast included (served at Nabucco café). Restaurants within walking distance.
Closed	Rarely.
Directions	10-minute walk from Santa Maria Novella train station. Exit station, Via Nazionale; 7th street on right (Via delle Ruote).

Cristina Gucciarelli
Via delle Ruote 14A, 50100 Florence
Tel   +39 0552 83955
Email   info@abacusreservations.com
Web   www.mrflorence.it

Relais Grand Tour & Grand Tour Suites

Step straight off the street into the 18th-century elegance of Giuseppe and Cristina's home. Your hosts are jolly, enthusiastic (as is Albert, the dog), a mine of information on all things Florentine. The welcoming bedrooms – three very large ones on the ground floor, four doubles on the second floor, all with showers – have traces of the original frescos and are furnished with family paintings and antiques. You're given a breakfast voucher for the famous Nabucco café-bar down the road (to be used at any time of day), but if you're staying upstairs, you have the option of breakfast, at extra charge, in your room. A charming bonus is an 18th-century theatre attached to the house, a fabulous room with original seats and Neapolitan tiles that Giuseppe and Cristina open to guests for recitals, readings and wine tastings. This is a terrific position in super-central Florence, with the Accademia Museum next door, and the Duomo and the market of San Lorenzo a five-minute stroll. If you come by car, you'll pay to park, but the station is within walking distance – come by train! *Minimum stay two nights.*

Price	€95–€110. Suites €110–€170.
Rooms	7: 3 doubles, 4 suites.
Meals	Breakfast included (served at Nabucco café). Restaurants within walking distance.
Closed	Never.
Directions	From Santa Maria Novella station onto Via Nazionale, straight on; then 4th left Via Guelfa, then right; 2nd left Via Reparata. Bus No. 1, 11, 16, 22, & 25.

Cristina Gucciarelli
Via Santa Reparata 21, 50129 Florence

Tel	+39 0552 83955
Email	info@abacusreservations.com
Web	www.florencegrandtour.com

Le Stanze di Santa Croce

A great find, this very old 'terratetto', nestled between its neighbours on a small street off the Piazza Santa Croce – perfect for those who want to stay in the historic centre. There's attention to detail at every turn; everything has been thought through beautifully. The four elegant rooms, one with a four-poster, aren't large but are beautifully presented, each named after famous Florentine bells, each with its own refined identity; they provide sanctuary from the heat of the city, while the jasmine-garlanded breakfast terrace is the perfect place from which to enjoy Mariangela's exceptional baking. Your charming host runs her own highly acclaimed Tuscan cookery courses so make sure you book a lesson during your stay. Freshly baked cakes, homemade jams and a variety of teas are in constant supply. There's a cool lobby with comfortable seating and plenty of books, the internet and useful local info on where to go and what to see, and cheery Mariangela is always on hand to tell you more: the best markets, the artisan workshops, the hidden corners. Fresh and inviting.

Price	€145–€160.
Rooms	4 doubles.
Meals	Restaurant 50m.
Closed	Rarely.
Directions	In historic centre. Details on booking.

Ethical Collection: Food.
See page 400 for details

Mariangela Catalani
Via delle Pinzochere 6, 50122 Florence
Mobile   +39 347 2593010
Email   info@lestanzedisantacroce.com
Web   www.lestanzedisantacroce.com

Residenza Casanuova

Live like a Florentine in the heart of the city, high above the madding crowds. The top floor of this handsome palazzo belonged to Beatrice and Massimiliano's grandmother, and is filled with her elegant taste. There are panelled doors and parquet floors, creamy walls and tall windows. Light-filled rooms are furnished with antiques, grand mirrors and pretty chandeliers, polished surfaces are dotted with china vases, walls hung with engravings, portraits and a collection of oils by great-grandfather. Calm, uncluttered bedrooms are soft and spacious, each with an amusing theme: a collection of umbrellas, hats or tin boxes. One has a magnificent Murano mirror. Breakfast on beautiful china in the handsome dining room or on the terrace before plunging into the hubbub of the city's museums, galleries and churches. The owners, with an apartment on the same floor, will help with tours, museums and shopping trips. Friendly and easy going, they're on hand when you need them or happy to leave you alone. Return to a private terrace for a glass of wine and rooftop views. *Ask about Gelato Lovers tours & tiramisu-making sessions.*

Price	€120–€170.
Rooms	5: 4 doubles, 1 single.
Meals	Restaurants within walking distance.
Closed	Never.
Directions	Exit Firenze Sud. Follow directions to city centre & S. Ambrogio market. Bus No. 6, 23, 14 or C2.

Beatrice & Massimiliano Gori
Via della Mattonaia 21, 50121 Florence

Tel	+39 0552 343413
Email	info@residenzacasanuova.it
Web	www.residenzacasanuova.it

Antica Dimora Firenze

Ring the buzzer and up you go – via the small lift or the wide stone stair. Enter the relaxed *residenza* where you come and go as you please; friendly reception is manned until 7pm. A treat to come back here, to a decanter of vin santo and a book of love stories by your bed. Perhaps even a four-poster or a jasmine-scented balcony… Italian love of detail is revealed in walls washed rose-pink and pistachio-green, in fabrics woven by local artisans, in striped sofas, silk curtains and little vases of dried lavender. Black and white 19th-century prints and antique cotto floors combine beautifully with waffle towels and walk-in showers, modems and satellite TV: it's the best of old and new. Settle down in the guest sitting room, dip into almond biscuits and a cup of tea and plan where to have dinner; all the info's there. Browse a glossy book or a magazine, choose a favourite DVD, be as private or as sociable as you like. There are homemade cakes and jams at breakfast, you are on a quietish street near the university area and it's brilliant value for the centre of Florence. *Ask about special packages. You cannot park in central Florence; ask about garage on booking.*

Price	€90–€150.
Rooms	6: 3 doubles, 3 twins.
Meals	Restaurant 30m.
Closed	Never.
Directions	In Florence "centro storico"; San Marco square, then Via San Gallo. 10-minute walk from train station.

Lea Gulmanelli
Via San Gallo 72, 50129 Florence

Tel	+39 0554 627296
Email	info@anticadimorafirenze.it
Web	www.anticadimorafirenze.it

Residenza Johlea

Experience living in a real Florentine *residenza*... a particularly charming home. The restored, late 19th-century building is in an area well-endowed with musuems (the Museum of San Marco and Michelangelo's David are just around the corner). It has good access to train and bus stations, and Laura, Giovanna or Anna will be there to greet you until 7.30pm. A lift transports you up to big bedrooms with long, shuttered windows, subtle colours and lovely fabrics. All are different and all are comfortable, with settees, polished floors and rugs, super bathrooms; all friendly and cosy. There are antiques and air conditioning, books, a shared fridge. There's no breakfast room, but you can enjoy buffet-style breakfasts in the seclusion of your own room. And there's a well stocked honesty bar available throughout the day. Like the rest of Lea's *residenze* (there are four altogether in this book and Antica Dimora Johlea, is right next door – see overleaf), this is excellent value considering its closeness to the city centre. *Ask about special packages. You cannot park in central Florence; ask about garage on booking.*

Price	€70–€120. Single €50–€80.
Rooms	8: 2 doubles, 4 twins, 1 single, 1 triple.
Meals	Restaurant 30m.
Closed	Never.
Directions	In Florence "centro storico"; San Marco square, then Via San Gallo. 10-minute walk from train station.

Lea Gulmanelli
Via San Gallo 76, 50129 Florence

Tel	+39 0554 633292
Email	johlea@johanna.it
Web	www.johanna.it

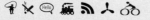

Antica Dimora Johlea

A cross between a B&B and a hotel – no room service but a friendly face on reception throughout the day – the *residenza* idea is perfect for the independent traveller. Lea Gulmanelli has got her *residenze* down to a fine art – and what's special about this one is that it has a roof terrace. Weave your way past antique pieces tucked under sloping ceilings and up to a wide, sun-flooded, pergola'd terrace for breakfasts and sundowners and a classic panorama of Florence – thrilling at night! Now that Antica Johlea has been redecorated, the entire top floor of this restored 19th-century palazzo feels bright, light and inviting. Furnishings are colourful and fresh; bedrooms – some lofty, some more intimate – have beautiful silk-canopied four-poster beds, delicate prints on walls and mozzie-protected windows. Luxurious extras include radios, WiFi and satellite TV, there's an honesty bar for drinks and polished tables for breakfast. Romantics could ask for a room with a balcony. Michelangelo's David is at the Accademia round the corner, the Duomo is a ten-minute walk. *Ask about special packages. You cannot park in central Florence; ask about garage on booking.*

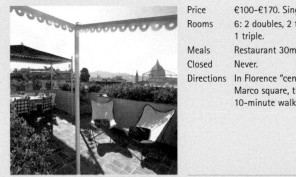

Price	€100–€170. Single €75–€120.
Rooms	6: 2 doubles, 2 twins, 1 single, 1 triple.
Meals	Restaurant 30m.
Closed	Never.
Directions	In Florence "centro storico"; San Marco square, then Via San Gallo. 10-minute walk from train station.

Lea Gulmanelli
Via San Gallo 80, 50129 Florence

Tel	+39 0554 633292
Email	anticajohlea@johanna.it
Web	www.johanna.it

Residenza Johanna I

Astonishingly good value in the historic centre of Florence — and what an attractive, friendly place to be. You really feel as though you have your own pad in town, away from tourist bustle. Owner Lea has several other *residenze* (see previous entries) which have been such a success that she and Johanna have opened this one in a lovely 19th-century palazzo, shared with notaries and an embassy. Up the lift or marble stairs to a big welcome on the second floor. Your hosts are charming, keen to make your stay a happy one. Graceful arches, polished parquet floors and soft colours give a feeling of light and space to the two parallel corridors, classical music wafts in the background and there are plenty of books and guides to browse through on rainy days. The bedrooms are big, airy and cool, silk drapes beautify beds (some four posters) and give the rooms a feeling of charm and elegance. All have excellent, stylish bathrooms. There's a new breakfast room, too. Slip out to a bar for a cappuccino and a panino before wandering happily off to the Duomo, the San Lorenzo market and the Piazza della Signora. *Ask about special packages. You cannot park in central Florence; ask about garage on booking.*

Price	€90–€120. Single €65–€80.
Rooms	10: 3 doubles, 6 twins, 1 single.
Meals	Restaurants nearby.
Closed	Never.
Directions	In Florence "centro storico"; San Marco square, then Via San Gallo. 10-minute walk from train station.

Mrs Ilanit
Via Bonifacio Lupi 14, 50129 Florence
Tel   +39 0554 81896
Email   lupi@johanna.it
Web   www.johanna.it

Relais Villa Antea

A 1900s villa a 15-minute walk from Piazza San Marco — with parking. Off a leafy residential square, close to restaurants, antique shops, botanic gardens and Russian Orthodox Church, is a friendly Italian-family concern, a lovely little find. The Antea is overseen from early morning until 8.30 at night by owner Delitta and her sister Serena — and, when they go home, housekeeper Reuben. Enjoy continental breakfast with fruits in season — even, sometimes, homemade 'bombolone' (mini doughnuts) — served at tiny round tables in a big elegant room. Up the white stone stair are large light bedrooms with tall windows and well-used parquet, decorated in yellows or greens with lavish silken drapes and net curtains, pristine covers, walk-in wardrobes, posies of plastic flowers. Extras include air con, a mini bar, WiFi and a restaurant guide put together by Delitta. Beds are extra-king in size and bathrooms are vast, with super-charged showers. Through the side gate is a courtyard shaded by horse-chestnut trees, and a pebbled courtyard makes a tranquil spot for an aperitivo before a night on the town.

Price	€100–€180.
Rooms	6 doubles.
Meals	Restaurant 2-minute walk.
Closed	Rarely.
Directions	15-minute walk from S. Lorenzo, Accademia or Piazza San Marco. Bus No. 12 from Piazza della Stazione to Via Ruffini.

Carlotta Ferrari
Via Puccinotti 46, 50129 Florence

Tel	+39 0554 84106
Email	info@villaantea.com
Web	www.villaantea.com

Villa La Sosta

It's a 15-minute walk to the Duomo, yet the 1892 villa on the Montughi hill stands in large landscaped gardens where songbirds lull you to sleep. The mansard-tower sitting room with sofas, books and views is a lofty place in which to relax, and there's billiards. Bedrooms, with large windows and wooden shutters, are equally stylish with striking toile de Jouy or checks and dark Tuscan pieces. Interesting, too, are the artefacts – ivory carvings and wooden statues – gathered from the Fantonis' days in Africa; the family ran a banana plantation there. Simple breakfast is served outside under an ivy-covered pergola in summer or in the dining room, just off the family's bright sitting room; over coffee the young, affable Antonio and Giusi – a brother-and-sister team – help you plan your stay. If the city's treasures start to pall they will organise a day in the vineyards or local pottery villages. There's parking off the main road and the number 25 bus, which stops outside the gates, will ferry you into the city or up into the hills. *Gluten-free breakfasts available.*

Price	€94-€130. Singles €85-€105. Triple €130-€160. Quadruple €160-€190.
Rooms	5: 3 doubles, 1 triple, 1 quadruple.
Meals	Restaurants 800m.
Closed	Rarely.
Directions	Signs for Centro & Piazza della Libertà, then Via Bolognese; villa on left. Bus No. 25 from r'way station; get off 800m after Via Bolognese begins, just before Total petrol station. Parking.

Antonio & Giuseppina Fantoni
Via Bolognese 83, 50139 Florence
Tel   +39 0554 95073
Email   lasosta@lasosta.com
Web   www.villalasosta.com

Torre di Bellosguardo

Breathtaking in its beauty and ancient dignity. The entrance hall is cavernous, glorious, with a painted ceiling and an ocean of floor; the view reaches through a vast, plaster-crumbling sun room to the garden. Imposing, mellow buildings, gorgeous gardens fashioned by a friend of Dante, magical views of Florence. A water feature meanders along a stone terrace, a twisted wisteria shades the walkway to a kitchen garden, there are goats, ponies and rabbits. A pool, gym and cane tables and chairs occupy the old orangery while another pool settles into a perfect lawn. Most of the bedrooms can be reached by lift but the tower suite, with windows on all sides, demands a long climb. The bedrooms defy modern convention and are magnificent in their simplicity, the furniture richly authentic, the views infinite. But do ask for a room with one of the newer beds. Signor Franchetti is often here, and his manners and his English are impeccable – unlike those of the irrepressible pink parrot. All this, and Florence a 30-minute walk, or a 10-minute cab ride, down the hill.

Telephone & internet connection in each room.

Price	€290. Single €160. Suites €340-€390.
Rooms	16: 8 doubles, 1 single, 7 suites.
Meals	Breakfast not included in winter €20-€25. Restaurant 2km.
Closed	Rarely.
Directions	A1 exit Firenze Certosa for Porta Romana/Centro; left at Porta Romana on Via Ugo Foscolo; keep right & take Via Piana to end; right into Via Roti Michelozzi.

Amerigo Franchetti
Via Roti Michelozzi 2,
50124 Florence

Tel	+39 0552 298145
Email	info@torrebellosguardo.com
Web	www.torrebellosguardo.com

Residenza Strozzi

Down a grand, pine-swayed drive through immaculately maintained, back-in-time grounds, two strikingly different, perfectly put together apartments next to the famous Villa Strozzi (the family, who live on-site, were peers of the Medici). Both feel warm, cosy, and have heaps of period charm. The Stables is grandly 18th-century, bright and cheery, with parquet flooring and original tiles, each pen, still partitioned with its original railings, now serving a new purpose: one a creamy, wood-panelled bedroom with a giant bed, another a dining room, the third a sitting room with a beautiful antique rug and a chic grey sofa. Upstairs, the old grooms' quarters have become a mezzanine living room with day beds and writing table. The Chapel is smaller, its nave now a bedroom with frolicking angels fresco'd high above you; the vestry is a sitting room, its walls hung with old botanic prints; two antique sofas invite you in. Superb bathrooms feature original ceramics, cute kitchens come fully stocked. There are also two beautiful B&B rooms in the villa itself. Ten minutes from the centre of Florence, and the views are pure Tuscan. *Min. stay two nights. Special deals for honeymooners.*

Price	€80-€120. Chapel & stables €85-€130 (€650-€950 per week). Extra bed €25.
Rooms	2 + 2: 2 doubles. Chapel for 2-4, Stables for 2-5.
Meals	Dinner €30-€50. Restaurant 300m.
Closed	Never.
Directions	Bus No. 10 or 67 dir. Settignano; get off at Ponte a Mensola or Bus No. 17 dir. Verga; get off at Verga 2.

Guido Casalone
Via Madonna delle Grazie 18/20,
50135 Florence
Tel   +39 0556 10068
Email   info@residenzastrozzi.it
Web   www.residenzastrozzi.it

Entry 141 Map 8

Relais Villa L'Olmo

With a bit of luck you will be greeted by Claudia, a lovely German lady of considerable charm, married to a Florentine whose family have owned the property since 1700. The Relais is a clutch of immaculately converted apartments, all looking down over the valley, all shamelessly *di lusso*. Imagine softly-lit yellow walls beneath chunky Tuscan beamed ceilings, nicely designed kitchenettes, white china on yellow cloths, smartly checked sofas, glass-topped tables, fresh flowers – even a private pool (and plastic loungers) for the two villas if you can't face splashing with others in the main one. And there's a new communal barbecue, so you can mingle if you wish. Claudia runs a warmly efficient reception and rents out mountain bikes and mobile phones; she organises babysitting, cookery classes and wine tastings, too. There's a cheerful restaurant and a pizzeria, and farm products for sale, Florence is 20 minutes away by car or bus and it's heaven for families. *Special rates for local golf, tennis & riding clubs.*

Price	Villas €190–€360. Apts €80–€245. Farmhouse €210–€470.
Rooms	11: 2 villas for 2-4; 8 apts for 2-5; 1 farmhouse for 6-8.
Meals	Breakfast €12. Restaurants nearby.
Closed	Never.
Directions	A1 exit Firenze-Certosa; at r'bout, signs for Tavarnuzze; there, left to Impruneta. Track on right, signed to villa; 200m past sign for Impruneta.

Claudia & Alberto Giannotti
Via Impruneta per Tavarnuzze 19,
50023 Impruneta
Tel +39 0552 311311
Email florence.chianti@dada.it
Web www.relaisfarmholiday.it

Villa di Riboia

Step over the threshold and into the arms of this Italian family. Three generations have lived in the 16th-century villa; you will be welcomed as friends and children will be adored. Wander where you will, among the comfy sofas and antiques of the sitting room, where doors open to the garden, beneath the frescoes (the work of Elisabetta's uncle) of the formal dining room, or over a cup of coffee in the rustic kitchen. For peaceful moments there's a guest sitting room at the top of the grand stone staircase. Beamed and tiled bedrooms ooze traditional comfort with their dark chests and iron bedsteads, patterned rugs and woodland murals, bathrooms are old-fashioned but spacious, fresh flowers abound. There are walks and cycle routes from the house, and the treasures of medieval Impruneta just up the road. Return to an Italian garden with steep steps in parts, a play area, a pool and views towards Florence. Dine on produce from their small organic farm under the gazebo in the summer. Embrace for a brief while Italian family life. *Minimum stay two nights. Welcome dinner with family for four-night stays.*

Price	€80–€90. Triple €110–€120.
Rooms	2: 1 double, 1 triple.
Meals	Dinner with wine, €20.
Closed	Never.
Directions	A1 exit Certosa dir. Firenze; right at lights in Galluzzo main square onto Viale Gherardo Silvani dir. Impruneta; pass Pozzolatico, then Mezzomonte; after Monteoriolo 1st sharp right onto Via di Riboia; on right.

Elisabetta Renzoni
Via di Riboia 2a,
50023 Monteoriolo

Tel +39 0552 374038
Email info@villadiriboia.it
Web www.villadiriboia.it

Entry 143 Map 8

La Canigiana Agriturismo

With Florence's Duomo glistening in the distance across a carpet of olive groves, this Tuscan farmhouse has the best of both worlds. Set amongst the sparkling air of the Chianti hills, it is 15 minutes from that glorious city. Producing organic olive oil, the farm has been in Alessandra's family for over 100 years. Her family and father still live on the estate – let yourself to be swept into their warm embrace. The apartments (with private entrances) share those glorious views. A cut above those of the average agriturismo, the bedrooms here are country comfortable with colourful bedspreads, wrought-iron beds, posies of fresh flowers and prints on white walls. Traditionally tiled floors, beams and shuttered windows add charm. Kitchen areas incorporated into the living room are fine for holiday cooking and there are pretty tablecloths for dinner; choose the ground-floor apartment for its lovely terrace, or take the two together. Those Tuscan jewels – Pisa, Lucca, Siena, Florence – are under an hour away, and there's an orchard-enclosed pool for your return. Bliss. *Minimum stay three nights.*

Price	€550–€750. Whole house €1,200–€1,400. Prices per week.
Rooms	2 apartments for 3.
Meals	Restaurant 1.5km.
Closed	December–February.
Directions	From A1 exit Firenze-Certosa dir. Firenze. At lights left dir. Montespertoli. Junc. after 6km, right to La Romola. House after 1km on left; signed.

Ethical Collection: Environment.
See page 400 for details

Alessandra Calligaris
Via Treggiaia 146, 50020 La Romola

Tel	+39 0558 242425
Email	info@lacanigiana.it
Web	www.lacanigiana.it

Azienda Agricola La Capannaccia

Originating in 1753, revived phoenix-like from an 18th-century fire, commandeered by the Americans in WW2, and renovated over 30 years by the current family, this country pile of an agriturismo (Chianti grapes, organic olive oil) is steeped in history and character. No pool but a large lawned garden with a hot tub to share, heaps of olive groves and vineyards to stroll, farm machinery all around and a stunning view from the top of the hill. As for the apartments, two occupy an extended wing, the other is in the main house. They exude an elegant simplicity with their solid wrought-iron beds, new fireplaces, mottled, clotted cream paint schemes, cotta floors, and classic, cosy kitchens. The flat in the main house is decoratively busier, with its many antiques and Murano glass chandeliers. Your hosts, the charming Luca and his parents, are warm, fun, love horses (the stables house six, plus two shaky-kneed foals) and happy to advise on everything; they'll even drive you to the restaurant down the road. Beautifully positioned for day trips to Florence, and a riding school nearby. *Minimum stay two nights.*

Price	€80-€250.
Rooms	3 apartments: 1 for 2, 2 for 2-4.
Meals	Basic breakfast included. Restaurants 1km.
Closed	Rarely.
Directions	A1 exit FI-Certosa dir. Florence. Left at 2nd lights; dir. San Casciano. After 4km, over x-roads to Scandicci. 2nd left, right into Via di Vingone; after approx. 4km right into Via Francesca, on for 1km, then right Via delle Selve; 1st house.

Luca Bini
Via delle Selve 5, 50018 Scandicci
Tel   +39 0552 41839
Email   info@lacapannaccia.com
Web   www.lacapannaccia.com

Entry 145   Map 8

Dimora Storica Villa Il Poggiale

This 16th-century villa is so lovely it's impossible to know where to start. Breathe in the scent of old-fashioned roses from a seat on the Renaissance loggia. Wander through the olive trees to the pool (note: some traffic hum from the next-door road). Retreat into the house for some 1800s elegance. Much loved, full of memories, this is the childhood home of two brothers, Johanan and Nathanel Vitta, who devoted two years to its restoration. Rooms are big, beautiful, full of light, and everything has been kept as it was. An oil painting of the Vittas' grandmother welcomes you as you enter; another, Machiavelli by Gilardi, hangs in the salon. Bedrooms are all different, all striking. Some have frescoes and silk curtains, others have fabrics commissioned from a small Tuscan workshop. The attention to detail is superb but in no way overpowering. The independent apartment is a restored farmhouse with original fireplace and stunning views over the rose garden. The staff really make you feel like wanted guests, breakfast is buffet, dinner is in the restored olive store and Florence is a 20-minute drive. *Honesty bar. Well-being & fitness area.*

Price	€130–€240. Suites €195–€240. Apartment €310.
Rooms	24 + 1: 21 doubles, 3 suites. Apartment for 5.
Meals	Dinner €30. Wine from €8. Restaurants 300m.
Closed	February.
Directions	Rome A1 exit Firenze-Certosa; superstrada Firenze-Siena, exit San Casciano; signs for Cerbaia-Empoli. After 3km, signs on left.

Monica Cozzi
Via Empolese 69,
50026 San Casciano

Tel	+39 0558 828311
Email	villailpoggiale@villailpoggiale.it
Web	www.villailpoggiale.it

Il Poggetto

A deliciously green and sunny Tuscan hilltop, surrounded by vineyards and olive groves. Once through the electronic gates, you'll be captivated by the views. The gardens are delightful, too: three hectares of rose-ridden lawns, fruit trees, azaleas and heather (always something in flower), with pines and cypresses for shade and a terrace dotted with lemon and mandarin trees. Ivana and her family moved to the 400-year-old *casa colonica* in 1974 and have renovated beautifully, using original and traditional materials. The apartments are attractive, uncluttered and full of light. All have big comfortable beds, antique furniture and private patios. La Loggia was once a hay barn; the huge, raftered living/dining area is superb and the old triangular air bricks are still in place. La Cipressaia, characteristically Tuscan in style and very private, is a conversion of the stable block, and sleeps five. Il Gelsomino, named after the jasmine outside the door, and La Pergola join each other. Everyone has use of the pool, which is set apart in a stunning position: you can watch the sun rise and set from your lounger. *Minimum stay three nights.*

Price	€70–€90 (€355–€1,120 per week).
Rooms	4 apartments for 2-5.
Meals	Restaurants 1km.
Closed	Rarely.
Directions	Milano-Roma A1 exit Scandicci; take Pisa-Livorno exit Ginestra; right for Montespertoli. In Baccaiano left uphill to Montagnana; signed after 1km. 1st left into Via Montegufoni, left at the church into Via del Poggetto.

Andrea Boretti & Ivana Pieri
Via del Poggetto 14,
50025 Montespertoli
Mobile   +39 339 3784383
Email   info@poggetto.it
Web   www.poggetto.it

Locanda le Boscarecce

A sparkling star in Tuscany's firmament. Susanna is full of life and laughter, her daughter Swan is equally warm – and an accomplished sommelier. Swan's husband, Chef Bartolo from Sicily, concocts dishes that people travel miles to discover. Fruits, vegetables, herbs and olive oil come from the grounds, there are 450 wines in the cellar and, outside, the biggest pizza oven you will ever see. The 200-year-old *locanda* is on a ridge, embracing fields and farms and heavenly sunsets. Bedrooms in the farmhouse are part rustic, part refined, with bold colours and pretty lace at the windows, each space unique. Beds are modern and comfortable, furniture 18th and 19th-century, bathrooms have bath tubs *and* showers, and some rooms have kitchenettes. Tennis, cycling, swimming – all are possible – or you may relax under the dreamy gazebo and dip into a book on art history from the library. Even the location is enticing, in a charmed triangle formed by Florence, Siena and Pisa. Heart-warming, creative, special. *Ask about cookery courses, wine, cheese & olive oil tastings.*

Price	€100–€145.
Rooms	12: 8 doubles, 3 triples, 1 quadruple.
Meals	Dinner €25. Restaurant 3km.
Closed	20 November–26 December.
Directions	From Castelfiorento, Via A. Vivaldi for Renai; right after dirt road, signed. Over bridge, road curves left, stay on paved road for 'di Pizzacalada'; T-junc. left; signed.

Ethical Collection: Community; Food.
See page 400 for details

Susanna Ballerini
Via Renai 19, 50051 Castelfiorentino
Tel +39 0571 61280
Email info@leboscarecce.com
Web www.leboscarecce.com

Fattoria Barbialla Nuova

An organic farm specialising in Chianina cattle, fragrant olive oil and white truffles; utter tranquillity 30 minutes from Florence. Delightful Guido and others have worked hard to provide somewhere stylish, bio-sensitive and beautiful to stay on this 500-hectare nature reserve/farm. Three farmhouses here, all with sweeping views, all on the top of a hill. Le Trosce – one floor but several levels – is for one big party. Doderi is divided into three apartments, simple and minimalist; Gianluca's bedcovers and 60s retro furniture add style, originality and colour. The apartments in Brentina, deeper in the woods, are a touch more rustic – designers will love their whitewashed simplicity. All have books, music and delicious bathrooms. Outside: chic patios and pools. Down at the farm: fresh produce, Slow Food dining, orchards, pigs and hens. Nature trails entice you to explore, so forage in the cool shade of the woods in the truffle zone or stumble upon a ruined 'casa colonica'. Lovely old Montaione, San Miniato and Certaldo Alto have festivals throughout the year. *Minimum stay three to seven nights.*

Price	Apts €450–€650 for 2; €680–€1,050 for 4; €850–€1,320 for 6. Farmhouse €1,420–€2,000. Prices per week.
Rooms	7 apartments: 2 for 2, 3 for 4, 2 for 6. Farmhouse for 8.
Meals	Restaurant 3km.
Closed	10 January–10 March.
Directions	From S.G.C. FI-PI-LI exit San Miniato; up hill to Montaione; 4km after Corazzano, on right opp. white 6km sign.

Àrghilo Società Agricola
Via Casastrada 49, 50050 Montaione

Tel	+39 0571 677259
Email	info@barbiallanuova.it
Web	www.barbiallanuova.it

Ethical Collection: Environment; Food.
See page 400 for details

B&B Del Giglio

You'll fall under Del Giglio's spell. What with the beauty, the history and your hosts' warmth and zest, you won't have a chance of resisting. Roberto and Laura bought the 12th-century house, part of delightful San Donato's fortified walls, years ago and have been working on it devotedly ever since. In the apartment, where polished antiques and Roberto's works of art blend beautifully with white walls and chunky rafters, you get a small dark wood kitchen (note, delicious continental breakfast is provided, brought to you on the terrace or the living room) and simple, comfortable bedrooms, one double, one twin, sharing a bathroom tiled with Valentino bluebirds; the double also has a basin and wc. No washing machine – but there is a tiny gym! Downstairs – through a courtyard with a fascinating little wine cellar – is a perfect garden, with resident tortoises and breathtaking views to San Gimignano. If you don't want to eat out, have a barbecue under the ancient olives. Once through the gate, there's walking for miles, among the olive groves and the rolling hills. Exceptional place, and people. *Minimum stay two nights.*

Price	€85. €170 for 4.
Rooms	Apartment for 2-4.
Meals	Restaurants 50m.
Closed	Rarely.
Directions	Florence-Siena road (4 corsi) to San Donato; dir. centre; park in any of free car parks then 3-minute walk.

Roberto Cresti
Via del Giglio 78,
50028 San Donato in Poggio
Tel   +39 0558 072894
Email   info@delgiglio.it
Web   www.delgiglio.it

Fattoria Le Filigare

Overlooking vineyards and green-cloaked hills, pretty gardens, shady patios and a statue-strewn terrace is this beautiful Tuscan estate. Now the Burchis have converted part of the main villa and farm buildings into stylish apartments with an authentic feel, owner Deborah combining traditional materials with an architect's feeling for space. Beams, raftered ceilings, archways, terracotta floors, cool white walls set the tone, rustic furniture does the rest – simple wrought-iron or wooden beds (some four-poster), painted wardrobes, copper pans. Contemporary sofas and art works add elegance; living areas are open-plan with smart kitchens tucked into corners. Some apartments have patios, others mezzanines, others jacuzzis. A further seven apartments are at Girasole, 200m up the hill: more gardens, more heavenly views. You get a summer swimming pool, a tennis court, a peacock (just one!), a play area, and wine tastings and visits to the cellars that are included in the price. Shops and restaurants are down the bumpy track, then a ten-minute drive. *Minimum stay two nights; one week in high season.*

Price	€650-€890 per week.
Rooms	7 apartments for 2, 4 or 6. Girasole: 7 apartments.
Meals	Restaurants 2km & 4km.
Closed	Rarely.
Directions	A1 exit Certosa; superstrada for Siena; exit San Donato in Poggio; well signed from Panzano road; 2km bumpy track.

Alessandro Cassetti Burchi
Loc. Le Filigare,
50020 Barberino Val d'Elsa

Tel	+39 0558 072796
Email	info@lefiligare.it
Web	www.lefiligare.it

Entry 151 Map 8

Fattoria Casa Sola Agriturismo

Atop a hill of lush greenery, this is exquisite. Count Giuseppe Gambaro and his wife Claudia tend the wine and oil production, as the family has done for generations – and the gates are shut at night to prevent wild boar from snaffling them! The two-storey apartments, 700 metres from the main house and pool, are cool, fresh, comfortable with whitewashed walls, tiled floors, traditional country bedspreads and vineyard views. Simply named Red, White and Yellow, each has a garden with roses to match. Your hosts are charming and courteous and passionate about their wine, and present you with a bottle on arrival. Once a week they take guests round the vineyards and wine-making facilities, rounding off the visit with a glass of Vin Santo and *cantucci* biscuits. Claudia is fond of children and often organises races and games. For grown-ups there are cookery and watercolour classes; you can also play tennis and horse ride nearby. Sample the creations of a personal chef; eat out in Barberino and San Donato. Or drive the 30 minutes to Florence or Siena. Perfection. *Minimum stay two nights. Free vineyard tours & wine-tasting.*

Price	€770–€2,430 per week.
Rooms	10 apartments: 3 for 2-3, 3 for 4, 3 for 4-6, 1 for 8.
Meals	Breakfast €5. Chef available, by arrangement. Restaurant 5km (special price for Casa Sola guests).
Closed	Rarely.
Directions	Firenze–Siena exit San Donato in Poggio; SS101 past S. Donato church; 1.5km, right to Cortine & Casa Sola.

Giuseppe Gambaro
Via Cortine 5,
50021 Barberino Val d'Elsa

Tel	+39 0558 075028
Email	vacanze@fattoriacasasola.com
Web	www.fattoriacasasola.com

Castello di Pastine

Enthroned atop an olive-terraced hill on a Chianti vineyard sea, this 14th-century castello encloses a number of comfortable self-catering apartments in two big ancient buildings and a house tucked away in the woods. Acres of landscaped grounds, wonderfully magical, perfectly maintained, have long and spectacular views past statues and cypresses, secret hideaways and jogging trails. There's a huge pool with snazzy parasols and pergolas, multiple terraces with barbecues, slides, swings, ping pong, volleyball and floodlit tennis, and a hot tub for the lazy. All feels nicely countrified and cared for, with terracotta floors, exposed brickwork, plentiful beams, big sofas piled with cushions, eclectic prints – testament to family travels – and well-stocked kitchens. Casa Colonica can be rented as a single unit but our favourite is the house that hides in the woods, one wall was once part of a cave. Young Guido knows all the secrets and stories: the Castello is his pride and joy. Cycle tours of vineyards beckon, San Gimignano is close, Florence is half an hour. A paradise for families. *Min. stay three-seven nights.*

Price	€68–€105. Apts €475–€1,400; cottage €1,290–€1,750 per week.
Rooms	8: 7 apts for 2-5, 1 cottage for 6.
Meals	Occasional dinner. Restaurant 3km.
Closed	Rarely.
Directions	A1 exit Firenze Certosa; SS Firenze-Siena, exit Tavarnelle Val di Pesa. Thro' town dir. Barberino Val d'Elsa; provincial rd No. 50 right; signs for Vico d'Elsa-Sant'Appiano. Left; signs for Pastine. 1st fork, right; right.

Guido Materi
2-4 strada di Vico - Pastine,
50021 Barberino Val d'Elsa

Tel	+39 0558 075176
Email	castellodipastine@gmail.com
Web	www.pastine.it

Sovigliano

A stone's throw from Tavarnelle, down a country lane, this ancient farmhouse stands among vineyards, olives, cypresses and pines. Though the setting is secluded you are in the middle of some of the most popular touring country in Italy; on a clear day, you can see the towers of San Gimignano. Every view is breathtaking. Sovigliano has been renovated by the family with deep respect for the architecture and traditional materials. The self-catering apartments – one palatial, with a glorious stone fireplace – are most attractive, all white walls, ancient rafters, good beds and country antiques. If you choose to go B&B, the double rooms are equally charming. The big rustic kitchen, with a private fridge for each guest, makes it easy to meet others should you wish to do so, and dinner can be arranged. Relax under the pines in the garden, take a dip in the pool, work out in the exercise area (here children must be supervised), enjoy a pre-dinner drink. Vin Santo, olive oil and grappa are for sale. Signora is most helpful and will insist you return!

Price	€135–€170. Apartments €158–€410.
Rooms	4 + 4: 2 doubles, 2 twins. 4 apartments for 2-4 (some rooms connect to make apt for 8).
Meals	Dinner with wine, €35.
Closed	Rarely.
Directions	SS2 Firenze-Siena exit Tavarnelle; on entering town, right & follow Marcialla. Sovigliano just out of town: left at 4th r'bout down lane signed Magliano; follow signs.

Patrizia Bicego
Strada Magliano 9,
50028 Tavarnelle Val di Pesa

Tel	+39 0558 076217
Email	info@sovigliano.com
Web	www.sovigliano.com

Palazzo Malaspina B&B

A special find. The medieval walls of San Donato are tucked away behind an arch, while the Renaissance façade belies a modern and spacious interior. Enter the big hall with its fine wooden doors and stylish staircase: sense the history. The palazzo is a listed building and Maria is enthusiastic about all she has to offer. She was born here, in Room 3, and now lives in the apartment downstairs with her pet dog. Breakfast, in your bedroom – or at a huge table on white runners and china – includes fruits, cheeses, croissants, jams. (Do try her delectable chocolate cakes.) Each of the bedrooms has a classic Tuscan charm with family antiques and fabrics from the House of Busatti in Anghiari. Luxurious bathrooms have mosaic tiles and huge white towels bearing the palazzo's emblem; three have a jacuzzi. From some of the rooms you can just glimpse the towers of San Gimignano, from others, little gardens that guide the eye to the countryside beyond and its treasures. There's a very small garden to the rear. Drop your baggage off outside; car parks are a five-minute walk.

Price	€70–€110.
Rooms	5: 3 doubles, 2 twins/doubles.
Meals	Restaurant next door.
Closed	Occasionally.
Directions	A1 exit Firenze-Certosa; SS Firenze-Siena for Siena; exit San Donato; signs for San Donato; thro' arch into "centro storico"; Via del Giglio, on left.

Maria Pellizzari
Via del Giglio 35,
50020 San Donato in Poggio

Tel   +39 0558 072946
Email   info@palazzomalaspina.it
Web   www.palazzomalaspina.it

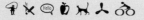

Villa Le Barone

The Marchesa, who has now passed away, wrote a delightful book about her passion for the countryside and the lovely old manor house that has been in the family for 400 years. It's a gorgeous place, with old-fashioned comforts and no TVs: truly unspoiled. Staff bustle with an easy-going friendliness under the supervision of the owners, a charming couple who spend part of the year here. Bedrooms vary, some in the villa, others in outbuildings around the estate; some are small, others on a grand scale; most have a warm Tuscan style and some charming pieces of furniture. The sitting room has an irresistible comfort, with a log fire for chilly nights and vast coffee-table books to whet your appetite for Italy. The airy dining room – once the wine cellar – is a fitting setting for leisurely Tuscan dinners and local wines. The gardens are no less appealing, full of roses, olive trees and lavender; you have tennis for the active, a parasoled terrace for the idle and a pool that is far too seductive for anyone intent upon a cultural holiday. That said, do visit the exquisite church of San Leolino, a step away.

Price	€180–€345.
	Half-board €110–€190 p.p.
Rooms	30: 29 twins/doubles, 1 single.
Meals	Light lunch €20. Dinner €39.
	Wine from €20.
Closed	Only three rooms open Nov–March.
Directions	Panzano (not marked on all maps) 7km from Greve in Chianti; hotel signed from Greve.

Aloisi de Larderel
Via San Leolino 19,
50020 Panzano in Chianti

Tel	+39 0558 52621
Email	info@villalebarone.com
Web	www.villalebarone.com

Fattoria Viticcio Agriturismo

You're on a hill above Greve, in Chianti Classico country. Alessandro's father, Lucio, bought the farm in the 1960s and set about producing fine wines for export. It was a brave move at a time when people were moving away from the countryside. Now the vineyard has an international reputation. Visit the vaults and taste for yourself. Nicoletta (also a sommelier) runs the agriturismo, helped by their daughters. The apartments are named after them – Beatrice, Arianna, Camilla – and lie at the heart of the estate. Much thought has gone into them. Plain-coloured walls, brick arches, beams and terracotta floor tiles give an attractively simple air, furniture is a charming blend of contemporary and antique pieces; kitchens are superb. One pool rests in a walled garden, with a small play area for children; a second lies within the olive groves. You may hear the occasional tractor – this is a working estate – but the farmyard is tidy and well-kept, with tubs of flowers everywhere. There's a family atmosphere, too, and wonderful views. *Minimum stay two nights; one week in apartments.*

Price	€115.
	Apartments €790–€1,200 per week.
Rooms	3 + 5: 2 doubles, 1 twin.
	5 apartments: 3 for 2-4, 2 for 4-6.
Meals	Breakfast €5. Restaurants 1km.
Closed	Rarely.
Directions	A1 exit Firenze Sud; via Chiantigiana SS222. In Greve, signs for pool ("piscina"): over small bridge past pool on right; take track for Viticcio, signed.

Alessandro Landini & Nicoletta Florio Deleuze
Via San Cresci 12a,
50022 Greve in Chianti

Tel	+39 0558 54210
Email	info@fattoriaviticcio.com
Web	www.fattoriaviticcio.com

Entry 157   Map 8

Corte di Valle Agriturismo

The British ambassador in the 1920s, Sir Ronald Graham (a reputed pro-fascist) lived here, and what was good enough for him... But it did go downhill, and Marco, who left banking after 35 years to pursue this dream, has had to pour money into it as well as affection. He has succeeded brilliantly: the old Tuscan farmhouse is a handsome, even stylish, place to stay and has not lost any of its dignity and character. Bedrooms are large, the décor is uncluttered but lovely, the shower rooms are immaculate and the beds very comfortable. The room at the top has its own terrace – an idyllic spot from which to watch the sun set and rise. Downstairs is a huge sitting room where you can gather with your friends and a cavernous hall; outside is a pool with a view. Occasional dinner is served in their hunting lodge restaurant across the yard. Marco enjoys food and wine and may offer tastings of his own vintage; Irene, gentle and shy, is proud of the herbs and saffrons she sells. All around you lies the lush and lovely Chianti countryside, and the idyllic little town of Greve is five kilometres away.

Price	€95–€115.
Rooms	8: 7 doubles, 1 twin.
Meals	Dinner €25–€30, on request. Wine €7–€9.
Closed	Rarely.
Directions	5km north of Greve in Chianti, on west side of S222, north of turning to Passo dei Paccorai. House visible from road.

Marco & Irene Mazzoni
Via Chiantigiana, Loc. Le Bolle,
50022 Greve in Chianti
Tel   +39 0558 53939
Email   cortedivalle@cortedivalle.it
Web   www.cortedivalle.it

Podere Torre Agriturismo

At the end of a long bumpy track, a little farmstead that exudes contentment; no wonder the roses do so well. They are coaxed and charmed by Cecilia, who has the same effect upon her guests. Hers is no run-of-the-mill B&B: here everything is intuitively presented. Next to the main house is 'La Stalla', a cool, ground-floor bedroom in the watchtower. 'Concimaia' (the name referring to its unpoetical origins as a manure store) is reached across a flowery terrace with table and chairs for two, and interconnects with 'Fienile', an apartment in the small barn – a useful set-up for a party of four. Cecilia gives you fluffy towels, cotton bed linen, blocks of Marsiglia soap, lavender bags and candles for evening relaxation. Swallows nest in the laundry room, where you can wash and iron, and you get the basics needed to rustle up a picnic supper and eat outside. Cecilia and Paolo run a small vineyard producing good-quality wine and olive oil. There is a taverna a mile away that you can walk to; at breakfast time we advise you stay put and be spoiled.

Price	€70 (€450 per week).
	Apartment €85 (€550 per week).
Rooms	2 + 1: 2 doubles. Apartment for 2.
Meals	Breakfast €10. Restaurants 2km.
Closed	Rarely.
Directions	From Greve in Chianti for Pieve di San Cresci; 3km on minor road, signed.

Cecilia Torrigiani
Via di San Cresci 29,
50022 Greve in Chianti

Tel	+39 0558 544714
Email	poderetorre@greve-in-chianti.com
Web	www.greve-in-chianti.com/poderetorre.htm

Podere La Casellina Agriturismo

Come here for life's slow rhythm – and for the gentle family. The Bensi grandparents moved here in 1936 (see picture below), when the local church put the *podere* into their careful hands; the family and young Michelangelo have worked the land ever since. Anyone wishing to experience the 'real' side of peasant life (*vita del contadino*) – and learn something of its history – should come here; so little has changed at La Casellina, inside or out, and there are few concessions to modernity. Guest bedrooms are in the old hayloft and stables, simple but comfortable, with views of the little San Pietro al Terreno church. The landscape, between Chianti and Valdarno, is exquisite; you have the chestnut woods of the Chianti mountains to one side, and oaks, cypresses and olives to the other. Learn to prune vines and pick olives on the farm; gather chestnuts and wild mushrooms in the woods. Go riding or biking, then return to Grandma's recipes – the grape flan is delicious. There's passion fruit for breakfast, and Michelangelo is a dear who speaks brilliant English. *Minimum stay two nights.*

Price	From €76.
Rooms	3 doubles.
Meals	Lunch with wine, €18.
	Dinner with wine, €24.
Closed	Rarely.
Directions	A1 exit Incisa; Figline road. Just before Figline, right to Brollo & Poggio alla Croce; 5km, on right.

Michelangelo & Silvia Bensi
Via Poggio alla Croce 60,
50063 Figline Valdarno

Tel	+39 0559 500070
Email	poderelacasellina@tin.it
Web	www.poderelacasellina.it

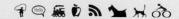

Locanda Casanuova

"The beauty of simplicity" is their motto. Casanuova was once a monastery, then an orphanage, then a farmhouse… Ursula and Thierry took it on years ago, rescuing the house and returning the land to organic use. They're a generous couple and the whole place exudes an air of serene simplicity. Delicious fresh menus are chalked up on the board each day and meals, served at large tables under the vines, are happy events. Off the refrectory is a library where you can pore over trekking maps at a big round table. The bedrooms, spotless and charming, are furnished with natural fabrics (and no TVs!) and have a serenely monastic air; bathrooms are equally delightful. By the old mulberry tree 800m from the house are two pleasing apartments for self-caterers, one up, one down. As well as being a talented cook, Ursula is an imaginative gardener: green secret corners, inviting terraces and unusual plants abound. Best of all, in a clearing in the woods, is an enchanting swimming 'pond', a natural, self-cleansing pool with lily pads, surrounded by decking, with a paddling pool for tinies alongside. *Yoga.*

Price	€90–€100. Half-board €80 p.p. Apartments €75–€100.
Rooms	18 + 2: 12 doubles, 4 singles, 2 suites. 2 apts: 1 for 2, 1 for 4.
Meals	Dinner €25–€30. Wine €10–€35.
Closed	7 November–15 March.
Directions	A1 from Rome exit Incisa Valdarno; dir. Figline, right for Poggio alla Croce; left before Poggio alla Croce for San Martino; on for 2km.

Ethical Collection: Food.
See page 400 for details

Ursula & Thierry Besançon
San Martino Altoreggi 52,
50063 Figline Valdarno

Tel	+39 0559 500027
Email	locanda@casanuova-toscana.it
Web	www.casanuova.info

Podere Le Mezzelune

A treat to find this house in the north Maremma. After a long, winding track, two big wooden gates; ring the bell and they swing open to reveal a tree-lined drive. This is a typical Tuscan, late 1800s farmhouse turned into a delightful B&B where you feel as though you are visiting friends. Downstairs, a huge dining table for breakfasts of fresh, home-baked pastries and seasonal fruits, and an open fire for winter. Upstairs are the bedrooms, two looking out to sea, all with their own terrace and a view. Painted white and cream, they have linen curtains, wooden floors, furniture made to the owners' design, candles, fresh fruit and vintage wooden pegs hung with an antique shawl. Bathrooms, too, are perfect. For longer stays there are two little private cottages in the garden, comfortable with open fires, dishwashers and beams. You are surrounded by cypresses, vines, flowers, herbs, 2,000 olive trees and seven hectares of woodland. This is a magical place, five minutes from the historic centre, 15 minutes from the sea and blissfully free of newspapers and TV. *Minimum stay two nights.*

Price	€160–€180. Cottages €180–€195.
Rooms	4 + 2: 4 twins/doubles. 2 cottages for 2-4.
Meals	Breakfast €13 for self-caterers, by arrangement. Restaurants 3km.
Closed	15 December–January.
Directions	SS1 exit La California towards Bibbona. Just before village, signs for Le Mezzelune on left. Follow for approx. 2km to farm gate.

Azienda Agricola Le Mezzelune
Via Mezzelune 126,
57020 Bibbona

Tel	+39 0586 670266
Email	relais@lemezzelune.it
Web	www.lemezzelune.it

Poggio ai Santi

International sports presenter Dominique knows what people yearn for when they're away. At Poggio ai Santi, he and his wife are channelling all their imagination and flair into providing it. Here are three buildings – the main house 19th-century, the other two modern – set among roses and with spellbinding sea views. Uneven paths wind through fabulously relaxing gardens planted with a hundred exotic trees; there's even a painting hut, so help yourself to art supplies and have a go at capturing the views. As for the restaurant, it is presided over by Danny, an exciting and passionate Michelin-starred chef. To eat here is a cosmic experience: the seafood and lobster bisque will linger long in the memory! Bedrooms are cool, Asian-chic and luxurious; bathrooms are gloriously decadently lush. The big, open-plan, parquet-floored suites have magnificent terraces and ingenious wardrobes that open to mini-kitchens. Enter the Royal Mare suite and you find a vast free-standing bath on the corner of your terrace... drink a toast to your good fortune as you soak, gazing across the sea to the isle of Elba.

Price	€146-€398.
Rooms	11 suites.
Meals	Dinner €35-€40. Wine €10-€100.
Closed	10 January-10 February.
Directions	A12 exit for SS to Vincenzo, right, then 4th right. Climb hill to top; go slow & look for hidden turning on right, big iron gates.

Francesca Vierucci
Via San Bartolo 100,
57027 San Vincenzo
Tel   +39 0565 798032
Email   poggioaisanti@toscana.com
Web   www.poggioaisanti.com

Tenuta Il Sassone

The views are inspirational, the gardens are beautiful and you feel welcomed into someone's much-loved home. Simona and her husband are charming, talented, funny, friendly, and Il Sassone is their dream. Unless you've booked in to a cookery workshop the kitchen is out-of-bounds, but you have the run of the rest: the pastel-pretty sitting room, the billiard room with library, the sunny terraces, the wildlife-rich woodland (rabbits, porcupine, deer), the organic orchards and the kitchen garden, and the saltwater infinity pool – with hydro jets and glorious views. Each calm, colour-themed bedroom has floral fabrics and hand-painted touches – an artist friend helped decorate the house; perfect bathrooms stock aromatics and towels. Flowers glamorise tables, sculptures dot sunny corners, tortoises and dogs doze, and, on a clear day, you can see the sea; beaches are a short drive. Return to a digestif before dinner with the lovely hosts, then join guests at the elegant table and prepare for a Tuscan feast. Breakfasts include sausage and eggs, cakes, crostata and Simona's amazing jams. *Min. stay one week in high season.*

Price	€160–€240.
Rooms	6 doubles.
Meals	Dinner €25–€45, on request.
Closed	Mid-January to mid-February.
Directions	A1 exit Certosa then Florence-Siena road; cont. onto Siena-Grosseto road. Exit Civitella Paganico dir. Roccastrada and Follonica (Strada Provinciale delle Collacchie). After 6-7km sign on the left for Il Sassone; right, on for 3km.

Simona Ceccherini
Tenuta Il Sassone 23,
Loc. Poggio Curzio,
58024 Massa Marittima

Tel	+39 0566 904230
Email	info@ilsassone.it
Web	www.ilsassone.it

Pieve di Caminino Historic Resort

A fallen column lying deep in the grass, woods, a quiet lake... so peaceful it's hard to believe what a history this settlement has had since it was first recorded in 1075. It is set in a huge natural amphitheatre, ringed by hills and medieval fortresses, and has its own magic spring. Once you've driven through the big rusty gates and down the tree-lined drive, you'll be greeted by your hosts in an 11th-century church – part of their private quarters. It's the most lovely, airy space, with battered columns, soaring arches and elegant furniture – a subtle study in cream, gold and brown. The suites (one a romantic cottage) and the apartments are beautiful too. Each has its own terrace or balcony and is simply furnished with family antiques and fine old paintings. Enchanting windows look over the grounds, the massive walls are rough stone or plaster, the ceilings beamed or vaulted. The 500-hectare estate has been in Piero's family since 1650 and produces its own olive oil and wine. The beautiful panoramic pool has distant views to the isle of Elba. *Min. stay three nights in high season. Complimentary wine in room.*

Price	€110-€170 (€600-€900 per week). Apts €180-€250 (€900-€1,300 per week).
Rooms	5 + 2: 5 suites for 2-3. 2 apts for 4-5.
Meals	Breakfast €10. Restaurant 6km.
Closed	Never.
Directions	From Milan m'way Bologna-Firenze exit Firenze-Certosa, for Siena-Grosseto, exit Civitella Marittima for Follonica. 5km before Montemassi right for Sassofortino. On right, 1km.

Piero Marrucchi & Daniela Locatelli
S.P 89, snc,
58036 Caminino
Tel +39 0564 569736
Email caminino@caminino.com
Web www.caminino.com

Ethical Collection: Environment; Food.
See page 400 for details

Montebelli Agriturismo & Country Hotel

Breathe in the scents of myrtle and juniper. Stroll to the ancient oak at the top of the hill and watch the sun go down. Explore this whole lovely area on horseback: Montebelli has plenty, and mountain bikes too. Little tracks lead you past gnarled oaks to vineyards, olive groves and a small lake. The farm is run organically by the Tosi family; son Alessandro oversees the hotel, aided by an efficient staff. Loungers line an elegant pool in manicured grounds; the farm produce – honey, jam, olive oil, grappa, wine – are displayed in reception, alongside a blackboard announcing the day's menu. The cooking is Tuscan/Neapolitan, the produce largely home-grown; cookery courses may be in the offing. Breakfast is served on the big shaded terrace; on a summer evening there could be a concert or a barbecue. Bedrooms, divided between the spanking new building and the much more characterful farmhouse, are cool, clean and welcoming, their white walls, wooden floors, understated furnishings and interesting pictures striking the right note of simplicity. The bathrooms are fabulous, the spa is out of this world.

Price	€160–€240. Suites €200–€270. Half board €25 extra p.p.
Rooms	45: 36 doubles, 9 suites.
Meals	Dinner €37. Wine from €15.
Closed	January–March.
Directions	From SS1 exit Gavorrano Scalo for Ravi-Caldana; 5km, turn for Caldana. After 2.5km, sign for Montebelli.

Ethical Collection: Environment; Food.
See page 400 for details

Carla Filotico Tosi
Loc. Molinetto, 58023 Caldana Bivio
Tel   +39 0566 887100
Email   info@montebelli.com
Web   www.montebelli.com

Villa Bengodi

A house that matches its owners: family orientated, gentle and with old-fashioned charm. Great-aunt Zia Ernesta lived in the room with the angel frescoes for most of her life; now Caterina shares the running of the B&B with her brothers and their wives. The villa and its gardens are their pride and joy. Bedrooms are generous, light and spotless and house a hotchpotch of furniture from past decades; some have ceilings painted in 1940, another a terrace; all have original floor tiles in varying patterns. Modern bathrooms are excellent, views are to the garden or sea. While away the days in the enchanting palm-fringed garden, or on the terrace where views reach to Corsica on a clear day. Beaches and mile upon mile of surf are a hop away – or you could walk the full mile to Talamone, where a family friend takes you out on his boat to fish and to swim; eat what you catch. The apartments sit on terraces below the villa and have their own gardens. Dine al fresco in summer; in winter under a chandelier made of antlers and pine cones. A personal home and a magical setting. *Minimum stay three nights.*

Price	€110–€170. Apartments €800–€1,500 per week.
Rooms	6 + 2: 6 doubles. 2 apartments for 2-4.
Meals	Dinner with wine, €30, by arrangement.
Closed	Rarely.
Directions	From Grosseto-Roma dir. Talamone. 1st left & where road ends near station right into Via Bengodi. 1st right again.

Famiglia Orlandi
Via Bengodi 2, Loc. Bengodi,
58010 Fonteblanda

Mobile	+39 335 420334
Email	info@villabengodi.it
Web	www.villabengodi.it

Ethical Collection: Community; Food.
See page 400 for details

Quercia Rossa

Although satnav-challengingly hard to find, Quercia Rossa is worth the test! Built in
the 1940s on the site of a Roman slave farm, the farmhouse sits on an estate of oak and
cypress-scudded fields of wheat, with poolside panoramas of the Tyrrhenian Sea and the
plains of Marsiliana. As for the interiors, they are quirky and design-mag cool. A huge
communal Maremma table beneath antique oil-lamps in a stunningly elegant dining room
forms the focus of meals enriched by stylish young Alessandro – and Chef bakes fresh cakes
for breakfast each day. Fabulous furniture from Victorian voyager Augusta Belloc (daughter
of Hilaire) – bought blind as a 'job lot' – catch the eye throughout: big gold mirrors and
pretty gilded sconces; cherrywood pieces with intricate swans carved into the legs; a huge
mahogany four-poster; an ornate bathroom mirror above an ancient marble basin; and, in
the red and white-tiled sitting room, beautiful antique armchairs in deep rich blue and
gold. It's wonderfully laid-back, yet classy and romantic at the same time. A special,
unusual place, made magical by Alessandro.

Price	€81-€143.
Rooms	6 doubles.
Meals	Dinner with wine, €25-€35.
Closed	Rarely.
Directions	A1 exit Orvieto; SS74 dir. Pitigliano/Manciano. Thro' Manciano dir. Albinia on SS74 for 23.8km La Sgrilla; signed from here. Right at entrance to Tenuta Cavallini; follow white road for approx. 5km.

Ethical Collection: Food.
See page 400 for details

Alessandro Bonanni
Montemerano, Santarello 89,
58014 Manciano
Tel   +39 0564 629529
Email   info@querciarossa.net
Web   www.querciarossa.net

Castello di Ripa d'Orcia

As you drive up the long, white road, the castle comes into view: a thrilling sight. Ripa d'Orcia dates from the 13th century, one of Siena's most important strongholds. The battlemented fortress (closed to the public) dominates the *borgo* encircled by small medieval dwellings. The family are descendants of the Piccolomini who acquired the estate in 1484 and are hugely proud of their heritage. Grand banquets and knights in shining armour may come to mind… children will love it here. Rooms and apartments have huge raftered ceilings and are furnished simply and well; many have breathtaking views. There's also a day room, filled with lovely furniture and heaps of books to browse. You breakfast in a small annexe off the main restaurant; there's a cellar for wine tastings and a shop for you to stock up on your favourites. A pool too, and a beautiful chapel in the grounds. The area is a paradise for walkers and there is enough on the spot to keep lovers of history and architecture happy for hours – before the 'official' sightseeing begins. *Minimum stay two nights; three in apt.*

Price	€110-€150. Apts €110-€155 for 2; €175-€190 for 4.
Rooms	6 + 8: 6 twins/doubles. 8 apartments: 5 for 2, 3 for 4.
Meals	Breakfast €12 for self-caterers. Dinner from €12. Wine from €10. Closed Mondays.
Closed	November-March.
Directions	From SS2 for San Quirico d'Orcia; right over bridge. Follow road around town walls for 700m. Right again, signed; 5.3km to Castello.

Famiglia Aluffi Pentini Rossi
Via della Contea 1/16,
53027 Ripa d'Orcia

Tel	+39 0577 897376
Email	info@castelloripadorcia.com
Web	www.ripadorcia.it

Entry 169   Map 11

Il Rigo

The fame of Lorenza's cooking has spread so far that she's been invited to demonstrate her skills in the US (she runs courses here, too.) So meals in the big, beamed dining room at pretty check-clothed tables are a treat. Irresistible home-grown organic produce, 60 local wines to choose from and a gorgeous Tuscan setting. There are two houses on the family farm, named after the stream running through it. Casabianca, reached via a cypress-flanked drive, is ancient and stone built. A vine-covered pergola shades the entrance; beyond the reception area is a courtyard full of climbing roses. The second house, Poggio Bacoca, is about 600 metres away. Once home to the farmworkers, it's red-brick built and has two sitting rooms and panoramic views. You walk (600m) to 'Casabianca' for those wonderful meals. Bedrooms are homely, pretty and inviting; all have embroidered sheets, appealing colour schemes and matching bathrooms. No televisions: it's not that sort of place. Lorenza and Vittorio hope and believe that their guests will prefer a relaxed chat over a glass of wine.

Price	€100–€124. Half-board €144–€170 for 2.
Rooms	15 doubles.
Meals	Lunch/dinner €22–€25, by arrangement. Wine from €12.
Closed	Never.
Directions	Exit A1 Certosa; follow SS, exit Siena South. SS.2 (Via Cassia) 2km south of S. Quirico d'Orcia; on left on 2km track, signed.

Vittorio Cipolla & Lorenza Santo
Podere Casabianca, 53027
San Quirico d'Orcia

Tel	+39 0577 897 291
Email	info@agriturismoilrigo.com
Web	www.agriturismoilrigo.com

Podere Salicotto

Watch sunsets fire the Tuscan hills; catch the sunrise as it brings the valleys alive.
Views from this hilltop farmhouse roll off in every direction. It is peaceful here, and
beautiful. Breakfast is a feast that merges into lunch, with produce from the organic
farm, and Silvia and Paolo, a well-travelled, warm and adventurous couple, are happy
for you to be as active or as idle as you like. Eat in the big farmhouse kitchen or
under the pergola, as deer wander across the field below. Paolo is full of ideas and
will take you sailing in his six-berth boat that has crossed the Atlantic – or organise
wine-tasting and cycling trips. The beamed and terracotta tiled bedrooms are airy and
welcoming, full of soft, Tuscan colours and furnished with simplicity but care: antiques,
monogrammed sheets, great showers. B&B guests are in the main house (private
entrance) while the studio is in the converted barn. Visit Siena, medieval Buonconvento,
Tuscan hill towns. Come back, rest in a hammock, laze around the pool with a glass
of wine and a fabulous view.

Price	B&B: €150 (€980 per week). Studio: €1,200 per week.
Rooms	6 + 1: 6 doubles. Studio for 2-4.
Meals	Breakfast €15 for self-caterers, on request. Restaurants nearby.
Closed	February & November.
Directions	From Siena via Cassia to Buonconvento. After Agip petrol station, 2nd left. After 2nd hill, house 2nd on right.

Silvia Forni
Podere Salicotto 73,
53022 Buonconvento

Tel   +39 0577 809087
Email   info@poderesalicotto.com
Web   www.poderesalicotto.com

Ethical Collection: Environment; Food.
See page 400 for details

La Locanda del Castello

Antique clocks and white truffles are just two of the treats here; the former are collected by your excellent host Silvana, the latter are a rare delicacy for which the region is famous. The hilltop village of San Giovanni d'Asso acts as a bridge between the Val d'Orcia (home of the celebrated truffle) and the breathtaking countryside of the Crete Senesi. At the heart of the town is an imposing 16th-century castle, and tucked into its walls lies La Locanda del Castello. There are only nine bedrooms in this lovely hotel; all are beautifully decorated and furnished with Silvana's family hierlooms. Bathrooms are luxurious and, as with everything in the hotel, built into the original shape of the castle. But the jewel in this particular crown is the restaurant – open to the public – where the chefs cook to old Tuscan recipes and guests feast on pecorino cheese, fine meats and an intoxicating selection of regional wines. And, of course, truffles. On balmy evenings, the canopy over the patio can be rolled back to allow diners to marvel at the moon. Breakfasts are every bit as delicious. *Ask about city tours, wine tours, hot air balloon trips and airport / train station transfers.*

Price	€80-€160.
Rooms	9 doubles.
Meals	Lunch/dinner with wine, €45.
Closed	10-31 January.
Directions	Florence-Roma A1 exit Valdichiana; 5km to Sinalunga; 10km Trequanda-Montisi; 5km to hotel. Park below castle.

Silvana Ratti Ravanelli
Piazza V. Emanuele II 4,
53020 San Giovanni d'Asso

Tel	+39 0577 802939
Email	info@lalocandadelcastello.com
Web	www.lalocandadelcastello.com

Bosco della Spina

The road sign for 'pizzeria' is misleading: nothing so mundane here. Tables overlook a magical garden of pergolas, waterfalls, vines and wisteria; Castle Murlo hangs in the distance. Imaginatively restored and landscaped, these former farmhouse cellars in medieval Lupompesi have strikingly modern interiors and old Tuscan beams and terracotta; architecturally it is an interesting restoration. The restaurant, a cool space of open arches, raftered ceiling and sleek furniture, serves classic regional dishes (pizza in the summer only) accompanied by 180 wines. Reached down a series of impersonal corridors, the super comfy suites, each with fridge, sink and dual hob, have terraces, big divans and furniture made by local craftsmen. Blankets are neatly rolled, colours white and conker brown, beds hi-tech four-poster, bedcovers faux suede, shower rooms designery. All this and a wine bar, library, small gym, slimline pool (suitable for lengths only) and garden spots filled with tinkling water and views. A smoothly run and relaxed operation, popular with wedding parties, too.

Price	€100–€200.
Rooms	14 suites for 2-4, 4-6, or 4-8.
Meals	Dinner €30. Wine from €7.
Closed	Rarely.
Directions	A1 for Siena; exit Siena south; SS2 for Rome-Buonconvento; 15km; Monteroni d'Arbia; right to Vescovado di Murlo just after r'bout; 8km; right for Casciano di Murlo; 1km; in Lupompesi, on left, signed 'Residence'.

Brigida Meoni
Lupompesi, 53016 Murlo

Tel	+39 0577 814605
Email	bsturist@boscodellaspina.com
Web	www.boscodellaspina.com

Ethical Collection: Food.
See page 400 for details

Montorio

As you pootle up the drive, you will be inspired by the Temple of San Biagio. A Renaissance masterpiece designed by Antonio Sangallo the Elder, it is an unforgettable backdrop to Montorio. The house stands on top of its own little hill, 600m above sea level, overlooking a vast green swathe of Tuscany. Made of warm stone walls and roofs on different levels, it was once a *casa colonica*. It is now divided into five attractive apartments, each named after a celebrated Italian artist or poet, each with a well-equipped kitchen and an open fire. White walls, beams and terracotta floors set a tone of rural simplicity; antiques, paintings and wrought-iron lights crafted by Florentines add a touch of style; leather chesterfields and big beds guarantee comfort. The terraced gardens – full of ancient cypress trees, pots of flowers and alluring places to sit – drop gently down to olive groves and vineyards. Stefania's other villa, Poggiano, is five minutes away and historic Montepulciano, full of shops and eating places, is close enough to walk. *Minimum stay three nights.*

Price	€100–€170 for 2 (€500–€1,200 per week). €200–€250 for 4 (€1,400–€1,650 per week).
Rooms	5 apartments: 3 for 2, 2 for 4.
Meals	Restaurants 500m.
Closed	December–January.
Directions	A1 exit Valdichiana for Montepulciano. In Torrita di Siena, left at lights to Montepulciano. There, follow signs to Chianciano. Right at x-roads Bilvio di S. Biagio.

Stefania Savini
Strada per Pienza 2,
53045 Montepulciano

Tel	+39 0578 717442
Email	info@montorio.com
Web	www.montorio.com

Frances' Lodge

You stay in a converted hilltop lemon house, a ten-minute bus ride into the city. Catch your breath at views that soar across olive, lemon and quince groves to the Torre del Mangia of Siena. The old farmhouse was built by Franca's family as a summer retreat. Now she and Franco – warm, charming, intelligent – have filled the lofty, light-filled *limonaia* with beautiful things: an oriental carpet, a butter-yellow leather sofa, vibrant art by Franca. Guests may take breakfast in this lovely room, divided by a glass partition etched with a lemon tree from the kitchen, Franca's domain. And the first meal of the day – in the historic garden in summer – is to be lingered over: Tuscan salami and pecorino, fresh figs, delicious coffee. Bedrooms burst with personality and colour – one, funky and Moroccan, another huge, white and cream, with an outside area with a view. Chic coloured bed linen, huge walk-in showers, a fridge stocked with juice and water, towels for the pool. And what a pool – curved, it lies on the edge of the house, filled with views. A special place with a big heart. *Minimum stay two nights. Over 18s only.*

Price	€180–€220. Suite €240–€380.
Rooms	6: 5 doubles, 1 suite for 2-4 (with kitchenette).
Meals	Restaurant 800m.
Closed	10 January-10 March.
Directions	Past Siena on Tangenziale ring road for Arezzo-Roma; exit Siena Est to big r'bout 'Due Ponti'; road to S. Regina; 1st right Strada di Valdipugna; signed on right.

Ethical Collection: Environment; Food.
See page 400 for details

Franca Mugnai
Strada di Valdipugna 2,
53100 Siena

Mobile	+39 337 671608
Email	booking@franceslodge.it
Web	www.franceslodge.it

Campo Regio Relais

Bustling, beautiful Siena. Step straight in from a quiet cobbled street to marble floors, frescoed walls and heavy antiques. A first-floor sitting room gleams with leather sofas and huge vases of fresh flowers, there are striped tablecloths on the breakfast tables and the terrace looks over rooftops to the Duomo. This building, which dates from the 16th-century, is known locally as 'stick of the parrot' thanks to its particular architectural structure: one bedroom has the view and a private terrace, another a window onto the view from its bed. All are generously sumptuous with monogrammed linen sheets, taffeta curtains, soft creams and pale lilacs, big buckets of scents and soaps and large-mirrored bathrooms; thoroughly pampering. It's strolling distance to restaurants, shops, street life. Then back for a nightcap from the honesty bar in the candlelit salon, as you watch the twinkling lights of the city below. Honeymooners will find it irrresistible, architecture buffs will swoon, children may prefer somewhere a touch more robust.

Price	€150–€650.
Rooms	6 twins/doubles.
Meals	Restaurants nearby.
Closed	Rarely.
Directions	From m'way exit Siena west; follow signs for stadium until x-roads with Basilica di San Domenico.

Livia Palagi
Residenza d'Epoca,
Via della Sapienza 25, 53100 Siena

Tel	+39 0577 222073
Email	relais@camporegio.com
Web	www.camporegio.com

Rocca di Castagnoli

Max truly wants this place to shine, and shine it does. Ancient Rocca di Castagnoli, one of Chianti's most prestigious wine-producing estates, is a one thousand-year old hilltop castle with an attached hamlet and – off a courtyard with time-polished cobbles – some swooningly beautiful self-catering apartments and rooms. Immaculately designed interiors with beamy ceilings and ancient cotta floors offset the sharply defined opulence of sleek modern fixtures, royalty-sized draped beds, gold embroidered curtains, mountains of cushions and perfectly placed antiques. Bathrooms have huge whirlpool showers and snazzy products. Kitchens and sitting rooms follow flawless suit. A communal billiards room opens onto a terrace with stop-and-stare views that are shared from the pool in the garden below. Breakfasts are predictably perfect; and there's an exquisite inn, Osteria al Ponte, a stroll away. Tour the vineyards and cellars, dig into your pool-side sunspot, let dashing manager Max advise you – in perfect English – on wine trails in Chianti, and postpone the return home. The place is a dream!

Price	€120-€180.
	Apartments €450-€800 per week.
Rooms	6 + 7: 6 doubles. 7 apts for 2-6.
Meals	Breakfast €12.
	Restaurant 5-minute walk.
Closed	Rarely.
Directions	FI-SI road exit Radda in Chianti; follow signs for Giaole in Chianti until signs for Rocca di Castagnoli; signed.

Max Adorno
Loc. Castagnoli,
53013 Siena

Tel	+39 0577 731909
Email	info@roccadicastagnoli.com
Web	www.roccadicastagnoli.com

Entry 177   Map 8

Antico Borgo Poggiarello

The 17th-century farm buildings in the woods — the *borgo* — have been transformed into holiday homes and linked by a circuit of well-considered paths. Poggiarello is a family set-up. Signora Giove does the cooking, son Roberto does front of house (he once worked in a tax office and has no regrets); Nino, Paolo and Ciro — the perfectly behaved English setters — are there when you need them. You can self-cater or do B&B here: arrangements are flexible. Most apartments are for two; some interconnect and are ideal for eight. Rooms are big and comfortable with wrought-iron beds, cream curtains and covers, tiled floors; all have patios and great views. One is excellent for wheelchair-users. Days are spent lolling by the pool, evenings sunset-gazing on the terrace. Though the treasures of Siena, Monteriggioni and Volterra lie a short drive away, it's hard to leave: there's a beautifully lit bath housed in a cave that's heated all year to 38 degrees (extra charge), and a terraced restaurant in the old stables where you can sample the best of Tuscan home cooking.

Price	€100–€130.
Rooms	10 apartments: 9 for 2, 1 for 4.
Meals	Breakfast €7. Dinner, 5 courses, €25; by arrangement. Wine from €10.
Closed	November–February.
Directions	From Florence-Siena m'way exit Monteriggioni. Right after stop sign, 1.4km, left for Abbadia a Isola & Strove. After 6km, left for Scorgiano. On for 4km, left at 'Fattoria di Scorgiano'. Signed for 2km.

	Roberto Giove
	Strada di San Monti 12,
	53035 Monteriggioni
Tel	+39 0577 301003
Email	info@poggiarello.com
Web	www.poggiarello.com

Fortezza de' Cortesi

Restoring the ruins of this lovely place was a labour of love for Cledy. The project took nine years, the results are stunning. An actress, Cledy has given the 10th-century *fortezza*-villa a charm and a distinction all of its own. Captivating features – vaulted ceilings, arched windows, rich stone, chestnut beams – mix with fabrics and colours in a most harmonious manner. The five bedrooms, all different, have sumptuous bathrooms and unforgettable views, while up in the tower is the most tempting of suites, with a big fireplace and a bath with hill views. (A tiny kitchenettte, too, for hot drinks.) Come for two nights of blissful B&B – or rent the whole lovely place. If you're into self-improvement, Cledy can rustle up courses: try cookery, ceramics or wine tasting. It was saffron that built San Gimignano and they grow the spice here; olive oil too. The house stands high in 12 hectares of land, with a terraced garden, gazebo, pool and views of San Gimignano's celebrated towers. Worth the drive to get here, but leave the children behind – it's exquisite! *Minimum stay two nights in B&B.*

Price	€148-€180. Suite €210-€270. Whole villa €6,600-€7,800 per week.
Rooms	6: 5 doubles, 1 suite.
Meals	Owner's restaurant in San Gimignano, 5km.
Closed	Rarely.
Directions	Exit Florence-Siena m'way at Poggibonsi Nord; signs for San Gimignano; after 8km, road forks, right for San Gimignano; 50m left into gravel road; signed.

	Cledy Tancredi Loc. Monti 26, 53037 San Gimignano
Tel	+39 0577 940123
Email	info@fortezzacortesi.com
Web	www.fortezzacortesi.com

Fattoria Guicciardini

A visit to San Gimignano is a must and this makes a charming base: nine self-catering apartments right in the centre, immaculately converted from a 15th-century complex of farm buildings. Two were granaries in a former life (their bedrooms on a mezzanine floor), another was the farm cook's house. Lovely cool rooms have huge raftered ceilings, others arched windows or original fireplaces and tiles; all have been furnished in a contemporary style with new sofas, kilim-style rugs, white curtains and the occasional antique. There are entrances from both outside the city walls and from the Piazza S. Agostino (and do sneak a look at the church's altar frescoes by Benozzo Gozzoli). Get up early and watch the mists fall away to reveal the vineyards all around, then drink in the astonishing art of San Gimignano before the army of tourists descends. Evening in the city is magical, too, when the city's fairytale towers are floodlit. This is the time of day at which San Gimignano – honey pot of Tuscan tourism, deservedly so – is at its most lovely.

Price	€120 for 2-4; €150 for 2-6 (€800-€1,000 per week).
Rooms	9 apartments: 6 for 2-4, 3 for 4-6.
Meals	Restaurant 100m.
Closed	Never.
Directions	Leave Florence-Siena m'way at S. Gimignano & Poggibonsi Nord exit. Fattoria in centre of S. Gimignano.

Tuccio Guicciardini
Viale Garibaldi 2/A,
Piazza S. Agostino 2,
53037 San Gimignano
Tel   +39 0577 907185
Email   info@guicciardini.com
Web   www.guicciardini.com

Tenuta di Camporsevoli: Le Capanne & Casa dei Neri

Just off a track winding up to the lovely private hamlet of Camporsevoli – 2,000m above sea level – is Le Capanne, a thick-walled farmhouse as aristocratic as its owners. Your well-kitted kitchen and large homely sitting room at ground level lead to a dining terrace with smart cypress-strewn lawns from which to admire stop-in-tracks views. Bedrooms are light, elegant and spacious with tall ceilings, exposed wooden beams, natural colours and cream borders around windows. Sumptuous beds, classy bathrooms; all feels beautifully understated. Casa dei Neri, in the heart of the hamlet, is less grand but utterly private. It is reached by a Tuscan stone outside stair, which opens into the dining room (with open fireplace) and kitchen. Bedrooms are cosy and uncluttered with exposed stone walls, a light, floral décor and clear, modern bathrooms. Outside, a terrace with plastic chairs and striped loungers makes a secluded spot for outdoor dining. A short walk along a pretty track leads to a shared infinity pool in the woods, with a changing room and shower and views: enchanting! *Ask about cultural & gastronomic tours.*

Price	Le Capanne €2,400-€5,000. Casa dei Neri €1,800-€3,000. Prices per week.
Rooms	2 houses: 1 for 8, 1 for 10.
Meals	Welcome breakfast included. Restaurants 3km.
Closed	Never.
Directions	A1 exit Chiusi/Chianciano. From Cetona to Le Piazze. In front of restaurant Bottega delle Nane, onto Via di Camporsevoli. On for 2km, left to Le Capanne. Ring for detailed directions.

Valentina Grossi Orzalesi
53040 Le Piazze

Mobile	+39 335 6595033
Email	info@camporsevoli.it
Web	www.camporsevoli.it

Fattoria Tregole

A vineyard and a private family chapel. What could be more Italian? The delightful Kirchlechners – he an architect, she a restorer – make Chianti Classico, grappa and olive oil from their Tuscan manor farm. They spent seven years restoring the buildings, keeping original features – raftered ceilings, terracotta floors, large fireplaces – and furnishing with a light, country-house touch. The airy apartments and the bedrooms, including a ground-floor suite with a terrace, feel like the family's rooms; all are lovely. Walls are eye-catching with Edith's hand-painted stencils, painted brass bedsteads are cleverly restored; there are traditional lampshades, dried flowers, patchwork quilts and crochet cushions. It is light, warm and inviting. Breakfast in the sunny dining room or on the patio; twice a week Edith cooks a Tuscan dinner, accompanied by the wine from the Tregole cellars. A beautiful pool, quiet views over olive groves and vine-clad hills, a garden with shady nooks, a tiny Renaissance chapel – it is intimate and homely. *Minimum stay three nights in apts.*

Price	€130–€150. Suite €180. Apts €200–€320.
Rooms	5 + 2: 4 doubles, 1 suite for 2. 2 apts: 1 for 4, 1 for 5.
Meals	Dinner €35, book ahead. Wine from €10. Restaurants 3km.
Closed	Mid-November to mid-March.
Directions	From Florence SS222 for Greve-Panzano-Castellina; 5km after Castellina in Chianti; sign for Tregole; 1km.

Edith Kirchlechner
Loc. Tregole 86,
53011 Castellina in Chianti
Tel   +39 0577 740991
Email   fattoria-tregole@castellina.com
Web   www.fattoria-tregole.com

Tenuta di Ricavo

Softly spoken Christina runs a charming tenuta – traditional, elegant, well-loved and well-used. Surrounded by rolling olive groves and vineyards, this is the ancient hamlet of Ricavo – 994AD! Immaculate gravel paths bring you to rose bushes, fruit trees and noble cypresses, there's a church to the side (services are still held), a restaurant at the heart and sensational views all around. You have the choice of two pools, spruce with sunloungers and blue parasols, and the use of the main house as and when you please. Sofas hand-stitched by Grandmama, walls dotted with paintings of and by the family, floors of polished mottled marble, log fires for cool evenings, books in every language… sit back and marvel at it all. The authenticity continues into bedrooms with their big comfy beds and old terra floors, good fabrics in white and cream, bright rugs and framed dolls, bathrooms are distinctly old-fashioned. Ask for the room with the terrace – you can see for miles. Local dishes in the restaurant, breakfasts to set you up for the day, nightingales to sing you to sleep, Siena a half-hour drive: you'll love it all.

Price	€150–€240. Apt €240–€400.
Rooms	23 + 1: 9 doubles, 7 twins, 5 suites, 1 cottage suite, 1 family room. 1 apartment for 6-8.
Meals	Dinner €37. Wine from €8. Menu à la carte available. Restaurant closed Sundays.
Closed	November-Easter.
Directions	A1 exit Certosa, then Florence-Siena road to San Donato dir. Castellina in Chianti; look out for signs to Pecora Nera Restaurant.

Alessandro Lobrano
Loc. Ricavo 4,
53011 Castellina in Chianti
Tel   +39 0577 740221
Email   ricavo@ricavo.com
Web   www.ricavo.com

Entry 183   Map 8

Podere Cogno

The deeper you follow the bumpy unlit road into the woods, the quieter it gets – until all you can hear are birds and crickets. When you alight, you find yourself in a secret place: a green clearing overlooking olive groves and hills. The land has been worked since Etruscan times and the mellow dignified house suits its setting: the tower is 13th century, the house a century younger. Marco and Giovanna love it dearly and their enthusiasm and generosity bubble over. From the billiard room and library at the top to the gym and the wonderful oak-floored sitting room below, there's masses of space. Bedrooms are restrained and stylish, with exposed beams and 18th-century furniture; bathrooms are sparkling, and supplied with a superabundance of towels. You'll have breakfast on the veranda and Giovanna, an excellent cook, will make you an evening meal if you book early in the day; all is homemade, much is home-grown. The garden is wonderful, with a pond full of frogs and goldfish, a deliciously scented rose garden (with a hot tub) and an elusive family of coypus. *Min. stay three nights in B&B; one week in apt & cottage.*

Price	€120–€230. Apt €1,015–€1,400 per wk. Cottage €1,365–€1,750 per wk.
Rooms	7 + 2: 1 double, 3 suites for 3, 3 garden suites for 2. 1 apt for 2, 1 cottage for 2.
Meals	Dinner €27. Restaurant 2km.
Closed	6 January–1st weekend in March.
Directions	A1 exit Firenze-Certosa dir. Siena; exit S. Donato in Poggio, dir. Siena. After Castellina in Ch., S.R. 222 (ex SS) Chiantigiana for 4km. At km 47.450 right dir. Caggiolo & Caggio. At x-roads sign for Cogno; on for 1.5km.

Marco Matteini
Loc. Cogno,
53011 Castellina in Chianti

Tel	+39 0577 740978
Email	marcomatteini@tin.it
Web	www.poderecogno.com

Palazzo Leopoldo

In a corner of the hall is a stone carving of a swaddled baby – 14th-century evidence of the hospital this once was. For the last few centuries Palazzo Leopoldo has been a manor house. It's surprisingly peaceful here, in the middle of beautiful, hilltop Radda, and it's walking distance to several *enoteche* nearby to taste the finest chiantis. The whole house, on different levels teeming with nooks and crannies, has a delightful feel: the hall is light, with white-painted arches, an old tiled floor, the occasional bright rug, and fresh flowers. Stroll onto the terrace and gaze over the lovely hills. Bedrooms range from suites to doubles in the eaves; all are big, generously equipped and have a rustic Tuscan feel. Some have the old bell-pulls for service, others the original stoves and frescoes; the owner has preserved as much as possible. A remarkable breakfast is served in a remarkable kitchen, replete with 18th-century range. Add to that an indoor pool and spa, a restaurant serving delicious food and truly delightful staff. Worth the steep and winding road to get here. *Ask about cookery classes.*

Price	€113–€225. Suites €315–€394.
Rooms	19: 14 doubles, 5 suites.
Meals	Breakfast €9.90. Lunch €25. Dinner €35.
Closed	January–February.
Directions	Signed in centre of Radda in Chianti.

Martina Rustichini
Via Roma 33,
53017 Radda in Chianti

Tel	+39 0577 735605
Email	info@palazzoleopoldo.it
Web	www.palazzoleopoldo.it

La Locanda

Admire the view from the pool – both are stunning. This is a magical place; a soft green lawn edged with Mediterranean shrubs slopes down to the pool, a covered terrace overlooks medieval Volpaia. (Some of the best chianti is produced here; the village itself is a 20-minute walk.) The house vibrates with bold colour and lively fabric. The beautiful raftered living room, with open fireplace, big, stylish sofas and pale terracotta floor, reveals photos of Guido and Martina, he from the South, she from the North. They scoured Tuscany before they found their perfect inn, renovated these two houses and filled them with fine antiques, delightful prints, candles and fun touches. There's a library/bar where you can choose books from many languages and where Guido is generous with the grappa. The bedrooms, some with their own terraces, are in a separate building and have big beds, great bathrooms and whitewashed rafters, as was the custom here. Martina cooks and gardens while Guido acts as host – they are a charming pair. Once settled in you'll find it hard to stir. *Minimum stay two nights.*

Price	€200–€280. Singles €180–€250. Suite €300.
Rooms	7: 3 doubles, 3 twins, 1 suite.
Meals	Dinner €35 (Mon, Wed & Fri). Wine €18–€70. Restaurants 4km.
Closed	November to mid-April.
Directions	From Volpaia village square take narrow road to right which becomes track. On for 2km past small sign for La Locanda to left; 1km further to group of houses.

Guido & Martina Bevilacqua
Loc. Montanino,
53017 Radda in Chianti

Tel	+39 0577 738832/3
Email	info@lalocanda.it
Web	www.lalocanda.it

Hotel Villa La Grotta

There are many treats in store. The first, glimpsed on your way in, is the marvellous Castello di Brolio. The second is the hotel itself, on the castle's 4,000-acre estate. Originally a ninth-century manor house and later a nunnery, it has been restored and converted into a delightful small hotel by its Swiss owner. A bottle of wine will be waiting to welcome you in a cool, inviting bedroom – all pastel walls, soft lighting, lovely old beds, colourful kilims on terracotta-tiled floors. All have four-posters and many have vineyard views, making this a popular honeymooners' retreat. General manager Doogie runs it all with panache and her own inimitable style – it's informal and fun. You're pampered, too, with a Turkish bath, jacuzzi baths and two swimming pools, the outdoor one with pillars sculpted by a famous artist. But perhaps the biggest treat of all is the restaurant, where fish and meat dishes are cooked to perfection, accompanied by well-priced wines and served in a stylish dining room (or al fresco, under an ancient walnut tree). No surprise that people travel from as far as Florence. *Minimum stay two nights.*

Price	€260-€280. Suites €360-€380.
Rooms	12: 10 doubles, 2 suites.
Meals	Dinner €35-€45. Wine €22-€320. Restaurant 3km.
Closed	November-March.
Directions	From Gaiole to Castello di Brolio; left of castle for Castelnuovo Berardenga for 1km, hotel up dirt track for 600m.

	Doogie Morley-Bodle Brolio, 53013 Gaiole in Chianti
Tel	+39 0577 747125
Email	info@hotelvillalagrotta.it
Web	www.hotelvillalagrotta.com

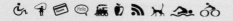

Castello di Tornano

The first thing you see is the ancient stone tower, peeking above the wooded hills and vineyards. Inside, a beautiful restoration that has enriched the glorious stonework, the spaciousness and the sense of history. Rooms are positively regal with deep rugs on tiled floors, sparkling chandeliers and richly coloured drapes and linen (plum, raspberry, royal blue, vermilion). The opulent Tower Room has its own jacuzzi and a terrace with stunning views. Self-catering apartments are uncluttered with exposed beams and stone walls, some with lovely vaulted ceilings. Bathrooms are a treat: neutral-toned mosaics blend in with the original stone, there are big mirrors and fluffy white towels and robes. Relax downstairs in the living room with its old font, soft-lighting and plush red drapes; request dinner and you are served fine Tuscan food. The hotel is also an agriturismo so chianti, olive oil, grappa and sweet vin santo are all produced here. Come for the friendly atmosphere and the lovely pool and garden, the wine tastings, the riding on the estate, the luxuriousness of it all, and the peace.

Price	€140-€520.
Rooms	11 + 7: 7 doubles, 2 suites, 2 triples. 7 apartments.
Meals	Breakfast €12 for self-caterers. Dinner €40, on request. Wine from €11. Restaurant 6km.
Closed	8 January-12 March; November-23 December.
Directions	A1 exit Valdarno for Cavriglia-Gaiole on road 408. Pass Gaiole, cont. for Siena for 5km; signed on left.

Maura Marasca
Loc. Tornano,
53013 Gaiole in Chianti
Tel   +39 0577 746067
Email   info@castelloditornano.it
Web   www.castelloditornano.it

L'Ultimo Mulino

The sense of space is stunning – the vast, medieval hall, the lofty ceilings, the stone walls, the flights of stairs... Original arches give glimpses of passageways beyond and many of the rooms are connected by little 'bridges' from which you can see the millstream far below. Outside the restored watermill is a large terrace for delicious breakfasts, a lovely long pool, and a small amphitheatre where occasional concerts are held. In the middle of nowhere you're surrounded by trees and it's immensely quiet – just the sound of water and birds. All feels fresh and clean, the atmosphere is welcoming and informal, and nothing is too much trouble for the staff. Sparsely, elegantly and comfortably furnished, the great hall makes a cool, beautiful centrepiece to the building – and there's a snug with a fireplace where you can roast chestnuts in season. Excellently equipped bedrooms have terracotta tiled floors and good, generously sized beds. You dine in the conservatory overlooking the stream, on mainly Tuscan dishes – be tempted by truffles and local delicacies. Historic Radda is a ten-minute drive.

Price	€112–€203. Suite €324–€370.
Rooms	13: 12 doubles, 1 suite.
Meals	Breakfast €9.90. Dinner €35–€45. Wine list €15–€80. Closed Mondays.
Closed	Mid-November to mid-March.
Directions	From Gaiole in Chianti 1st right on road to Radda. Mulino on right after bend; signed.

Lorenza Padoan
Loc. La Ripresa di Vistarenni,
53013 Gaiole in Chianti

Tel	+39 0577 738520
Email	info@ultimomulino.it
Web	www.ultimomulino.it

17 Via dei Goti

Just south-east of Siena, this medieval hill town buzzes with its weekly market and year-round inhabitants. Catch brilliant views of surrounding hills through entrance arches in ancient walls; Porta dei Tintori is a fine place to sit with a glass of wine in the evening. Your perfect townhouse is tall and narrow, on four floors, cool in the summer yet cosy in winter; rusts, blues and whites bathe its walls. You enter the open-plan dining area off the street; through an arched wall is a fully-stocked kitchen. (Take what you need – wine included – then simply replace.) On the first floor are a double bedroom and an elegant living room with a beamed ceiling, an open fireplace, a cream sofa and chairs, lovely art work and books galore. A second salon and another bedroom are on the third floor, then right at the top (not for the un-nimble) is the master bedroom, splendid with its French antiques and embroidered linen curtains and sheets. The bathroom has a claw-foot bath from which you may gaze over rooftops, and candles are waiting to be lit. Fabulous.

Price	€450–€650 per week.
Rooms	House for 6 (3 doubles).
Meals	Restaurant 50m.
Closed	Rarely.
Directions	Directions on booking.

Sheri Eggleton & Charles Grant
53040 Rapolano Terme

Tel   +44 (0)117 9081949
Email sherieggleton711@googlemail.com
Web   www.17viadeigoti.co.uk

Hotel Borgo Casabianca

A medieval hamlet on top of a hill, meticulously restored. In theory a farm, this has more the feel of a country estate. In the 'Villa Padronale'- with a tiny chapel standing alongside – are terracotta-floored bedrooms grandly endowed with elaborate ceilings and rich drapes and chandeliers; some have their 18th-century wall decorations. The surrounding stables and barns have become 20 self-contained, individually furnished apartments, nicely rustic with white walls, old beams and chunky terracotta. Each has its own little garden; many have balconies or terraces with stupendous forest views over the estate. You will find everything you need in the farm's on-site shop, from wine to olive oil and homemade biscuits: this is an ideal set-up for self-caterers and families. There are wonderful walks in the surrounding countryside and bikes for further afield; you can meander down to the lake to fish, relax at the poolside bar or hide away in the secluded cloister garden. The bright and inviting restaurant is in the old wine cellars, still with its vats and press.

Price	€170–€198. Suites €240–€360.
	Apts €245–€420 (€950–€1,995 per week).
Rooms	9 + 20: 3 doubles, 6 suites.
	20 apartments: 15 for 2, 5 for 4–6.
Meals	Breakfast €12 for self-caterers.
	Dinner €35. Wine from €10.
Closed	January–March.
Directions	A1 exit 28 for Valdichiana, Sinalunga,
	Asciano. After Asciano, 9km on right.

Luigi Scaperrotta
SP 10, Loc. Casabianca,
53041 Asciano

Tel	+39 0577 704362
Email	casabianca@casabianca.it
Web	www.casabianca.it

Castello di Gargonza

A fortified Romanesque village in the beauty of the Tuscan hills, whose 800-year-old steps, stones, rafters and tiles remain virtually intact. Today it is a private, uniquely Italian marriage of exquisitely ancient and exemplary modern. Seen from the air it is perfect, as if shaped by the gods to inspire Man to greater works: a magical maze of paths, nooks and crannies, castellated tower, great octagonal well, a heavy gate that lets the road slip out and tumble down, breathtaking views. You're given a map on arrival to help you navigate your way round. No cars, no shops, but a chapel, gardens, pool and old olive press for meetings, concerts and breakfasts by the fire. A restaurant sits just outside the walls. The Count and Countess and their staff are passionate about the place and look after you well. Bedrooms and apartments are 'rustic deluxe' with smart modern furnishings, white-rendered walls, superb rafters, open fireplaces, tiny old doors reached up steep stone staircases. There's an ancient ambience, as if time has stood still. Intriguing, delightful. *Min. stay two nights; one week in apts.*

Price	€120-€180. Suites €175-€190. Apartments €875-€2,065 per week.
Rooms	24 + 8: 21 doubles, 3 suites. 8 apartments for 2-10.
Meals	Breakfast €9 for self-caterers. Lunch/dinner with wine, €25-€35.
Closed	10 January-1 March; November (weekends only).
Directions	Exit A1 at Monte S. Savino; SS73 for Siena. Approx. 7km after Monte S. Savino right for Gargonza; signed.

Roberto Guicciardini
Loc. Gargonza,
52048 Monte San Savino

Tel	+39 0575 847021
Email	gargonza@gargonza.it
Web	www.gargonza.it

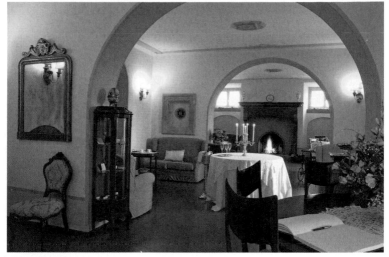

Villa Marsili

Always refreshing to come to Cortona, set so magnificently on the top of a hill. And the site of this beautifully run palazzo-hotel is steeped in history: in the 14th century the church of the Madonna degli Alemanni stood here, built to house the miraculous image of the Madonna della Manna. Beneath, an Oratory was linked by a flight of stairs (still to be seen in the breakfast room); in 1786 the church was demolished and an elegant mansion built on the site. The owners have carefully preserved many of the original architectural features hidden over the centuries, and the hall and the light-filled bedrooms are immaculately and individually decorated with trompe l'œils and hand-painted borders. Colours are gentle yellows, bathrooms are gorgeous, most rooms are large, some are tiny, all windows have views. The front of the house looks onto a garden with a pergola where an excellent breakfast buffet is enjoyed – along with a stunning panorama of the Valdichiana and Lake Trasimeno. On the northern side is a winter garden, with the Borgo San Domenico a mesmerising backdrop. *Complimentary evening aperitif. Ask about cooking classes & vineyard tours.*

Price	€130–€230. Singles €80–€130. Suites €250–€340.
Rooms	26: 18 doubles, 5 singles, 3 suites.
Meals	Restaurants 5-minute walk uphill.
Closed	9 January-February.
Directions	A1 exit Val di Chiana, then Siena & Perugia m'way; 2nd exit for Cortona. Follow signs for "Cortona Centro". Parking nearby.

Stefano Meacci
Viale Cesare Battisti 13,
52044 Cortona

Tel	+39 0575 605252
Email	info@villamarsili.net
Web	www.villamarsili.net

Casa Bellavista

A glass of wine at a table in the orchard. Birdsong for background music – or occasionally foreground, if the family rooster is feeling conversational. And a panorama of Tuscan landscape. Bellavista is well-named: its all-round views take in Monte Arniata, Foiano della Chiana and the old Abbey of Farneta. There was a farm here for 200 years but the house was extensively restored about 30 years ago. It still has the original brick exterior, now softened by creepers, and a welcoming, family atmosphere (Simonetta and her husband, Guido, have two teenage children). There's an assured, uncluttered country elegance to the rooms, and pretty, airy bedrooms are furnished with family antiques and interesting textiles; two have their own balcony with views onto the garden. Simonetta's kitchen has a huge marble table top for kneading bread and she cooks farmhouse food for her guests: it is delicious; breakfasts are lavish, cookery lessons are a treat. Roam the Arezzo province in true Italian style: vespas and bikes are free! Italian family B&B of the very best sort.

Price	€120–€140.
Rooms	3: 1 double, 2 twins/doubles.
Meals	Dinner €35, by arrangement. Wine from €19.
Closed	Rarely.
Directions	Autostrada Valdichiana exit Perugia; exit Foiano. After 400m, right for Fratta-S. Caterina. On for 2.8km, right next to ruined building. After 1km, right at junc.; keep to left-hand road. After 600m, right onto dirt road.

Simonetta Demarchi
Loc. Creti C.S. 40,
52044 Cortona

Tel	+39 0575 610311
Email	info@casabellavista.it
Web	www.casabellavista.it

La Palazzina

There is an English inflection to La Palazzina, with its quirky 14th-century watchtower planted inexplicably beside the main house. And it makes a most unusual self-contained retreat with luscious views across the wooded valley. You get a well-equipped kitchen, a wood-burner for cosy nights, a winding stair to a half-moon double and, at the top, a twin with a stunning, brick-beehive ceiling. The honeysuckle-strewn terrace is just as you would wish, with cypress trees marching sedately up the hill alongside, and birdsong to disturb the peace. The grounds, including a saltwater swimming pool with views, are for you to explore, and lead to some of the loveliest walks in the valley. David and Salina are great company and will prepare dinner for you on your first evening, left in the fridge for your arrival. Hannibal defeated the Roman army at nearby Lake Trasimeno and there is little that David doesn't know about the historical importance of this area – his enthusiasm is contagious. The garden is a delight; the tower magical. *Minimum stay one week.*

Price	£695–£995 per week.
Rooms	Tower for 4 (1 double, 2 singles).
Meals	Dinner first evening, with wine, €30; by arrangement. Restaurants 15-minute drive.
Closed	Rarely.
Directions	Directions on booking.

David & Salina Lloyd-Edwards
Sant'Andrea di Sorbello,
52040 Mercatale di Cortona

Tel   +39 0575 638111
Email   davidle47@btinternet.com
Web   www.palazzina.co.uk

Relais San Pietro in Polvano

Paradise high in the hills. The adorable Signor Protti and his wife run this enchanting hotel with their son and daughter-in-law and the care they lavish on the place is apparent at every turn. Bedrooms have shutters and gorgeous old rafters, wide wrought-iron beds, elegant painted wardrobes, rugs on tiled floors, straw hats on white walls. For cool autumn nights there are cream sofas and a log fire. The pool, on a terrace just below, must have one of the best views in Tuscany: keep your head above water and you are rewarded with the blue-tinted panorama for which Italy is famous. There is a restaurant for guests serving delicious local food and their own olive oil; bread comes fresh from the bread oven. In summer you dine at beautifully dressed tables on a terrace overlooking the gardens, full of cool recesses and comfy chairs, and the olive-grove'd valley beyond. An atmosphere of luxurious calm and seclusion prevails, and your hosts are a delight. For those who choose to venture forth, note that gates close at midnight. *Children over 12 welcome. Minimum stay two nights.*

Price	€130-€300.
Rooms	10: 4 doubles, 1 single, 5 suites.
Meals	Dinner €20-€30. Wine from €10.
Closed	November-March.
Directions	A1 Rome-Milan exit Monte San Savino for Castiglion Fiorentino. At 3rd lights, left for Polvano. After 7km, left for Relais San Pietro.

Luigi Protti
Loc. Polvano 3,
52043 Castiglion Fiorentino

Tel	+39 0575 650100
Email	info@polvano.com
Web	www.polvano.com

Il Pero

A lab called Molly, a pony called Topsy, cats, chickens and a pool with long views – this is a brilliant place for families. It is lived and worked in by delightful William and Miranda, who, with their two young girls, have poured their hearts into a new life in Italy. Il Pero is a work in progress, a lovely old Tuscan farmhouse (1782) set in a flat plain and surrounded by barley and sunflowers, plus a haybarn, an olive press (they produce their own oil) and a kitchen garden you can help yourself to. You get four super apartments with good kitchens, cheery bright bedrooms, big wet rooms and little pergolas for private outdoor spaces – and a romantic bedroom in the square tower, with an ancient wine barrel for the shower! All is new or cleverly recycled, from the mattresses that can be adjusted to suit your requirements to the lovely old floorboards from a nearby convent. Don't miss the minstrel's gallery, illuminated by a chandelier with 120 candles (a wow for big celebrations) or the pizza evenings – great fun. As for cobbled hilltop Arezzo, it is stuffed with fine churches and frescoes, pretty shops and irresistible *gelatos*. *Ask about photography courses.*

Price	€150. Apts €800–€1,500 per week.
Rooms	1 + 4: 1 double. 4 apts: 2 for 2, 1 for 5, 1 for 6.
Meals	Breakfast €15 for self-caterers. Welcome pack. Occasional dinner with wine, €30. Restaurants 5km.
Closed	Rarely.
Directions	A1 exit Monte S. Savino. At Montagnano dir. Rigutino & Frassineto. Leaving Frassineto left off main road; past cemetery, gravel track, stone house with towers; left after farm. Right into drive, signed.

Miranda Taxis
Loc. Manziana 15,
52100 Policiano

Tel	+39 0575 979593
Email	info@ilpero.com
Web	www.ilpero.com

Il Palazzetto

An unassuming barn conversion up a steep drive, this self-catering treat combines traditional architecture with fresh homely furnishings and underfloor heating. A 2.5-acre garden of fruit orchards and olives with long vistas to ancient hill-topped Tuscan towns ensures birdsong and herb-tinted peace and tranquillity. Bedrooms are understated, simple and comfortable with plenty of wood and natural colours. The spacious sitting room is made snug by an open fire in winter, while French windows keep it breezy in summer. Behind the house is a rose-rambled terraced dining area and a covered pergola; down some steps through the olive trees to the field below lies a lovely large saltwater infinity pool, a secluded sun trap for relaxing with far-reaching views; bliss too for a night-time, underwater-lit dip. There's loads to do in the area, from truffle snuffling, fishing and riding to meandering through the alley'd mazes and markets of nearby medieval towns Città di Castello, San Sepolcro and Anghiari. A well-converted, well-furnished space whose gardens, given time, will mellow.

Price	€825–€2,090 per week.
Rooms	House for 8.
Meals	Restaurants 1.5km.
Closed	Never.
Directions	In Monterchi centre at large sq., over bridge on right. Follow road round old town (don't go into old town). Exit Monterchi, 1st right to Ripoli & Pianezze. On for 1.5km until small bridge on left. Over bridge, onto gravel road. At x-roads, left track for 0.2km. New drive on right; very steep.

Diane Noel
Loc. Borgacciano, 52031 Monterchi

Mobile	+44 (0)7956 841895
Email	diane@noelfamily.co.uk
Web	www.il-palazzetto.com

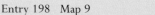

Villa I Bossi

Fifty people once lived on the ground floor of the old house and everything is as it was – the great box that held the bread, the carpenter's room crammed with tools, the robes hanging in the sacristy, the oven for making charcoal… Francesca loves showing people round the house that has been in her husband's family since 1240; it is brimful of treasures. There's even a fireplace sculpted by Benedetto da Maiano in the 1300s – his 'thank you for having me' to the family. Sleep in faded splendour in the main villa or opt for the modern comforts of the orangery: simple and beautiful. This is a magical place, full of character and memories, overseen by the most delightful people. As for the park-like gardens… set among gentle green hills, they have been enriched over the centuries: to one side of the swimming pool, a hill covered in rare fruit trees, to the west, Italian box hedges and camellias, peonies and old-fashioned roses, avenues, pond, grassy banks and shady trees, enticing seats under arching shrubs, olives and vines… And they make their own chianti and oil. *Ask about cookery courses.*

Price	€125–€165.
Rooms	10 + 1: 2 doubles, 2 twins. Orangery: 2 doubles, 2 triples, 2 quadruples. Apartment for 2.
Meals	Dinner, 4 courses with wine, €35; by arrangement. Restaurant 200m.
Closed	January-February.
Directions	In Arezzo follow signs to stadium. Pass Esso petrol station & on to Bagnoro. Then to Gragnone; 2km to villa.

Francesca Viguali Albergotti
Gragnone 44/46, 52100 Arezzo

Tel	+39 0575 365642
Email	franvig@ats.it
Web	www.villaibossi.com

Casa Simonicchi

After a blissful drive through the Casentino National Park you arrive at a hamlet of stone houses. This one is a farmhouse with a barn attached, made comfortable to the point of luxury by sculptress Jenny. In the top barn (six entrance steps only) is a family apartment simply, charmingly furnished with natural colours, Italian and English pieces, paintings and sculpture. The two bedrooms, each with a shower, are placed at either end; the spacious sitting room and well-equipped kitchen lie between. Best of all is the roof terrace, and its breathtaking panorama of sweet-chestnut forests. Bask in the sun or the shade, take a cool shower, dine al fresco, stargaze – there's a reflector telescope. Below are flowery terraces, lavender and olives – and a sculpture garden. Jenny also does B&B in her farmhouse and gives you two bedrooms, one romantically over the arch. Expect beams, antiques, a huge fireplace. Warm, generous, knowledgeable, Jenny can tell you all about the historic towns to visit; the countryside of Michelangelo and St Francis of Assisi; the welcoming taverna down the road. *Minimum stay two nights.*

Price	€175; €350 for 4. Apt €675–€975 per week.
Rooms	1 + 1: 1 suite for 4. Apt for 4 (1 double, 1 twin).
Meals	Dinner with wine, from €30, by arrangement. Restaurant nearby.
Closed	Christmas-April.
Directions	Exit A1 Arezzo; north for Sansepolcro; signs for Caprese Michelangelo; left for Lama; right for Chiusi della Verna; after cypress-filled cemetery, house on 3rd right-hand bend; sharp descent.

Jennifer Frears-Barnard
Via Simonicchi 184,
Caprese Michelangelo, 52033 Arezzo
Tel   +39 0575 793762
Email   jenniferbarnard@alice.it
Web   www.simonicchi.com

Galealpe Agriturismo

The road winds ever higher to Alessandra and Andrea's olive farm on the top of a hill, surrounded by Tuscan beauty. The olives are organically farmed, the house has been restored with local materials. The two apartments, bright and country simple, each with its own entrance and a private spot in the garden, have ivory walls and well-stocked kitchens, comfy sitting rooms and wood-burners for chilly evenings. Bedrooms are a good size, and charming. Your lovely young hosts make it easy for you to enjoy 'la dolce vita' and are passionate about the environment and the great outdoors. Come for their guided tours of the Prato Magno range – on horseback or in your boots; mountain bikes are yours to borrow, trails start close by. A ten-kilometre drive brings you to Arezzo and its Saturday market, so stock up with delectable cheeses, hams, breads, tomatoes, then head for the hills and a picnic. Or take it back to your terrace overlooking the pretty garden and valley views that reach to Arezzo's Duomo. Florence is an hour away – perfect for a day trip if the peacefulness overwhelms you! *Minimum stay two nights.*

Price	€54–€66.
Rooms	2 apartments: 1 for 2-4, 1 for 4-6.
Meals	Breakfast €6, by arrangement. Restaurant 5km.
Closed	Never.
Directions	A1 Florence-Rome exit Arezzo dir. Bibbiena; at shopping centre 'Il Magnifico' r'bout follow Ponte Buriano, then Pieve San Giovanni.

Alessandra Cerulli & Andrea Pesce
Pieve San Giovanni 76, 52010 Arezzo
Tel   +39 0575 451309
Email   info@galealpe.it
Web   www.galealpe.it

Rendola Riding Agriturismo

One of the forerunners of agriturismo in Tuscany, Jenny started Rendola back in the 70s and gives you the best possible way of seeing Chianti — on horseback. You need to be able to ride, and the minimum age for riders is ten. Equestrians may expect excellent conditions and an English (not western) style. Choose between lessons with set timetables, relaxed treks and three-day forays. How wonderful, after a long sticky day in the saddle, to return to showers and homely rooms! Then, at the rustic ring of a cow bell, guests, family and stable workers gather in the dining room for dinner, where sprightly Pietro serves wholesome organic Tuscan dishes washed down with chianti — and regales the assembled company with many a tale. It's all delightfully laid back: chickens, ducks, turkeys, horses, dogs in the courtyard; music, books, an open fire in the sitting room; jackets on the backs of chairs... Non-riders will appreciate generous Jenny's advice on what to see and do in the area. *Minimum stay two nights. Pick-up from Montevarchi train station.*

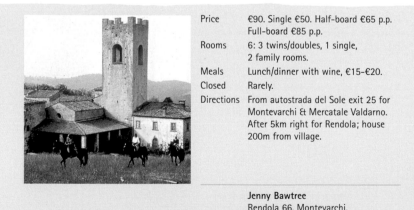

Price	€90. Single €50. Half-board €65 p.p. Full-board €85 p.p.
Rooms	6: 3 twins/doubles, 1 single, 2 family rooms.
Meals	Lunch/dinner with wine, €15–€20.
Closed	Rarely.
Directions	From autostrada del Sole exit 25 for Montevarchi & Mercatale Valdarno. After 5km right for Rendola; house 200m from village.

Jenny Bawtree
Rendola 66, Montevarchi,
52025 Arezzo

Tel	+39 0559 707045
Email	info@rendolariding.it
Web	www.rendolariding.it

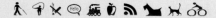

Borgo Iesolana Agriturismo

At the centre of an immaculate patchwork of fields, vineyards and woods, this irresistible group of old buildings. Mellow stone and warm brick blend, flowers tumble from terracotta pots, arches invite you in out of the sun, a pool beckons. Giovanni and Francesco inherited the estate from their grandfather and live here with their young families. They have created nine apartments, all different, from the farm buildings, and it is a solid, sensitive conversion. The décor is an upmarket, uncluttered mix of traditional and new: good beds and fabrics, super kitchens, thoughtful lighting. And if you prefer not to self-cater, you can breakfast in the 'wine bar' across the way. This, too, is an impeccable restoration, with modern Italian furniture and big windows. Lunch and dinner are available on request; local produce and traditional Tuscan fare. The farm is beautifully run (the very vines are edged with roses) and produces wine, olive oil, grappa and honey. It lies alongside an old Roman road that once linked Siena with Florence, with views on all sides of Chiantishire. *Min. stay two-seven nights depending on season.*

Price	€830–€2,595 per week (€130–€180 two nights low season).
Rooms	11 apartments: 3 for 2, 3 for 4, 3 for 6, 2 for 8.
Meals	Breakfast €10. Lunch/dinner €25–€30, by arrangement. Wine €9–€12.
Closed	Never.
Directions	A1 Firenze-Roma exit Valdarno; at toll, right for Montevarchi dir. Levane/Bucine; thro' Bucine, left to Pogi. Left for Iesolana, 150m left; over narrow bridge & cont. to Borgo.

Giovanni & Francesco Toscano
Loc. Iesolana,
52021 Bucine
Tel   +39 0559 92988
Email   info@iesolana.it
Web   www.iesolana.it

Odina Agriturismo

You are 650 metres above sea level and feel on top of the world – the Arno valley reaches out before you and the air is pure. Paolo is a talented gardener and each bush, tree and herb has been chosen with care, posing magnificently next to the solid, blue-shuttered house. The interiors of the house and apartments are delightfully rustic and contemporary. Each is different: kitchen surfaces are of granite, or local *pietra serena*, bathroom walls are softly ragged in varying shades. All have French windows to a patio with wooden outdoor furniture. Oil, vinegar, sugar, coffee, salt and washing-up liquid are provided; ask in advance and they'll provide more (for which you pay). The reception is in a beautifully restored, de-consecrated chapel, with an old bread-making chest and a 'shop' selling Odina olive oil, honey, lavender and beans. Take a dip in the pool, go for long, lazy walks in the olive groves and chestnut woods, prepare a barbecue. Garden courses and visits – highly recommended – are held here in May. *Minimum stay one week; three nights in low season. Private chef available.*

Ethical Collection: Environment; Food.
See page 400 for details

Price	€525–€945 for 2; €800–€1,750 for 4-5. Farmhouse €2,100–€3,700. Prices per week.
Rooms	4 apartments for 2, 5, 6, or 7. Farmhouse for 8-10.
Meals	Restaurants 5km.
Closed	Mid-January to mid-February.
Directions	Florence-Rome A1, exit Valdarno. In Terranuova, follow Loro Ciuffenna.

Paolo Trenti
Loc. Odina, 52024 Loro Ciuffenna
Tel   +39 0559 69304
Email   info@odina.it
Web   www.odina.it

Umbria

Locanda Palazzone

An imposing palazzo in the Umbrian countryside, Locanda Palazzone is full of contrasts. Built by a cardinal as a resting place for pilgrims to Rome, it was designed with an urban sophistication: buttressed walls, mullioned windows, vaulted hall. It later fell from grace and became a country farmhouse – until Ludovico's family rescued it, planting vineyards and restoring the buildings. Despite the rusticity of the setting, the interiors are cool, elegant, chic. The sitting room (once the Grand Hall) is light and airy, its huge windows overlooking the garden. Bedrooms – split-level suites, mostly – are understatedly luxurious, their modern and antique furnishings set against pale oak floors, cream walls, exposed stone. Red, claret and purple cushions add warmth; white linen sheets, Bulgari bath foams and specialist herb soaps soothe. Meals – regional, seasonal – are served on rainbow porcelain on the terrace, accompanied by the estate's wines. Your generous hosts are eager to please, the pool is surrounded by delphiniums and roses, and views sweep to vineyards and forests. A remarkable place. *Minimum stay two nights June-August.*

Price	€165-€290.
Rooms	7 suites: 5 for 2, 2 for 4.
Meals	Dinner, 4 courses, €38; by arrangement.
Closed	10 January-20 March.
Directions	A1 Florence-Roma, exit Orvieto; 1.8km dir. Orvieto; at bridge for funicular, right for Allerona; on. to Sferracavallo junc.; on for Allerona; 200m, left toward Castel Giorgio, keeping petrol station on right; 2.5km, signed.

	Lodovico Dubini
	Loc. Rocca Ripesena, 05010 Orvieto
Tel	+39 0763 393614
Email	info@locandapalazzone.com
Web	www.locandapalazzone.com

Locanda Rosati Agriturismo

From the moment you turn off the road – whose proximity is quickly forgotten – the atmosphere is easy. The house has been gently modernised but remains firmly a farmhouse; the summer-cool rooms on the ground floor – with open fires in winter – have been furnished with an eye for comfort rather than a desire to impress, and wild flowers, books and magazines are scattered. Dinner is the thing here; it's rustic, delectable and Giampiero and Paolo are natural hosts, full of stories and enthusiastic advice on what to do and where to go. Tables are laid with simple cloths, glass tumblers and butter coloured pottery, the recipes have been handed down the Rosati generations and the wines come from a wonderful cellar carved out of the tufa seven metres below ground. Bedrooms are simple, with new wooden beds, pristine bed linen, spotless showers. Much of the furniture comes from the famous Bottega Michelangeli in Orvieto, whose jigsaw-like carved animal shapes characterise this region. From the gardens you can see the spiky skyline of Orvieto: delightful. *Ask about cookery courses.*

Price	€110–€150. Singles €90–€110. Half-board option available.
Rooms	10: 4 doubles, 1 single, 5 family rooms.
Meals	Dinner with wine, €37.50.
Closed	7 January-February.
Directions	Exit A1 at Orvieto; on for Viterbo, Bolsena & Montefiascone; 10km; on right.

Giampiero Rosati
Loc. Buonviaggio 22, 05018 Orvieto
Tel   +39 0763 217314
Email   info@locandarosati.it
Web   www.locandarosati.it

Locanda di Colle dell'Oro

Candles flicker alongside the path, illuminating your way as you return from the garden restaurant. It's an imaginative touch, in keeping with the Locanda's ethos. Gioia delights in her family's country home and you will too, from the moment you step into the striking entrance hall and breathe in the heady scent of jasmine. In spite of occasional music and four lively dogs, the restored 19th-century house feels harmonious and calm. Large, lovely bedrooms, named after plants, have neutral colour schemes and bleached wooden furniture that Gioia has painted with flowers. Ask for a room with a view. Sheets and towels are of the purest linen and the bathrooms are beautifully planned; the luxury is real and understated. French windows lead from the breakfast room to the terrace looking down over sprawling Terni, and a garden full of birdsong and geraniums, jasmine, roses, hydrangeas; the swimming pool is hidden on a lower terrace. Yoga classes three times a week, cookery classes out of season.

Price	€70–€100. Suites €130. Triples €110. Half-board €20 extra p.p.
Rooms	10: 5 doubles, 1 suite, 4 triples.
Meals	Lunch/dinner €30.
Closed	Rarely.
Directions	From A1 Orte exit Terni Ovest. Follow signs for Norcia Cascia until signs for Locanda. Hotel on left.

Gioia Iaculli
Strada di Palmetta 31, 05100 Terni

Tel	+39 0744 432379
Email	locanda@colledelloro.it
Web	www.colledelloro.it

Eremo del Sole

Once through the impressive estate gates you follow a lavender-clumped drive to a lavishly renovated collection of apartments — all perched on a pine-forested ridge on a 124-acre estate. Take care not to let the astonishing view distract you from appreciating what spreads out before you: a seductive pool prefacing the forest and a split-level garden brimming with flowers and bustling with butterflies, birds and bees. Potted lime trees, outsized urns, a herb garden, an olive grove, ducks, donkeys and stabled horses: every inch is perfectly groomed. An unusually sumptuous medieval theme runs through these three immaculately renovated apartments: opulently draped four-posters, tapestries and medieval style paintings, heavy curtains with medieval seals hanging at arched windows of leaded glass; the odd stained-glass piece or fresco; and arched porticos leading to covered patios and terraces. Kitchens are country-homely and modern and Federica, your generous hostess, will organise trips to bucolic markets for supplies and recommend restaurants, ten-minutes down the windy roads, in Spoleto.

Price	€880-€1,900 per week.
Rooms	3 apartments for 4-8.
Meals	Lunch/dinner from €30, on request. Restaurants 3km.
Closed	Never.
Directions	SS3 exit Spoleto (API petrol station immed. after you turn off); follow signs to hospital. Past hospital; on until Collerisana. Left towards Rubbiano, cont. on windy road until end.

Federica Marini
Loc. Rubbiano, 06049 Spoleto
Tel   +39 3479 700850
Email   federica@ourspoleto.com
Web   www.eremodelsole.com

Villa Campo Verde

Renovated over a period of five years, with the involvement of local craftsmen and architects, this vast, cavernous 17th-century farmhouse, resplendent amid terraced orchards and groves, still has paintings and pottery scattered about from its incarnation as an artists' commune in the Seventies. The work has been extensive and no corner has been cut: a fantastic manicured pool area with wooden deck, matching furniture and outdoor wood-fired oven for eating outside; smartly done bedrooms with antique furniture, striking rugs from the Middle East, underfloor heating and creaky old doors; wonderful bathrooms of granite and marble, wooden vanities with modern sinks and perhaps a tub recessed into the wall like a work of art; living rooms with oriental carpets and armchairs and sofas around large fireplaces... an inviting bar room, massive beams and secretive balconies, a suspended staircase, an old wine barrista sunk into the ground and covered with glass flooring. And, of course for somewhere that sleeps 25, a vast kitchen with a dining room to match. Bohemian rhapsody Italian style. *Minimum stay five nights.*

Price	June–September €9,000; October–May €6,000.
Rooms	Villa for 25 (7 suites for 3-4; 2 sharing bath).
Meals	Restaurants nearby.
Closed	Never.
Directions	From Assisi, south on SS3 past Trevi, Campello sul Clitunno; exit Eggi. In Eggi left towards lower piazza. At right end of piazza, Via del Campo Verde, to end; green gates.

	Beverley Willcox
	Via Campo Verde 35, 06049 Eggi
Tel	+39 0743 520858
Email	beverley.willcox@yahoo.co.uk
Web	www.villacampoverde.com

B&B & Self-catering   Umbria

Le Logge di Silvignano

Wrought-iron gates swing open onto a courtyard… and there is the house, in all its unruffled, medieval beauty. Thought, care and talent have gone into its restoration. And the setting: the Spoleto hills with views to Assisi! Alberto's love of roses has been awoken in Diana and is wonderfully evident, while the recent planting preserves as many of the old inhabitants as possible: prune, Japanese persimmon and two ancient figs, source of breakfast jams. The graceful open gallery with octagonal stone pillars dates from the 15th century but the main building has its roots in the 12th. Guest suites, big and charming, have Amalfi-tiled bathrooms, pretty sitting rooms with open fireplaces, tiny kitchens for snacks and drinks, sumptuous fabrics woven in Montefalco look perfect against stone walls and massive beams. Diana and Alberto are delighted if you join them for a glass of wine in the newly restored 'club house' before you set off to dine, or even for a nightcap on your return. They're warm, interesting people, genuinely happy to share their corner of paradise. *Minimum stay four nights.*

Price	€700–€1,600 per week.
Rooms	3 + 2: 3 suites for 2-3. 2 apartments for 4-5. Kitchenette available for drinks for guests.
Meals	Breakfast €10. Restaurants 1.5-4km.
Closed	10 November-10 March (open New Year's Eve & upon request).
Directions	A1 Florence-Bologna exit Bettolle-Sinalunga, then E45 for Perugia-Assisi-Foligno. SS3 Flaminia until Fonti del Clitunno, then dir. Campello-Pettino; 3km after Campello right for Silvignano, 1.5km.

Alberto & Diana Araimo
Fraz. Silvignano 14, 06049 Spoleto
Tel   +39 0743 274098
Email   mail@leloggedisilvignano.it
Web   www.leloggedisilvignano.it

Entry 210   Map 12

Casa del Cinguettio

The twists and turns require skilful negotiation but the rewards on arrival are great. Tucked out of sight from the village street, beneath a medieval castle, the beautifully restored barn appears to hang on to the side of the hill – and the views from pool and terrace over the Spoleto valley are stupendous. A night swim almost leaves you feeling suspended in space! As for the recently refurbished, split-level interiors, they combine traditional, solid, cave-like Umbrian architecture with funky modern touches. Slabs of wood from the wall make a glass-banistered staircase, there are white marble floors, a glass-topped dining table, a groovy, steep-stepped mezzanine, modern sinks atop marble vanitics; the contrasts and colours are gorgeous. Ethnic spreads, an oriental rug and a corner fireplace add warmth to the sitting room on cool evenings in, while the fully kitted kitchen leads onto a barbecue terrace for lazy lunches under the olives trees. Herbs scent the air. The hills are laced with walking and riding paths, the area is rich with history, Assisi is a short drive. *Parking available for 2 cars.*

Price	£950–£1,900 per week.
Rooms	House for 6-8.
Meals	Restaurants 10-minute drive.
Closed	Rarely.
Directions	Directions on booking.

Berenice Anderson
06042 Campello Alto

Tel	+44 (0)1865 553244
Email	bma161@hotmail.com
Web	www.casadelcinguettio.co.uk

Pianciano

The old borgo buildings (some 16th century) are now self-contained apartments; come for deep delicious comfort on a working, self-sufficient estate. Wander down the terraced orchards to a huge pick-your-own vegetable garden overlooking a sauna and sleek pool – and tables and chairs under a vine canopy, an idyllic setting for lunch. Beyond are olive groves, vineyards and pastures – space galore to explore. Lavender-scented bedrooms are touched with elegant details: jade-coloured vases arranged just so, divine hand-detailed linen, old doors mounted as headboards, antique frames holding romantic paintings. Neutral coloured throws complement beamed ceilings, terracotta floors and sturdy wooden pieces, bookshelves hold handsome tomes, framed copies of old letters and antique architectural plans dot walls. High-ceilinged sitting rooms and a cavernous dining room hewn from the hillside provide heart-warming living space; knock-out views across the valley mean you'll keep the curtains open. Visit the wonderful little villages of the Valnerina, fall in love with this magical place. *Ask about pizza nights.*

Price	€750–€1,600 per week.
Rooms	3 apartments for 6-8.
Meals	Breakfast €10. Chef available, by arrangement. Restaurant nearby.
Closed	Never.
Directions	Exit Eggi-San Giacomo from SS; right at lights, then right dir. Passo d'Acera. At Tamoil garage straight on, reach 6km milestone, on for 300m, then right at sharp bend onto dirt road. Through gate Pianciano (please close behind you) and on for 200m to estate.

Claudia Bachetoni
Loc. Silvignano, 06049 Spoleto

Tel	+39 0743 521535
Email	pianciano@pianciano.it
Web	www.pianciano.it

I Mandorli Agriturismo

I Mandorli is aptly named: there's at least one almond tree outside each apartment. The blossom in February is stunning and, in summer, masses of greenery shades the old *casa padronale*. Once the centre of a 200-hectare estate, the shepherd's house and the olive mill in particular are fascinating reminders of days gone by. Mama Wanda is passionate about the whole, lovely, rambling place and will show you around, embellishing everything you see with stories about its history. Widowed, she manages the remaining 47 hectares, apartments and rooms, *and* cooks, aided by her three charming daughters: home-grown produce and excellent gnocchi every Thursday. Bedrooms are sweet, simple affairs with new wrought-iron beds and pale patchwork quilts; small bathrooms are spotless. Children will love the wooden slide and seesaw, the old pathways and steps on this shallow hillside, the new pool – wonderful to return to after cultural outings to Assisi and Spoleto. This is olive oil country so make sure you go home with a few bottles of the best. *Laundry facilities: small charge.*

Price	€40-€85 (€265-€650 per week). Apts €65-€150 (€360-€700 per week).
Rooms	3 + 3: 1 twin/double, 2 triples. 3 apts: 1 for 2, 2 for 4.
Meals	Breakfast €5 for self-caterers. Restaurants 500m.
Closed	Rarely.
Directions	SS3 exit Trevi-Montefalco for Bovara; signed from main road.

Famiglia Zappelli Cardarelli
Loc. Fondaccio 6,
06039 Bovara di Trevi
Tel   +39 0742 78669
Email   info@agriturismoimandorli.com
Web   www.agriturismoimandorli.com

Casale Campodoro

The interior of this restored 18th-century building has been embellished with style and a quirky humour: imagine an Indonesian hippo's head over a fireplace and a plastic goose as a lamp. Piero, a gentle, humorous and intelligent Italian, lives here with Carolina, four cats and three daft, friendly and boisterous dogs. In one shower room, a muscular plaster-cast juts out of the wall and serves as a towel rail; elsewhere, Scottish grandmother's clothes – lace interwoven with scarab beetles – have been framed and hung. By the pool are plastic yellow Philippe Starck sofa and chairs; on the walls, religious icons. The garden sits on an Umbrian hillside and has little steps leading to hidden corners and a large aviary, whose birds escape and return at night. There are lovely views across to an old abbey, and other, more edible delights: breakfast brings warm, fresh, homemade bread and tasty jams. Once a week, guests get together for dinner with everyone contributing a national dish. Don't mind the animals or the odd bit of peeling paint – this is a joyously individual and eccentric place.

Price	€50–€60 (€420 per week). Apts €80–€130 (€480–€700 per week).
Rooms	3 + 3: 3 doubles. 3 apartments for 3–5.
Meals	Restaurants nearby.
Closed	Rarely.
Directions	From Perugia-Cesena exit Massa Martana (316) to Foligno/Bastaro; left to San Terenziano; 1km; right to Viepri; 100m, track on left; 1st on right.

	Carolina Bonanno Fraz. Viepri 106, 06056 Massa Martana
Tel	+39 0758 947347
Email	camporo@libero.it
Web	www.casalecampodoro.it

Tenuta di Canonica

The position is wonderful, on a green ridge with stunning views. The house was a ruin (17th century, with medieval remnants and Roman foundations) when Daniele and Maria bought it in 1998. Much creativity has gone into its resurrection. There's not a corridor in sight – instead, odd steps up and down, hidden doors, vaulted ceilings, enchanting corners. Cool, beautiful reception rooms are decorated in vibrant colours, then given a personal, individual and exotic touch: family portraits, photos, books; there's even a parrot. The bedrooms are vast, intriguingly shaped and alluring, with rugs on pale brick or wooden floors and gorgeous beds and fabrics. The dining room opens onto a covered terrace surrounded by roses and shrubs, a path sweeps down to the pool; there's good walking on the 24-hectare estate. This is a house that reflects its owners' personalities. Daniele and Maria are vivid, interesting and well-travelled and, while they are away, Giovanna is on hand to welcome guests to the rich tapestry of rooms. *Minimum stay two nights.*

Price	€150–€235. Apartments €950–€1,100 per week.
Rooms	11 + 2: 11 doubles. 2 apartments for 3-4.
Meals	Dinner €40. Wine €10-€40. Restaurant 5km.
Closed	December-February.
Directions	Florence-Rome A1 exit Valdichiana; E45 Perugia-Terni exit Todi-Orvieto; SS448 for Prodo-Titignano; 3km, Bivio per Cordigliano; 1km, signed. Do not turn right to Canonica, continue until Cordigliano sign, then on left.

Daniele Fano
Loc. Canonica m.75/76, 06059 Todi

Tel	+39 0758 947545
Email	tenutadicanonica@tin.it
Web	www.tenutadicanonica.com

La Palazzetta del Vescovo Relais

Only the bells from a nearby convent or the hum of the tractor will disturb you. Paola and Stefano love to pamper their guests and there's a 'wellness' room in the cellar. Widely travelled and from the corporate world, they decided in 2000 to hang up their business suits and do something different. They bought this 18th-century hilltop palazzetta – once a summer residence for bishops, utterly abandoned in the 1960s – and restored it to its former glory. An informal elegance prevails. The four sitting rooms are cool, elegant and inviting; the bedrooms, each individual, each lovely, are composed in subtle, muted colours: pale walls, fine rugs, muslin'd four-posters, antique Neapolitan beds. What they have in common is a matchless view over steeply falling vineyards and the Tiber valley. On a clear day you can see as far as Perugia. The newly-planted gardens and the pool make the most of the outlook, too – as does the terrace, where you can enjoy an aperitif before Paola's Umbrian cuisine. She, like her house, is a delight – serene, smiling and friendly.
Minimum stay two nights. All alcoholic drinks included.

Price	€180–€260. Singles from €140.
Rooms	9 doubles.
Meals	Light lunch, from €15. Dinner, 4 courses, €35. Wine from €10. Restaurant 4km.
Closed	Rarely.
Directions	A1 Rome-Florence exit Perugia onto E45; exit Fratta Todina. On for 7km, left for Spineta, thro' Spineta; house on right after vineyard, up track behind gates.

Paola Maria & Stefano Zocchi
Via Clausura 17, Fraz. Spineta,
06054 Fratta Todina
Tel   +39 0758 745183
Email   info@lapalazzettadelvescovo.it
Web   www.lapalazzettadelvescovo.com

Agriturismo Madonna delle Grazie

There are rabbits, dogs, horses, ducks and hens, and Renato will pluck a cicada from an olive tree and show you how it 'sings': children (and adults) who love animals will be in heaven. This is a real farm – not a hotel with a few animals wandering about – so don't expect luxury; it's agriturismo at its best and you eat what they produce. The simple guest bedrooms in the 18th-century farmhouse are engagingly old-fashioned; all have a terrace or balcony and the bathrooms are spotless. The farm is now fully organic and the food in the restaurant delicious, so make the most of Renato's own salami, chicken, fruit and vegetables, olive oil, grappa and wine. There's also a big playground for children, and table football in the house. The youngest offspring, free from the tyranny of taste, will love the Disney gnomes dotted around the picnic area. For the grown-ups there's riding, archery, a discount at the San Casciano Terme spa... and views that stretch to Tuscany in one direction, Umbria in the other. A great little place.

Price	€100–€140.
Rooms	6 doubles.
Meals	Dinner €22. Wine €8–€12.
Closed	Rarely.
Directions	From A1 north: exit Chiusi-Chianciano, right to Chiusi & Città della Pieve. From A1 south: exit Fabro, turn left; left after 1km to Città della Pieve.

Ethical Collection: Environment; Food.
See page 400 for details.

Renato Nannotti
Madonna delle Grazie 6,
06062 Città della Pieve
Tel   +39 0578 299822
Email   info@madonnadellegrazie.it
Web   www.madonnadellegrazie.it

Entry 217   Map 12

Villa Lemura

Live like an aristocrat but without the pomp or circumstance. This 18th-century building, once the country villa of Umbrian nobility, has an opulent but faded grandeur. Delightful Emma, Luca and family have made it their home: don't be surprised to find a bicycle propped against the gracious pillars of the entrance hall. Rooms will make you gasp — frescoed ceilings, richly tiled floors, Murano chandeliers — yet it all feels charmingly lived-in. Furniture is a comfortable mismatch of antiques and brocante finds. The high-ceilinged, elegant bedrooms might include an antique French bed, a chaise longue or a painted ceramic stove. Most have frescoes, one has a private terrace. Sink into sofas in the ballroom-sized salon, browse a book in the library, breakfast on the terrace above the Italian garden. Dinner can be arranged — or you may rustle up your own in the delightful orangery. Lake Trasimeno, Perugia and Assisi wait to be discovered; or find a quiet spot in the villa's shady gardens, full of terraced pool, mossy statues, fountains, olive grove and views.

Price	€100–€150. Whole house on request.
Rooms	7: 3 doubles, 1 twin, 1 triple; 1 double, 1 twin sharing bath.
Meals	Dinner €30 (min. 8), on request. Wine from €10. Restaurant 1km.
Closed	Occasionally.
Directions	From A1 exit Chiusi for Perugia; exit Perugia/Magione (not Panicale); signs to Panicale; thro' Macchie & Colgiordano (not up to Panicale); left to Lemura, Villa 1st on left.

Emma & Luca Mesenzio
Via Le Mura 1,
06064 Panicale
Tel   +39 0758 37134
Email   villalemura@alice.it
Web   www.villalemura.com

Villa di Monte Solare

A hushed, stylish, country retreat in a perfect Umbrian setting. This noble villa, encircled by a formal walled garden, has been transformed into a small hotel with uniformed staff, elegant rooms and fine restaurant. The grounds, which include the little chapel of Santa Lucia and a small maze, envelop the hotel in an atmosphere of calm. Bedrooms are spacious and lovingly tended, full of local fabric and craftmanship. The public rooms have kept their charm, their painted cornices and friezes, huge fireplaces, ancient terracotta floors. The restaurant, a gorgeous beamed room with a roaring fire in winter, seats bedroom capacity, so non-residents may only book if guests are dining out. Cappuccino from a bar machine at breakfast; at dinner, superb designer food and a choice 380 wines. The owners live for this place and eat with guests every night, the mood is refined and jackets are usually worn, though not insisted upon. In the old glass *limonaia* is a new beauty spa, for guests only. There are bikes to rent, pools to swim, even concerts and talks on Umbrian history. The view stretches out in every direction.

Price	€200–€240. Single €130–€145. Suites €300–€450.
Rooms	25: 14 doubles, 1 single, 10 suites.
Meals	Lunch €45–€65. Dinner with wine, €45–€65.
Closed	Never.
Directions	Exit A1 at Chiusi–Chianciano; right to Chiusi; right for Città della Pieve; signs for Perugia, wall on left; left for Perugia-Tavernelle (SS220); 1km after Tavernelle, left for Colle S. Paolo. 4km to Villa.

Ethical Collection: Environment; Food.
See page 400 for details

Rosemarie & Filippo Iannarone
Via Montali 7, Colle San Paolo,
06068 Tavernelle di Panicale

Tel	+39 0758 32376
Email	info@villamontesolare.it
Web	www.villamontesolare.it

The Country House Montali

Irresistible: a sympathetic restoration, a sensational setting and, some say, the world's best vegetarian cuisine. Chefs drop by from all over to be tutored in the art of vegeterian cooking, such is their reputation for fine food 'with a twist of Umbria and a splash of Brazil.' Standing on a plateau surrounded by woodland, reached by a long bumpy track, the gardens open to the hills and drop down to Lake Trasimeno, while the bedrooms, in three single-storey buildings, have verandas with views and a colonial air. White walls show off hand-carved teak furniture and oil paintings by the owner's brother; terracotta floors are graced by Indian rugs. After a wonderful day striding the hills, return to the serene little restaurant and colourful food exquisitely presented: roulade of crepes stuffed with the crunchiest vegetables, aubergine tart with caper parsley sauce, creamy saffron risotto and black truffles from Norcia. Alberto's wife Malu is head chef, Alberto sees to the wines – the best of local. Keen musicians both, they occasionally hold concerts too. Readers heap praise – no wonder. *Ask about cookery courses.*

Price	Half-board €200–€220 for 2.
Rooms	10 doubles.
Meals	Half-board only.
Closed	November–March.
Directions	A1 from Rome, exit Fabro dir. Città della Pieve and Piegaro. 2km after Tavernelle, left for Colle San Paolo. Up hill 7km, following signs. Left at top of hill, hotel 800m on left.

Alberto Musacchio
Via Montali 23,
06068 Tavernelle di Panicale
Tel　　+39 0758 350680
Email　montali@montalionline.com
Web　　www.montalionline.com

Umbria

Umbria

Villa Aureli

Little has changed since the Villa was built in the 18th century and became the country house of the Serègo Alighieri family 100 years later. The ornamental plasterwork, floor tiles and decorative shutters reflect its noble past, it is known to all the locals and is full of precious and historic treasures (walled up by a perspicacious housekeeper during the Occupation) which inspire the interest, attention and care of Sperello (descendent of Dante!). The house in fact has its origins in the 16th century, and the grounds are suitably formal – overgrown here, tamed there, with lemon trees in amazing 18th-century pots in the *limonaia* and a swimming pool created from an irrigation tank. The apartments are big and beautiful, the one on the second floor the largest and grandest, with balconies and views. Floors have mellow old tiles, ceilings are high and raftered, bedrooms are delightfully faded. You are a step away from the village, so can walk to the few shops and bar. A quietly impressive retreat, wonderfully peaceful – and special. *Minimum stay one week in high season; two nights in low season.*

Price	€700–€1,500 per week.
Rooms	4 apartments: 1 for 4, 1 for 4–8, 1 for 5, 1 for 6.
Meals	Occasional dinner with wine, €36. Restaurant 2km.
Closed	Never.
Directions	From A1, exit Valdichiana for Perugia, exit Madonna Alta towards Città della Pieve. At square, sign for Bagnaia; on left after 200m. Alternatively, go to centre of Castel del Piano and ask.

Sperello di Serègo Alighieri
Via Luigi Cirenei 70,
06132 Castel del Piano

Mobile	+39 340 6459061
Email	villa.aureli@libero.it
Web	www.villaaureli.it

Brigolante Guest Apartments

In the foothills of St Francis' beloved Mount Subasio the 16th-century stone farmhouse has been thoughtfully restored by Stefano and Rebecca. She is American and came to Italy to study, he is an architectural land surveyor – here was the perfect project. The apartments feel very private but you can always chat over an aperitif with the other guests in the garden. Rooms are light, airy and stylishly simple, combining grandmother's furniture with Rebecca's kind touches: a rustic basket of delicacies from the farm (wine, eggs, cheese, honey, olive oil, homemade jam), handmade soap and sprigs of lavender by the bath. Pretty lace curtains flutter at the window, kitchens are well-equipped, and laundry facilities are available. This is a farm with animals, so ham, salami and sausages are produced as well as wine. Feel free to pluck whatever you like from the vegetable garden – red peppers, fat tomatoes, huge lettuces. Warm, lively, outgoing and with two young children of their own, your hosts set the tone: a charming place, and bliss for families and walkers. *Minimum stay one week in high season.*

Price	€275–€550 per week.
Rooms	3 apartments: 1 for 2, 2 for 2-4.
Meals	Restaurant 1km.
Closed	Rarely.
Directions	Assisi ring road to Porta Perlici, then towards Gualdo Tadino, 6km. Right, signed Brigolante. Over 1st bridge, right, over 2nd wooden bridge, up hill 500m, right at 1st gravel road.

	Rebecca Winke Bagnoli Via Costa di Trex 31, 06081 Assisi
Tel	+39 0758 02250
Email	info@brigolante.com
Web	www.brigolante.com

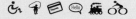

Romantik Hotel Le Silve & Agriturismo

The setting, deep in the heart of the Umbrian hills, takes your breath away. It's as beauiful and as peaceful as Shangri-La – so remote you'd do well to fill up with petrol before leaving Spello or Assisi. The medieval buildings have been beautifully restored and the whole place breathes an air of tranquillity. Superb, generous-sized bedrooms have stone walls, exquisite terracotta floors, beautiful furniture, old mirrors and (a rarity, this!) proper reading lights. Bathrooms are similarly rustic with terracotta floors and delicious pampering extras. The apartments are spread across three converted farm buildings. We loved the restaurant, too – intimate and inviting indoors and out. The produce is mostly organic, the bread is homemade, the cheeses, hams and salami are delectable. There are tennis and table tennis, a pool with a bar, a hydromassage and a sauna, and hectares of hills and woods in which to walk or ride or walk. A happy, friendly place, and popular – be sure to book well in advance. *Minimum stay two nights in apartments.*

Ethical Collection: Community; Food.
See page 400 for details

Price	Half-board €210–€300 for 2. Apartments €100 per night, €600 per week.
Rooms	20 + 13: 20 doubles. 13 apartments for 2-4.
Meals	Breakfast €10 for self-caterers. Dinner €40. Wine from €15. Restaurant 6km.
Closed	Hotel: November-April. Agriturismo: never.
Directions	Milan A1 exit Valdichiana for Perugia, then Assisi. Signs for Gualdo Tadino then Armenzano, km12; signs for hotel, 2km.

Marco Sirignani
Loc. Armenzano,
06081 Assisi

Tel	+39 0758 019000
Email	info@lesilve.it
Web	www.lesilve.it

Agriturismo Alla Madonna del Piatto

The road winds up and up through woods and off the track to a simple, centuries-old farmhouse in a hidden corner of Umbria. The position is stupendous. Views stretch over olive groves and forested hills to Assisi and its basilica, yet you are an easy distance from Perugia, Assisi, Spoleto. The old farmhouse was abandoned for decades until these Italian-Dutch owners fell in love with the view, then restored the building with sympathy and style, then replanted the olive groves. Bedrooms are airy, uncluttered, their country antiques mixed with Moroccan delights picked up on Letizia's travels; one room has a loo with a view. Lovely Letizia – a walking encyclopedia of the area – joins you for breakfast (her own breads and jams) at mosaic-topped tables, in a fresh, modern space of white and rose walls, with sofa and open fire. Your hosts are approachable and share their home gladly. If you can tear yourself away from the terraces and their panoramas, there are walks, medieval hill towns and all of Umbria to explore. And be sure to dine at Il Pioppo! *Minimum stay two nights; three in May & Sept. Cookery courses.*

Price	€80–€110.
Rooms	6: 5 twins/doubles, 1 family room for 3.
Meals	Restaurant 1km.
Closed	Mid-December to mid-March.
Directions	From Assisi SS147 for Perugia; after Ponte San Vittorino turn right, Via San Fortunato; uphill 6.5km; right; Via Petrata. Ask owner for detailed directions.

Letizia Mattiacci
Via Petrata 37, Pieve San Nicolo,
06081 Assisi

Tel	+39 0758 199050
Email	letizia.mattiacci@gmail.com
Web	www.incampagna.com

Casa Rosa

Once you've wrenched your gaze from pool-side panoramas over the forested flanks of Mount Subasio National Park, and had your senses tickled by the sweet orchestra of lavender, Russian sage and Mediterranean herbs that assail you – strategically planted to waft their perfumes into the apartments – let wonderful host Jennifer welcome you in. An expat artist whose mural and decorative work embellishes these homely, colourful, bohemian interiors, she will relate Elysian tales of living off the land and raising a family on the 17-acre farm estate. Antique kettles and pots, bunches of dried herbs suspended from ceilings, well-stocked wine racks and flora 'n' fauna painted surrounds to mirrors and French windows, all lend themselves to a relaxed vibe, while an organic vegetable garden, and a yurt tucked away in the woods, add to the communal, convivial idyll. There's WiFi if you need it but it won't distract you from the views; lap them up from your balconied terrace. Better still, take the book of local walks provided, add a picnic, and head for the wooded hills. *Minimum stay one week.*

Price	€640–€1,130 per week.
Rooms	4 apartments for 2–5.
Meals	Dinner €20, on request. Community freezer stocked with meals. Restaurants 3km.
Closed	Rarely.
Directions	From Assisi road ss.444 for Gualdo Todimo. After 6km right on Santa Maria Lignano. After 2.5km left for Casa Rosa. House 1km on right.

Jennifer Holmes
Santa Maria Lignano,
06081 Assisi

Tel	+39 0758 02322
Email	jennifer@casa-rosa.it
Web	www.casa-rosa.it

San Lorenzo della Rabatta Agriturismo

Near Perugia but in another world, this tiny medieval hamlet is guarded by densely wooded hills. The houses congregate around a central space, their walls covered with ivy, wisteria and roses. This is a good place to bring children – pleasant, practical – and they'll be entertained by the agricultural touches: the rickety farm stools, the cattle stall converted into a seat, the wine barrel acting as a side table. One bed has an old gate for a bedhead and there are some four-posters too (draped in white nylon). The living spaces are open-plan, with gingham much in evidence; most have a fireplace and a big rustic basket of wood. The kitchen areas and bathrooms are small and basic but clean and adequate. Outside, narrow steps bordered with miniature roses lead you down to the pool and lovely views to the hills. There s also table tennis and a small play area for children set amongst the olive trees. It's all wonderfully peaceful, but more apartments are planned. Teodora, who lives on site and has a lovely smile, will, given a day's notice, cook you a five-course meal. *Minimum stay two nights.*

Price	€80–€120.
Rooms	8 apartments for 2-8.
Meals	Dinner, 5 courses, €16 (served in your apartment).
Closed	January-February.
Directions	A1 south exit Valdichiana. From south exit Orte. E45 dir. Perugia exit Madonna Alta. Follow signs for Cenerente & S. Marco. At Cenerente right after church; signed.

Paola Cascini
Loc. Cenerente,
06134 Perugia
Tel +39 0756 90764
Email info@sanlorenzodellarabatta.com
Web www.sanlorenzodellarabatta.com

Le Torri di Bagnara - Country Medieval Resort

Aided by a staff of 30, Signora Giunta runs her empire with professionalism and pride. Hers is a huge and magnificent estate, 1,500 acres of pastoral perfection with vast views, a pristine pool (bathing hats on, please!), a 12th-century tower, an 11th-century abbey, three castles and many terraces. It is a medieval framework for a modern, holiday enterprise and you feel you're on top of the world. Four rustic but pretty apartments fill the tower, each on a different floor. Some have barrow-vault ceilings and Romanesque windows, strokeable fabrics and fine old furniture, tiny galley kitchens and wonderful views. On the ground floor is a dining and sitting area for the sociable; outside, figs, peaches, olives, herbs and a shared laundry. Bedrooms in the abbey feed off a delightful paved courtyard with small church and tower and are as luxy as the rest. The restaurant serves fresh, seasonal dishes or try the local specialities only three miles away; the motorway is conveniently close. Cookery classes, wine tastings, free mountain bikes... Signora Giunta has thought of everything. *Bus stop 500m. Minimum stay two nights.*

Price	€130–€240. Apts €460–€1,450 per week.
Rooms	7 + 4: 4 doubles, 3 suites.
	4 apts: 1 for 2, 2 for 4, 1 for 5.
Meals	Breakfast €10 for self-caterers.
	Dinner from €35. Wine from €8.
	Restaurants 5km.
Closed	January-March.
Directions	E45 exit Resina; north for Pieve San
	Quirico Bagnara; 4km, signed on left.

Ethical Collection: Food.
See page 400 for details

Zenaide Giunta
Strada della Bruna 8, Solfagnano,
06134 Perugia
Tel   +39 0755 792001
Email info@letorridibagnara.it
Web   www.letorridibagnara.it

Villa Rosa

The beautifully restored farmhouse looks out over fields and farms to the villages of Solomeo and Corciano, with Perugia in the distance. Distant church bells, the hum of a tractor, the bray of a donkey... yet you are five kilometres from the superstrada. You couldn't find a better spot from which to discover Tuscany and Umbria. Megan, who is Australian, and Lino are a helpful and hospitable couple, and will help you enjoy every aspect of your stay: hunt for truffles (or cashmere, in Solomeo!), book in for a twice-weekly cookery class with a chef from Perugia, take advantage of a personalised tour. There are two apartments here. For a family, the two-storey *casetta* at the end of the garden is perfect – a delightful mix of recycled beams and terracotta tiles, with open fire, air con, jacuzzi and perfect views. The flat on the ground floor of the farmhouse is similarly good – new bunk beds in the living area, cool in summer, a great terrace. There's a saltwater pool to cool you down, and the views from two of the apartments are wonderful. *Minimum stay three nights in apts.*

Price	Cottage €160–€180 (€600–€1,200 per week). Apts €95–€120 (€425–€750 per week).
Rooms	1 cottage for 6. 2 apartments: 1 for 3, 1 for 4.
Meals	Restaurant 1km.
Closed	Rarely.
Directions	Exit Perugia-Bettolle at Corciano, for Castelvieto thro' village (via underpass & bridge) to shrine. Left & on to 2nd shrine; right uphill; house after couple of bends.

Megan & Lino Rialti
Voc. Docciolano 9, Montemelino,
06060 Magione

Tel   +39 0758 41814
Email   meglino@libero.it
Web   www.villarosaweb.com

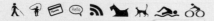

Castello di Petroia

Brave the loops of the Gubbio-Assisi road and arrive at the castle at dusk. The front gate is locked, you ring to be let in; an eerie silence, and the gates creak open. Inside, dim lighting, stone walls, a splendid austerity. Come morning, you will appreciate the vast-fireplaced magnificence of the place, and the lovely terrace that catches the all-day sun. With a full house, dinner is a sociable affair, graciously presided over – in English and Italian – by the tweed-clad count. It takes place in one of two grand dining rooms and is rounded off by the house speciality, a fiery liqueur. Then up the stairs – some steep – to bedrooms with polished floors and shadowy corners, dark furniture and flowery beds. A feeling of feudalism remains – four staff serve 12 guests – and the landscape is similarly ancient. The castle is set on a hillock surrounded by pines in beautiful, unpopulated countryside and a marked footpath running through it. Walk to Assisi – it takes a day – then taxi back. Or take the bus into Gubbio and the funicular into the hills – the views are stupendous. And return to your 900-acre estate.

Price	€110–€160. Suites €170–€210.
Rooms	8: 4 doubles (1 in tower), 4 suites.
Meals	Dinner with wine, €30–€38. Restaurant 5km.
Closed	January–March.
Directions	S298 from Gubbio south for Assisi & Perugia. After Scritto, just before Biscina & Fratticiola, take stony road signed to Castello.

Carlo Sagrini
Scritto di Gubbio, 06020 Gubbio
Tel   +39 0759 20287
Email   info@petroia.it
Web   www.petroia.it

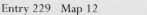

Locanda del Gallo

A restful, almost spiritual calm emanates from this wonderful home. In a medieval hamlet, the *locanda* has all the beams and antique tiles you could wish for. Light, airy rooms with pale limewashed walls are a perfect foil for the exquisite reclaimed doors and carved hardwood furniture from Bali and Indonesia; your charming hosts have picked up some fabulous pieces from far-off places and have given the house a colonial feel. Each bedroom is different, one almond with Italian country furniture, another white, with wicker and Provençal prints; some have carved four-poster beds. Bathrooms are gorgeous, with deep baths and walk-in, glass-doored showers. A stunning veranda wraps itself around the house: doze off in a wicker armchair, sip a drink at dusk as the sun melts into the valley. The pool is spectacular, like a mirage clinging to the side of the hill; and there's a huge lime tree. Jimmy the cook conjures up food rich in genuine flavours, with aromatic herbs and vegetables from the garden; he and his wife are part of the extended family. Paola and Erich are interesting, cultural and warm. *Minimum stay two nights. Spa.*

Price	€120–€140. Suites €200–€240.
	Half-board €75–€90 p.p.
Rooms	9: 6 doubles, 3 suites for 4.
Meals	Lunch €12. Dinner €28.
	Wine from €10.
Closed	Rarely.
Directions	Exit E45 at Ponte Pattoli for Casa del
	Diavolo; for S. Cristina 8km. 1st left,
	100m after La Dolce Vita restaurant;
	continue to Locanda.

Paola Moro & Erich Breuer
Loc. Santa Cristina, 06020 Gubbio

Tel	+39 0759 229912
Email	info@locandadelgallo.it
Web	www.locandadelgallo.it

Ethical Collection: Environment; Food.
See page 400 for details

Le Cinciallegre Agriturismo

This was once a tiny 13th-century hamlet on an ancient crossroads where local farmers met to buy and sell their produce. It's an incredibly peaceful spot, overlooking valley, meadows and woods, reached via a long, unmade road. Fabrizio used to be an architect and his conversion of these old houses is inspired: all feels authentic and delightful. In the cool, beamed living room, comfortable seats pull up around a 200-year-old wood-burning stove; there's lots of rustic furniture and a fine old dresser. The simple, comfortable bedrooms, named after birds, have their own terrace areas and immaculate bathrooms. You can cook in the outhouse but Cristina is a wonderful chef serving real country food and Umbrian wines so you're likely to leave her to it. Fabrizio and Cristina are warm, hospitable, interesting people, passionate about the environment, their natural garden, which is lovely, and the ten organic hectares of land full of wildlife. Fabrizio will be happy to tell you about the walking; indeed, he'll be disappointed if you don't have time to explore.

Price	€70–€100.
Rooms	7: 3 doubles, 1 single, 1 family room, 2 triples.
Meals	Dinner €30, on request. Guest kitchen.
Closed	October–March.
Directions	A1 exit Val di Chiana for Perugia & follow E45 to Cesena. Exit Umbertide Gubbio. Follow 219 for Gubbio. Signed from Mocaiana.

Fabrizio & Cristina de Robertis
Fraz. Pisciano, 06024 Gubbio

Tel	+39 0759 255957
Email	cince@lecinciallegre.it
Web	www.lecinciallegre.it

Monte Valentino Agriturismo

On top of the world in Umbria. Woods fall away, hills climb to snow-scattered heights. It's the perfect escape, the only route in a steep, winding, two-kilometre dirt track. All around you lie 60 hectares of organically farmed land – mushrooms are gathered from the woods, cereal and vegetables from the fields, fruit from the trees. These new apartments are contemporary yet cosy with simple wooden furniture, tiled floors and throws on the striped sofas. All have small balconies and kitchens and clean, fresh shower rooms; two have access to beautifully designed, red-brick terraces, where the views sweep and soar away. The swimming pool is delightful, surrounded by deck chairs and olive trees. Fabrizia, who lives next door, is enthusiastic and charming with an engaging smile, and proud of her new venture – meet her over simple breakfasts in her homely kitchen. This is perfect cycling terrain – for the experienced! You can also swim in the river, horse riding is six miles away, cookery lessons can be arranged, and Fabrizia's husband Nicola will give you archery lessons if you fancy something different.

Price	€70-€80 (€450-€560 per week).
Rooms	4 apartments for 2-3.
Meals	Restaurants 12km.
Closed	Never.
Directions	SS E45 Orte-Cesena exit Montone-Pietralunga; SP201 to Pietralunga. At km12, Carpini (before Pietralunga); right at x-roads, signed.

Fabrizia Gargano & Nicola Polchi
Loc. Monte Valentino, 06026 Pietralunga

Tel	+39 0759 462092
Email	info@montevalentino.it
Web	www.montevalentino.it

La Buia

When Lucie and Richard moved to Umbria 20 years ago, La Buia was in desperate need of a facelift. Who better to assign to the task than an artist and a garden designer? This is a fantastically welcoming home with glorious gardens and raw forest to roam. Snuggle in to the cosy guest room with its private entrance off the stone walkway – all soothing blues and a flowing mosquito net over the bed – or the more romantic, peachy-pink bedroom upstairs, with its own basin but sharing a bathroom with the family. In either case Lucie's gorgeous paintings adorn the walls – almost outshone by terrific views of the countryside from every window. Start the day slowly savouring the generous breakfast, served out under the arbour at the big antique table. Plan your day: if you feel like exploring, medieval towns are a short drive. Or stay put and wander the estate's three hectares, winding up with a swim in the rosemary and lavender-fringed pool. Now the Shelbournes are busy exercising their creative powers in the renovation of an old tobacco tower – we can't wait to see their new rooms! *Tower for 6-8 to rent, opening in 2010.*

Price	€85-€150.
Rooms	2: 1 double; 1 double sharing family bathroom.
Meals	Dinner €35. Restaurants 5km.
Closed	Rarely.
Directions	A1 exit north Arezzo; follow signs for Città di Castello. In Monterchi, follow signs to Monte S. Maria Tiberina. Past Lippiano turning, up hill; right down hill into valley.

Richard & Lucie Shelbourne
Voc. La Buia 43,
06010 Lippiano

Tel	+39 0758 502007
Email	richardshelbourne@virgilio.it

la Preghiera Residenza d'Epoca

Shady terraces, a sunken garden, a flower-filled loggia and a private chapel. So many tranquil spots in which to recharge batteries. This glorious 12th-century monastery, hidden in a wooded valley near Gubbio and Cortona, was a pilgrim's resting place. Now it is owned by the Tunstills (architect and interior designer) who have restored with English country-house flair and Italian attention to detail. The large sitting and dining rooms are elegantly scattered with sofas, paintings and antiques; there is a billiard room, and a library of books and DVDs. Bedrooms combine original features – beamed and raftered ceilings, terracotta floors, wooden shutters, exposed stone – with sophisticated details. Bed linen is cotton and silk, furniture is hand-crafted, wardrobes have interior lights, bathrooms are marbled. Breakfast on the terrace, take afternoon tea by the pool, dine by candlelight on local boar and truffles. There are vintage bikes to borrow, horse riding and golf, medieval hilltop towns to visit, lovely staff to look after you. You can even book a massage by the pool. *Ask about half-priced deals.*

Price	€120–€310. Whole house on request.
Rooms	11 twins/doubles.
Meals	Dinner with wine, 4 courses, €50; by arrangement. Restaurant 800m.
Closed	December–February.
Directions	Exit E45 at Promano dir. Città di Castello; left at r'bout; next r'bout right thro' Trestina; right to Calzolaro; before bridge left to Vecchio Granaio; road bears right; along river, hotel on left, 300m.

Liliana & John Tunstill
Via del Refari, 06018 Calzolaro

Tel	+39 0759 302428
Email	info@lapreghiera.com
Web	www.lapreghiera.com

La Molinella

Eat, sleep and dream in the little old watermill in the Umbrian hills – an enchanting bolthole for two. Though you can reach Perugia in under an hour it is fairly remote; but the hiking and riding are easy. Potted lavender, herbs and tidy vines are plentiful, and apple trees and a few olives up by the cool circular pool (all yours, with views)... the 'shabby chic' of the interior repeats itself outside so you barely notice where the gardens end and nature begins. Loveliest of all is the dappled veranda complete with daybed for outdoor R&R. Back inside, ceilings are low, floors are old wood or terracotta, beams are rustic, pale blue paintwork is deliberately worn, and the kitchen, with its antique marble-topped table and old-fashioned pellet stove in one corner, will make you giddy with delight. (It also has loads of workspace and a modern oven.) Owner Annie is here when guests arrive, lives nearby should you need her, and moves back in in winter! At the top is the snug bedroom with romantic bed and sweet white linen, below is a sitting room with deep sofa and open fire. Honeymoon heaven. *Minimum stay one week.*

Price	€995 per week.
Rooms	House for 2-3.
Meals	Welcome pack with breakfast & dinner. Restaurant 15-minute drive.
Closed	November-April.
Directions	From A1 exit Valdichiana/ Betolle/ Sinalunga dir. Perugia; stay on 75 bis carriageway to Tuoro exit. Follow signs for Tuoro, Umbertide, Lisciano Niccone and Mercatale. Thro' Mercatale, then small village Mengaccini; Annie will send directions from here on booking.

Annie Bradbery
Voc. La Molinella,
06010 San Leo Bastia

| Mobile | +39 340 6349783 |
| Email | annie.bradbery@googlemail.com |

Casa San Gabriel

Enjoy David's wine on arrival, absorb the view of cultivated and wooded hills and unwind. Chrissie and David, warm, generous, thoughtful, bought the farmstead in a ruinous state and did it up it all up in under a year. The little 'houses', private but close, each with its own terrace, are suitable for singles, couples or families so take your pick. For further space there's a living room in the main house with books and open fire. The restoration is sympathetic, unpretentious, delightful, the off-white décor and soft furnishings enhancing undulating beams and stone walls; the bathrooms are so lovely you could spend all day in them. Supplies are left for breakfast on your first morning and should last until you're ready to venture out. You may also pick produce from the vegetable gardens. David cooks on Tuesdays, and Thursday is pizza night – your chance to use an original wood-fired oven. Bliss to have Perugia so near by – a 20-minute drive – and to return to a pool with views down the valley all the way to Assisi, a bottle of chilled Orvieto by your side. *B&B option October-April only.*

Price	B&B: €80.
	Self-catering: €400–€1,025 per week.
Rooms	3 apartments: 1 for 2, 1 for 2-4,
	1 for 4.
Meals	Dinner €25 (Tues); pizza €15 (Thurs).
	Wine €10. Restaurant 5km.
Closed	Rarely.
Directions	E45, exit Pierantonio for Castle
	Antognolla; after 4.5km, left for Santa
	Caterina; 1.5km on white road.

Christina Todd & David Lang
CP No 29, V. Petrarca No 2,
06015 Pierantonio
Tel   +39 0759 414219
Email   chrissie@casasangabriel.com
Web   www.casasangabriel.com

Il Convento Mincione

Big Apple chic meets Italian tradition: an unexpected but elegant marriage in a 12th-century convent deep in Umbria. With that attention to detail that only a New Yorker can give, Joan has achieved a classy and minimalist mood. And she has created rooms you really want to spend time in. There are seven apartments of varying sizes on the ground and first floors, each named after a lucky Tarot card, each with its own outdoor space. One, 'Dieci', has metre-thick walls and is thought to have been an old chapel. All have open-plan sitting, dining and kitchen areas, white or bare stone walls, fireplaces and rich old brick floors. Furnishings have been imaginatively thought through sumptuous fabrics, comfortable sofas, tall wrought-iron candlesticks – and there's a refreshing absence of clutter. A large communal kitchen, used for cookery courses, is also available. The convent buildings are of creamy stone, clustered round a central courtyard (a real suntrap) with an old font set in the wall; all around are open pasture, rolling hills and old oak woodland. Fabulous. *Minimum stay three nights.*

Price	€500–€1,200 per week. Whole house on request.
Rooms	7 apartments: 2 for 2, 1 for 2-3, 3 for 2-4, 1 for 4-6.
Meals	Breakfast €6 for self-caterers. Restaurants 2-5km.
Closed	Rarely. Ask about Christmas group bookings.
Directions	E45 dir. Umbertide exit Pierantonio; left to Antognola & Pantano; right to Piano di Nese; Right at fork, signed Preggio; sharp right. Gates on right after 200m. Signed.

Joan Halperin
Val Racchiusole, Case Sparse 467,
06019 Umbertide

Tel	+39 0759 415169
Email	joan@thisoldconvent.com
Web	www.thisoldconvent.com

Casa San Martino

Perhaps this is the answer if you are finding it impossible to choose between Tuscany and Umbria — a 250-year-old farmhouse on the border. Sit with a glass of wine in your Umbrian garden, watch the sun set over the Tuscan hills. The lovely, rambling house is alive with Lois's personality and interests: she's a remarkable lady who has lived in Italy for years and is a fluent linguist. Her charming big kitchen is well-equipped; an arch at one end leads to a comfortable family room, a door at the other to a pretty veranda with a stone barbecue. Up the narrow staircase is a large light sitting room with flowery sofas, books and an open fireplace — perfect for roasting chestnuts. The whitewashed bedrooms and bathrooms are cosy and attractive. Lois lives next door, is there when you need her and offers guests an enticing number of courses to choose from (cookery, fresco-painting, hiking, the history of Italian gardens); she can even book you a chef. The big garden with its dreamy pool looks across the Niccone valley and there are two villages with shops close by. *Minimum stay three nights.*

Price	€140. Whole house €3,000 per week.
Rooms	4: 1 double, 1 twin/double; 2 twins/doubles sharing bath.
Meals	Dinner with wine, €30. Restaurants 3km.
Closed	B&B: November-April. Self-catering: May-October.
Directions	A1 exit Valdichiana. Then 75 bis for Perugia, then for Tuoro & for Lisciano Niccone. At Lisciano N., left to S. Martino. Follow signs to S. Martino. On right-hand side near top of hill.

Lois Martin
San Martino 19,
06060 Lisciano Niccone

Tel	+39 0758 44288
Email	csm@tuscanyvacation.com
Web	www.tuscanyvacation.com

Casa Panfili

A steep, bumpy approach – but the welcome more than makes up for it. As for the position, overlooking the wooded hills and olive groves of the Niccone valley, it is glorious. The farmhouse, once used for drying and storing tobacco (spot the old ventilation bricks in the walls), has been rescued from ruin and is now immaculate. Typically Italian rooms – white-painted walls, arches, terracotta floors – have been given the English treatment with masses of books and rugs, old wooden chests and lacy cloths, prints and family photos. Beds have silky smooth sheets, spotless bathrooms are fragrant with fresh flowers, and Al and Betty, who were stationed in Naples for three years and decided they couldn't face returning to Whitehall, are generous, friendly hosts. They produce their own wine and olive oil and Betty offers Italian cookery classes in her kitchen. Meals are at a dining table gleaming with cut glass and silver, or outside under a vine-covered pergola. The gardens are tranquil and pretty, the olive trees screen the pool from the house and the nightingales serenade you at night. *Minimum stay two nights.*

Price	€110–€130.
Rooms	3: 2 doubles, 1 twin.
Meals	Lunch €10. Dinner with wine, €30; book ahead.
Closed	November-Easter.
Directions	Directions on booking.

Alastair & Betty Stuart
San Lorenzo di Bibbiano 14,
06010 San Leo Bastia
Tel   +39 0758 504244
Email   bettyalstuart@netemedia.net
Web   www.casapanfili.com

Le Marche • Abruzzo • Molise

Photo: istock.com

Locanda della Valle Nuova

In gentle, breeze-cooled hills, surrounded by ancient, protected oaks and on the road that leads to glorious Urbino, this 185-acre farm produces organic meat, vegetables and wine. It is an unusual, unexpectedly modern place whose owners have a special interest in horses and in the environment. Signora Savini and daughter Giulia – forces to be reckoned with! – make a professional team and cook delicious meals presented on white porcelain and terracotta. The breads, pastas and jams are homemade, the wines are local, the water is purified and de-chlorinated, the truffles are gathered from the woods nearby. The conversion has given La Locanda the feel of a discreet modern hotel, where perfectly turned sheets lie on perfect beds, and it's worth asking for one of the bigger rooms, preferably with a view. The riding school has a club house for horsey talk and showers; there are two outdoor arenas as well as lessons and hacks, and a fabulous pool. If you arrive at the airport after dark, Giulia kindly meets you to guide you back. *Minimum stay three nights; one week in apts.*

Price	€110. Half-board €85 p.p. Apartments €680 per week.
Rooms	6 + 2: 5 doubles, 1 twin. 2 apartments for 2.
Meals	Dinner €30. Wine from €9.
Closed	Mid-November to May.
Directions	Exit Fano-Rome m'way at Acqualagna & Piobbico. Head for Piobbico as far as Pole; right for Castellaro; on 3.5km, signed. Or, bus from Pesaro or Fano to Fermignano; owners will pick up.

Ethical Collection: Environment; Food.
See page 400 for details

Giulia Savini
La Cappella 14,
61033 Sagrata di Fermignano
Tel   +39 0722 330303
Email   info@vallenuova.it
Web   www.vallenuova.it

Villa Cartoceto

A stay at the reverentially restored Villa Cartoceto is an intimate one. You're welcomed into Axel and Judith's home – and immediately feel part of the small Italian community they have embraced. Bedrooms, off a large, multi-windowed sitting room, are modest, spotless, personal and off-beat, displaying a medley of original furniture and artwork from the previous owners plus endearing modern touches: large wooden armoires and antique chandeliers meet vibrant blown-up shots of figs and butterflies. Beds and showers are deliberately big. The view from the shaded, herb-scented rooftop terrace – used for breakfast, wine time and relaxing – is absurdly beautiful. Suspended on the edge of town, you can while away the day enjoying the hills and olive groves that open up to you then return to a perfect pre-dusk aperitif. They take food seriously here, as their popular osteria down the street attests, and are keen supporters of the Slow Food movement: ingredients are organic and the results full-flavour. Try truffle-hunting, wine, cheese and olive tours, or boat jaunts to catch your dinner.

Price	€75-€82.
Rooms	4 doubles.
Meals	Lunch/picnic €15. Dinner €9-€45. Wine €4-€35. Owner's restaurant 50m.
Closed	Rarely.
Directions	A14 exit Fano; SS dir. Rome. Exit Lucrezia & follow signs to Cartoceto. In Cartoceto follow signs to "centro storico". Villa Cartoceto is 1st house on right after Gastronomia Beltrami.

Judith Volker
Via Umberto I,
61030 Cartoceto
Tel   +39 0721 893020
Email   info@villacartoceto.com
Web   www.villacartoceto.com

Ethical Collection: Environment; Food.
See page 400 for details

Villa Giulia

Pines, cypress oaks and roses surround the Napoleonic villa, wisteria billows over the lemon house wall. The gardens merge into the family olive farm and an ancient wood. No formality, no fuss, just an easy, calm and kind welcome from Anna, who moved here a year ago with her youngest son. The villa was named after an indomitable great-aunt (the first woman to climb Mont Blanc!) and the family furniture remains – large wooden mirrors, stunning antiques – along with a candle burn on the mantelpiece left by the Nazis. Bedrooms, the best and most baronial in the villa, have shuttered windows and old-fashioned metal beds; one noble bathroom has its own balcony, another is up a winding stair. The two suites in La Dependenza have kitchenettes, while the apartments proper are divided between the Farmhouse and the Casa Piccola. Sitting rooms are grand but easy, the dining room's chairs are gay with red checks and summer breakfasts are taken at pink-clothed tables on a terrace whose views reach to the Adriatic (the beach is a mile away). Atmospheric, historic, beautiful, and good for all ages.

Price	€120-€260.
	Apartments €800-€1,800 per week.
Rooms	9 + 5: 3 doubles, 6 suites.
	5 apartments for 3-6.
Meals	Dinner €30-€50. Wine €8-€36.
	Restaurants nearby.
Closed	January-March.
Directions	SS16 from Fano for Pesaro, 3km north of Fano turn left; signed.

Anna Passi
Via di Villa Giulia, Loc. San Biagio 40,
61032 Fano

Tel   +39 0721 823159
Email   info@relaisvillagiulia.com
Web   www.relaisvillagiulia.com

Castello di Monterado

Orlando's great-great-grandfather bought the Castello, parts of which go back to 1100. The renovation continues, and is glorious! Orlando and Kira, quietly spoken, charming, are deeply passionate about the family home whose exquisite revival has been achieved floor by floor. The Music Room, its terrace overlooking the Caseno valley and the distant sea, is a living museum, the Library combines vast armchairs with ancient tomes, there are frescoes on every wall and ceiling, antiques, art work, chandeliers – the sheer beauty will thrill you. There's a lovely balcony for al fresco breakfasts, or a dining room for drearier mornings (overseen by Bacchus and Arianna, of course). Bedrooms, all vast, all generously different, ǹǹǹ ǹǹ ǹǹ ǹ ǹǹ ǹǹ ǹǹǹǹ ǹǹǹǹ each other across ceilings, beds are soberly but beautifully dressed, cupboards have been crafted from the cellar's barrels, one suite has its hydromassage bath positioned so you gaze on gardens as you soak. Very special; very good value.

Price	€200.
Rooms	4 suites.
Meals	Restaurants within walking distance.
Closed	Never.
Directions	A14 exit at Marotta, right for Pergola; after 7km left for Monterado. Signed.

Orlando & Kira Rodano
Piazza Roma 18,
60010 Monterado

Tel	+39 0717 958395
Email	info@castellodimonterado.it
Web	www.castellodimonterado.it

Castello di Monterado - Apartments

Cut off from western Italy by the Apennines is Le Marche; peaceful, charming and unsought-out. At the top of a steep wooded hill is Monterado, a small medieval town of cobbled streets and fabulous views. Beyond is the sea. On a small square in town, opposite the Castle of Monterado (see previous entry) is a solid old stone building housing six apartments with a contemporary and luxurious feel. One is on the ground floor, two are on the first and two are on the second; Anemone, the largest, spreads itself over two levels. Lofty walls are plastered white, floors are polished parquet, styling is minimalist, classy and sleek. In the town are a handful of restaurants and shops, a swimming pool and tennis and, in May, a hog roast festival to which locals flock; the region is the home of *porchetta*. If you want beach resorts with a Sixties feel, then head west for the resorts of Le Marche. After a day's touring, return to the peaceful garden of the Castello, with its cedar trees and scented roses and, beyond, a landscaped woodland with winding paths.

Price	€385-€595.
Rooms	6 apartments: 3 for 4, 2 for 5, 1 for 6.
Meals	Restaurants within walking distance.
Closed	Never.
Directions	A14 exit Marotta, dir. Pergola. After 7km left for Monterado; signed.

Orlando & Kira Rodano
Piazza Roma 26,
60010 Monterado
Tel   +39 0717 958395
Email   info@castellodimonterado.it
Web   www.castellodimonterado.it

Caserma Carina Country House

Nothing is too much trouble for Lesley, whose easy-going vivacity makes this place a delight. Cots, toys, DVDs, a bottle of wine at the end of a journey, a welcoming smile – she and Dean provide it all. The apartments are immaculate, the gardens prettily landscaped, the pool has long views. A 15-minute walk down the hill from historic Mogliano (three restaurants, shops, banks and bars) is this magnificent 19th-century country house, its four new apartments spanning three floors. The unrestored part sits quietly, rustically alongside. Inside, all is new, inviting and spotlessly clean. Showers have cream tiles and white towels, kitchens are quietly luxurious, sofas gleam in brown leather, cushions add splashes of red, wooden furniture is stylish and new; italian shutters cut out early morning light, and views are of rolling hills. You are in the heart of the lovely, unsung Le Marche, an easy drive from historic Macerata, and not much further from the Adriatic coast. Couples will love it and foodies will be happy: out of season cookery courses are planned. An all-year-round treat. *Shared laundry.*

Price	£400–£825 per week.
Rooms	4 apartments: 1 for 2, 2 for 2–4, 1 for 4–5.
Meals	Restaurant within walking distance.
Closed	Rarely.
Directions	Directions on booking.

Lesley McMorran
Contrada Mossa 16,
62010 Mogliano
Tel +39 0733 557990
Email info@caserma-carina.co.uk
Web www.caserma-carina.co.uk

Casa Canaletti

It is luxurious, chic, immaculately put together. The perfectionism is a match for the world's finest hotels, yet Casa Canaletti is child-welcoming, charming and great fun. This is thanks to Alan, Italiaphile and designer, who took the plunge to move to the Marche, find a big derelict farmhouse, transform it and transport it to another level. You have the entire ground floor to yourselves, Alan has the rest of the house; there are no other paying guests. Of course the views are breathtaking but it's the details that will keep you smiling: the geometric lawns framing gravel plots of olive trees, the mirrored bar alongside the saltwater pool. White beams and walls, cool polished concrete, dark wood: such is the palette; brick arches and recessed rectangular windows remind you of the history. Bedrooms have braided rugs, bathrooms have custom-made sinks, along the corridor is a Chinese lacquer armoire. There's a barbecue with a Moroccan bed and outdoor lighting for meals under the stars. You can hike in the Sibillini mountains, ski near Sarnano, visit the ruins of Urbisalia — all are close. *Shared use of pool.*

Price	£800-£1,000 for 4 (2 bedrooms); £1,000-£1,500 for 6 (3 bedrooms), except July-Aug. Prices per week.
Rooms	Apartment for 4-6 (2 doubles, 1 twin). Extra bed available.
Meals	Restaurants nearby.
Closed	Rarely.
Directions	Bologna-Ancona A14 exit Macerata-Civitanova Marche; SS77 exit Macerata Ovest dir. Sarnano; SS78. 5km; left dir. S. Lorenzo. At T-junc. right to S. Lorenzo. Call from here, Alan will meet you.

Alan Saunders
C. da Appezzana 47,
62020 Loro Piceno

Mobile	+39 334 9548131
Email	alan.saunders@casa-canaletti.com
Web	www.casa-canaletti.com

Torre Tenosa

Hard to believe this is the old watchtower – it's so peaceful now. The wooded hills and pastures of Sibillini National Park end in the snow-tipped southern Apennines; a gentle breeze ruffles the trees and grass. Drink in the stunning view (and a glass of local wine) from the terrace. Inside is open plan, with ruddy terracotta tiles underfoot and solid beams overhead. Downstairs you have a well-equipped kitchen area, a good-sized dining table and a jolly red sofabed. The bedroom is up on the wide open mezzanine. At night, sink into a red-striped, down-filled duvet; in the morning, peer out of a dear little stone-framed window from your bed. A smart, clean shower room and small utility room are up on a further level. Environmentally-sound behind-wall heating keeps everyone snug, the internet keeps you in touch. Karen, Frank and their young family live next door but you feel nicely private here, and have your own drive. Karen runs yoga retreats nearby, and the National Park is ten minutes – hike, bike, ski, or just tuck into delicious local food. Perfect for a couple, or close friends.

Price	€475–€525 per week.
Rooms	House for 2.
Meals	Restaurants within 5km.
Closed	Never.
Directions	From Camerino SE for Sfercia; left after 2km; right-hand bend signed 'Arcofiato'; phone Frank from here.

	Frank Schmidt
	Loc. Santa Lucia 13,
	62032 Camerino
Tel	+39 0737 633500
Email	frank@torretenosa.it
Web	www.torretenosa.it

Le Valicelle

At the end of a long driveway this big friendly villa is embraced by gardens discreetly tended by the English owners in the (early) morning, cradled in a landscape of cherry trees and olive groves, surrounded by natural beauty with not a soul to be seen. And there's space to spread. Imagine a pool fringed by palms, a yard for sandbox and games, a rose-clambered arbour, a pretty wicker-chaired loggia, a barbecue, hammock and glider swing… heaven for families. A border of low hedges encloses it all and beyond are lovely views of hilltop Sant'Angelo (two kilometres away). Inside, all is comfortable, relaxing and clean: a great big living space (a huge leather chesterfield, a sturdy table topped by a basket of local goodies, a kitchen with two ovens), and five bedrooms spread over three floors; a funky fun bannister made of branches leads to the kids' hideout in the attic. Add functional bathrooms, heaps of storage and well-restored shutters. This part of the Marche is fantastic for pootling around in: get lost in the rolling hills, discover wonderful medieval towns and gastronomic festivals. *Min. stay two nights in low season; one week in high season.*

Price	€50–€80. Family room €70–€100. Whole house €900–€2,000 per week.
Rooms	B&B (winter only): 2 doubles, 1 family room for 2-3. Whole house available (summer only).
Meals	Restaurants 2km.
Closed	Rarely.
Directions	Bologna A14 dir. Ancona; exit Macerata-Civitanova Marche dir. Mac. Exit Mac. Ovest dir. Sforzacosta. SS77 for 25km, dir. S. Ginesio/Sarnano; then S. Angelo in Pontano. Phone from village; owner will meet you.

Piero Milozzi
C. da Collezampone 23,
62020 Sant'Angelo in Pontano
Mobile   +39 333 4322 804
Email   levallicelle@alice.it
Web   www.levallicelle.com

Villa Vinci

Villa Vinci has a fairytale setting, grandly on the top of a hill overlooking medieval Fermo. Popes, kings and Garibaldi graced the 16th-century villa with their presence, Giovan Battista Carducci and Porcinai with their brilliance. The former is responsible for the neoclassical architecture, the latter for the designs of the classic gardens that spill out from your apartment. As refined as it is – with its sparkling marble floors, gorgeously preserved antiques and Gajassi cherubs adorning warm butter walls (and functional kitchen tucked away) – the apartment only just competes with the setting. Throw open the French doors and let in the sunlight and the panoramas of the Sibillini mountains and the Adriatic sea: marvellous. Take a stroll through the manicured parks of the two his tori estate, spend a quiet morning at the duomo across the street, sally forth to discover yet more medieval treasures. Your hosts – former Ambassador Vinci Gigliucci and his wife – have impeccable charm, a perfect reflection of their estate. You will be as enchanted by them as you are with this magical place. *Ask about short breaks.*

Price	€2,500 per week.
Rooms	Apartment for 6 (1 double, 2 twins).
Meals	Restaurant 500m.
Closed	Rarely.
Directions	A14 Fermo/Porto San Giorgio exit; dir. Fermo. In Fermo signs to Piazza del Popolo, then to Duomo. Villa is directly opp. Duomo.

Giulio Vinci Gigliucci
Piazzale Girfalco 1,
63023 Fermo

Tel	+39 7342 28760
Email	info@villavincifermo.com
Web	www.villavincifermo.com

Casa di Siobhan

Past the flags, down the drive and there is Siobhan's smartly restored but relaxing farmhouse. Tuck into a cosy bedroom for homely B&B – tiny antique clocks and large wicker trunks at the end of beds, beaded lamps, floral paintings – or self-cater in the light, bright apartment at the back. B&B guests start the day with a pre-packaged breakfast in a cute room with lavender cupboards and a whimsical mural of eggplants and artichokes – or under the arbour in summer, with gorgeous views of the Marche hills. The pool too looks onto the hills, making it hard on a summer's day to pull yourself away; and with Siobhan's dinners based on the best local produce, you may find yourself eating in every night. The petite wood and stainless steel kitchen and outdoor barbecue invites self-catering guests to whip up their dinners outside; in much comfort, thanks to outdoor sofas and armchairs. Mountains and coast are a very short drive and cyclists will love the quiet country roads. If you are looking for tranquillity, pluck some figs from the garden and find a peaceful spot just for you.

Price	€80. Apartment €900–€1,200 per week.
Rooms	2 + 1: 2 doubles each with separate bathroom. Apt for 5.
Meals	Dinner with wine, €30. Restaurants in Capparuccia.
Closed	Never.
Directions	A14 exit Fermo Porto San Giorgio; follow signs to Grottazzolina. On for approx. 14km until sign for Capparuccia on right. Right & up hill until drive with small European and Italian flags.

Siobhan Shalaby
Contrada Capparuccia 18,
63020 Ponzano di Fermo
Tel   +39 0734 632743
Email   info@casadisiobhan.co.uk
Web   www.casadisiobhan.co.uk

Agriturismo Contrada Durano

Spend a few days at this tranquil agriturismo and you'll never want to leave. The hillside farm, built in the late 18th century as a refuge for monks, has been lovingly restored by two generous, delightful and energetic owners: Englishman Jimmy and Italian Maria Concetta. No clutter, no fuss, just tiled floors, white walls, dark furniture. The bedrooms are simple and some are small, but the bar and sitting areas give you masses of space. And if you're after a room with a view — of olive groves, vineyards and perched villages — ask for rooms 1 or 2. There's dinner most evenings: food to make your heart sing — home-grown or local organic ingredients, prosciutto, pecorino, their own bread and wine. As you feast your eyes from all three dining rooms on distant mountains you may ask yourself, why go elsewhere? In spring and summer, walk through wild flowers up to the village of Smerillo. And do visit the 'cantina' and stock up with Durano bounty: olives, preserved apricots and beetroot, wines from Le Marche and homemade passata — an Italian summer in a bottle. *Minimum stay two nights.*

Price	€90.
Rooms	7 doubles.
Meals	Dinner with wine, €38.
Closed	Rarely.
Directions	A14 Ancona-Bari exit Porto San Giorgio for Amandola, 38km. 10km after Servigliano, sign on left; house 2km off road.

Maria Concetta Furnari
Contrada Durano, 63020 Smerillo
Tel   +39 0734 786012
Email   info@contradadurano.it
Web   www.contradadurano.it

Ethical Collection: Environment; Food. See page 400 for details

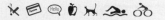

Casa Pazzi

You know there's fun in store when you spot the vintage Fiat 600 against the ancient stone walls. In renovating this 18th-century palazzo, the designers chose to introduce an unusually playful touch. The result is a series of apartments whose décor is whimsical but elegant, humorous but sophisticated… every room will make you smile. Carved painted headboards complement each apartment's theme – Palm, Garden, Orient – gorgeous curtains dress windows, bathrooms are bright and cheery, fittings are sleek and modern, and there are breathtaking views of the sea. You get swirls on bannisters and retro touches in kitchens – and big chandeliers. Whip up your own breakfast or request it from Noemi or Sabrine – professional, helpful hosts – and take it to tables under the young citrus trees on the verdant grassed terrace. Note, too, the oversized, flower-spilled urns. Grab one of the cute palazzo bikes for trips down the hill to some of Italy's cleanest beaches. Or zip around town: you're smack dab in the middle of it, beautifully elevated, behind private gates.

Price	€120-€150. Apartments €150-€200.
Rooms	1 + 4: 1 double. 4 apartments for 2-4.
Meals	Breakfast €10. Restaurant 50m.
Closed	Rarely.
Directions	Directions on booking.

Roberto Pazzi
Via Sotto le Mure 5,
63013 Grottammare

Tel   +39 0735 736617
Email   info@casapazzi.com
Web   www.casapazzi.com

Relais del Colle

Patrizia has succeeded brilliantly in merging luxury with being green. Her home and B&B are on an eight-hectare biodynamic farm, so the wines you enjoy, the wheat that makes your delicious breads and pastas and the vegetables that beautify your plate are all home-grown. Not only is the food organic but the fluffy towels, bathrobes and bed linen are too; all are of organic cotton. Crisp, country-chic guest rooms, each with a piece of balcony or terrace, give a sweet nod to the past: white linen curtains made of antique fabric stitched by the former owner's grandmother; the occasional charming antique. Bathrooms are über-sleek. Relais del Colle may be off the beaten track but perfectionist Patrizia has thought of everything to keep you happy, including a romantic grotto with a huge hot tub, a massage room and a Turkish colour therapy bath – heated with solar energy, of course – and an elegantly smart dining room for the restaurant. Come for the inviting bedrooms, the gorgeous setting, the vineyard rambles, the organic spa and the lovely, leisurely meals. Worth a very long weekend.

Price	€65–€140. Triple €165–€195. Quadruple €210–€240.
Rooms	6: 4 doubles, 1 triple, 1 quadruple.
Meals	Lunch/dinner €30–€50 (Fri, Sat & Sun). Restaurant 3km.
Closed	Never.
Directions	A14 exit Grottammare; right after toll. Left at lights, straight on for 12km until S. Maria Goretti. Right at sign to village; after 10m sign to Trivio di Ripatransone. Up hill, left at stop sign. 450m, right; left after 200m on Contrada S. Greg; to end.

	Patrizia Weiszflog
	Trivio, Contrada S. Gregorio,
	63038 Ripatransone
Tel	+39 0735 987003
Email	info@relaisdelcolle.it
Web	www.relaisdelcolle.it

Casa San Ruffino

In a land that venerates the 'bella figura', Claire and Ray Gorman, transplants from London, keep their rural B&B running on perfectly oiled wheels and a huge dose of style. The four smart guest rooms in their recently renovated 19th-century farmhouse are decorated in neutral tones in sympathy with clean white walls, beamed ceilings and beautiful old terracotta floors. Beds with crisp white linen, neatly folded fuzzy blankets and four lush pillows will cradle you to sleep, while pinch-me views from sparkling French windows will welcome you in the morning. Plan your day over homemade breads and cakes in the neat, chic breakfast room or outside at your own little garden table. The medieval towns of Montegiorgio and Fermo, and the Adriatic beaches, are a short drive. If, however, you can't tear yourself away from this glorious country spot, trot down the gravel path, past sweet-smelling lavender and perfectly potted lemon trees, to the pool, and take your fill of the rolling vineyard hills, the silvery olive groves and the distant snow-capped mountains. Who would not fall in love with this place?

Price	€110–€130.
Rooms	4 doubles. Child's bed available.
Meals	Dinner €25. Wine €7.
Closed	Rarely.
Directions	From Francavilla d'Ete dir. Montegiorgio, past Montegiorgio sign, blue street sign for Contrada Montese on right; next right after 500m, sign for house on corner points right. 1st house on left after 250m; dirt track to house, silver post box on left. Phone for detailed directions.

Ray & Claire Gorman
Contrada Montese 13,
63025 Montegiorgio

Tel	+39 0734 962753
Email	info@casasanruffino.com
Web	www.casasanruffino.com

Vento di Rose B&B

House, orchards, breakfasts, roses, people… in the foothills of Monterubbiano, ten minutes from the sea, is a place to relish, an unexpected treasure. Your gentle, happy, delightful hosts, with a little English between them, fill the house with artistic flourishes and love doing B&B. Emanuela's sunny personality infuses everything; on the first night Emidio will take you to a local restaurant to ensure you don't get lost. The kitchen/breakfast room, exquisitely Italian, is all blues and creams, its white lace tablecloth strewn with rose petals, then laden with garden cherries, peaches, pears, fresh frittata of artichokes, mulberry fruit tarts, warm bread from Moresco – a different treat every day. The garden's shady bowers are scented with roses, honeysuckle and jasmine; the views are long; the pillows carry sprigs of lavender at night. Bedrooms are bright and airy with pale colourwashed walls and embroidered linen, each with a sitting area; you are also welcome to share the lounge. A paradise of hospitality, tranquillity and blissful breakfasts. *Hot tub in garden.*

Price	€80-€95.
Rooms	3: 1 double, 2 family rooms for 2-4.
Meals	Picnic available. Restaurants 4km.
Closed	January-February.
Directions	A14 exit Pedaso dir. Monterubbiano. After 200m, left at lights; on for 7km. After Bar Giardino on left, cont. 2km. On right, signed.

Emidio di Ruscio
Via Canniccio 7,
63026 Monterubbiano
Tel +39 0734 59226
Email ventodirose@libero.it
Web www.ventodirose.it

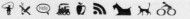

Modus Vivendi

Walkers, birdwatchers, outdoorsy types will love it here. Views stretch over rolling hills dotted with towns while the mountains of the Majella National Park rise behind. Hospitable Emilia is a trained guide, keen on birds and flowers, and can suggest walks or even join you. Passionate about conservation, she's restored her creamy stone house using local artisans and friendly materials; there are ecological paints, wood-burning stoves, solar panels, recycled rainwater. Cool white and exposed stone walls, timbered ceilings and terracotta floors make rooms light and airy, while furnishings are traditional but uncluttered – wrought-iron or carved beds, richly coloured bedspreads, an antique armoire or a handsome chair. Bathrooms sparkle with chrome and pretty mosaics; all is fresh, new, pristine. The apartments have open-plan living areas with kitchens to one side, and terraces for dining. Or let Emilia cook, Abruzzese style. Everything is homemade, and the produce is local organic. In the summer, eat under the pergola and raise a glass of home-produced liqueur to those views.

Price	€60-€80. Apts €540-€775 per week.
Rooms	5 + 2: 5 doubles. 2 apartments for 4.
Meals	Lunch/dinner from €20.
	Restaurant 5-minute drive.
Closed	Rarely.
Directions	A25 Rome-Pescara exit Scafa.
	Follow signs for Abbateggio for 10km;
	house signed.

Ethical Collection: Environment; Community; Food. See page 400 for details

Dario de Renzis
Via Colle della Selva,
65020 Abbateggio

Tel	+39 0858 572136
Email	Info@ecoalbergomodusvivendi.it
Web	www.ecoalbergomodusvivendi.it

Dimora Del Prete di Belmonte

The old palace hides among the cobbled streets of the medieval centre – a gem once you step inside. Venafro, a Roman town, lies in the lovely valley of Monte Santa Croce, ringed by mountains. The first thrill is the enchanting internal garden with its lush banana palms and citrus trees, where a miscellany of Roman artefacts and olive presses lie scattered among tables and chairs. Next, a frescoed interior in an astonishing state of preservation; painted birds, family crests and *grotteschi* adorn the walls of the state rooms and entrance hall. Bedrooms are furnished in simple good taste, one with a big fireplace and a sleigh bed, another with chestnut country furniture, most with views. Shower rooms are small – bar one, which has a bath. Dorothy is a wonderful hostess and has fantastic local knowledge, she and her son are a great team. They also run an organic farm with 1,000 olive trees (many of them over 400 years old), vines, walnut-trees and sheep. An area and a palace rich in content – and relaxed, delicious dinners do full justice to the setting. Breakfasts are as good. *Easy access by train.*

Price	€120. Suite €150. Apartment €500 per week (€200 for weekend).
Rooms	5 + 1: 4 doubles, 1 suite. Apartment for 2-4.
Meals	Lunch/dinner with wine, €30.
Closed	November-March.
Directions	Leave A1 Rome-Naples motorway at S. Vittore from north; follow signs for Venafro, Isernia and Campobasso. The Palace is easy to find in the historical centre of Venafro.

Ethical Collection: Food.
See page 400 for details

Dorothy Volpe del Prete
Via Cristo 49, 86079 Venafro
Tel   +39 0865 900159
Email   info@dimoradelprete.it
Web   www.dimoradelprete.it

Lazio

Photo: istock.com

Casa in Trastevere

If you're independent souls, fortunate enough to be planning more than a fleeting trip to Rome, this apartment is a great base, a ten-minute walk from the old quarter of Trastevere. The area, though residential, has a great buzz at night and the shops, bars and restaurants are a treat to discover. Signora Nicolini, once a specialist restorer, has furnished this sunny first-floor flat as if it were her own home. She has kept the original 19th-century red and black terrazzo floor and has added contemporary touches: a cream sofa, an all-white kitchen (no microwave or oven, but you won't mind, with so many tempting restaurants on your doorstep), kilims and modern art. You have a large open-plan living/dining room with screened kitchen, a double and a twin bedroom, each with a white bathroom, and an extra sofabed. All is fresh and bright, and the big bedroom is very charming with its hand-quilted bedspread. Marta is a delight and does her best to ensure you go home with happy memories. Put your feet up after a long day, pour yourself a glass of wine... then set off to explore some more of this magical city. *Minimum stay four nights.*

Price	From €140 for 2; from €180 for 4; from €200 for 5-6.
Rooms	1 apartment for 2-6.
Meals	Restaurants nearby.
Closed	Rarely.
Directions	From Ponte Sisto cross Piazza Trilussa. Right into Via della Lungara, left into Via dei Riari, right into Vicolo della Penitenza. From Termini bus line H. From Trastevere station, bus No. 8.

Marta Nicolini
Vicolo della Penitenza 19,
00165 Rome

Tel	+39 335 6205768
Email	info@casaintrastevere.it
Web	www.casaintrastevere.it

Buonanotte Garibaldi

Cross the Tiber into maze-like Travestere. Turn right for boisterous bars, left for cobblestoned tranquillity. Here lies a place that is small and special – an artistic find behind solid green doors. Fashion and textiles designer Luisa, as welcoming as can be, has transformed her studio and home into a vibrant three-bedroom B&B. Built around a beautiful sun-dappled courtyard, it is a showcase for her creations. Two bedrooms, Orange and Green, are on the ground floor opening to the courtyard (orange trees and magnolias, a marvel in spring) while Blue is above with its own big terrace, heaven for honeymooners. Walls are clean and minimalist, bathrooms mosaic'd and sparkling; splashes of colour come from hand-painted organza. Yours to retire to – a winter treat – is a salon with stylish settees and books on art and Rome. Charming staff, friendly and discreet, serve breakfast at an oval dining table surrounded by silk panels: fresh fruits, breads, meats, eggs how you like them, lavender shortbread, baked peaches; a wonder. All this in Rome's old heart – and Luisa's lovable dog, Tinto.

Price	€220-€280.
Rooms	3 twins/doubles.
Meals	Restaurants within walking distance.
Closed	15 December-January; 15-30 August.
Directions	Off Via Garibaldi in Trastevere.

Luisa Longo
Via Garibaldi 83, 00153 Rome
Tel   +39 0658 330733
Email info@buonanottegaribaldi.com
Web   www.buonanottegaribaldi.com

Entry 259   Map 12

Hotel Santa Maria

All around are cobbled streets, ancient houses and the bustle of cafés, bars and tiny shops that is Trastevere. Just behind the lovely Piazza de Santa Maria – whose church bells chime every 15 minutes – is a pair of green iron gates that open to sudden, sweet peace and the fragrance of honeysuckle. On the site of what was a 17th-century convent is this secluded single-storey hotel, its courtyards bright with orange trees. The layout is a tribute to all those earlier cloisters: rooms here open onto covered, brick-pillared terraces that surround a central, gravelled courtyard where you can sit out in summer. Authentic materials have been used – Peperino marble for the floors, walnut and chestnut for the ceilings – while the breakfast room has the original terracotta floor. Newly decorated bedrooms have soft yellow walls, high ceilings, big beds. There's no sitting room but a good bar, and the internet and bikes are free. Stefano, the owner, runs a courteous staff and you are well looked after. He's also a qualified guide and has recently opened a sister hotel, Residenza Santa Maria (see next entry), just around the corner.

Price	€170-€220. Suites €260-€480. Triple €200-€280. Quadruple €230-€320.
Rooms	18: 8 doubles, 5 suites for 4, 5 or 6, 4 triples, 1 quadruple.
Meals	Restaurants 10m.
Closed	Never.
Directions	15-minute taxi from Termini station.

	Paolo Vetere Vicolo del Piede 2, 00153 Rome
Tel	+39 0658 94626
Email	info@hotelsantamaria.info
Web	www.htlsantamaria.com

Residenza Santa Maria

Secreted away off the atmospheric cobbled lanes of Trastevere, wonderfuly central – an olive-stone's throw from Piazza Santa Maria – this 18th-century building came up with a few surprises when the owners renovated a few years ago. In unearthing a Roman cistern in the basement – now a long, cavernous cellar dining room – they discovered various artefacts, bas-relief tiles and pieces of friezes; these now adorn recessed alcoves. Ancient arches lead through to reception and a covered courtyard, where murals of classical Rome add colour to an otherwise neutral palette. There's simple oak wood furniture and cedar wood ceilings throughout; beds have brocaded floral spreads that create a bit of a splash. Just a simple décor, the same throughout: a writing desk, an abstract painting, cotto floors, and stencilled designs beneath the beams. Breakfasts are abundant and many excellent osteria lie within a hand-in-hand stroll. Take advantage of the complimentary bicycles from their sister operation a minute's walk away, the Hotel Santa Maria. Prepare to get lost in Trastevere!

Price	€220. Triple €270. Quadruples €300.
Rooms	6: 2 doubles, 1 triple, 3 quadruples.
Meals	Restaurants nearby.
Closed	Rarely.
Directions	15-minute taxi from Termini station.

Stefano Donghi
Via dell'Arco San Calisto 20,
00153 Rome
Tel   +39 0658 335103
Email   info@residenzasantamaria.com
Web   www.residenzasantamaria.com

Guest House Arco de' Tolomei

Up the graceful sweep of the dark wooden staircase and you enter a fascinating little B&B in the peaceful old Jewish quarter of Trastevere. The house has been in Marco's family for 200 years and those sedate gentlemen framed on the blue walls are just some of the past inhabitants. Marco and his wife Gianna are great travellers and have filled the family home with bits and pieces from their journeys abroad. Floor to ceiling shelves heave under the weight of books in the red drawing room, gorgeous pieces of art and sculpture beautify walls and tables, and floors are laid with exquisite parquet; there's plentiful dark wood and every square inch gleams. The long oval dining table awaits guests eager to sample Gianna's breakfasts. Bedrooms, reached through a cugote' sitting room, have bold flowers – pinks, reds, yellows – or pinstripes on the walls, a backdrop to handsome bedsteads and great little bathrooms, while the best have miniature staircases up to private terraces with views that roll down over the terracotta patchwork of Trastevere's tiny terracotta roofs.

Price	€160–€220.
Rooms	5: 4 doubles, 1 triple.
Meals	Restaurants 50m.
Closed	Never.
Directions	From Ciampino airport to Trastevere train station; line H to Piazza Sonnino, then Via della Lungaretta to Piazza in Piscinula.

Marco Fè d'Ostiani
Via dell'Arco de' Tolomei 27,
00153 Rome

Tel	+39 0658 320819
Email	info@inrome.info
Web	www.inrome.info

Hotel San Francesco

Trastevere — Rome's stylish and bohemian quarter — is at its best on a sleepy Sunday morning when the flea market unfurls and the smell of spicy *porchetta* infuses the air. But first, enjoy one of the most generous breakfasts Rome has to offer, served in a long, light room that overlooks a 15th-century cloister complete with friar, garden and hens... Built in 1926 as a training school for missionaries, this young hotel runs on well-oiled wheels. There's a black and white tiled sitting room with black leather armchairs, big white lilies and a piano, and a stylishly furnished roof garden with canvas parasols and views to the Vatican; gorgeous by day, ravishing by night. Marble stairs lead to carpeted corridors off which feed small, comfortable bedrooms — lined curtains at double-glazed windows, fabulous bathrooms, garden views at the back. Pop into the Santa Cecilia next door for a peep at Bellini's *Madonna*, stroll to the sights across the river, rent a bike. Not truly central — you'll be using the odd taxi — but a very pleasant launch pad for discovering the city.

Price	€69–€310.
Rooms	24 doubles.
Meals	Restaurants nearby.
Closed	Never.
Directions	From Termini station, bus No. 75, 44 or line H. Airport train to Travestere (35 mins).

Daniele Frontoni
Via Jacopa de' Settesoli 7,
00153 Rome

Tel	+39 0658 300051
Email	info@hotelsanfrancesco.net
Web	www.hotelsanfrancesco.net

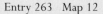

Dépendance Valle delle Camene

Pick your way through the shady gravel garden – past weathered statues posing discreetly amongst ferns, palms and soaring magnolias – and up to the handsome 19th-century villa that sits, proudly, in this Roman garden. This is where Viviana lives; she and her daughter, Stefania, have breathed life into the guest annexe that lies to one end. It is small but beautifully formed, and you have the whole place to yourself. Blue and yellow tiles wash floors with colour, their vibrancy barely diminished after 200 years; there are chunky marble hand basins, their curves deliciously smooth from centuries of use, and walls and beamed ceilings that are refreshingly white. Modernity is cleverly concealed: the fabulously stylish jacuzzi bath hides behind a thick hessian curtain, the new bed lies under an embroidered quilt. Breakfast in your private little courtyard where the original Roman walls offer total seclusion. In the open-air sitting room at the front: plump cushions on wicker sofas encircled by young orange trees in portly ceramic urns – a blissful spot for a flop and a glass of something chilled after a day's amble round the city. *Min. stay two nights.*

Price	€160. Sofabed €30.
Rooms	1 double (+ sofabed).
Meals	Restaurants within walking distance.
Closed	Rarely.
Directions	Metro: Line B to Circo Massimo, then 5-minute walk.

Stefania Agnello
Via di Valle delle Camene 3C,
00184 Rome
Tel　　+39 3288 181181
Email　info@valledellecamene.com
Web　　www.valledellecamene.com

Caesar House Residenze Romane

A calm, comfortable oasis above Roman din. The Forum can be glimpsed from one window, elegant cafés, shops and restaurants lie below, and the Colosseum is a five-minute stroll. Up the lift to the second floor of the ancient palazzo; grand reception doors open to a bright, welcoming space. Charming, stylish sisters, Giulia and Simona, run things together with the help of Grandma: a family affair. Bedrooms, named after celebrated *italiani*, have warm red ceramic floors, heavy curtains in maroon or blue, matching sofas and quilted covers, a choice of blankets or duvets, vestibules to keep luggage out of the way and every modern thing: air con, minibar, internet, safe, satellite TV. You breakfast in your room – it's big enough – or in the pretty dining room with its tables draped in cream linen, and modern art dotted here and there. There's even a gym for those who have surplus energy after a long day's sightseeing around the city's ancient ruins. The service here is exemplary – maps, guided tours, airport pick up, babysitting, theatre booking, bike hire. It's thoroughly professional, and personal too.

Price	€170–€230. Singles €150–€200. Extra bed €20.
Rooms	6: 4 doubles, 2 twins.
Meals	Restaurants nearby.
Closed	Never.
Directions	Metro: line B from Termini station to Cavour, then 5-minute walk or bus No. 74 or 40 down Via Cavour.

	Giulia & Simona Barela
	Via Cavour 310, 00184 Rome
Tel	+39 0667 92674
Email	info@residenzeromane.com
Web	www.caesarhouse.com

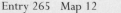

Casa Trevi I & II

A hop, skip and a jump from Italy's most famous fountain, the Casa Trevi is a treasure. Find yourself in an astonishingly peaceful courtyard, all olive trees, scented oranges and a fountain inhabited by small turtles. Though you're in Rome's most vibrant heart, not a sound penetrates from outside. The apartments are on the ground floor of one of the old buildings and open directly off the courtyard. Interiors are bright, soothing and minimalist in the most beautiful way: white walls and terracotta, glass shelving and concealed lighting, a mix of modern and brocante finds. There are no windows as such but the double glass-paned doors let in plenty of light. Hobs and fridges are provided in the airy, white kitchens, but serious cooking is not catered for (who wants to eat-in in Rome?). Shower rooms are gorgeous. On three sides are 17th-century buildings in yellows, ochres and reds; on the fourth, a modern monstrosity. Marta could not be sweeter, and the security – a big plus – is excellent, with a porter and security camera in the main entrance. Good value for central Rome. *Minimum stay four nights.*

Price	€140. €180 for 4.
Rooms	2 apartments: 1 for 2-3, 1 for 4.
Meals	Restaurants nearby.
Closed	Rarely.
Directions	Directions on booking; no parking in pedestrianised area. 10-minute taxi from Termini station. Metro: Piazza Barberini.

Marta Nicolini
Via in Arcione 98, 00187 Rome
Tel +39 335 6205768
Email info@casaintrastevere.it
Web www.casatrevi.it

Casa Trevi III

This, too, is five minutes from the Trevi Fountain – most breathtaking by night – but in a separate street from Casas Trevi I and II. Marta – full of warmth, a busy bee – has waved her stylish wand again and created a deeply desirable place to stay. She employed one of the top restoration experts in Rome to make ceiling beams glow and terracotta floors gleam – and the result? Old Rome meets new. Up a tiny lift to the third floor and into an open-plan sitting, dining and kitchen area – black, white, grey, chic, with a polished wooden floor. A discarded shutter for a frame, an antique door for a bedhead, air con to keep you cool, double glazing to ensure quiet. The white-raftered twin and double rooms share a sparkling, 21st-century shower in beige marble. Modigliani prints beautify cream walls, mirrored doors reflect the light, silk cushions sprinkle the sofa and shutters are painted dove-grey. Never mind the tourists and the street vendors, Rome lies at your feet. And you have the unassuming Trattoria della Stampa, where the locals go, in the very same street. *Minimum stay four nights.*

Price	€140–€200.
Rooms	Apartment for 3-5.
Meals	Restaurants nearby.
Closed	Never.
Directions	No cars in pedestrianised area; 10-minute taxi from Termini station. Metro: Piazza Barberini. Directions on booking.

Marta Nicolini
Via dei Maroniti 7, 00187 Rome

Tel	+39 335 6205768
Email	info@casaintrastevere.it
Web	www.casatrevi.it

Hotel Modigliani

There's a sense of anticipation the moment you enter the marble hall, with its deep, pale sofas and fresh flowers – Marco's wide smile and infectious enthusiasm reinforce the feeling. This is an unusual, delightful place, hidden down a side street just five minutes' walk from the Spanish Steps and Via Veneto. The house belonged to Marco's father, and Marco and Giulia (he a writer, she a musician) have turned it into the perfect small hotel. Marble floors and white walls are a dramatic setting for black-and-white photos taken by Marco, their starkness softened by luxuriant plants. The bread oven of the 1700s has become a dining room – all vaulted ceilings, whitewashed walls, cherrywood tables, fabulous photos. Bedrooms are fresh and elegant; some have balconies and wonderful views, all have small, perfect bathrooms. There's a lovely new sitting room and bar for guests to use. The whole place has a sweet, stylish air, it's unusually quiet for the centre of the city and there's a patio scented with jasmine. Marco and Giulia will tell you about Rome's secret corners – or grab a copy of Marco's new guide and discover Rome for yourselves.

Price	€150–€195. Suites €208–€340. Family suite €330–€440. Apartments €200–€250.
Rooms	23 + 2: 20 twins/doubles, 2 suites, 1 family suite for 4–6. 2 apartments: 1 for 3, 1 for 6.
Meals	Breakfast included for all. Restaurant 10m.
Closed	Never.
Directions	Metro: Line A, 2nd stop Piazza Barberini. 5-minute walk from Spanish Steps.

Giulia & Marco di Tillo
Via della Purificazione 42, 00187 Rome

Tel   +39 0642 815226
Email   info@hotelmodigliani.com
Web   www.hotelmodigliani.com

Villa Ann

Gentle, charming Lismay is a trained cook so dinners (Italian) and breakfasts (English) are delicious; John is a golfing enthusiast and will tell you where to play… and who would guess Italy's oldest golf course was so near? Indeed, the whole family is sports-mad which is why they originally chose this area, excellent for sailors and windsurfers, hand-gliders, hikers and bikers. The modern villa, named after John's mother, sits in its own olive grove and palm-filled gardens with a pool in the orchard, which you may use for early morning and pre-dinner swims. Small basic bedrooms on the first floor are reached via an outside stair and lead off a modest landing (furnished with a table and dining chairs) where John's office tucks behind a curtain. One room has no hanging space but the beds are comfy and the sheets are new, and two rooms share a large balcony, full of morning sunshine with views to the hills. Wine tastings at Frascati are a short drive and the Rome express train gets you to the city in 20 minutes; your very helpful hosts will drive you to and from the station. *30 minutes from Ciampino airport.*

Price	€30-€60.
Rooms	3: 1 twin/double; 2 twins/doubles sharing bath. Whole house available during holidays.
Meals	Dinner with wine, €20.
Closed	Rarely.
Directions	Directions on booking.

John & Lismay Garforth-Bles
Via Mole del Giardino 4,
00049 Velletri

Tel	+39 0696 453398
Email	j.garforth@tiscali.it
Web	www.villa-ann.com

Villa Monte Ripone

Slip through glass doors into a cool, welcoming space of fresh flowers, comfy sofas and richly tiled floors. This handsome country house, with its golden colours and olive green shutters, was Anna's family home. The open-plan, ground floor – all vaulted ceilings, polished tiles and beautiful antiques – includes an elegant dining room and comfortable sitting room. Upstairs is a maze of unexpected spaces, little steps up and steps down. Airy, boldly-coloured bedrooms are a mix of much-loved antiques and modern functional furnishings. Some are grander than others but all share dreamy views over fields and the family's olive groves and fruit trees. The views from the pool, hidden below the house, are equally enchanting. There are walks directly from the house and peaceful shady spots in the garden. Eat out in Nazzano (a five-minute drive) or here: it's regional cooking with organic veg from the garden. Anna, Renzo and their two children live next door and the atmosphere is family-friendly and easy. *Minimum stay three nights.*

Price	€80–€90. Family room €120. Whole house on request.
Rooms	5: 2 doubles, 1 twin/double, 1 suite, 1 family room for 4.
Meals	Dinner with wine, €25, by arrangement.
Closed	November–March.
Directions	A1 Roma-Firenze exit Ponzano Sorrate for Nazzano; 2km after Ponzano Romano right fork for Rome; ignore turning to Nazzano; Via Civitellese on right; 200m on right, signed.

Anna Clarissa Benzoni
Via Civitellese 2,
00060 Nazzano

Tel   +39 0765 680302
Email   monteripone@virgilio.it

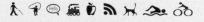

Azienda Agrituristica Sant'Ilario sul Farfa

Straightforward good value, and an hour from Rome by car. The approach, along a steep, unmade track, is marked by that typically Italian juxtaposition of the electric gates and an olive tree of staggering antiquity. This little farm sits on one of the steeply terraced hills above the river Farfa, with views from its terrace to the Sabine hills. Susanna Serafini is a chatty and creative hostess whose dinners – delivered on request, and using farm produce – are brilliant value. The aspect of the place is rather ranch-like, with bedrooms in two single-storey farm buildings, white with wooden shutters. Bedrooms are snug and wood-panelled with some fine antique bedheads, white walls and showers. The two apartments in the main house have small kitchens for simple meals: great for families. A pleasing tangle of trellises extends across the garden – more farmyard than formal. Take a dip in the pool or the river, spin off on a mountain bike, book onto an olive – or grape – harvesting weekend. There are painting classes for grown-ups, cookery and craft classes for children and little ones love it.

Price	€80. Half-board €55-€60. Apartment €480-€850 per week.
Rooms	6 + 3: 2 doubles, 4 family rooms. 3 apts: 1 for 3, 1 for 4, 1 for 5.
Meals	Dinner/Sunday lunch with wine, €20. Restaurants 2km.
Closed	January.
Directions	From SS4 Rome-Rieti exit to Osteria Nuova dir. Poggio Nativo. Just after Monte S. Maria sharp left onto Via Sant'Ilario signed to Sant'Ilario sul Farfa.

Susanna Serafini
Via Sant'Ilario, 02030 Poggio Nativo
Tel   +39 0765 872410
Email   info@santilariosulfarfa.it
Web   www.santilariosulfarfa.it

La Torretta

Casperia is a joyful, characterful, car-free maze of steepish streets in the Sabine hills. La Torretta has the dreamiest views from its terrace, and easy interior spaces that have been wonderfully designed by architect Roberto. A huge ground-floor sitting room with beautiful frescoes around the cornicing welcomes you... an old stone fireplace, modern sofas and chairs, books, paintings, piano. The upper room – opening onto that terrace – is a stunning, vaulted, contemporary living space with an open stainless-steel kitchen and views through skylights to the church tower and valley. Maureen, warm-hearted and hospitable, is passionate about the region and its food. She arranges cookery courses and will cook (on request) using the best olive oil and whatever is in season – mushrooms, truffles, wild boar. Whitewashed, high-ceilinged bedrooms are charming in their simplicity; beds are made and towels changed regularly; bathrooms are a treat. Don't worry about having to leave your car in the square below the town: Roberto has a buggy for luggage. Fine breakfasts, too – among the best in Italy!

Price	€90. Single €70. Family room €150.
Rooms	7: 5 doubles, 1 single, 1 family room (2 connecting rooms) for 4.
Meals	Dinner with wine, €30, by arrangement. Restaurant 50m.
Closed	Rarely.
Directions	From North, A1 exit Ponzano Soratte towards Poggio Mirteto. Continue on SS657 for 5km to T-junc. Left on SS313 to Cantalupo towards Casperia.

Roberto & Maureen Scheda
Via G. Mazzini 7, 02041 Casperia
Tel +39 0765 63202
Email latorretta@tiscali.it
Web www.latorrettabandb.com

L'Ombricolo- Country House Hospitality

Two decades years ago it was a ruin. Now it's a mellow stone house with a warmth and character all of its own. Dawne has employed local materials and craftspeople to restore the vaulted ceilings and flagged floors, and filled the interiors with her creativity. Where cattle once slept – their rub marks against the stone arches remain! – is now an inviting sitting room with a beautiful fireplace, cream sofas, music and books. The pretty bedrooms are equally individual: steps here and there, odd corners and turns, beamed sloping ceilings. But the glorious heart of the house, created from an old, dismantled grocery store in Rome, is Dawne's kitchen. Here you will find her unhurriedly preparing a meal when you return from a day away, ready with a glass of wine and a smile. She's a fascinating person to talk to, has lived in Italy for 40 years, worked in the film industry in Rome and travelled the world. Her garden is as relaxing as her home: charming, not spic and span; plants swoop over the veranda, there are shady trees for hot days and dogs and cats galore. Thrill to the stars at night.

Price	€120–€130. Extra bed €40 (ground floor room only).
Rooms	5 doubles.
Meals	Dinner €45. Restaurant 1km.
Closed	Rarely.
Directions	Exit A1 at Bomarzo. Follow signs for Castiglione in Teverina (12 km). Restaurant Molla Solis on left; over bridge look for sign to L'Ombricolo, on left before grain silos.

Dawne Alstrom
01020 Civitella d'Agliano

Tel	+39 0761 914735
Email	dawne@lombricolo.com
Web	www.lombricolo.com

Locanda Settimo Cielo

Bounce down the track through olives and orchards to the vine-smothered arbour, park up and enter an exotic oasis of rusticity and peace. Built in the early 19th century to house the estate's sharecroppers, this sturdy farmhouse sits grandly atop a cliff of tuff surrounded by elms, pines and splendid views of forested, wildlife-stuffed hills. A stroll down stepped paths cut into the rock and tunnelled fruit trees reveals a secluded, deck-fringed pool, while a fabulous covered patio terrace with solid tables and chairs provides lovely outdoor space. Interiors are gorgeous, rustic and reminiscent of a safari lodge: massive hand-carved beds and tables; looming wardrobes; framed African tapestries. Ambient lighting and an enormous fireplace illuminate a high-ceilinged, decadently comfortable sitting room – heaven – while lovely Francesca's breakfasts of homemade breads and juices harvested from the estate set you up for a day's hiking in the hills, touring the vineyards or visiting medieval villages. Or simply stay put and nod off to the birdsong with a book.

Price	€120.
Rooms	9: 5 doubles, 3 triples, 1 quadruple.
Meals	Restaurant 5km.
	Occasional dinner, €25.
Closed	Rarely.
Directions	From A1 exit Orvieto; follow signs to Todi then to Lubriano. Stay on street until Strada Sterrata Locanda Santa Caterina N. Dal 28 al 34. Left; on to B&B.

	Francesca Anghileri
	Loc. Santa Caterina 28,
	01020 Lubriano
Tel	+39 0761 780451
Email	info@settimocieloagriturismo.com
Web	www.settimocieloagriturismo.com

La Locanda della Chiocciola

Perhaps the name has something to do with the pace of life at 'The House of the Snail'. This is an unhurried place. Maria Cristina and Roberto have turned a 15th-century stone farmstead in the Tiber valley into an entrancing small hotel and restaurant. Gardens full of flowering shrubs and peaceful walkways are set in 25 hectares of woods, olive groves and orchards, and there's a wonderful pool. Be welcomed by mellow, gleaming floors and furniture, and the intoxicating smell of beeswax. A beautiful staircase sweeps up to the bedrooms, each of which has its name painted on the door: 'Mimosa', 'Coccinella', 'Ciclamine'... they are arresting rooms – big, uncluttered, individual – some with four-posters, one with a vast bath. Terracotta tiles contrast with pale walls and lovely fabrics, family antiques with elegant modern furniture or pieces that Maria Cristina and Roberto have collected on their travels. They're a charming and gentle young couple, proud of what they have created. The food is delicious and the new Turkish bath, sauna and jacuzzi are a treat.

Price	€130–€170. Half-board €95–€115 p.p.
Rooms	8: 3 doubles, 2 suites, 1 family room, 2 triples.
Meals	Dinner €35. Wine from €10. Menu à la carte also available.
Closed	Mid-December to mid-January.
Directions	Exit autostrada at Orte for Orte Town. Before Orte, dir. Penna in Teverina. After 2.5km, sign for La Chiocciola on left.

Roberto & Maria Cristina
de Fonseca Pimentel
Seripola, 01028 Orte
Tel   +39 0761 402734
Email   info@lachiocciola.net
Web   www.lachiocciola.net

Campania

Photo: istock.com

Masseria Giosole Agriturismo

A wonderful place for families. Sixty hectares of olives and fruit trees – help yourself! – a children's playground, a stunning pool, free bikes, tennis and a relaxed, no-rules atmosphere. Children scamper safely, parents flop around lazily… occasionally ambling off via the orchards to the river with just the birds for company. The di Maglianos, a handsome lively couple whose family have farmed here for three centuries, have created a place that reflects their gracious, easy-going nature. Rooms in the sprawling, peachy coloured *masseria* are large and airy with terracotta or wooden floors, high beamed ceilings and pale washed walls, and lightly sprinkled family antiques. Colourful textiles add dash. Bedrooms, some with a garden terrace, are uncluttered and restful, their bathrooms small but spotless. Nearby are ancient churches and palazzi in Capua, the Royal Palace at Caserta, and Naples and Pompeii are under an hour's drive. Come back to a delicious meal of local dishes – home-produced, naturally – dining around the fire in winter, in the garden in summer. *Minimum stay two nights.*

Price	€86–€120. Suites €110–€150. Apts €90–€125.
Rooms	5 + 2: 3 doubles, 2 suites for 2-4. 2 apts: 1 for 2-4, 1 for 6-8.
Meals	Breakfast €8 for self-caterers. Dinner €25, by arrangement. Restaurants 1km.
Closed	Rarely.
Directions	A1 Rome-Naples exit Capua. Follow signs for Capua and Agriturismo Masseria Giosole for 7km. Past San Giuseppe church on right; after 500m, right. On for 1.5km; signed.

Barone Alessandro & Baronessa
Francesca Pasca di Magliano
Via Giardini 31, 81043 Capua
Tel   +39 0823 961108
Email info@masseriagiosole.com
Web   www.masseriagiosole.com

Giravento

Stay here and tread lightly on the planet. Sweet Serena is a passionate environmentalist
– but never sacrifices comfort. The new handsome pink farmhouse oozes character and
charm. Built to high environmental standards (local bricks, naturally treated wood
floors, old-fashioned terracotta tiles) on a site surrounded by olive groves and orchards
with views of the Taburno Camposauro regional park, the whole place is a paradise for
birds, wild flowers and animals. Bedrooms, with private entrances, are light, airy and
thoroughly natural: voile curtains, stripped floors, eco lighting, solid country furniture,
and jewel-like splashes from rugs and bed throws. Heaps of space and walk-in showers,
too. Flop around the pool, or in the open-plan living area with those views across the
valley and a delicious wood-burner for winter. Share a meal around the table and
discover Serena's passion for cooking – and her delectable 'invention' *ciocannurca*, slices
of low-sugar apples dipped into bitter chocolate. Raise a glass and watch the magical
fireflies perform. *Minimum stay two nights.*

Price	€90.
Rooms	3: 1 double, 1 triple, 1 quadruple.
Meals	Summer brunch €15. Dinner with wine, €30, by arrangement.
Closed	Rarely.
Directions	M'way Milan-Naples exit Caianello; on to Telesina on SS372 dir. Benevento. After 35km dir. Fondo Valle Isclero-Napoli, S. Agata de' Goti. Exit Melizzano, Amorosi, Solopaca, MEG Museo Engastronomico.

Serena Bova
Vicinale Castagneto 7,
82030 Melizzano
Mobile   +39 347 2708153
Email   info@giravento.it
Web   www.giravento.it

Ethical Collection: Environment; Community;
Food. See page 400 for details

Il Cortile Agriturismo

Arriving here is a memorable moment. The black door in the suburban street opens onto a beautiful flagged courtyard rich in jasmine and oranges – ravishing in spring. The villa was built as a summer retreat for Arturo's forebears, and now includes two self-contained suites facing the courtyard with secluded entrances. Guests have their own sitting room/library filled with family antiques, comfortable sofas and pictures, and cool, spacious bedrooms, with pale washed walls, tiled floors and some good antiques; shower rooms are crisply white. Access to one bedroom is through the other, making this absolutely perfect for families with children. Dutch Sijtsken is charming and thoughtful, serves truly delicious food and brings you little vases of flowers from her and Arturo's lushly lovely garden. This *giardinello delle delizie* – a little garden of delights – is surprisingly large. Three tall date palms, two ancient magnolias, beds stuffed with calla lilies, hedges of glistening roses and camellia, paths that meander... choose a deckchair and dream. Special people, special place.

Price	€66-€90.
Rooms	2 suites: 1 for 2-3, 1 for 4-5.
Meals	Dinner €25. Wine from €5.
Closed	Never.
Directions	From Rome or Naples: highway to Bari exit Nola. Follow signs to Cimitile & Cicciano. House 10-minute drive from highway.

Sijtsken, Giovanna & Alessandra Nucci
Via Roma 43, 80033 Cicciano

Tel	+39 0818 248897
Email	info@agriturismoilcortile.com
Web	www.agriturismoilcortile.com

Relais Castelcicala

Live like a prince in a country villa. Restored with care and passion, this raspberry pink, 18th-century mansion was the holiday home of the Princes of Castelcicala; Gherardo is the architect son of the current prince. In a family home, shared wtih charming wife Barbara and three daughters, you will be swept up by their welcome, and their love of family history. Expect Sicilian liqueurs and generous bathroom goodies; you almost feel you're staying as a family friend. Guest rooms are in the former stables, a smart spotless mix of old and new: an antique washstand, a modern floor lamp, polished terracotta tiles, old beams, a white corner bath. Most rooms have sitting areas, one has its own garden, and there's a salon with deep sofas and a winter fire. For summer; a sun terrace and a small curvy pool. Naples, Pompeii, Herculaneum are 30 minutes away and the spectacular Amalfi coast not much further. Return to the villa's orchards, olive groves and jasmine-scented gardens. Where to dine? Their own lovely restaurant is just 500 metres up the hill, a favourite with locals. Perfect pampering far from the crowds.

Price	€75–€100. Suites €75–€120.
Rooms	6: 2 doubles, 4 suites for 2–4.
Meals	Dinner €25. Wine €10.
Closed	Rarely.
Directions	A16 Napoli/Salerno exit Nola onto SS7 bis dir. Avellino; then dir. Casamarciano, then Nola. On for 2km, left after hospital into Via Castelcicala; right after 200m; house on left.

	Gherardo & Barbara Sallier de la Tour
	Via Cappuccini 1, 80035 Nola
Tel	+39 081 5105667
Email	relais@castelcicala.com
Web	www.castelcicala.com

Ethical Collection: Food.
See page 400 for details

Megaron Rooms & Breakfast

In the fashionable-funky heart of Naples, a stylish, minimalist B&B. The crumbling frontage of the noble 1900 palazzo and sober internal courtyard conceal a luxurious interior; the whole feel is one of silence, serenity and calm. A lift glides past the *piano nobile* up to the third floor where a smart 24-hour reception is revealed and large double doors open to large, light-filled bedrooms or suites – each a symphony in cream and black. Imagine muslin curtains at tall windows, big beds, deep sofas which convert into extra beds and antique tables and chairs. Bathrooms are exquisite in grey marble, with every little luxury. The suites have two bedrooms each and two bathrooms; one is on two levels linked by a fine walnut stairway. The breakfast room is similarly splendid. At your feet lies the enchantingly faded grandeur of one of Europe's liveliest cities: the bohemian Piazza Dante comes alive at night when the street musicians play and by day with its fantastic market. Find an outdoor table at the pizzeria of the same name and watch the literati drift by, drop into Cafe Mexico for the best coffee in town. Naples and the Megaron are a treat.

Price	€80–€100.
Rooms	5: 3 twins/doubles, 2 suites.
Meals	Restaurants 200m.
Closed	Never.
Directions	A1 Rome-Naples, follow Tangenziale (ring road) exit Capo di Monte; follow '"centro" for Piazza Dante. On right after National Museum.

Alex Ponzi
Piazza Dante 89, 80135 Naples
Tel +39 0815 446109
Email bnb@megaron.na.it
Web www.megaron.na.it

Parteno Bed & Breakfast

From the Neapolitan courtyard, steps lead to a glass and wrought-iron door – and, with luck, Alessandro, who, with Italian charm, impeccable English, and a delightful English-speaking staff, settles you in with welcoming words and a cup of tea. The bedrooms, some with balcony, are named after flowers; from 'Petunia' to 'Orchid' they spell out 'Parteno'. The décor is charming: wrought-iron mirrors, tables, chairs, beds and chandeliers have been crafted by local artisan Mazzella, and the gorgeous hand-painted bathroom tiles by an artist from Vietri sul Mare. The early 20th-century décor has been restored and the raftered ceilings will delight you: this feels more like a charming Italian home than a swish hotel. Modernity is revealed in air conditioning, small fridges and walk-in showers. The Parteno is in a lovely part of Naples, almost on the waterfront, near bustling cafés, restaurants and beautiful squares. Choose the bedroom at the front: it's a joy to eat breakfast looking out over the bay of Naples and the ferries heading for Sorrento, Capri and Ischia, or in the lovely breakfast room with equally delightful views.

Price	€99–€165.
Rooms	6: 4 doubles, 2 triples.
Meals	Lunch/dinner from €20. Wine from €8.
Closed	Never.
Directions	A1 Rome-Naples; follow Tangenziale (ring road) exit Fuorigrotta for centre. Parteno 1st building right off Piazza Vittoria, across from sea.

Alex Ponzi
Lungomare Partenope 1, 80121 Naples

Tel	+39 0812 452095
Email	bnb@megaron.na.it
Web	www.parteno.it

Palazzo San Teodoro - Riviera 281

Naples is vibrant and brimming with history. Right at its heart, the luxurious Palazzo soothes and calms. Elegantly neoclassical yet warmly inviting – thanks to Elena and her team, who speak good English are are full of smiles – it has a peachy position in a smart residential area, five minutes from the palm tree-edged waterfront. Through an archway, a lift whisks you to the third floor and a vast apartment of parquet floors, white walls, sofas with silk cushions, huge windows, and rattan chairs on terraces with views to the waterfront and the rosy rooftops. Bedrooms, all with private terraces, are airy modernist spaces, a mix of antique and contemporary jazzed up with bold art and colourful fabrics. Bathrooms indulge in marble, glass and chrome. Breakfast on the terrace then plunge into the city's heady mix of museums, galleries, markets – most within walking distance. Elena, who lives below, is a joyful, generous Neapolitan, and will help with restaurants, theatres, the sights. Return to a nightcap and the lights of Naples below you. Heaven to take the whole place.

Price	€140-€170. Whole apartment €3,150 per week.
Rooms	3: 2 doubles, 1 suite.
Meals	Restaurants nearby.
Closed	Rarely.
Directions	Directions on booking.

Elena Basile
Via Riviera di Chiaia 281,
80121 Naples
Tel   +39 0817 641427
Email   info@riviera281.it
Web   www.riviera281.it

La Murena Bed & Breakfast

Views from your rooftop terrace stretch to chestnut forests and the Gulf of Naples below. Here, high on the slopes of Vesuvius, the peace is palpable and the air cool and pure. Giovanni and his son live on the ground floor of this modern house, while the guests have the option of self-catering or B&B: the three bedrooms and kitchen are upstairs, and you share Giovanni's living room (with a fascinating display of Giovanni's hand-carved jewellery) below. There's also a large outside area for children to romp in. Breakfast appears each evening in the fridge as if by magic: peaches, apricots and oranges from the garden, cheeses and homemade jams. The larger of the bedrooms has a fancy wrought-iron bed with a golden cover, writing desks are antique with marble tops and floor tiles are patterned blue. The kitchen, too, is prettily tiled, there's blue glassware in a sea-blue cupboard, a white-clothed table, no shortage of mod cons and a good sofa to curl up into. For lovers of archaeological sites the place is a dream: Herculaneum, Pompeii, Torre Annunziata, Boscoreale, Paestum. *Minimum stay three nights. Airport pickup.*

Price	€80. Singles €60.
	Whole house €240 (€1,500 per week).
Rooms	3 doubles.
Meals	Restaurants nearby.
Closed	Rarely.
Directions	From autostrada Napoli-Pompei-Salerno exit Torre del Greco; follow signs for Il Vesuvio (via Osservatorio).

Giovanni Scognamiglio
Via Osservatorio 10,
80056 Herculaneum

Tel	+39 0817 779819
Email	lamurena@lamurena.it
Web	www.lamurena.it

Villa Giusso

It's a steep and challenging climb to get here but the rewards are immense. The villa, once a monastery, stands high on a promontory overlooking the Bay of Naples and the views from the terrace are breathtaking. So too are the sunsets. You may expect an effusive welcome from Erminia, Giovanna and the rest of the Giusso family who'll settle you into your rooms – rather romantic with their vintage iron beds, quirky 18th-century furnishings and big old paintings. Then explore: there are endless sitting rooms and the tour ends in the attic, almost a family museum. Dinner, plentiful, locally sourced and delicious, is served at the vast communal table – an occasion to relish. Breakfasts are taken in a vaulted kitchen tiled with 17th-century ceramics; over fruits, cakes and fresh ricotta, plan a day touring the Amalfi coast. Drive to Sorrento, Positano, Pompeii, take the boat to Naples or Capri. Return to a gentle stroll through the estate's vineyards and olive groves and recoup on the terrace, accompanied by a glass of homemade walnut liqueur and those views over Ischia and Vesuvius. *Minimum two nights.*

Price	€90-€130.
Rooms	7: 5 doubles, 1 suite for 4; 1 double with separate bath.
Meals	Dinner with wine, €28 (except Mondays). Restaurants 5km.
Closed	November-Palm Sunday.
Directions	A3 Napoli-Salerno exit Castellammare di Stabia; signs for Sorrento. At Seiano, after Moon Valley Hotel, left for M. Faito; cont. for 4.6km, right after Arola sign, follow signs to Astapiana Villa Giusso.

Famiglia Giusso Rispoli
Via Camaldoli 51, Astapiana, Loc. Arola,
80069 Vico Equense

Tel	+39 0818 024392
Email	astapiana@tin.it
Web	www.astapiana.com

Entry 284   Map 13

Agriturismo La Ginestra

There is a fresh, rustic feel to this farmhouse, and its position, 680m above sea level, is incredible. From the flower-rich terraces, sea views stretch in two directions: the Bay of Naples and the Bay of Salerno. The hills behind hold more delights, particularly for serious walkers: the 'Sentieri degli Dei' is a stone's throw away, and some of the paths, especially those down to Positano, are vertiginous and tough. The delightful owners do not speak English but will happily organise guided nature walks; they are also hugely proud of their organic farm status. Bedrooms and shower rooms are charming and mostly a good size, some with their own terrace. Some of the farm's produce – nuts, honey, vegetables, olive oil – is sold from a little cottage; it's also served in the stable restaurant, where delicious Sorrento dishes are served at check-clothed tables to contented Italians. Sunday lunch is a joyous affair. This is quite a tribute to La Ginestra as it is not the most easily accessible of places – but not so inaccessible that the local bus can't make it up the hill. Great value. *Minimum stay three nights.*

Price	Triples €125–€165. Half-board €90 p.p.
Rooms	7 doubles/triples.
Meals	Half-board or full-board only. Lunch/dinner €23. Wine €5.
Closed	Never.
Directions	A3 exit Castellammare di Stabia; SS145 coast road to Vico Equense; SS269 to Raffaele Bosco; at Moiano-Ticciano follow road to Santa Maria del Castello.

Antonetta Starace
Via Tessa 2, Santa Maria del Castello, 80060 Moiano di Vico Equense

Tel	+39 0818 023211
Email	info@laginestra.org
Web	www.laginestra.org

Azienda Agricola Le Tore Agriturismo

Vittoria is a vibrant presence and knows almost every inch of this wonderful coastline – its paths, its hill-perched villages, its secret corners. She sells award-winning organic olive oil, vinegar, preserves, nuts and lemons on her terraced five hectares. The cocks crow at dawn, distant dogs bark in the early hours and fireflies glimmer at night in the lemon groves. It's rural, the sort of place where you want to get up while there's still dew on the vegetables. The names of the bedrooms reflect their conversion from old farm buildings – 'Stalla', 'Fienile', 'Balcone' – and are simply but solidly furnished. We are told by those who stay that dinners are abundant and delicious, so do eat in, and get to meet Vittoria and your fellow guests. Breakfast is taken at your own table under the pergola, and may include raspberries, apple tart and fresh fruit juices. You must descend to coast level to buy your postcards, but this is a great spot from which to explore, and to walk – the CAI 'Alta via di Lattari' footpath is nearby. Le Tore is heaven to return to after a day's sightseeing, with views of the sea.

Ethical Collection: Community; Food.
See page 400 for details

Price	€90. Apartment €700–€1,000 per week.
Rooms	6 + 1: 4 doubles, 1 twin, 1 family room for 4. Apartment for 5.
Meals	Dinner €25, by arrangement. Wine €8. Restaurant 5-minute walk.
Closed	November to Palm Sunday. Apartment available all year.
Directions	A3 Naples-Palermo, exit Castellammare di Stabia for Positano. At x-roads for Positano, by restaurant Teresinella, sign for Sant'Agata; 7km, left on Via Pontone; 1km.

Vittoria Brancaccio
Via Pontone 43,
Sant'Agata sui due Golfi,
80064 Massa Lubrense

Tel	+39 0818 080637
Email	info@letore.com
Web	www.letore.com

Villa Oriana Relais

Leave Sorrento's busy piazza below, enter through a pair of electronic gates, and breathe in the scent of jasmine, honeysuckle and lemons. This is a world away (yet just a 15-minute walk) from Sorrento bustle. The sleek white villa – decked with terraces like a cruise ship – enfolds you in coolness and calm. And you are immediately drawn to the living room with its wide terrace and spectacular bay-of-Naples views; the main rooms – uncluttered spaces of white walls, terracotta floors, crisp furnishings – are above the bedrooms to make the most of them. Family warmth fills the place, thanks to Pasquale and his mother Maria – and what a way to start the day, breakfasting on Maria's homemade breads, jams, cakes and fruit juices. Bedrooms are equally cool and airy, furnished with a mixture of antique and modern; linen curtains and Murano chandeliers, a walnut writing table, a lacy bedcover. Marbled bathrooms are luxurious and pristine. Restaurants are an easy walk down, a steep climb up... reward yourself with a swirl in the rooftop jacuzzi-with-views on your return. *Parking available. Scooters available to rent.*

Price	€59–€210.
	Suite & family rooms €90–€315.
Rooms	6: 3 twins/doubles, 1 suite for 2,
	2 family rooms for 3-4.
Meals	Restaurants nearby.
Closed	Never.
Directions	From Naples A3 dir. Salerno; 25km,
	exit Castellammare di Stabia to
	Sorrento; left after Agip petrol station
	into Via San Martino. Villa on right.

	Famiglia d'Esposito
	Via Rubinacci 1,
	80067 Sorrento
Tel	+39 0818 782468
Email	info@villaoriana.it
Web	www.villaoriana.it

Entry 287   Map 13

Casa Albertina

Positano is a honeycomb of houses clinging to the hillside between beach and high coast road – the famous 'Costiera Amalfitana'. Among the colourful façades you cannot miss the deep-red Casa Albertina. Mere minutes from the summer-thronged one-way road system, you climb to get here – or catch the bus to the top and walk down – leaving car and luggage in the able hands of the hotel staff. (There is a charge and you need to pre-book, or phone as you approach.) Here is the one-time refuge of the playwright Pirandello – a historic and unexpectedly peaceful *casa* with heavenly views. Air-conditioned bedrooms are comfortable and hotel-smart, many with terraces. No bar, no pool, but a wonderful roof deck and a stylish restaurant serving regional food, including the local *azzurro* (blue) fish. The wine list is pricey but long. Lorenzo, whose family owns the hotel, combines impeccable manners and relaxed charm with good English and his staff are delightful. A charming spot from which to visit Amalfi, Sorrento, Pompeii or Paestum. Or take the boat to popular Capri.

Price	€120–€240.
Rooms	20 twins/doubles.
Meals	Restaurants nearby.
Closed	Rarely.
Directions	From m'way, exit Castellammare di Stabia for Sorrento & then Positano. Hotel short walk from main street (call staff to pick up car & luggage).

Lorenzo Cinque
Via della Tavolezza 3, 84017 Positano

Tel	+39 0898 75143
Email	info@casalbertina.it
Web	www.casalbertina.it

Residenza Pansa

Gorgeous Amalfi. Like Venice, Pisa and Genova, Amalfi was a maritime republic, and you are in its heart, guarded by the watchtowers that kept an eye on the sea. Up 68 steps from tourist-central Piazza Duomo is a new hotel in an old palazzo – an exciting venture for the Pansa family, owners of the Pasticceria Pansa (est. 1830) on the square below – source of delicious breakfast croissants! Lovely young Eva welcomes all. Her bedrooms, bright, cheerful and airy, are furnished with built-in wardrobes, comfortable beds and every modern thing, from soundproofing to mini bars to bathrooms with showers *and* baths. The best open to a shared balcony, furnished with curly iron tables and chairs, divided by planters. Lovely to have breakfast up here (note, no breakfast room) with a view of the glittering sea; ask for a room with a sea view. The welcome is lovely and the position is amazing; make the most of it. There's a bus stop at the bottom of the steps so exploring the breathtaking coastline could not be easier. Visit exquisite Ravello, then walk the 3,000 steps down to Minori and the sea…

Price	€60–€120.
Rooms	6 doubles.
Meals	Restaurants within walking distance.
Closed	Rarely.
Directions	In centre of Amalfi. From Piazza Duomo, 1st left by Oro d'Amalfi jewellery shop; Piazza dei Dogi; to right of restaurant Da Barracca, flight of steps; up then left again (68 steps in total). Ask about parking.

Roberto Pansa
Via Salita dei Greci 11, 84011 Amalfi
Mobile   +39 3349 846029
Email   info@residenzapansa.it
Web   www.residenzapansa.it

Boccaccio B&B

Between the post office and the hardware store, no ordinary village house. Climb the marble staircase, step into your room and your heart will skip a beat. Just the other side of the road, one thousand feet below, is the dizzying curve of the Bay of Salerno. Vineyards, lemon groves, white houses, all cling to the steep valley sides in apparent defiance of gravity; almost impossible to pull yourself away from the view! And all four rooms have it. This is a family affair; grandmother had these rooms and the family still live on the upper floor. Bonaventura and his family have refurbished the house in an understated modern style that has a welcoming simplicity: beech wood furniture, crisp bed linen, sleek lighting and sunny, hand-painted Vietri floor tiles. Bathrooms are spotless, with walk-in showers. Two minutes from Ravello's picture-perfect piazza (tourist-busy in season), and the Rufolo and Cimbrone gardens, Boccaccio's position is enviable. Your host worked 35 years in the film industry, and he and his family are warm, charming and very thoughtful. *Discounted parking: book ahead.*

Price	€75-€95.
Rooms	4 twins/doubles.
Meals	Restaurants 100m.
Closed	Rarely.
Directions	2-min walk from central pedestrian square of Ravello.

Bonaventura Fraulo
G. Boccaccio 19,
84010 Ravello
Tel   +39 0898 57194
Email   infoboccaccio@hotmail.com
Web   www.boccaccioravello.com

Villa en Rose

You really get a feel here of what life must have been like before roads and motorised transport came to these steep hillsides; this is a place for walkers. The position is stunning, halfway between Minori and Ravello on a marked footpath which was once a mule trail. In fact, the only way to get here is on foot, with about 15 minutes' worth of steps down from the closest road. (Lugging your provisions up here could be a challenge in bad weather!). The open-plan apartment is modern-functional not aesthetic and the bedroom is in an alcove off the sitting room, but the views are wonderful and the house is set amid lemon groves. You are miles from the crowds clustering around the coast, and the pool means you don't have to venture down to the beach. The second, much smaller apartment is on the owner's floor above, and has no seating space as such. If you don't feel like cooking, the walk up to the main square in ravishing Ravello would certainly earn you a cappuccino and a brioche. And don't miss the glorious gardens of the Villas Rufolo and Cimbrone. *Minimum stay three nights. Air conditioning extra charge.*

Price	From €104.
Rooms	2 apartments: 1 for 2-4 (+ sofabed), 1 for 2-3.
Meals	Breakfast €6. Restaurants in Ravello, 1km.
Closed	Rarely.
Directions	Details on booking. Valeria will meet you in Ravello.

Valeria Civale
Via Torretta a Marmorata 22,
84010 Ravello
Tel +39 0898 57661
Email valeriacivale@yahoo.it
Web www.villaenrose.com

Hotel Villa San Michele

Stone steps tumble down – past lemon trees, palms, bougainvillea, scented jasmine – to the rocks below, and a dip in the deep blue sea. It is a treat to stay in this small, intimate, family-run hotel, with its smiley staff and dreamy views. It may be situated at the junction of the coast road and the road to Ravello but its terraced gardens and bedrooms are truly peaceful. Dining room and reception are at the top – light, airy, cool. Almost everyone gets a balcony or terrace, and at night you are lulled to sleep by the lapping of the sea. Floors are cool and pale-tiled, some in classic Amalfi style, some white; beds have patterned bedspreads, shower rooms are clean. It is all charming and unpretentious, from the white plastic tables to the blue stripy deckchairs from which you can gaze on the sea and watch the ferries slip by, heading for Positano or Capri. Delectable aromas waft from a cheerful kitchen where Signora is chef; the menu is short and just right. Atrani and Amalfi are walkable, though traffic is heavy in summer; for the weary, a bus stops in front of the hotel. *Use of pool at Villa Scapariello.*

Price	€100-€190.
Rooms	12 doubles.
Meals	Dinner €28. Wine from €15. June-Sept half-board only.
Closed	7 January-14 February; 7 November-25 December.
Directions	A3 to Salerno exit Vietri sul Mare; follow signs to Amalfi; hotel 1km before Amalfi on left. Discuss parking on booking.

Nicola Dipino
SS 163 Costiera Amalfitana,
84010 Castiglione di Ravello

Tel	+39 0898 72237
Email	smichele@starnet.it
Web	www.hotel-villasanmichele.it

La Mola

You'll catch your breath at the views as you step onto your balcony. La Mola is perched high up in the old town, way above the tourists who congregate down the hill in Santa Maria. It is a grand old 17th-century palace and incorporates a 12th-century tower — an interesting building in its own right. The balconies are superb and wrap around the house; the terraced garden is lovely; the restaurant a joy. The huge round stone olive press found in the cellars during restoration gives the B&B its name; now it forms the base of a vast glass-topped drinks table. The sea is everywhere — your room looks onto it, as does the communal sitting room, and the terrace where you take summer meals. Furnishings are pristine, bedrooms have tiled floors, wrought-iron bedsteads with embroidered linen and the odd antique, bathrooms are charming. La Mola is the ancestral home of Signor Favilla, who spends every summer here with his wife, running the B&B with admirable and amiable efficiency. Away from the seafront resorts the countryside up here is lovely, and Paestum, Agropoli and Velia are a short drive away.

Price	€114-€124. Singles €80.
Rooms	5 doubles.
Meals	Dinner with wine, €40. Restaurant 50m.
Closed	November-March.
Directions	From Naples A30 south to Battipaglia, then Agropoli-Castellabate. La Mola is in 'centro storico'.

Francesco & Loredana Favilla
Via Adolfo Cilento 2,
84048 Castellabate
Tel   +39 0974 967053
Email   info@maisonlamola.com
Web   www.maisonlamola.com

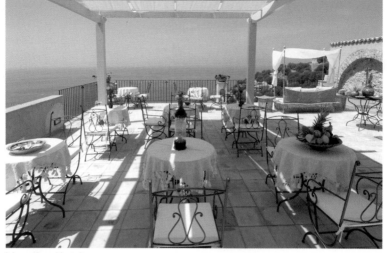

Marulivo Hotel

Cool – in both senses of the word. Metre-thick walls give the whole place that delicious damp-ancient smell, a constant reminder that you are staying in a 14th-century monastery. Architect Lea, and Massimo, lovely people, have revived the ruin after 100 years of abandonment. Open to the elements, its topsy-turvy layout is intriguing, the kind of place that cries out to be explored the moment you duck under the archway. Gorgeous bedrooms have exposed brickwork, terracotta floors, balconies and super beds with curly-whirly headboards – and heaps of individual touches: dividing the bedrooms of one suite is the 'window' of a confessional unearthed during the restoration. The terrace and the blue views will leave you giddy; sink into the cushioned wicker sofa and toast the beauty with a lovely glass of the local greco. This is a place that won't play on your eco conscience either; they've won awards for their green efforts. Potter around exquisite medieval Pisciotta, scramble down through the olive groves to the harbour, visit the famous grottos. New to us, but a favourite already. *Min. stay two nights in cottages.*

Price	€80-€130. Suites €130-€200. Cottages & house €400-€1,725 per week.
Rooms	11 + 4: 9 doubles, 2 suites. 3 cottages for 2-6, 1 house for 5.
Meals	Breakfast €7 for self-caterers. Restaurant 40m.
Closed	November-February.
Directions	From Naples A3 Salerno-Reggio Calabria exit Battipaglia; SS dir. Agropoli-Sapri exit Poderia; follow signs to Palinuro, then Pisciotta; in Pisciotta off Piazza Pinto.

Lea Pinto
Via Castello,
84066 Pisciotta

Tel	+39 0974 973792
Email	info@marulivohotel.it
Web	www.marulivohotel.it

Calabria • Basilicata • Puglia

Photo: istock.com

La Bouganville

You could spend weeks here, there's so much to do – snorkelling, sailing, swimming in caves. And to see: the town of Praia, the grottos of Dino Island, the Tower of Fiuzzi, waterparks and beaches. Softly-spoken Giovanni will meet you and settle you in; he and his son live in Herculaneum (see La Murena, entry 283) and in August this is their holiday home. On its peaceful residential street you can barely see the house for the flowers and the trees; the garden was established 25 years ago when the house was built. The garden, enclosed and perfect for little ones, is full of scents and shade; a gardener comes several mornings a week and from the terrace is a fantastic view of tiny Dino Island. Inside, rooms are simple and comfortable: cheerful bedcovers on plain wooden beds, a gleaming white bathroom and a shower, a well-equipped kitchen and a brightly tiled sitting/dining room with a sofabed, a pine table and chairs and a hearth for winter. You can walk to the resort of Praia a Mare and the beaches are special, with crystal clear water and fine sands. Excellent for families. *Minimum stay one week. Cycle track nearby.*

Price	€450–€600 for 2; €750–€850 for 4. Prices per week.
Rooms	1 apartment for 2-5.
Meals	Restaurants nearby.
Closed	August.
Directions	Autostrada Napoli-Salerno exit Lagonegro Nord; continue for Praia a Mare. Ask owner for detailed directions.

Giovanni Scognamiglio
Parco Bouganville,
87028 Praia a Mare
Tel   +39 0817 779819
Email   lamurena@lamurena.it

Entry 295   Map 15

Il Giardino di Iti Agriturismo

The farm, peaceful, remote and five minutes from the Ionian sea, has been in the family for three centuries. A massive arched doorway leads to a courtyard and vast enclosed garden (rabbits for the children, pigs, goats and cats too). Meals are served here in summer; at night, the lemon and orange trees glow from little lights tucked into their branches. The large, cool bedrooms have been simply and prettily decorated. Ask for one that opens directly off the courtyard, its big old fireplace (lit in winter) and brick-paved floors intact. Each room has a wall painting of one of the farm's crops, and is correspondingly named: 'Lemon', 'Peach', 'Sunflower', 'Grape'. The bathrooms are old-fashioned but charming, the apartment kitchens basic. Courses are held here on regional cooking, weaving, too. If neither appeals, revel in the atmosphere and the gastronomic delights of the restaurant and atone for the calories later. There's a host of activities on offer in the area, and, of course, heaps of history. Signora is gentle and charming. You'll be sad to leave.

Price	Half-board €40–€55 p.p. Full-board €50–65 p.p.
Rooms	12 + 2: 10 family rooms; 2 doubles sharing bath. 2 apartments for 3-4.
Meals	Half-board or full-board only. Wine from €18. Limited self-catering in apts.
Closed	Never.
Directions	A3 Salerno-Reggio Calabria exit Sibari. Rossano road (SS106) to contrada Amica, then towards Paludi.

Francesca Cherubini
Contrada Amica,
87068 Rossano
Tel   +39 0983 64508
Email   info@giardinoiti.it
Web   www.giardinoiti.it

San Teodoro Nuovo Agriturismo

A haven in a green sea of citrus and olive groves. Bougainvillea disguises the lower half of the delightful Marchesa's old rose-tinted mansion; shutters peep from above. Rent an apartment furnished with family antiques in a wing of the house, or choose one of four beautifully converted ones a short stroll away – in the old stables where the restaurant is housed. All rooms are large and light, some with marvellous vaulted ceilings, and elegantly and charmingly furnished; they even have small parterre gardens. A whitewashed chapel alongside adds a Mexican feel, and there's a fine pool. You will appreciate the range of Basilicata cuisine here; breakfasts and dinners – candlelit, atmospheric – are excellent, the vegetarian choices are superb and you'll probably want to book into a cookery class after sampling the food. Follow the routes taken by 18th-century travellers, visit workshops devoted to reproducing classical antiques. You are five minutes from the Ionian Sea and white sands, golf courses are nearby, archaeological sites abound. *Minimum stay two nights. Ask about cookery courses.*

Price	€120–€140 (€840–€980 per week). Half-board €80–€90 p.p.
Rooms	9 apartments for 2, 4 or 6.
Meals	Dinner with wine, €25–€30, by arrangement.
Closed	Never.
Directions	Directions on booking.

Maria Xenia d'Oria
Loc. Marconia, 75015 Pisticci

Tel	+39 0835 470042
Email	doria@santeodoronuovo.com
Web	www.santeodoronuovo.com

Foresteria Illicini

Come for the views of the tiny islands of Matrela and Santojanni, the caves and rocky coves, the water lapping at the beach. This bewitching location could be a setting for *The Tempest*. Guglielmo's father bought the whole spectacular promontory and surrounding park of olive trees, holm oaks and myrtles 50 years ago; they spent every family holiday here. Now Guglielmo, a gentle architect, and his wife Diane have turned it into a deliciously unmanicured resort. Foreigners have barely discovered the area, so, outside the Italian holiday months, the five-acre park, the two small beaches and the large pool are beautifully peaceful, though the bar and the restaurant close. Plastic chairs abound, but the setting is the thing! The small room for buffet breakfast also overlooks the sea, The bedrooms are housed in little cottages just a few yards back from the shoreline, each with a deckchair'd terrace and a view of the sea. Each is neatly and simply furnished, with tiled floors, comfortable beds and a spotless bathroom. The sunsets are exceptional. Good value, great for families.

Price	€70–€190. Half-board €190 (August only).
Rooms	11: 8 doubles, 1 single, 2 family rooms for 3-4.
Meals	Lunch €15–€30 (July-August only). Dinner €30 (August only). Wine from €10.
Closed	Mid-October to mid-May.
Directions	From A3, exit Lagonegro nord. SS 585, exit Maratea sud. SS 18 to Maratea, left at km 236.7.

Guglielmo & Diane Rivetti
Loc. Illicini, 85046 Maratea

Tel	+39 0973 879028
Email	staff@illicini.it
Web	www.illicini.it

Villa Cheta Elite

Villa Cheta Elite is a godsend in an area with few really nice hotels. It's a gracious Art Nouveau villa a twisty drive up from the coast road, with a terraced garden of winding paths, tropical trees, scented plants and views that keep you rooted to the spot. Relax in the shade of the gardens, or cross the road and plunge down 165 steps for a swim in the clear green waters below. (Then trek up again!). Bedrooms are classic Italian: antiques and fine fabrics, marble floors, large windows and plenty of light, the loveliest with a view of the sea. The public rooms, with ornate cornices and mouldings, are exquisitely furnished with good paintings and a number of portraits of previous occupants. There's also a small sitting room, and a library where you can bone up on the history of the region. The restaurant is fabulous: delicious food served beneath Murano glass chandeliers on embroidered linen. In summer you dine on the terrace with views of the sea and the moon. It's an undeniably romantic spot; you may hear nightingales sing. Stefania and Piero are delightful hosts, their staff courteous and kind.

Price	€140–€280. Half-board €196–€364 for 2.
Rooms	20 doubles.
Meals	Lunch/dinner €35–€45. Wine €18.
Closed	November–Palm Sunday.
Directions	From A3 exit Lagonegro-Maratea; 10km, SS104 right to Sapri. In Sapri left onto coast road for Maratea. Villa 9km along coast, above road on left.

Stefania Aquadro
Via Nazionale, 85041
Acquafredda di Maratea
Tel   +39 0973 878134
Email info@villacheta.it
Web   www.villacheta.it

La Chiusa delle More

The Italians flock here in August. Out of season, the lovely beaches and fresh-fish restaurants are wonderfully uncrowded; on the seafront, you can watch the fishermen sort their catch. Foreign tourists have not yet discovered Peschici, so come out of season. Francesco and Antonella's 16th-century farmhouse is 500 metres from the sea: park under an ancient olive tree and climb up to the reception terrace from where you can drink in the views. Nearby, on another terrace, teak loungers flank a sparkling pool, and the air is scented with citrus. The B&B rooms, in a small block to one side, are light, cool and simply furnished, with small but good shower rooms. Francesco and Antonella, a delightful pair, vibrant and full of fun, have five hectares of olive groves and a big kitchen garden. The olive oil and vegetables supply their restaurant and the food is divine – hard not to love the typically Puglian dishes and the local wines. Breakfast on the terrace is a treat too, a wonderful start to a day discovering the splendours of the Gargano National Park.

Price	€160–€200.
Rooms	10: 8 doubles, 2 family rooms for 4.
Meals	Dinner €30. Wine €5–€50.
Closed	October–April.
Directions	1.5km from Peschici; signed from Peschici.

Francesco & Antonella Martucci
Loc. Padula, 71010 Peschici

Tel	+39 3470577272
Email	lachiusadellemore@libero.it
Web	www.lachiusadellemore.it

Cefalicchio Country House

In 1901 the Rossi brothers built a present for their mother: a grandiose country house, an extension of their almond farm. Their descendants developed this into a successful biodynamic winery; now it is also a beautiful place to stay. The architecture is unusual for this area; rather than simple and rustic it is romantic and grand, with a zigzagging external staircase. The first floor houses two spectacular suites, with museum-worthy antiques and floor-to-ceiling windows; the gloriously tiled original kitchen is used for cooking lessons. The second floor contains 'loft' guest rooms, simpler but just as elegant, pale-walled and furnished with polished wood. There are also two characterful apartments, one on the ground floor with tall arched ceilings, the other, ideal for families, next to the tree-framed pool. Wine lovers will adore it, but there's plenty for everyone, with the rambling grounds, the remote setting, the impressive restaurant and the rustic-chic spa: indulge in wine-based therapies — not drinking, but bathing. Lovely young Katrin and Livio look after you well.
Ask about gourmet weekends.

Ethical Collection: Environment; Food.
See page 400 for details

Price	€130. Suites €170. Apartments €150.
Rooms	11: 7 doubles, 2 suites, 2 apartments for 2-4.
Meals	Lunch/dinner €30.
Closed	January-February.
Directions	Milan-Taranto (A14) or Naples-Bari (A16) to Canosa di Puglia exit; thro' Canosa to state road 98 (now regional road 6), then provincial road 143; follow signs for Cefalicchio (3km).

Famiglia Rossi
Contrada Cefalicchio, SP143,
70053 Canosa di Puglia

Tel	+39 0883 642123
Email	info@cefalicchio.it
Web	www.countryhouse.cefalicchio.com

Lama di Luna - Biomasseria Agriturismo

The sister of Pietro's great-grandmother lived here until 1820; Pietro bought the farm in 1990, then discovered the family connection. It was "meant to be". Lama di Luna is the most integrated organic farm in Italy: 200 hectares of olives and wines, 40 solar panels for heat and hot water, beds facing north, feng shui-style. Pietro, who lives here with his family, is young, lively, charming, passionate about the environment and this supremely serene place. The farm goes back 300 years and wraps its dazzling white self around a vast courtyard with a central bread oven, its 40 chimney pots "telling the story" of the many farm workers that once lived here. Each bedroom, complete with fireplace and small window, once housed an entire family. Pietro searched high and low for the beds, the natural latex mattresses, the reclaimed wood for the doors. There's a library for reading and a veranda for sunsets and stars, and views that reach over flat farmland as far as the eye can see. Breakfast here on homemade cakes and jams, orchard fruits, local cheeses. Remote, relaxing, memorable. *New pool.*

Price	€140–€160. Suites €230–€300. Extra bed €40.
Rooms	11: 9 twins/doubles, 2 suites for 3-4.
Meals	Dinner with wine, €25. Restaurants 3km.
Closed	Never.
Directions	A14 exit Canosa di Puglia; right for Monervino Murge, Canosa-Andria, turn off for Montegrosso. After Montegrosso, 3.5km dir. Minervino; on left.

Pietro Petroni
Loc. Montegrosso,
70031 Andria
Tel +39 0883 569505
Email info@lamadiluna.com
Web www.lamadiluna.com

Ethical Collection: Environment; Food.
See page 400 for details

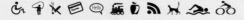

Entry 302 Map 14, 15

Masseria Serra dell'Isola

Spirits may fall as you lose your way down tiny lanes in a featureless landscape… no matter. Rita's smile as she scoops you up to guide you home brings instant cheer. Step over the threshold of the somewhat gaunt white *masseria* and you'll feel even better. The great hall with its uneven stone floor was once part of an olive mill (see where the presses used to stand) and, like the rest of the house, is filled with portraits and antiques with stories to tell. The light, gracious bedrooms are named after the women who once occupied them – Donnas Angelina, Ritella, Annina – and the elegant old beds bear new mattresses. The house has been in the family since 1726 and Rita is passionately proud of her heritage. You're welcome to browse through her impressive library of history books; she'll also gladly tell you about less well-known local places to visit. She organises courses, too, in art, antiques, restoration, cookery; dine by candlelight and you'll sample ancient family recipes and liqueurs from the time the Bourbons reigned in southern Italy. Unusual and authentic. *Minimum stay two nights.*

Price	€130.
	Whole house €3,300-€3,900 per week.
Rooms	6: 4 doubles, 2 twins/doubles.
Meals	Dinner, 3 courses, €35-€40.
	Wine €12-€18.
Closed	Rarely.
Directions	SS16 Bari-Brindisi exit Mola-Rutigliano, dir. Mola. When you reach bridge call Rita to come & guide you.

Rita Guastamacchia
S.P 165 Mola, Conversano n.35,
70042 Mola di Bari

Mobile	+39 349 5311256
Email	info@masseriaserradellisola.it
Web	www.masseriaserradellisola.it

Masseria Due Torri

At this graceful masseria expect immaculate rooms and heart-warming service from Elizabeth and Douglas. Their big country house has two bedrooms and a self-catering apartment on the ground floor; they live upstairs. The B&B rooms are inviting with chintz curtains, wrought-iron chairs and pretty eiderdowns on comfy mattresses, while the apartment has a charming sitting room with a high arched ceiling and original beams, three sofas, a pristine kitchen. There's a further kitchen on the ground floor, where a sumptuous breakfast is served in warm weather you eat at a canopied table outside, surrounded by lush and lovely gardens. There are six hectares here of olives (they produce their own oil), figs, prickly pears, garden flowers, wild flowers – green fingers are at work. The pool is nearby, with sunbeds, hammock and a bamboo-shaded picnic area alongside. In the grounds too is a new-build self-catering villa with its own access road and an arty modern décor. Books, magazines, outdoor games, indoor games, DVDs, a taxi service to and from local restaurants… it's all here.

Price	€80-110. Apt €540-€900. Villa €940-€2,100.
Rooms	2 + 2: 1 double, 1 twin/double. Extra bed/cot available. Apartment for 4-5. Villa for 8.
Meals	Breakfast €10 for self-caterers. Wine from €10. Restaurants 1km.
Closed	Rarely.
Directions	From Monopoli SP114 dir. Conversano; right after 3km at refuse bin. Masseria 200m on right.

Elizabeth & Douglas Manuel
Contrada Due Torri 187,
70043 Monopoli

Tel	+39 0802 146007
Email	info@masseria2torri.com
Web	www.masseria2torri.com

Masseria Alchimia

The masseria, a whitewashed, history-steeped, 350-year-old building – once with a watchtower – lies at the end of a cypress-lined drive and, at first glance, looks a little stark: a hint of the contemporary aesthetic to come. Not far from the main road, yet peaceful, eco-friendly and surrounded by seven acres of olive and fruit trees with sitting areas dotted around – some with a sea view – there's a sense of stillness. True design mag material: the building is unadorned, with clean, square lines despite its age, and part of it (the Romantic studio suite, ask for it) is new but blends seamlessly. Bright, well-lit studios and suites filled with designer classics – Panton chairs, Man Ray mirrors, lots of Eames, Starck, etc – are, like Swiss owner Caroline, cool, chic and urbane. There are concrete floors and perfect kitchenettes; imagine whites, greys, black-and-white photos and flashes of colour, say a purple or yellow chair, all beautifully timed. Each room has a sun terrace and there are private beaches guests can make use of on request. A sophisticated break from the rustic Pugliese norm. *Minimum stay three nights; seven in August.*

Price	€75-€235.
Rooms	8 studios/family suites for 2-4.
Meals	Restaurants 1km.
Closed	Never.
Directions	Bari-Brindisi SS16; from south exit Taranto; follow signs for Masseria Alchimia 1km dir. Adriatic coast.

Caroline Groszer
Contrada Fascianello,
72015 Fasano

Mobile	+39 335 6094647
Email	info@masseria-alchimia.it
Web	www.masseria-alchimia.it

B&B Masseria Piccola

Who could fail to be enchanted by the round walls, the conical roofs, the charming little rooms? These *trulli* were built a century ago by Nicola's great-grandfather; now they have been converted into one delightful, good value, B&B. You are on a quiet side street in Casalini di Cisternino, with a terrace in front of you and a patch of garden behind. A wicker sofa and chairs in the entrance hall invite you in. Snug, spotless bedrooms have pale walls and stone arches and are furnished with country antiques; beds are very comfortable, shower rooms are well-equipped and breakfast is at the big table in the kitchen or out under the flowers on the terrace. Nicola, shy, young, charming, looks after his guests well and you have a half-board option of a fixed-price dinner at a restaurant a ten-minute walk away... La Terrazza del Quadrifoglio has a great terrace, an authentic atmosphere and is popular with the locals (most of them Nicola's relatives!). The town is nothing special but Cisternino, with its lively weekly market, is well worth the visit.

Price	€80. Half-board €20 extra p.p.	
Rooms	4: 3 doubles, 1 single.	
Meals	Wine from €8. Restaurant 1km.	
Closed	Rarely.	
Directions	A14 Bari-Lecce exit Cisternino-Ostuni, then SP7 & SP9.	

Ethical Collection: Food.
See page 400 for details

Nicola Fanelli
Via Masseria Piccola 56,
72014 Casalini di Cisternino
Tel   +39 0804 449668
Email   info@masseriapiccola.it
Web   www.masseriapiccola.it

Masseria Impisi

Hidden but not hard to find, close to lovely hilltop Ostuni, is a 15th-century masseria and two inspirational new builds. Artistic, friendly David and Leonie have lived in Italy for 20 years and in Puglia for five; his sculptures dot the grounds, her mosaics shine like jewels. There's art in the bedrooms too; simple, tranquil spaces with cool Trani stone underfoot, they are havens on a hot day. The apartment is in the old gatehouse, its door washed in blue, its kitchen/dining area serene. All the bedrooms are quietly stylish, their walls white plaster or creamy stone, their bed frames made by David. None are huge but they open onto a colonnaded area, creating a feeling of space. Wet rooms have tiles that echo the Trani stone; towels are white and pristine. Wake to hot rolls and homemade jams, local cheeses and fruits from the garden, served above an olive mill that dates to the 10th century. The semi-wild grounds are filled with Pampas grass, cacti, olive trees, shady corners and a gorgeous natural pool; ancient cisterns still harvest rainwater. Bikes to borrow, boules to play, a beach a mile away… heaven in Puglia. *Minimum stay two nights in B&B.*

Price	€75-€95.
	Gate house €425-€770 per week.
Rooms	4 + 1: 1 double, 3 twins/doubles.
	Gate house for 2.
Meals	Restaurants 2.5km.
Closed	November-February.
Directions	Exit Gorgognolo on SS379 (E55). Take road parallel to SS, dir. Brindisi. 500m right at traffic island; left-hand narrow road 3km. Signed on left just before railway bridge. Detailed directions on booking.

Leonie Whitton & David Westby
Il Collegio, Contrada Impisi,
72017 Ostuni

Mobile	+39 340 360 2352
Email	info@ilcollegio.com
Web	www.ilcollegio.com

Villa Cervarolo

This trulli house, marooned in rolling countryside dotted by fruit and olive trees, is a beautiful Puglian blend of ancient vernacular and minimalist modern. A surprising find at the end of an unpaved track, this is a designer dream: exquisitely chic, sublimely inviting. The living spaces are open plan. Via the unobtrusively swish kitchen (modish appliances, Smeg fridge) you enter the sitting room, with DVDs (no TV: no signal!) and built-in sofa. Beyond, a study with a dusky pink chaise-longue. Bedrooms are a serene marriage of gleaming linen, sheepskin rugs, pale velvet cushions, cool polished cement. Bathrooms ooze style, one with a tub with views: gaze on the garden as you soak. A beach-style pool (unheated) is an invitation to laze, with its outdoor 'room' alongside: relax on the traditional living boat, recline on Moroccan kilims, cook up a storm in the outdoor kitchen, dine at table hewn out of rock. If you don't feel like cooking you can always employ a chef, and other treats can be arranged, from yoga to massage. Make sure you find time to explore the lovely wine villages of Valle d'Itria. *Min. one week.*

Price	£2,000–£3,250 per week.
Rooms	House for 6 (2 doubles, 1 twin/double).
Meals	Welcome pack with wine. Restaurants 7km.
Closed	Rarely.
Directions	Directions on booking.

Ostuni

Email	info@homeinpuglia.com
Web	www.homeinpuglia.com

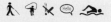

Masseria Il Frantoio Agriturismo

So many ravishing things! An old, white house clear-cut against a blue sky, mysterious gardens, the scent of jasmine — and private beaches five kilometres away. Armando and Rosalba spent a year restoring this 17th-century house (built over a sixth-century oil press) after abandoning city life. Inside — sheer delight. A series of beautiful rooms, ranging from fairytale (a froth of lace and toile) to endearingly simple (madras bedcovers and old desks) to formal (antique armoires and doughty gilt frames)… a gloriously eclectic mix. Dinner is equally marvellous — put your name down. Rosalba specialises in Puglian dishes accompanied by good local wines; Armando rings the courtyard bell at 8.30 and the feast begins, either in the arched dining room or outside in the candlelit courtyard. It will stay long in your memory — as will other details: an exterior white stone stairway climbing to a bedroom, an arched doorway swathed in wisteria. Armando is deeply passionate about his totally organic *masseria*, surrounded by olive groves and with a view of the sea; Silvana is on hand ensuring you bask in comfort. *Minimum stay two nights.*

Ethical Collection: Community; Food.
See page 400 for details

Price	€176–€220; children €54–€65. Apartment €319–€350.
Rooms	8 + 1: 3 doubles, 2 triples, 3 family rooms. Apartment for 2-4.
Meals	Dinner with wine, €55, by arrangement. Cold supper €31. Restaurant 5km.
Closed	Never.
Directions	Bari airport, E55 exit Pezze di Greco dir. Ostuni. On SS16, watch out for Ostuni km874 sign. Right into drive.

Silvana Caramia
SS 16km 874, 72017 Ostuni

Tel	+39 0831 330276
Email	prenota@masseriailfrantoio.it
Web	www.masseriailfrantoio.it

Vivificante

Vivacious Jane Shaw is a potter, textile designer and former teacher, who gives tailormade courses in her workshop. She has carried out extensive works on her house, at the heart of which is a delightful little trullo… it's a lovely vibrant place in which to live and work. There are just two rooms in the guest wing (let to one party) with a private bathroom between. The bedrooms are charming – terracotta floors, a Deco bed from Naples, her daughter's artwork, garden views – and have a happy, homely feel. Guests are also free to relax in Jane's large sitting room with its sofas and wood-burner. You breakfast – lavishly – in the wonderfully lofty kitchen, with three skylights and a wall of wood-framed glass. This overlooks the garden, a work in progress… so far Jane has planted oranges and lemons alongside 40 established olive trees, a goat-shaped piece of driftwood and a small hexagonal plunge pool for bobbing about. There's also an outdoor eating area, all mismatched wooden furniture and lanterns – lovely. *Minimum stay two nights. Ask about pottery workshops.*

Price	€70-€90.
Rooms	2: 1 double, 1 twin/double, sharing bathroom.
Meals	Dinner €15. Restaurants 4km.
Closed	Never.
Directions	From Ceglie Messapica SP23 'Fedele Grande'. After 4km right at x-roads; 1st house on left.

Ethical Collection: Environment; Community. See page 400 for details

Jane Shaw
1 Tratturo delle Vache,
Contrada Circiello,
72013 Ceglie Messapica
Tel +39 0831 380987
Email vivificante@rocketmail.com
Web www.vivificante.com

Trullo Solari

At the end of a bumpy unpaved lane, three conical trulli framed by pine, olive and fruit trees: a delightful sight. Inside is just as good, open plan with a dining area and a compact, fully-equipped kitchen. But it's the sitting room that dazzles, with its eight-metre wall of glass overlooking the pool. Fold the doors back in summer and merge your living space with the beautiful outside. This is a fabulously renovated house and you can really spread out. You get four big whitewashed bedrooms, simply furnished and served by sleek bathrooms. There's a terrace attached to the master bedroom, a rooftop sundeck, and an outdoors dining area with a barbecue and a pizza oven. There are a couple of other trulli in sight, but that doesn't stop you feeling private and remote. The lovely laid-back owners live nearby, leave you a luxurious welcome pack and lend you a pre-programmed Tom Tom so you don't get lost finding their recommended places! They're keen greenies — solar-fired underfloor heating, ecological products — and will help you plant a tree of your choice to reduce your carbon footprint. We loved it all.

Price	£1,200-£3,500 per week.
Rooms	House for 8 (2 doubles, 2 twins/doubles).
Meals	Restaurant 500m.
Closed	Never.
Directions	2km from Ceglie Messapica. Directions on booking.

Ethical Collection: Environment.
See page 400 for details

Cathy & Keith Upton
Contrada Petrelli,
72013 Ceglie Messapica
Tel   +39 0831 342153
Email   cathyupton@hotmail.it
Web   www.trullosolari.com

Palazzo Bacile di Castiglione

The palazzo's 16th-century walls dominate Spongano's Piazza Bacile; behind is a secret oasis. The charming *barone* and his English wife offer you a choice of apartments for couples or families, and B&B for groups; the history is interesting, the comforts seductive. On the first floor, a series of large terraces and four bedrooms open off a vaulted baronial hall – beige check sofas, an open fire (replete with home-grown cones and logs), a grand piano. Expect choice fabrics and new four-posters, pink, yellow or marble bathrooms, wardrobes dwarfed by lofty ceilings, kitchens for cooks. The outbuildings at the end of the long garden are similarly swish: olive wood tables, big lamps, framed engravings, books and CDs; kitchens reveal the owners' passion. (They are also keen greens, saving energy, going solar and composting madly.) The garden is lovely, all orange trees and wisteria, secluded walkways and corners, old pillars and impressive pool; at twilight, scops owls chime like bells. Beyond lie the baroque splendours of Lecce, Gallipoli and Otranto – and the coast. Borrow the bikes! *Minimum stay four nights.*

Price	€900–€2,770 per week.
Rooms	7 apartments: 2 for 2, 3 for 4, 1 for 6, 1 for 8.
Meals	Restaurant 500m.
Closed	Never.
Directions	SS16 dir. Maglie/S M di Leuca; pass Maglie, then SS275 to Leuca until signs for Spongano on left.

Sarah & Alessandro Bacile di Castiglione
73038 Spongano

Tel	+39 0832 351131
Email	albadica@hotmail.com
Web	www.palazzobacile.it

Ethical Collection: Environment.
See page 400 for details

La Macchiola

The palazzo's courtyard walls drip with creepers and geraniums; in front, across a little road, is a verdant citrus grove worth resting in. This *azienda agricola*, dating from the 17th century, is devoted to the production of organic olive oil (massages available) and Anna's family turn out some of Puglia's finest. Through the massive gates the narrow and unremarkable streets of Spongano village are left behind and you enter, via a Moorish arched portico, a white-gravelled, white-walled courtyard dotted with elegant wrought-iron tables and chairs. Off the creeper-clad inner courtyard, ground-floor apartments have been carefully converted into a series of airy and beautifully furnished rooms. Walls are colourwashed warm yellow and soft blue, sleeping areas are separated by fabric screens, ceilings are lofty and stone vaulted. One apartment for two has a 'dining room' squeezed into an ancient fireplace, bathrooms have pretty mosaic mirrors and most of the kitchenettes are tiny. *Marmellata* and cakes for breakfast, a vast roof terrace, beaches a short drive. *Minimum stay three nights.*

Price	€80–€100.
	Apartments €570–€1,500 per week.
Rooms	4 + 3: 2 doubles, 2 family rooms for 4.
	3 apartments for 2, 4 or 6.
Meals	Breakfast €6 for self-caterers.
	Restaurants 300m.
Closed	9 January–16 March;
	5 November–22 December
Directions	Directions on booking.

Anna Addario-Chieco
Via Congregazione 53/57,
73038 Spongano

Tel	+39 0836 945023
Email	lamacchiola@libero.it
Web	www.lamacchiola.it

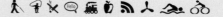

Masseria Varano

Wines and olive oils from the estate, local breads, pasta and cheeses — the generous welcome sets the tone for your stay. Victoria and Giuseppe, an Anglo-Italian couple, combine the best of English and Italian hospitality — gentle, warm, easy — reflected in their handsome creamy stone and green-shuttered *masseria*. The apartments, each with private entrance and terrace, are in the main house and two cottages. Elegant and airy, with creamy tiled floors, white walls and handsome chestnut fittings, rooms are decorated with modern furniture and old family pieces. Dotted with family photographs, Victoria's paintings, pretty fabrics and objects collected from travels, there's a gentle country-house feel, a home from home; the best wows you with a fleet of French windows and a vast terrace. Kitchens are light and modern, equipped to please the serious cook. Masses to do: beaches, Gallipoli, the harbours of Tricase and Santa Maria di Leuca… or just make the most of the pretty walled gardens and the pool. The owners are happy to leave you alone or have a chat over a glass of wine.

Price	€400–€1,400 per week.
Rooms	4 apartments: 1 for 2, 3 for 2-4.
Meals	Restaurant 4km.
Closed	November-Easter.
Directions	M'way Brindisi-Lecce, take Tangenziale (ring road) west of Lecce, exit 13 dir. Gallipoli; exit Taurisano. After 3km, before slow down sign overhead, left onto Via Trappeto di Varano. Left at x-roads; follow road to estate with high walls, 2nd set of double gates with intercom.

	Giuseppe & Victoria **Lopez y Royo di Taurisano** Contrada Varano, 73056 Taurisano
Tel	+39 0833 623216
Email	lopezyroyo@hotmail.com
Web	www.masseriainsalento.com

Entry 314   Map 16

Sicily • Sardinia

Photo: istock.com

Hotel Quartara

You arrive by boat; waves glitter in the sun, white houses dazzle on the shore. The exterior of this beautiful hotel may be typically Aeolian but bedrooms are eclectic: Melanesian, Chinese and Indonesian hand-crafted furniture, Sicilian crocheted bedspreads and tiled floors. Four overlook the sea. Bathrooms have soft lighting and a generous supply of lotions and potions, and every room has a terrace. The solarium is a family-popular retreat, thanks to wide terraces equipped with teak loungers, cool shade, endless sea views and pool. Out of season will be quieter – though too quiet for some. Breakfast on figs, pears, honey, prosciutto, yogurt; dine on risotto with prawns and saffron. The restaurant has arched ceilings, crisp white linen decorated with special seashells, art on the walls. This is a laid-back family affair: Signor Cappelli's garden supplies fragrant basil, lemons and glossy aubergines, attentive Maria and her sisters are usually around and the children stop by to say hello. The lovely isle of Panarea, a refuge for the rich and famous, has three villages and golf carts for cars.

Price	€180-€450.
Rooms	13: 10 doubles, 2 singles, 1 triple.
Meals	Dinner €30-€40. Wine from €18.
Closed	November-March.
Directions	Arrange pick-up from port of Panarea. By electric shuttle, or on foot; from port, right onto Via S. Pietro. Hotel 200m up lane.

Maria Pia Cappelli
Via San Pietro 15,
98050 Panarea, Aeolian Islands
Tel   +39 0909 83027
Email   info@quartarahotel.com
Web   www.quartarahotel.com

Hotel Signum

Leave the car and Sicily behind. Salina may not be as famous as some of her glamorous Aeolian neighbours (though *Il Postino* was filmed here) but is all the more peaceful for that. The friendly, unassuming hotel sits so quietly at the end of a narrow lane you'd hardly guess it was there. Dine on a shaded terracotta terrace with chunky tile-topped tables, colourful iron and wicker chairs; gaze out over lemon trees to the glistening sea. Traditional dishes and local ingredients are the norm. Then wind along the labyrinth of paths, where plants flow and tumble, to a simple and striking bedroom: cool pale walls, pretty antiques, a wrought-iron bed, good linen; starched lace flutters at the windows. The island architecture is typically low and unobtrusive and Clara and Michele (Luca's parents) have let the hotel grow organically as they've bought and converted farm buildings. The result is a beautiful, relaxing space where, even at busy times, you feel as if you are one of a handful of guests. Snooze on a shady veranda, take a dip in the infinity pool – that view again – or clamber down the path to a quiet pebbly cove.

Price	€130–€360.
Rooms	30: 28 doubles, 2 singles.
Meals	Dinner à la carte, €35–€60. Wine from €18.
Closed	Mid-November to mid-March.
Directions	By boat or hydrofoil from Naples, Palermo, Messina & Reggio Calabria. If you want to leave your car, there are garages in Milazzo.

Luca Caruso
Via Scalo 15, Malfa,
98050 Salina, Aeolian Islands
Tel +39 0909 844222
Email salina@hotelsignum.it
Web www.hotelsignum.it

Green Manors

Your hosts spotted the remote and dilapidated 1600s manor house years ago; it has been gloriously revived. Bedrooms, some with terraces, are rustic-refined: rich colours, tiled floors, heavy curtains, Sicilian patchwork, laced linen, family antiques, flowers... tapestries and paintings are illuminated by chandeliers, tapered candles stand in silver candelabra. Bathrooms come with huge baths or showers, delicately scented homemade soaps and waffle towels. Chris, Paolo and Pierangela have also been busy establishing their bio-dynamic orchard and you reap the rewards at breakfast, alongside silver cutlery, antique napkins and linen. The homemade jams are divine – cherry, apricot, ginger; the juices are freshly squeezed. Languid dinners are delicious and served outside behind a curtain of shimmering plants, or by the huge fireplace when the weather is cooler. There's a charming wooden cabin in the olive groves, with outside kitchen and bathroom; a lush tropical park with peacocks and ponies; occasional summer concerts beneath the mulberry tree. Exceptional. *Minimum stay two nights.*

Price	€100–€180. Cabin €80 (summer only). Cottage €200–€260.
Rooms	9 + 2: 5 doubles, 1 single, 3 suites. 1 cabin for 2, 1 cottage for 4-6.
Meals	Dinner €35. Wine €10-€60. Restaurants 1km.
Closed	Rarely.
Directions	Messina-Palermo, exit Barcellona dir. SS113 Palermo; immed. before Terme bridge, sharp left. Signed.

	Pierangela & Paolo Jannelli Verzera & Chris Jannelli Christiaens Borgo Porticato, 98053 Castroreale
Tel	+39 0909 746515
Email	info@greenmanors.it
Web	www.greenmanors.it

Ethical Collection: Environment; Community; Food. See page 400 for details

Entry 317 Map 18

Le Case del Principe

This vast walled estate with an impressive 17th-century palazzo amid an ocean of citrus trees lives up to its name; your host Gabriele is a prince. Overlooking a vineyard, across a labyrinth of pot-holed tracks linking the various parts, are a villa and five converted farm buildings. The villa, with its own garden and gazebo-covered terrace with tiled banquettes, has a 12-seater dining room with lacquered cane ceiling, a living room with an open fire and formal bedrooms with large beds, all quirkily decorated with unusual period pieces. The terraced row of single-storey cottages, backing onto a quiet road, have hedged-off terraces, cotto floors, neat kitchens, mezzanine bedrooms for children (with ladders) and pretty, traditional bathrooms tiled top-to-toe in blues and whites. Tucked away in the formal garden, a rose-smothered, thyme-scented pergola provides shady recess and a discreet pool with sleek recliners has a good view of the smoking volcano. Taormina with all its cultural hot spots, and Etna with all of hers (lava flows are visible during eruptions) are a short drive, as are the beaches.

Price	€400–€6,000 per week.
Rooms	5 cottages for 2, 4 or 6. Villa for 10.
Meals	Dinner for groups only. Wine €40. Restaurant 2km.
Closed	Never.
Directions	Directions on booking.

Principe Alliata di Villafranca
Tenuta Alliata, 98039 Taormina
Mobile   +39 349 7880906
Email   info@lecasedelprincipe.it
Web   www.lecasedelprincipe.it

Casa Turchetti

Turn back the clock a hundred or so years and you would have heard Puccini or Vivaldi resounding from deep within this 19th-century townhouse. The music academy is no more, but Casa Turchetti has not let go of its musical past: you'll spot the little lyre, the B&B's motif, dotted all over the place. Cheerful hosts Pino and Francesca are understandably proud of their restoration and will be as hands on or off as you want. Big bedrooms are elegant and supremely comfortable: soft yellow walls, generous red swags at balconied windows, marble floors that sparkle, embroidered white linen on antique beds. Bathrooms are designed for serious grooming; you'll want to spend far longer than necessary in here, wrapped in a fluffy towel or relaxed under a rain shower. Breakfasts are a talking point — the great book is heaped with praise. Catch your breath on the rooftop terrace: the Greek amphitheatre to your left, smouldering Etna to your right, the uninterrupted sweep of blue straight ahead, the hum of Taormina just below. All without having to step foot outside the door. *Minimum stay four nights.*

Price	€200–€250. Suites €350–€450.
Rooms	6: 3 doubles, 1 twin, 2 suites: 1 for 2, 1 for 4.
Meals	Restaurants within walking distance.
Closed	November–20 March.
Directions	Hotel in "centro storico".

Pino & Francesca Lombardo
Salita dei Gracchi 18/20,
98039 Taormina

Tel	+39 0942 625013
Email	info@casaturchetti.com
Web	www.casaturchetti.com

Hotel Villa Belvedere

It is perfectly named – stunning views sweep down over the botanical gardens to the azure sea below. Each front room has a balcony or bougainvillea-draped terrace; tantalizing glimpses of the sea can be caught from every angle. The five rooms on the first floor have beautiful big private terraces (no. 25 is particularly lovely, with arched windows and alcoves), those on the second have pretty little French balconies, and the bright-white 'attic' rooms on the top floor are delightful, with smaller terraces. The family rooms are at the back with views to the hills. The hotel has been in the family since 1902. Monsieur Pécaut, great-grandson of the founder, is French, his wife Italian, and they are helpful and very hands-on. There is no restaurant but delicious light lunches of pasta, sandwiches and snacks can be taken by the pool, a cool oasis shaded by subtropical vegetation and dotted with waving, century-old palms. A short walk away is a cable car that takes you down to the sea; medieval, cliff-hung Taormina, where Lawrence wrote *Lady Chatterley's Lover*, is known as the St Tropez of Italy.

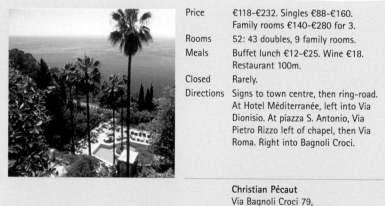

Price	€118–€232. Singles €88–€160. Family rooms €140–€280 for 3.
Rooms	52: 43 doubles, 9 family rooms.
Meals	Buffet lunch €12–€25. Wine €18. Restaurant 100m.
Closed	Rarely.
Directions	Signs to town centre, then ring-road. At Hotel Méditerranée, left into Via Dionisio. At piazza S. Antonio, Via Pietro Rizzo left of chapel, then Via Roma. Right into Bagnoli Croci.

Christian Pécaut
Via Bagnoli Croci 79,
98039 Taormina

Tel	+39 0942 23791
Email	info@villabelvedere.it
Web	www.villabelvedere.it

Hotel Villa Schuler

Late in the 19th century, Signor Schuler's great-grandfather travelled by coach from Germany and built his house here, high above the Ionian Sea. He chose the site well – the views of the Bay of Naxos and Mount Etna are a joy – and he built on a grand scale. When he died in 1905, Great Grandmama decided to let out some rooms, and the villa has been a hotel ever since. Though restored and brought up to date, it still has an old, elegant charm and a relaxed, quiet atmosphere. Lavish breakfasts are served in the chandelier'd breakfast room or out on the terrace. Individual bedrooms vary: some have beautifully tiled floors, antique furniture and stone balconies, while the more modern top-floor suites have beamed ceilings and large terraces. All come with jacuzzi showers and look out to sea or over the garden: vast, sub-tropical, scented with jasmine and magically illuminated at night. Hidden away behind a stone arch is a delightful, very private little apartment. A path leads through the gardens and out into the town's pedestrianized Corso Umberto. *Minimum stay two nights mid / high season.*

Price	€99–€212. Apartment €258 for 2; €400 for 4.
Rooms	26 + 1: 17 doubles, 5 suites, 4 triples. Apt for 2-4.
Meals	Breakfast for self-caterers included. Restaurants 100m (special prices for Hotel Villa Schuler guests).
Closed	Mid-November to February.
Directions	A18 exit Taormina; 3km; at 'Lumbi' car park into 'Monte Tauro' tunnel; around 'Porta Catania' car park to Piazza S. Antonio; right at P.O. into Via Pietro Rizzo; right into Via Roma.

Christine Voss & Gerhard Schuler
Piazzetta Bastione, Via Roma,
98039 Taormina

Tel	+39 0942 23481
Email	info@hotelvillaschuler.com
Web	www.hotelvillaschuler.com

Ethical Collection: Environment.
See page 400 for details

Villa Carlotta

There's a pretty, peaceful village above (Castelmola), a private beach below (Lido Stockholm), and a roof terrace that catches the sea breezes. Breakfasts up here are a joy, with their views of Mount Etna. The setting is perfect, the hotel is comfortable, the staff are attentive and friendly: this must be one of the best-loved hotels in Sicily. The building is an aristocratic villa built at the end of the 19th century with 15th-century pretensions, renovated in modern style with theatrical flourishes. Breakfast chairs are dressed in pleated linen, dove-grey sofas front glassy tables that mirror the sea, bedrooms trumpet generous beds and swagged curtains, a square blue pool nestles in a lush garden, and shaded loungers line up on two sides. Here a barman serves stylish drinks on silver platters – magical at night. No lounge but an exotic bar in the Roman catacombs (there's a Roman road in the gardens, too: perfectly preserved); no restaurant but plenty in clifftop Taormina, a stroll away, or a hotel shuttle. It's a pretty place but gets busy when the cruise ships drop by. Better by far to be here.

Price	€130-€320. Suites €200-€550.
Rooms	23: 7 doubles, 16 suites.
Meals	Restaurants within walking distance.
Closed	Mid-January to mid-February.
Directions	A18 exit Taormina. In town, left on Via Pirandello.

Andrea & Rosaria Quartucci
Via Pirandello 81, 98039 Taormina
Tel   +39 0942 626058
Email   info@villacarlotta.net
Web   www.villacarlotta.net

Entry 322   Map 18

Hotel Villa Ducale

The ebullient Dottor Quartucci and his family have restored this fine old village house with panache, re-using lovely old terracotta tiles and mixing family antiques with local fabrics and painted wardrobes and chests. Taormina, with its fabulous bays and young clientele, is the chicest resort in Sicily, and rich in archaeological and architectural sites. From the terrace high on the hill, distance lends enchantment to the view. You can see the sweep of five bays and the looming presence of Mount Etna as you breakfast on delicious Sicilian specialities – linger as long as you like. Flowers are the keynote of this romantic little hotel: bunches in every room, pots placed like punctuation marks on the steps, terraces romping with geranium and bougainvillea. Bedrooms, not large, are full of subtle detail, each one with a terrace, shower rooms come with slippers and robes, five of the suites lie across the road. The style is antique-Sicilian; the extras – air conditioning, internet, satellite TV – entirely modern. The buses don't run very often into Taormina so the shuttle to the private beach is handy.

Price	€130-€250. Suites €250-€440.
Rooms	17: 11 doubles, 6 suites for 2-4.
Meals	Lunch/dinner €20. Wine €18-€45. Restaurant 200m.
Closed	10 January-10 February.
Directions	From Taormina centre towards Castelmola; signed.

Andrea & Rosaria Quartucci
Via L. da Vinci 60, 98039 Taormina
Tel   +39 0942 28153
Email   info@villaducale.com
Web   www.villaducale.com

Palmento La Rosa Agriturismo

A chunky ten-metre beam dominates the vast living area: a reminder that Palmento la Rosa housed a wine press. Now it is a sophisticated wine estate ('palmento') and a charming place to stay, 700 metres above sea level (never too hot), surrounded by acres of Etna vines. Your stylish, lively, delightful hosts, Zora and Franz, have swapped Paris for this green haven at the foot of Europe's most celebrated volcano, sharing their passion for life, culture, sunshine and good food with guests. Served at one big granite table on the terrace in summer, meals are fresh and colourful Sicilian, desserts are magnificently baroque, wines are from Biondi and Benanti. There is true generosity of spirit here, visible in the large rooms with their sweeping chestnut floors, the sprawling sofas, the several fireplaces, the original art and the bedrooms flooded with light. Those on the ground floor open to palm trees and roses, those on the first have sea views. Trek in the National Park or climb the lower craters of Etna; cable cars can replace legs if need be! *Minimum stay two nights.*

Price	€120–€160.
Rooms	4: 3 doubles, 1 twin.
Meals	Dinner €35–€45. Wine list from €15.
Closed	8 January–15 February.
Directions	Directions on booking.

Franz & Zora Hochreutener
Via Lorenzo Bolano 55,
75030 Pedara

Tel	+39 0957 896206
Email	info@palmentolarosa.com
Web	www.palmentolarosa.com

Borgopetra

The renovation is complete – an exquisite revival of a 400-year-old farmstead, an oasis of beauty and peace. Five years ago journalist Cristina left the high life in Milan to join Toto in the restoration of his family *borgo*. On the southern slopes of Mount Etna, self-contained yet unremote, your luxurious apartments wrap themselves around a square courtyard scented with jasmine. The attention to detail is second to none, from the ergonomic beds to the soaps hand-made in Catania, from the Mascalucia olive oil in the kitchens to the thyme-infused honeys at breakfast. In the guest quarters, stunning antique rubs shoulders with stylish modern: perhaps a chic red basin on an ancient terracotta floor, an old country wardrobe, a sleek chaise-longue. Among apricot and orange trees and the pergola of an ancient vine is a cool pool, in the old marionette theatre, a massage room, gym, bar, and shelves crammed with Cristina's crime mysteries and board games. Cristina and Toto are the warmest pair you're ever likely to meet. A fine beginning for them… one to watch!
Minimum stay two nights.

Price	€100-€220.
Rooms	4 + 2: 1 double, 3 suites: 1 for 2-3, 2 for 3 (all with kitchenette). 2 apartments for 6.
Meals	Restaurant 300m.
Closed	8 January-15 February; 20 November-20 December.
Directions	15km from Catania; from m'way, exit Gravina-Etna. Detailed directions on booking.

Cristina Pauly
Via Teatro 9,
95030 Mascalucia

Tel	+39 0957 277184
Email	info@borgopetra.it
Web	www.borgopetra.it

Entry 325   Map 18

Limoneto Agriturismo

Dogs doze in the deep shade of the veranda. In the lemon grove, ladders disappear into trees, and shake as another basket is lowered down. This is 'rustic simplicity' at its best. The main house is modern and white, with as many openings as it has walls, through which chairs, tables and plants burst out on all sides. Lemon and olive trees (look forward to homemade *limoncello* after dinner) stop short of the terrace, where meals are taken throughout the summer. Bedrooms, straightforward, air-conditioned and TV-free, have wrought-iron beds, floral fabrics, tiled floors, spotless showers. Those in the main house look out across the garden to a play area; the larger family suites, in the pale pink *casa* across the courtyard, sleep five, their twin beds on a mezzanine. The owners, Adelina and husband Alceste, believe in the traditions of the region and are full of ideas for your stay: head for Noto, Palazzolo or the soft sands of Siracusa. The restaurant is sometimes hired out for weddings and parties; if you're concerned, please check in advance. *Child discounts.*

Price	€90–€120. Singles €70.
Rooms	10: 4 doubles, 3 family rooms, 3 triples.
Meals	Sunday lunch (except July & August) €22. Dinner €22. Wine from €10.
Closed	November.
Directions	From Catania towards Siracusa; on m'way exit Palazzolo & follow signs for 'Limoneto'.

Adelina Norcia
Via del Platano 3, 96100 Siracusa
Tel   +39 0931 717352
Email limoneto@tin.it
Web   www.limoneto.it

Entry 326   Map 18

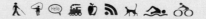

Monteluce Country House

In deep country, just four miles from gorgeous sleepy baroque Noto, Monteluce is a jewel of design and warm-heartedness. Architect-designers Claudio and Imelda have created a discreet wilderness bolthole from the grey urban north and genuinely welcome guests who bring news of the outside world. As carefully as these two houses lie respectfully low among their 12 hectares of olive and citrus groves, their sense of space and style will wrap you gently in colour, texture, excitement (Imelda's paintings, Claudio's gliding shots) and extreme Italian comfort. Brilliant, individually tiled bathrooms, some fun furniture, superb beds, fine detailing, nothing tacky, and each room with its own garden. If you are self-catering in one of the apartments, your kitchen will be another delight of colour and style, your beds may be on really generous mezzanines. A perfectly complementary couple, they share the caring: Claudio makes breakfast (different cake every day) which is brought to your table, inside or out, and Imelda entertains with her fascinating talk of north and south, Sicilian life. *One hour from Catania Airport.*

Price	€140–€220.
	Apartments €1,050–€1,400 per week.
Rooms	3 + 3: 1 double, 2 suites (with kitchenette). 3 apartments: 1 for 3, 2 for 2.
Meals	Restaurant 7km.
Closed	Rarely.
Directions	M'way dir. Gela exit Noto, then Noto-Pachino-Villa Romana del Tellaro; left for Noto; at x-roads, left for Pachino Portopalo on SP19; at km 5.5, right onto SP 22 dir. Vaddeddi-Villa Romana del T. After 2km, on right.

Imelda Rubiano
Contrada Vaddeddi,
Villa Romana del Tellaro, 96017 Noto

Mobile	+39 335 6901871
Email	info@monteluce.com
Web	www.monteluce.com

Bed & Breakfast Villa Aurea

Once the family's summer house, Villa Aurea is now a gentle, friendly place to stay, thanks to the owner's son, Enrico, who has given up city hotels for this. His father shaped these surroundings, his architect's eye and his attention to detail ensuring the place feels calm, spacious and uncluttered; his mother bakes fabulous cakes and tarts and delivers a divine breakfast, enjoyed in the garden in summer. Cupboards blend discreetly into the walls, stylish shutters soften the Sicilian light and low round windows are designed to allow moonlight to play in the corridor. Bedrooms are minimalist with bright white walls and bold bedcovers. Upstairs rooms share a long terrace shaded by a huge carob tree; two rooms interconnect for families. Tiled bathrooms – some huge, with sea views – sparkle and use solar-heated water. A tree was planted to mark the birth of each of the three children and the garden is now luscious and filled with all kinds of tree: banana, orange, lemon, almond… you can idle in their shade, work up a steam on the tennis court, or cool off in the striped pool. *New hotel opened in Pozzallo, 5km.*

Price	€60-€110.
Rooms	7 doubles.
Meals	Restaurants 1.5km.
Closed	Rarely.
Directions	Motorway Siracusa-Gela, exit Rosolini. SP46 Ispica-Pozzallo for Pozzallo, house 4km. Signed.

Francesco Caruso
Contrada Senna,
97014 Ispica
Tel +39 0932 956575
Email villa.aurea@gmail.com
Web www.marenostrumpozzallo.it/villaaurea/index.htm

Entry 328 Map 18

Cambiocavallo Unesco Area & Resort

On the main road to Modica, the blinding white, blue and terracotta of this ancient house – once a resting place for horses – suggest that they do things differently here. Step in to a high tech, high design look straight from an architectural magazine: sharp, stark, very zen. Windows and doors are stained black, walls are exposed stone or colourwashed, furniture is clean-limbed, lighting is funky. The effect is rich yet soothing. Bedrooms are clutter-free zones of crisp black or metallic pieces (with four-posters in the suites), polished black floors and chestnut beamed ceilings. Bold flowers and giant photographs add colour. Bathrooms are super-modern, unspeakably high tech! Relax on your private decking overlooking the olive and almond groves, or among the palms, cactus and orange trees of the newly created garden. In the summer, breakfast is served in the courtyard, a cool combination of white and blue walls, clipped box hedging and an ancient carob tree. After discovering the baroque towns (Unesco-protected), the fish restaurants and the local beaches, wonderful to return to this clean, spare space and chill.

Price	€100–€235.
Rooms	8: 6 twins/doubles, 2 suites.
Meals	Restaurants nearby.
Closed	November.
Directions	Siracusa-Gela exit Rosolini; then Ispica-Pozzallo. In Ispica, at r'bout dir. Pozzallo (do not go into Ispica). Before Pozzallo, blue sign Cambiocavallo; overpass for Sampieri, left. Signs for Cambiocavallo on right. 1st exit Pozzallo Nord, follow exit to junction, right dir. Modica; cont. on SP45 3km.

	Salvatore Tringali & Rosanna La Rosa
	Contrada Zimmardo Superiore,
	97015 Modica
Tel	+39 0932 779118
Email	info@cambiocavallo.it
Web	www.cambiocavallo.it

Nacalino Agriturismo

Concetta and Fillippo have bags of enthusiasm for their agriturismo, their food (it's exceptional), their children, and their eventful lives. They've been doing B&B in this pretty area of southern Sicily for over a decade now but there's no sign of their slowing down; everything is done with Sicilian energy, humour and flair. Simple bedrooms in the old stables border a grassy square with tables and chairs so you can sit out in the sun, while the rooms above the restaurant are more elegant, with high ceilings and polished chests at the foot of handsome beds. Dinner is a fabulous regional experience and everything is home-produced, from the olive oils to the wines. It's a great spot for families too – children will enjoy getting to know the friendly donkeys, and there's a communal sitting room stuffed with books and games for dreary days. The sea isn't far; Modica is a half-hour drive. Little English is spoken here but you'll leave with new friendships made – even if you haven't managed to exchange a single word in the same language! *Owners also have self-catering apartments 5km away.*

Price	€70-€130.
Rooms	12: 3 twins/doubles, 2 triples, 7 family rooms: 4 for 3, 3 for 4.
Meals	Dinner with wine, €25.
Closed	Rarely.
Directions	From Catania, m'way SR-Gela exit Rosolini; dir. Ispica, then Modica, then signs to Ragusa on SS115. Left for Marina di Modica after 7km, then right for Contrada Nacalino; on for 1.8km.

Filippo & Concetta Colombo
Contrada Nacalino, sn, 97015 Modica

Tel	+39 0932 779022
Email	info@nacalinoagriturismo.it
Web	www.nacalinoagriturismo.it

Palazzo Failla Hotel

Straddling a busy corner in spire-embellished Modica (there are dozens of churches on your doorstep) is this grand old hotel. Hemmed in by a lively café bar on one side, and its Michelin-starred restaurant on the other, the place buzzes with locals and tourists. The very smart exterior, with its red-carpeted stone steps and handsome red awnings, belies the atmosphere inside: informal, relaxed and friendly. Cheerful staff welcome you through sparkling glass doors and whisk you up wide stairs, through a beautiful old room with original floor-to-ceiling wood panelling, and into opulent bedrooms. Polished marble floors are decorated in exquisite geometric patterns; cherubs dance across high frescoed ceilings; and beautiful antiques from all corners of Italy pose against sumptuously papered walls. Chandeliers, gilt-framed paintings, rich embroidered bed linen: it's fabulous. Further rooms are found off a lovely sunlit courtyard a minute's walk from the main hotel. Have breakfast in the café, supper in the restaurant, and spend every hour in between exploring this beautiful town.

Price	€80–€195.
Rooms	10: 6 twins/doubles, 2 singles, 1 triple, 1 quadruple.
Meals	Restaurant next door. Wine €3–€12.
Closed	Never.
Directions	From Ragusa, 12km, 1st exit Modica Alta. Hotel is 300m after Duomo di San Giorgio, Piazza S. Teresa.

Paolo Failla
Via Blandini 5, 97015 Modica
Tel   +39 0932 941059
Email   info@palazzofailla.it
Web   www.palazzofailla.it

Hotel Locanda Don Serafino

The hotel lies in the heart of the stepped city, rich with baroque churches and mansions – a World Heritage Site. The sitting and breakfast room are cool all year round, their rock walls revealing that this part of the 19th-century building was hewn straight from the hillside – and most inviting with their cream couches and bright red rugs. Doubles are small, suites larger; your bathroom could be as narrow as a corridor or house a tub of Olympian proportions. But all bedrooms are delightfully simple, spotless with mod cons, their wooden furniture designed by a local architect, some with balconies, some with direct access from the street. And you'll sleep well: there are deeply comfortable mattresses and a choice of pillows, soft or firm. The staff here are wonderful, thanks to gentle, friendly Guiseppe. Homemade breads and hot chocolate are served for breakfast; for dinner, there's the family's restaurant, a ten-minute walk to the stables of an 18th-century mansion – elegant, intimate, very good. *Flexible breakfasts & check-out times.*

Price	€148-€195. Singles €118-€165.
Rooms	10: 4 doubles, 1 single, 5 suites.
Meals	Owner's restaurant 10-minute walk.
Closed	Never.
Directions	Ragusa-Ibla road. Down Corso S. Mazzini to Piazza della Repubblica; along Via della Repubblica; 50m past Chiesa del Purgatorio; right into Via XI Febbraio.

Famiglia La Rosa
Via XI Febbraio 15, 97100 Ragusa Ibla

Tel	+39 0932 220065
Email	info@locandadonserafino.it
Web	www.locandadonserafino.it

Fattoria Mosè Agriturismo

The town creeps ever up towards the Agnello olive groves but the imposing house still stands proudly on the hill, protecting its private chapel and a blissfully informal family interior. In the main house, high, cool rooms have superb original floor tiles, antiques and family mementos. The B&B room is plainer, has an old-fashioned idiosyncratic bathroom and olive-grove views. Breakfast is in a huge, shutter-shaded dining room or on the terrace, the dumb-waiter laden with homemade jams served on silver. Chiara's family used to come to escape Palermo's summer heat: a cooling breeze frequently blows. Your hostess, a quietly interesting ex-architect, has converted the stables into six airy modern apartments with high, pine-clad ceilings, contemporary fabrics and good little kitchens, plain white walls, paper lampshades, no pretensions. Most have their own terrace, all spill onto the lovely plant-packed courtyard (with barbecue), and there are Chiara's olive oils, almonds and fruits and vegetables to buy. The 'Valley of the Temples' is a short and hugely worthwhile drive. *Minimum stay two nights.*

Price	€100. Apts €500 for 2; €869 for 4; €1,092 for 6. Apt prices per week.
Rooms	1 + 6: 1 double. 6 apartments for 2, 4 or 6.
Meals	Breakfast €8 for self-caterers. Dinner by arrangement. Restaurants 2km.
Closed	7 January-March; November-22 December.
Directions	From Agrigento SS115 for Gela-Siracusa. At end of Villaggio Mosè road (past supermarkets, houses) left at sign for Fattoria Mosè; signed.

Chiara Agnello
Via M. Pascal 4, 92100 Villaggio Mosé
Tel   +39 0922 606115
Email   info@fattoriamose.com
Web   www.fattoriamose.com

Ethical Collection: Food.
See page 400 for details

Entry 333   Map 18

Agriturismo Sillitti

Drive through rolling farmland, up past the almond and olive groves, until you can climb no further. This is it: stunning 360 degree views over the island and, on a clear day, Mount Etna in the distance. Silvia's family have farmed for generations. She's passionately organic – grows olives, almonds, wheat, vegetables – and loves to share both recipes and kitchen garden. The farmhouse is new, its apartments bright and simple, furnished in unfussy style with cream floor tiles, modern pine and colourful fabrics. Open-plan living areas include tiny kitchens for rustling up simple meals. Rooms won't win design prizes but are spotless and airy and have superlative views. Silvia and Bruno (a doctor in nearby Caltanissetta) are open and welcoming; you'll be won over by their warmth and her cooking. Breakfast on homemade bread, cakes and jams; dinner is a feast of Sicilian dishes. A great spot from which to explore the island – castles, temples, Palermo, Taormina – or enjoy the views from the lovely large garden, with pool, terrace and shady pavilion. Space, peace, delightful people. *Minimum stay two nights.*

Price	€80. Apts €500–€960 per week.
Rooms	5 + 3: 5 doubles.
	3 apartments for 2-5.
Meals	Dinner with wine, €25.
	Restaurants 5km.
Closed	Rarely.
Directions	From Catania or Palermo A19 exit Caltanissetta onto SS640. Cont. on SS640 past Caltanissetta dir. Agrigento. After 10km exit for Serradifalco & Roccella. Stop here and phone Silvia.

Ethical Collection: Food.
See page 400 for details

Silvia Sillitti
Contrada Grotta d'Acqua,
93100 Caltanissetta

Tel	+39 0934 930733
Email	info@sillitti.it
Web	www.sillitti.it

Villa Mimosa

Nearby are the breathtaking temples of the Greek city of Selinunte, a short drive along the main road that passes close to Villa Mimosa. A crumbling ruin among umbrella pines and olive groves, the house was rebuilt as traditionally as possible by Jackie – who has managed to collect a goodly number of stray cats and dogs along the way. The great thing is you can self-cater here or go B&B: Jackie does both breakfasts and dinners. Three of the apartments stretch along the back and open onto a long, pergola-shaded terrace and a garden of olives and orange trees – bright with poppies in spring. The fourth apartment is on the first floor, with a balcony. Each is open plan, with a simple shower room and a kitchenette – homely spaces traditionally furnished with chunky carved Sicilian armchairs, high antique beds, good linen. If you dine with Jackie, it's outside on the terrace on her side of the house, or in her *salotto* on cool evenings. She's lived in Sicily for years, is very knowledgeable about the island and will steer you towards the nature reserves and the beautiful beaches. *€10 extra for one night stays.*

Price	€70-€100. Apts €400-€600 per week.
Rooms	4 apartments: 3 studio apts for 2-3, 1 apt for 2-3.
Meals	Dinner, 3 courses with wine, €35-€40. Restaurants 6km.
Closed	Rarely.
Directions	From Agrigento SS115 to very end, exit Castelvetrano. At end of slip-road sharp right; 2nd entrance on left.

Jackie Sirimanne
La Rocchetta, Selinunte,
91022 Castelvetrano
Tel   +39 0924 44583
Email   j.sirimanne@virgilio.it
Web   www.aboutsicily.net

Zarbo di Mare

A simple stone-built house, slap on the sea, on a beautiful stretch of coast to the north-west tip of the island, designed to catch the sun. Sun worshippers can follow the progress of the rays by moving from terrace to terrace through the day; those who prefer the shade will be just as happy. A vine-clad courtyard behind the house is a lovely place to take breakfast; you might move to the large shady terrace with a barbecue at the side of the house for lunch, and take dinner on the front terrace looking out to sea. There are two bedrooms, each with two beds, and an open-plan sitting-room with a pine-and-white kitchen. Below the house are steps down to a private swimming platform, fine for the sprightly; the sea is deep here, and perfect for snorkelling. (Families with small children may prefer to swim from the beach nearby at San Vito, where the water is shallow.) There are some lovely things to see in this part of Sicily; visit the extraordinary Greek temple at Segesta, standing gravely and peacefully at the head of the valley. *Contact number is in Belgium. Bikes for hire in village. Ask about shorter stays in low season.*

Price	€700–€850 per week.
Rooms	House for 2-4.
Meals	Restaurant 4km.
Closed	7 July–25 August.
Directions	Approx. 120km from Palermo airport. Motorway to Trapani, exit Castellammare del Golfo. Coast road SS187 to Trapani. San Vito clearly signed. House 5km after village.

Barbara Yates
Contrada Zarbo di Mare 37,
91010 San Vito Lo Capo

Tel   +32 (0)2 512 4526
Email barbara.yates@belgacom.net

Casa Hermosa

A must for theatre buffs, sandwiched between the Massimo and Politeama theatres (Sicily's finest): dazzling opera is a short stroll. Three floors up, on a blissfully quiet street in chaotic, beautiful Palermo, is this friendly, homely little find. And it's no surprise to learn that Silvia herself lived here as a child. These days she's busy nurturing olives and vines on her organic farm outside the city, but has transformed her little flat into a restful and comfortable place to stay. You enter a spacious L-shaped living room with some lovely family pieces scattered about (Nonna's handsome walnut armoire still stands by the front door); framed acrylic flowers cheer up white walls and cherry-red sofas sit comfortably on perfectly polished parquet. A neat little kitchen hides behind frosted doors, and simple bedrooms down the corridor have a narrow balcony each. Of course, if the theatre isn't your thing, Palermo's throbbing centre is still an easy walk; and it's a comfort to know you've got this little place to come home to when your eyes can feast on no more.

Price	€100–€200.
Rooms	1 apartment for 2–4.
Meals	Restaurant 100m.
Closed	Never.
Directions	10-minute walk from from Piazza Politeama. Or, from train station bus No. 101 to Via Roma, then Via Cavour; 50m walk to apt. Detailed directions on booking.

Silvia Sillitti
Via Villaermosa 26,
90139 Palermo
Tel   +39 0934 556637
Email   info@sillitti.it

Sicily

Chez Jasmine

Down by the 27-centuries-old Phœnician port you are enveloped in the history of Palermo and some breathtakingly fine buildings. Jasmine stands in a 10th-century courtyard in the old Arab town, just reviving from centuries of neglect. Irish-turned-Sicilian (almost), the delightful Mary lives round the corner, leaves fresh breakfast in your super kitchen, is involved in conservation, and can keep you entertained for hours with her insights into local mores. Her vertical, newly renovated 'doll's house' is adorable. It starts on the first floor (and you can barbecue in the courtyard). Expect a pleasing little all-Italian shower room and a bedroom with its own wicker sofa and writing table; then up to an open-plan living area, well-lit and comfortably furnished, marrying northern sobriety with southern colour. Finally, an iron spiral leads to a pretty terrace shaded by bamboo blinds, decorated with eager creepers and plants. Kalsart, a feast of music, art and many talents, makes summer evenings in La Kalsa so very pleasurable. *Minimum stay three nights.*

Price	€110-€130.
Rooms	House for 2-4.
Meals	Restaurants on doorstep.
Closed	Rarely.
Directions	From port road in Palermo go towards La Kalsa; at Piazza Kalsa, right; house to left of Chiesa della Pietà.

Mary Goggin
Vicolo dei Nassaiuoli 15,
90133 Palermo

Tel   +39 0916 164268
Email   info@chezjasmine.biz
Web   www.chezjasmine.biz

Palazzo Cannata

The stone escutcheon over the door justifies the palatial name, the tenderly scruffy yard inside tells today's humbler tale. One of the most exuberantly hospitable men you could hope to meet, Carmelo inhabits the top of the former bishop's palace; you can see Palermo's domes from the terrace. All her treasures are within walking distance (and quite a bit of the traffic). The flat is as full of eclectic interest as Carmelo's captivating mixed-lingo conversation. He teaches mechanics, with deep commitment, and breathes a passion for dance and music. Everywhere are paintings and photographs, bits of furniture and cabinets of mementos, yet there's plenty of space for everything to make sense. One could explore the details for hours, including the madonnas in the high-bedded double room and the painted beds in the triple. A fount of insight into his home town, Carmelo will tell you all. After the pastry breakfast he has prepared before going to work, you will discover his fascinating city. You will also meet friends Argo, the superb bouncing dog, and Enzo, his sociable master from next door.

Price	€80-€90.
Rooms	2: 1 double, 1 triple, sharing bath.
Meals	Restaurants nearby.
Closed	Rarely.
Directions	In Palermo, from Palazzo dei Normanni; left down small street off Via del Bastione.

Ethical Collection: Environment.
See page 400 for details

Carmelo Sardegna
Vicolo Cannata 5,
90134 Palermo
Tel +39 0916 519269
Email sardegnacarmelo@hotmail.com

Casa Margaret

Here are three adorable, unusual, freshly converted stone houses perched thrillingly on top of a hill. Surrounded by ancient gnarled olive trees and views of snow-capped mountains and sea, reached by a very rough wiggling track (be warned!), each has its own gorgeous character. Margherita, the highest, feels calm and laid back; a large covered terrace, wooden ceilings, stone floors, colourful objets old and new, vases of flowers, sofas before an open fire. There's a glass-topped dining table and a mod-conned kitchen, and comfortable bedrooms with hand-painted details. Rosita, the largest house, is robust yet cosy, with lots of bare stone, an iron candelabra above a snazzily tiled dining room, and a children's bedroom under the eaves. Bianca, dinky and cute, has a peek-over mezzanine to the living room below, lined with pots and characterful tomes. All have fantastic barbecue terraces for sensational views and are far enough apart for privacy and hidden by olive trees – yet close enough for a bunch of friends to enjoy. Plenty to do locally, and acres of ancient olive estate to roam wild in.

Price	€600-€1,850.
Rooms	3 cottages: 1 for 2, 1 for 4, 1 for 5.
Meals	Restaurant 2km.
Closed	Rarely.
Directions	A29 dir. Palermo, then A19 dir. Messina-Catania. After 50km x-road; follow Catania. 1st exit for "Buonfornello-Piano Zucchi-Sito Archeologico Imera". SS113 dir. Messina. After 4.6km right for Campofelice; road 9 of Madonie (SP9) dir. Collesano. After Campofelice stay on road; after 2km 1st gate, right.

Margherita Carducci Artenisio
Km 4 della strada provinciale 9,
Pizzillo, 90016 Collesano

Tel	+39 0916199221
Email	info@casamargaret.it
Web	www.casamargaret.it

Ca' La Somara Agriturismo

A short drive to the coast, a far cry from the fleshpots of Costa Smeralda, Ca' La Somara's white buildings stand out against the peaceful wooded hills and jutting limestone crags of Gallura. As you'd expect from the name, donkeys feature here – they're one of Laura's passions. She's an ex-architect who gave up city life and has converted the stables with charm and flair. Once used to shelter sheep, they are now ranch-rustic. You get a striking, galleried living/dining room, its stone walls decorated with harnesses and lanterns, farm implements, baskets and the odd amphora, and bedrooms small and simple, with whitewashed walls, carved beds and little shower rooms with hand-painted tiles. Don't miss the pretty village of San Pantaleo, an artists' community just up the hill. Return to cushioned benches in the garden or hessian hammocks in the paddock, with views of the valley and its windswept cork oaks. Dinner is fresh Mediterranean, served with Sardinian wines. It's all deliciously restful and undemanding – and there's a sparkling pool. *Relaxation therapies available.*

Price	€58-€136.
Rooms	9 doubles.
Meals	Dinner €20.
Closed	Rarely.
Directions	From Olbia, S125 dir. Arzachena. Look out for track on right, signed San Pantaleo; through village, dir. Porto Cervo. Signed at bottom of hill on right.

Alberto & Laura Lagattolla
Loc. Sarra Balestra, 07021 Arzachena

Tel	+39 0789 98969
Email	info@calasomara.it
Web	www.calasomara.it

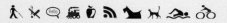

Li Licci

Not so long ago, this tranquil place was inaccessible. Deserted after the death of Gianmichele's grandfather, it was rescued by Jane and Gianmichele in 1985. Once they had moved in, the almost nightly entertaining of friends began. English-born Jane is an inspired cook of Sardinian food and the entertaining grew into the creation of a delightful restaurant (now with a Michelin mention) that is based on home-grown, organic produce: pecorino, ricotta, salamis, hams, preserves, liqueurs. And they have added four immaculate, simple, white-walled bedrooms, each with a shower. Jane looks after guests as she would like to be looked after herself, so staying here is like being in the home of a relaxed and hospitable friend. Li Licci has its own wells, producing the most delicious clear water, and a 2,000-year-old olive tree. Breakfast is outside in summer, overlooking the oak woods and hills of Gallura, or by the fire in the converted stables in winter: either way, a superb start to a day's walking, climbing or sailing… or lazing on the north coast beaches. *Minimum stay two nights.*

Price	€100. Half-board €65–€75 p.p.
Rooms	4: 2 doubles, 1 twin, 1 family room for 4.
Meals	Dinner with wine, €30–€40.
Closed	Epiphany-Easter.
Directions	Through S. Antonio to r'bout, then dir. Olbia. After 3.5km, right at sign. From Olbia Airport dir. Palau exit S. Mariedda-Tempio. 2km after Priatu, left at sign.

	Agri Mar s.r.l. Via Capo d'Orso 35, 07020 Palau
Tel	+39 0796 65114
Email	info@lilicci.com
Web	www.lilicci.com

Villa Las Tronas Hotel & Spa

It could be the setting for an Agatha Christie whodunnit (Hercule Poirot perhaps?): a crenellated, late 19th-century hotel dramatically set on a rocky spit of land jutting into the sea. The outer walls, gate and entry phone give the requisite aloof feeling and the atmosphere within is hushed and formal. Originally owned by a Piemontese count, it was bought by the present owners in the 1950s and they take huge pride in the place. The big reception rooms and bedrooms – formal, ornate, immaculate – have a curiously muted, old-fashioned air, while the high ceilinged bathrooms are new – vibrant with modern fittings and green and blue mosaic tiles. On all sides, windows look down at accusatory fingers of rock pointing into azure Sardinian waters. There's a little lawned garden, a swimming pool and restaurant area poised immediately above the rocks; delightful to hear the waves lapping below as you dine. Close by is the pretty, interesting old quarter of Alghero, and there are fabulous beaches and good restaurants up and down the coast. *Brand new Wellness Centre.*

Price	€178–€418. Suites €378–€620.
Rooms	25: 20 doubles, 5 suites.
Meals	Dinner €75. Wine from €20.
Closed	Never.
Directions	Leave Alghero, signs for Bosa/Lungomare. Hotel on right.

Vito La Spina
Lungomare Valencia 1, 07041 Alghero

Tel	+39 0799 81818
Email	info@hvlt.com
Web	www.hvlt.com

Su Dandaru

A totter down a cobbled alley in Bosa's impossibly quaint old town brings you to a prettily painted 1700s house with a red and yellow exterior. In contrast to the lovely old arches, the wooden beams, the stone floors is a fresh and imaginative décor. Four bedrooms are spread over three floors. The first, earth themed, is warmly hued and cosy with a big wrought-iron bed. The second, inspired by the river, is in greens and yellows, with linen curtains and a basket-weave bed; off the room, just before the bathroom, is a small room with a single bed. The third room, the suite, is all sea blues and greens, with a French armoire and antique lace curtains. Charming and inviting one and all, with small but perfectly formed bathrooms. Above is a sitting room with a comfy sofa, and a big roof terrace with views up to the medieval castle, down to the rooftops of Sa Costa; lovely for an evening under the stars. Or a chilled chianti after a day's boating on the river or lazing on the beach. You breakfast in an Italian café and can dine anywhere in town, perhaps at the owner's own little place, by the river under the palms. *Minimum stay two nights in high season.*

Price	€50–€125. Singles from €35.
Rooms	4: 1 double, 1 family room for 3; 1 double, 1 single sharing bathroom.
Meals	Restaurants within walking distance.
Closed	Rarely.
Directions	Coast road from Alghero to Bosa. In Bosa, left into town. Follow road, veer left, then 1st right, straight to end to r'bout/square. Park here; B&B is 2-minute walk.

Giacomo Forte
Via del Pozzo 25, Bosa
Mobile +44 (0)7595 996446
Email info@sardiniabandb.com
Web www.sardiniabandb.com

Hotel Su Gologone

Lavender, myrtle and rosemary scent the valley. The dazzling white buildings of Hotel Su Gologone stand among ancient vineyards and olive groves at the foot of the towering Supramonte. The hotel takes its name from a nearby spring and began life in the 1960s as a simple restaurant serving simple Sardinian dishes – roast suckling pig, wild boar sausages, ice cream with thyme honey. Now the restaurant is known throughout Europe. Run by the founders' daughter, Giovanna, it employs only local chefs and has a terrace with views to the mountains. In this wilderness region of the island this is an elegant and magical place, only 30 minutes from the coast and wonderful beaches. Juniper-beamed bedrooms have intriguing arches and alcoves and make much of local craftwork and art: embroidered cushions, Sardinian fabrics, original paintings, ceramics and sculpture. Browse a book about the island from the library, curl up in one of many cosy corners. Hiking can be arranged, the pool is fed by cold spring water, and there's an outdoor jacuzzi. Marvellous. *Book in advance May-September.*

Price	Half-board €310–€510 for 2.	
Rooms	69: 54 twins/doubles, 15 suites.	
Meals	Half-board only. Wine from €10.	
Closed	Rarely.	
Directions	From Oliena towards Dorgali. Right at sign for Su Gologone; hotel on right.	

Luigi Crisponi
Loc. Su Gologone, 08025 Oliena
Tel +39 0784 287512
Email gologone@tin.it
Web www.sugologone.it

Many of you may want to stay in environmentally friendly places. You may be passionate about local, organic or home-grown food. Or perhaps you want to know that the place you are staying in contributes to the community? To help you we have launched our Ethical Collection, so you can find the right place to stay and also discover how each owner is addressing these issues.

The Collection is made up of places going the extra mile, and taking the steps that most people have not yet taken, in one or more of the following areas:

• Environment Those making great efforts to reduce the environmental impact of their Special Place. We expect more than energy-saving light bulbs and recycling – in this part of the Collection you will find owners who make their own natural cleaning products, properties with solar hot water and biomass boilers, the odd green roof and a good measure of green elbow grease.

• Community Given to owners who use their property to play a positive role in their local and wider community. For example, by making a contribution from every guest's bill to a local fund, or running pond-dipping courses for local school children on their farm.

• Food Awarded to owners who make a real effort to source local or organic food, or to grow their own. We look for those who have gone out of their way to strike up relationships with local producers or to seek out organic suppliers. It is easier for an owner on a farm to produce their own eggs than for someone in the middle of a city, so we take this into account.

How it works

To become part of our Ethical Collection owners choose whether to apply in one, two or all three categories, and fill in a detailed questionnaire asking demanding questions about their activities in the chosen areas. You can download a full list of the questions at www.sawdays.co.uk/about_us/ethical_collection/faq/

We then review each questionnaire carefully before deciding whether or not to give the award(s). The final decision is subjective; it is based not only on whether an owner ticks 'yes' to a question but also on the detailed explanation that accompanies each 'yes' or 'no' answer. For example, an owner who has tried as hard as possible to install solar water-heating panels, but has failed because of strict conservation planning laws, will be given some credit for their effort (as long as they are doing other things in this area).

We have tried to be as rigorous as possible and have made sure the questions are demanding. We have not checked out the claims of owners before making our decisions, but we do trust them to be honest. We are only human, as are they, so please let us know if you think we have made any mistakes.

The Ethical Collection is still a new initiative for us, and we'd love to know what you think about it – email us at ethicalcollection@sawdays.co.uk or write to us. And remember that because this is a new scheme some owners have not yet completed their questionnaires – we're sure other places in the guide are working just as hard in these areas, but we don't yet know the full details.

Ethical Collection online

There is stacks more information on our website, www.sawdays.co.uk. You can read the answers each owner has given to our Ethical Collection questionnaire and get a more detailed idea of what they are doing in each area. You can also search for properties that have awards.

Ethical Collection in this book

On the entry page of all places in the Collection we show which awards have been given.

A list of places in our Ethical Collection is shown below, by entry number.

Environment

2 • 7 • 25 • 30 • 40 • 74 • 98 • 144 • 149 • 165 • 166 • 171 • 175 • 204 • 217 • 219 • 230 • 240 • 241 • 251 • 256 • 277 • 301 • 302 • 310 • 311 • 312 • 317 • 321 • 339

Community

52 • 74 • 148 • 167 • 223 • 256 • 277 • 286 • 309 • 310 • 317

Food

4 • 22 • 25 • 27 • 40 • 49 • 74 • 91 • 99 • 111 • 121 • 123 • 132 • 148 • 149 • 161 • 165 • 166 • 167 • 168 • 171 • 173 • 175 • 204 • 217 • 219 • 223 • 227 • 230 • 240 • 241 • 251 • 256 • 257 • 277 • 279 • 286 • 301 • 302 • 306 • 309 • 317 • 333 • 334

Photo: Podere Cogno, entry 184

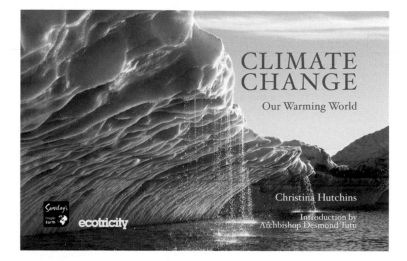

Climate Change Our Warming World   £12.99

"Climate Change presents in a clear and unique way the greatest challenge facing humanity. It is illustrated with telling photography and sharply written text. It is both objective and passionate. To read it is to know that urgent action is needed at every level in all societies." Jonathan Dimbleby

Climate Change is the greatest challenge facing humanity today. In the coming decade a tipping point may be reached triggering irreversible impacts to our planet. This book is not just for scientists or academics, it is for everyone concerned about the future of the earth.

Also available in the Fragile Earth series:

Ban the Plastic Bag A community action plan **£4.99**
One Planet Living A guide to enjoying life on our one planet **£4.99**
The Little Food Book An explosive account of the food we eat today **£6.99**

To order any of the books in the Fragile Earth series call
+44 (0)1275 395431 or visit www.fragile-earth.com

Money Matters
Putting the eco into economics £7.99
This well-timed book will make you look at everything from your bank statements to the coins in your pocket in a whole new way. Author David Boyle sheds new light on our money system and exposes the inequality, greed and instability of the economies that dominate the world's wealth.

Do Humans Dream of Electric Cars? £4.99
This guide provides a no-nonsense approach to sustainable travel and outlines the simple steps needed to achieve a low carbon future. It highlights innovative and imaginative schemes that are already working, such as car clubs and bike sharing.

The Book of Rubbish Ideas £6.99
Every householder should have a copy of this guide to reducing household waste and stopping wasteful behaviour. Containing step-by-step projects, the book takes a top-down guided tour through the average family home.

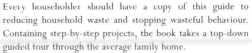

The Big Earth Book
Updated paperback edition £12.99
This book explores environmental, economic and social ideas to save our planet. It helps us understand what is happening to the planet today, exposes the actions of corporations and the lack of action of governments, weighs up new technologies, and champions innovative and viable solutions.

What About China? £6.99
Answers to this and other awkward questions about climate change
A panel of experts gives clear, entertaining and informative answers arguing that the excuses we give to avoid reducing our carbon footprint and our personal impact on the earth are exactly that, excuses.

Have you enjoyed this book? Why not try one of the others in the Special Places series and get 35% discount on the RRP *

British Bed & Breakfast (Ed 14)	RRP £14.99	Offer price £9.75
British Bed & Breakfast for Garden Lovers (Ed 5)	RRP £14.99	Offer price £9.75
British Hotels & Inns (Ed 11)	RRP £14.99	Offer price £9.75
Devon & Cornwall (Ed 1)	RRP £9.99	Offer price £6.50
Scotland (Ed 1)	RRP £9.99	Offer price £6.50
Pubs & Inns of England & Wales (Ed 6)	RRP £15.99	Offer price £9.75
Go Slow England	RRP £19.99	Offer price £13.00
Ireland (Ed 7)	RRP £12.99	Offer price £8.45
French Bed & Breakfast (Ed 11)	RRP £15.99	Offer price £10.40
French Holiday Homes (Ed 4)	RRP £14.99	Offer price £9.75
French Châteaux & Hotels (Ed 6)	RRP £14.99	Offer price £9.75
French Vineyards (Ed 1)	RRP £19.99	Offer price £13.00
Go Slow France	RRP £19.99	Offer price £13.00
Paris (Ed 1)	RRP £9.99	Offer price £6.50
Italy (Ed 6)	RRP £14.99	Offer price £9.75
Go Slow Italy	RRP £19.99	Offer price £13.00
Spain (Ed 8)	RRP £14.99	Offer price £9.75
Portugal (Ed 4)	RRP £11.99	Offer price £7.80
India & Sri Lanka (Ed 3)	RRP £11.99	Offer price £7.80
Green Europe (Ed 1)	RRP £11.99	Offer price £7.80
Morocco (Ed 3)	RRP £9.99	Offer price £9.10

*postage and packing is added to each order

To order at the Reader's Discount price simply phone +44 (0)1275 395431 and quote 'Reader Discount IT'.

If you have any comments on entries in this guide, please tell us. If you have a favourite place or a new discovery, please let us know about it. You can return this form or visit www.sawdays.co.uk.

Existing entry

Property name: _____

Entry number: _____ Date of visit: _____

New recommendation

Property name: _____

Address: _____

_____

Tel/Email/Web: _____

Your comments

What did you like (or dislike) about this place? Were the people friendly? What was the location like? What sort of food did they serve?

_____

_____

_____

_____

Your details

Name: _____

Address: _____

_____

_____ Postcode: _____

Tel: _____ Email: _____

Please send completed form to:
IT6, Sawday's, The Old Farmyard, Yanley Lane, Long Ashton, Bristol BS41 9LR, UK

Photo: Trullo Solari, entry 311

412 Index by town

Abano Terme	48
Abbateggio	256
Acquafredda di Maratea	299
Albignasego	49
Alghero	343
Amalfi	289
Andria	302
Arezzo	199-202
Arzachena	341
Asciano	191
Assisi	222-225
Barbarano Vicentino	47
Barberino Val d'Elsa	151-153
Bardolino	38
Barolo	11
Bibbona	162
Bologna	80
Bordighera	86
Borgo San Lorenzo	120-123
Bosa	344
Bovara di Trevi	213
Brisighella	83
Bucine	203
Buonconvento	171
Cadenabbia di Griante	15
Calco	22
Caldana Bivio	166
Caltanissetta	334
Calzolaro	234
Camaiore	102
Camerino	247
Caminino	165
Campello Alto	211
Canosa di Puglia	301
Capua	276
Carpineti	79
Cartoceto	241
Casalborgone	9
Casalini di Cisternino	306
Casperia	272
Castel del Piano	221
Castelfiorentino	148
Castellabate	293
Castellina in Chianti	182-184
Castelnuovo di Garfagnana	101
Castelrotto	35
Castelvecchio di Rocca Barbena	88
Castelvetrano	335
Castiglion Fiorentino	196
Castiglione di Ravello	292
Castroreale	317
Ceglie Messapica	310-311
Cellarengo	6
Cerro di Laveno Mombello	14
Cicciano	278
Città della Pieve	217
Civitella d'Agliano	273
Colle di Buggiano	110
Collesano	340
Colognola ai Colli	44
Cortina di Alseno	78
Cortona	193-194
Courmayeur	1
Crespina	115

① B&B & Self-catering   Friuli-Venezia Giulia ②

③
④ **Agriturismo La Faula**
An exuberant miscellany of dogs, donkeys and peacocks on a modern, working farm where rural laissez-faire and modern commerce happily mingle. La Faula has been in Luca's family for years; he and Paul, young and dynamic, abandoned the city to find themselves working harder than ever. Yet they put as much thought and energy into their guests as into the wine business and farm. The house stands in gentle countryside at the base of the Julian Alps – a big, comfortable home, and each bedroom delightful. Furniture is old, bathrooms new. There is a bistro-style restaurant where wonderful home-reared produce is served (free-range veal, beef, chicken, lamb, just-picked vegetables and fruits); on summer nights there may be a barbecue. An enormous old pergola provides dappled shade during the day; sit and dream awhile with a glass of estate wine or acquavita. Or wander round the vineyard and *cantina*, watch the wine-making in progress, practice your skills with a golf club on the residents' driving range, cool off in the river, visit the beaches of the Adriatic. Perfect for families. *Minimum stay two nights.*

⑤ Price	€80. Apartments €455 per week.	
⑥ Rooms	9 + 4: 9 twins/doubles. 4 studio apartments for 2–4.	
⑦ Meals	Lunch/dinner €18. Wine €10. Restaurant 500m.	
⑧ Closed	16 September–14 March.	
⑨ Directions	A23 exit Udine Nord dir. Tarvisio & Tricesimo. From SS13 Pontebbana dir. Povoletto-Cividale. At r'bout, right dir. Povoletto. At Ravosa, pass Trattoria Al Sole on left; right after 20m. Signed.	

Paul Mackay & Luca Colautti
Via Faula 5, Ravosa di Povoletto,
33040 Udine
Mobile   +39 334 3996734
Web   www.faula.com

Ethical Collection: Environment; Community; Food. See page 400 for details ⑩

⑪   Entry 74 Map 5 ⑫